P9-CRM-788

THE BIG BOOK OF TELL ME WHY #2

BY ARKADY LEOKUM

BARNES & NOBLE BOOKS
NEW YORK

TELL ME WHY, #4

Copyright © 1986, 1972 by Arkady Leokum.
Illustrations copyright © 1986
by Grosset & Dunlap, Inc.,
a member of The Putnam & Grosset Group, New York.
Original ISBN 0-448-22504-2.
Abridged from the original book entitled
Lots More Tell Me Why.

TELL ME WHY, #5

Copyright © 1988, 1977, 1974 by Arkady Leokum.
Illustrations copyright © 1988
by Grosset & Dunlap, Inc.,
a member of The Putnam & Grosset Group, New York.
Original ISBN 0-448-19069-9.
Abridged from the original books entitled
Another Tell Me Why and

Tell Me Why/Love, Sex, & Babies.

TELL ME WHY, #6

Copyright © 1992, 1972 by Arkady Leokum.
Illustrations copyright © 1972
by Grosset & Dunlap, Inc.,
a member of The Putnam & Grosset Group, New York.
Abridged from the original book entitled
Lots More Tell Me Why.

Copyright © 1992, 1977 by Arkady Leokum.
Illustrations copyright © 1977
by Grosset & Dunlap, Inc.,
a member of The Putnam & Grosset Group, New York
Abridged from the original book entitled
Another Tell Me Why

THE BIG BOOK OF TELL ME WHY 2

Published in 1992 by Marboro Books Corp.,
a division of Barnes & Noble Inc., by
arrangement with Grosset & Dunlap, Inc., a member of
The Putnam & Grosset Group, New York.
ISBN 0-88029-999-1
Printed in the U.S.A.

PRINTED ON RECYCLED PAPER

CONTENTS

Chapter 3
The Human Body

Chapter 4
How Other Creatures Live

Chapter 5
How Things Are Made

CHAPTER 1
OUR WORLD

WHAT IS RADIATION?

Looking at it very simply, radiation is the sending out of waves of energy. You have known about it since you were a baby—though you didn't know what it was. When you held your hand in front of a hot stove or radiator, or a light bulb, you felt radiant heat. When you sat in the warm sun, a type of radiation called ultraviolet rays was striking your skin.

All these are examples of electromagnetic radiation. The other major type of radiation is called radioactive radiation, and it comes from either radioactive material or nuclear reactions. In radioactive radiation, particles, as well as waves of energy, are given off.

Since electromagnetic radiation is the sending out of waves of energy, we should know something about those waves. The distance between the waves is called the wavelength. The number of waves passing a given point each second is the frequency. And when all the waves within a certain range of wavelengths are grouped together, we call them the spectrum.

The group with the shortest wavelength is the X-ray spectrum. Next comes the ultraviolet spectrum. Then comes the visible-light spectrum; we can see these waves. The waves get still longer, and we can no longer see them. This is the infrared spectrum. Even longer waves (Hertzian waves) are used for radio, television, and radar.

What produces all these waves? In some cases machines are required; in others they are produced naturally. Naturally made waves come from the sun. To produce any radiation requires energy. In the case of the sun, atomic energy is produced by a reaction called fusion. In the case of X-rays, a target must be bombarded with particles.

Radioactive radiation is the process of change or decay that certain elements undergo. Such elements are radioactive. They radiate particles (and waves, too) as the nuclei of their atoms break up.

WHAT ARE UFO'S?

The popular name for them is "flying saucers." UFO stands for "unidentified flying object."

Do they really exist? Many books have been written about them and thousands of people claim they have seen them; some even claim they have photographed them. And no matter what scientific investigations reveal, there will still be people who believe they exist.

Studies of saucer reports show that UFO's are very different from one another. Some people report having seen flat saucers; others see saucers shaped like spheres, cigars, or doughnuts.

The colors of saucers seem to be as different as their sizes. Saucers of nearly all colors have been reported. Some seem to change color as they are being watched.

Saucers have been seen to move in every direction and at nearly every speed. They can turn at right angles, move straight up or straight down, or travel in a zigzag path. They can hang motionless in the air, and make either a hissing noise or a roar.

When the United States Air Force started to investigate the reports about flying saucers, it discovered that people weren't "imagining" what they saw. Everyone who reported a flying saucer had seen something. But what?

In some cases, the "something" was actually a weather balloon. In other cases, it was a satellite, a cloud, a meteor, a star, a bird, a comet, a planet, or fireworks. It was also what are called sun dogs. These are images of the sun reflected through ice crystals. Many flying-saucer stories have been traced to fireballs, which are formed by lightning.

If saucers were really spaceships, there would be a certain pattern in the reports about them. But there is no such pattern. The reason is that people are not seeing spaceships but many other things. So scientists believe that there is no evidence that we are being visited, watched, or invaded by intelligent beings from other worlds.

WHY DO ALL THE PLANETS LOOK DIFFERENT?

The reason each of the planets looks different to us is that each one seems to be made up of different substances. Even though they are all planets revolving around the sun and part of the solar system, their composition varies.

We actually know very little about what the planets are made of, and this is one of the questions man hopes to answer with the space explorations that are presently going on and those that are being planned for the future.

Let's take a brief look at each of the other planets and see what is known of their make-up. Mercury is a small, rocky world. It has some dark areas on its surface, and has a very thin atmosphere of carbon dioxide.

Venus is a white globe with some hazy markings. It is completely covered by a layer of white clouds. The clouds contain carbon-dioxide gas, and some nitrogen and oxygen may also be present. We still don't know whether the surface of Venus is very hot or not. If it is not hot, there may be oceans on Venus. If it is very hot, then it is probably a vast and lifeless desert.

Mars is a small, rocky world. Parts of Mars are darker than others, but we still don't know whether these markings are canals or not. Mars has little if any oxygen, so the question about life on Mars is still a mystery.

Jupiter appears as a yellowish globe with darker bands of color crossing it. Jupiter is covered by a layer of clouds that may be thousands of miles deep. We still don't know whether Jupiter has a rocky core or whether the main body of the planet is made up of solid hydrogen.

Saturn is also covered by clouds. It has bands of color—yellowish at the equator, greenish at the poles. It may have a small, rocky core. Uranus looks slightly green with a band of silvery color. Neptune is a dim greenish object, with a few bands of color. Very little is known about Pluto. It may be a small, rocky planet like the earth. It is so cold that any atmosphere it has must be frozen.

As you can see, man still has a great deal to find out about the other members of the solar system.

WHAT ARE THE SIZES OF THE PLANETS?

A planet is very different from a star. A star is a huge ball of hot gases that gives off heat and light. A planet is a much smaller body that shines by reflected light.

Let's start with the planet nearest to the sun and move outward. The first one is Mercury. Mercury's diameter is 2,900 miles—about the width of the Atlantic Ocean. So it's only a fraction of the earth's size.

The next planet we meet is Venus. It is very nearly the same size as the earth. Its diameter is 7,600 miles, while that of the earth is 7,913 miles. By the way, an odd fact about Venus is that it rotates backward; that is, from east to west. The next planet is our earth, and then comes Mars.

Mars shines in the sky with a reddish color. It has a diameter of 4,200 miles, a little more than half that of the earth. Mars has interested scientists more than most planets because of its markings that look like channels or canals. It seems the most likely planet other than ours to have life on it, perhaps some kind of plant life.

Jupiter, the next planet, is far away from the sun. It takes about 11.9 years to complete one orbit. Jupiter is the largest of the planets. It has a diameter of 86,800 miles, nearly 11 times the diameter of the earth.

Saturn, the next planet, is another giant. It has a diameter of 71,500 miles, which is about nine times that of the earth. An unusual thing about Saturn is the group of flat rings that circle it. These rings are made up of billions of tiny particles.

Uranus, the next planet, is much larger than the earth. It has a diameter of 29,400 miles. Uranus is tilted over on its side. Its axis is tilted over at an angle of 98 degrees. (The earth tilts at an angle of

23½ degrees.) Neptune, the next planet, is 28,000 miles in diameter. And finally, the last known planet, Pluto, is believed to have a diameter of about 3,600 miles. It is so far from the sun that the sun appears to it as only a bright star in the sky.

WHAT IS THE CORONA OF THE SUN?

Have you ever seen photographs of a total eclipse of the sun? All around the dark sun, there is an uneven glow of light, and this light is called the corona.

To understand what the corona is, we have to know some things about the sun. To begin with, the sun, at least at its surface, is not a solid like the earth. This surface, which is all that we can observe of the sun, is composed of gases.

In fact, the sun is surrounded by four layers of gaseous matter that hide what is underneath. The innermost of these layers is called the photosphere. The next two layers are known as the reversing layer and the chromosphere. Together they form the sun's atmosphere. The outermost layer is the corona.

Let's see what each of these layers of gas is. The photosphere (or "light sphere") is what we see when we look toward the sun. Most of the time, dark sunspots can be seen on this bright surface.

The "reversing layer," which is made of gaseous vapors, extends

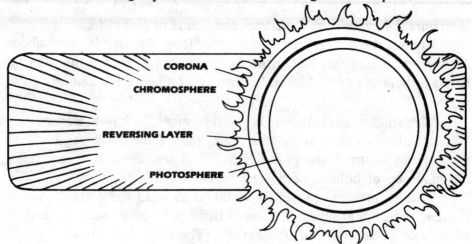

CORONA
CHROMOSPHERE
REVERSING LAYER
PHOTOSPHERE

several hundred miles out from the photosphere of the sun. This layer is never seen, but it can be studied by an instrument called the spectrograph.

Outside the reversing layer is the chromosphere, or color sphere. It is about nine thousand miles thick and is made up mostly of hydrogen and helium gases. At the time of a total eclipse, it shines out around the dark disk with a brilliant scarlet light. From this red border, flame-colored clouds of the same material shoot out to great heights, sometimes even as much as one million miles! They are called prominences, and they look like great flames of fire.

Then comes the outer layer, which is called the corona. It is composed of light, gaseous matter, and has two parts. The inner corona, lying next to the red chromosphere, is a band of pale yellow. The outer corona is white, with streamers extending out millions of miles from the edge of the sun.

All of this describes only the layers that surround the sun. What is beneath them still remains a mystery!

WHAT ARE ULTRAVIOLET RAYS?

Light rays, heat rays, X-rays, and ultraviolet rays are all forms of radiation. Radiation wavelengths have an amazingly large span. The longest are radio waves; the shortest, gamma rays. About halfway between the longest and shortest wavelengths are light waves, or visible radiation.

Light waves themselves have a great variety of wavelengths. Each color is a different wavelength. Red light is the longest wavelength visible to man. Next is orange, followed by yellow, green, blue, and violet, which is the shortest wavelength radiation that can be seen.

Just past the violet-light wavelength are the radiations in what scientists call the ultraviolet range. The sun emits these rays, as do certain man-made lamps specially produced for this purpose. Ultraviolet wavelengths range from just above those of violet light to more than 2,500,000 waves per inch.

Because ultraviolet rays are shorter than other rays, they are penetrating. From the sun these rays, along with heat, reach the nerves in your skin. Still, only about half the ultraviolet rays from the sun ever reach the ground. Many are absorbed high up in the earth's atmosphere.

IS THE EARTH ALWAYS THE SAME DISTANCE FROM THE SUN?

Do you know why it's hot in summer and cold in winter? It's because the position of the earth's axis with respect to the sun changes as the earth revolves around the sun. Now, this change is very slight, when you consider the great distance of the earth from the sun. Yet that small change is enough to make us broil in summer and freeze in winter!

Can you imagine then what life would be like if the distance of the earth from the sun were to change a great deal? If we wandered farther away, life might become impossible because of the cold. If we came much nearer, we might all burn up in the heat! So the distance from the earth to the sun remains pretty much the same at all times, and that distance is, in round numbers, ninety-three million miles.

But the orbits of the planets around the sun are not quite circular, and in the case of many other planets the distance from the sun does change quite a bit during the year.

For example, the planet Mercury, nearest the sun, has an orbit that is less like a circle than the path of any other planet. The planet Venus varies in its distance from the sun from sixty-seven million to sixty-eight million miles.

Mars, the first planet beyond the earth, takes 687 days for its journey around the sun. During this trip its distance from the sun varies, but it averages about 141,700,000 miles.

Jupiter, the next planet away from the sun, provides an example of a planet whose distance from the sun varies a great deal. So we find that in discussing distance from the sun, an "average" figure is given for all the planets, including the earth. The reason for the variations is the pull on each planet by the others in our solar system.

WHY DON'T WE FEEL THE ROTATION OF THE EARTH?

Until a few hundred years ago, men believed that the earth stood still; that the sun, the moon, and the stars went around it. It's easy to understand why this was so. After all, that's the way it looked. And nobody could feel the earth moving. If the earth moved, why didn't objects fly off it, including the water in the oceans?

Today, of course, we know that the earth is moving constantly in two ways. It is going around the sun, and it is rotating on its axis. The reason we don't feel it is that we go along with the surface as it moves, and so does the air that surrounds us. Gravity holds everything on earth down, including the water in the oceans.

But the rotation of the earth is known to us from many things that we observe and feel. It is this rotation that causes day and night. If the earth didn't rotate, the side facing the sun would always have daylight, and the side facing away from the sun would be in darkness. But every point on the earth is carried around to the light side and then the dark side every twenty-four hours.

Another important motion of the earth that we can't "feel," but that makes a difference in our lives, is the trip the earth takes around the sun. It is this motion that causes the change of seasons, and you know how different our life becomes with each changing season. In fact, this trip around the sun, which takes about 365¼ days, and which we call a year, is the way we measure history, the length of our lives, and so on.

The change of seasons is caused by the slant of the earth's axis. This slant or tilt is 23½ degrees from the vertical. Each pole leans toward the sun half the year and away from the sun the other half. So for six months the northern part of the earth receives more sunlight and thus more heat (summer), and during the other months it receives less sunlight and has its cooler season.

HOW MUCH DOES THE EARTH WEIGH?

Since the earth is suspended in space, "weighing" it is not the same thing as putting an object on a scale. When we speak of the weight of the earth, we mean the amount of matter that makes it up. This is called its mass.

The earth's mass is about 6.6 sextillion tons. To give you an idea of how that number looks, here it is: 6,600,000,000,000,000,000,000. How did scientists find out that this was the mass of the earth?

To do this, they used a principle based on the fact that any two objects attract each other. This is what the force of gravity depends on. Put in simple terms, the law of gravity states that two objects are attracted by a force that depends on their mass and their distance apart. The bigger the objects, the greater the force that pulls them together. The farther apart they are, the smaller the force.

To measure the weight of the earth, the following is done: A small weight is suspended from a string. The exact position of that weight is measured. Now a ton of lead is brought near the hanging weight. There is an attraction between the weight and the lead, and this causes the weight to be pulled just a tiny bit out of line. (Actually, it is less than one-millionth of an inch, so you can see how carefully the measuring must be done.)

After this is measured, scientists can use mathematics to figure out the weight of the earth. They have measured the power of the earth's attraction on the weight, and they have measured the power of the one-ton lead's attraction on the suspended weight. The relative difference can be calculated and tells them the mass of the earth.

What is this mass made of? There is the crust of solid rock; then a layer called the mantle, which is also solid rock and goes down about one thousand eight hundred miles; and then the innermost part, which is the core and is about two thousand one hundred miles in radius. The material of the core is liquid because of the great heat at the center of the earth.

WHAT IS ST. ELMO'S FIRE?

St. Elmo's fire is one of the many interesting phenomena connected with lightning, and to understand it we must review what takes place when lightning occurs.

All matter is made up of two kinds of particles, positive and negative. The two kinds of particles strongly attract each other, and if they are separated, they have a great tendency to reunite.

14

When a strong negative or positive charge is built up in the base of a cloud, it induces an opposite charge below it on the earth. Electrons start moving from the region of the negative charge to the positive. They gradually build up a channel or channels of charged particles between the earth and the cloud, and when there is a great surge of electrons, a lightning flash occurs.

Now suppose that instead of allowing the charges to build up until the strain is too great and must be broken, there were some way of enabling the charge from the earth below to "leak off." Instead of a lightning stroke, the charge would leak off in the form of a "brush discharge." This, by the way, is exactly the way a lightning rod works. The point of the lightning rod enables the electrons to leak off.

St. Elmo's fire is the glow that accompanies such a "brush discharge" of atmospheric electricity. It appears as a tip of light on the ends of pointed objects, such as church towers or the masts of ships during stormy weather. We usually hear a crackling or fizzing noise at the same time.

Another place St. Elmo's fire is commonly observed is on the edge of propellers, and along the wing tips, windshields, and noses of airplanes when they are flying in dry snow or in the vicinity of thunderstorms. This discharge may sometimes be strong enough to cause static in the radio of the airplane.

IS THE EQUATOR THE HOTTEST
PLACE ON EARTH?

When we talk about places on earth being "hot" or "cold," we are talking about "climate." And in a general way all climate is determined by the heat of the sun.

It is the heat of the sun that warms the land, the oceans, and the atmosphere. The heat of the sun draws moisture into the atmosphere, and thus makes rain possible. The sun's heat causes differences in air pressure, which creates winds, and together the sun's heat and the winds produce ocean currents. So, in discussing the climate of a particular location, it is important to consider the sun's heating effect on that area.

Now, because the surface of the earth is curved, the heating effect of the sun is greatest at the Equator and least at the Poles. At the Equator, the rays from the sun strike the earth vertically. Above and below the equatorial region, the rays strike the earth at an angle, or slant. This means that the regions above and below the Equator, the Temperate Zones, receive fewer rays from the sun than the areas in the region of the Equator, the Tropical Zone. The regions of the earth farthest from the Equator, in other words, receive the least amount of heat.

When a ray of sunlight strikes the earth at an angle, it has to pass through more atmosphere, and so some of its heat is absorbed by the air—and that's another reason the other zones receive less heat.

All of this makes the region of the Equator the hottest region on earth. But we have been talking about what is called solar climate, climate depending only on the sun's heat. There are many other factors, however, that enter into the picture to determine what is called physical climate, the actual climates found on the earth.

The most important of these other factors are water, land, and altitude. The waters of the oceans and ocean currents, the existence of large land areas, and the altitude of the land all can combine to create different climates regardless of the location on earth. That's why, at any particular time, it may be hotter at a point far from the Equator than it is at the Equator itself, although the equatorial region is the hottest on earth.

WAS THE SAHARA ALWAYS A DESERT?

The Sahara desert is the world's hottest region in summer and the world's largest desert. It is bigger than the United States and has an area of over 3,500,000 square miles.

Yet at one time most of the Sahara was under water! In ages gone by, there were rivers and valleys and gorges. In fact, some people believe that the sand of the Sahara comes from the time when it was the bottom of a great sea. But this theory is not accepted by most authorities.

We do know that at one time the Sahara had the climate of a moist temperate or subtropical region. There were probably grass and trees growing there. But gradually the vegetation disappeared and the region became arid. This dried out the soil, and wind erosion broke up the particles until the sand was formed. There are still some patches of oases, however, where trees and grasses grow, and where springs and natural wells may be found.

The Sahara is kept dry by the winds in the region. They are northeast trade winds that blow steadily toward the Equator. As the air moves toward the Equator, it gets hotter and is able to hold more moisture. So the air takes up moisture like blotting paper and keeps the desert dry and hot.

In July, there are many places in the Sahara where the average temperature is 100 degrees Fahrenheit. At a place called Azizia near Tripoli, the world's record heat was recorded in 1922. It was 136.4 degrees! When the sun goes down, however, the land cools very quickly. The temperature may drop 30 to 50 degrees, and in some oases in winter, there is even frost at night!

Despite the dryness of the land, there is some animal life there, such as the desert antelope, which carries a water supply in a special sac in its body.

HOW ARE LAKES FORMED?

Lakes are inland bodies of water that occupy depressions in the surface of the land. These depressions are called basins.

Lakes result from the flow of water into low areas. Lake water comes largely from rainfall and melting snow. The water enters a lake basin through brooks, streams, rivers, underground springs, and ground water.

The lake basins themselves are formed in several ways. Many lakes are the result of faulting or warping in the earth's crust. Lake Superior in North America is an example of such a lake.

Sometimes lakes are created by volcanoes. A lava flow may block the outlet of a valley and form a lake basin. Sometimes the crater of an extinct volcano fills with water. Crater Lake in southern Oregon is an example of this.

Many lakes occupy basins formed by glacial erosion. All the Great Lakes (except Lake Superior) and Lake Winnipeg in Canada are examples of lakes that were formed by glaciers.

Along coastal areas, waves and shore currents sometimes close inlets and temporarily create lakes out of bays and estuaries. Sometimes the main stream of a river may build up its flood plain by depositing silt (mud and soil) when the river overflows. As a result, tributary valleys are flooded and lakes are formed.

In places where limestone underlies the land, ground water may dissolve and remove enough limestone to produce great sinkholes that form lake basins. Florida contains many lakes of this type.

Lakes may also be artificially made. When a dam is built across a river valley, it will block the flow of water and form a lake. Lake Mead was formed when Hoover Dam was built on the Colorado River.

WHAT ARE THE LARGEST WATERFALLS IN THE WORLD?

A waterfall is any stream of water which descends suddenly from a higher to a lower level. If the volume of water is small, it is called a cascade; if large, it is called a cataract.

Some falls plunge hundreds of feet in a single narrow stream of water. Others are famous for their breadth and for the immense volume of water that pours over their ledges. Here are some of the great waterfalls of the world:

Angel Falls, in the Guiana Highlands of Venezuela, are the world's highest falls (3,212 feet), with the longest uninterrupted drop

(2,648 feet). The falls were discovered in 1935 by an American aviator, James Angel.

The longest waterfall in Asia is the Gersoppa Falls in India. It is a cataract that falls in four sections for a total of 830 feet. The falls that discharge the largest volume of water of any waterfall are the Guaira Falls, which are on the border of Brazil and Paraguay. They discharge over 470,000 cubic feet of water per second. There are 18 falls, but the total drop is only about 200 feet.

One of the world's highest single waterfalls is Ribbon Falls in Yosemite National Park. It is a narrow stream that drops 1,612 feet down a cliff into the Merced River.

The second highest falls in the world are found in South Africa. They are the Tugela Falls. The falls plunge 2,800 feet in five jumps.

And then, of course, there are Niagara Falls, among the most famous in the world. They are located in the Niagara River, about 16 miles northwest of Buffalo, New York. Actually, Niagara Falls consist of two cataracts—the Horseshoe (or Canadian) Falls and the American Falls. The international boundary line between Canada and the United States passes through the center of Horseshoe Falls.

About 94 percent of Niagara's waters, or some 84,000,000 gallons, flows over the Horseshoe Falls every minute.

American Side of Niagara Falls

WHAT IS HARD WATER?

Water is a tasteless, odorless, colorless compound of two gases: hydrogen, a very light gas, and oxygen, a heavier, active gas. Water exists in three states: as a liquid; as a solid, called ice; and as a gas, called water vapor.

But when we discuss the various properties of water, we discover that water as it occurs in nature is never pure in the true sense. It contains dissolved mineral material, dissolved gases, and living organisms. So it is very seldom that we are dealing with just "water."

For example, chemically pure water is tasteless. But we all know there often is a slight taste to water. Part of this taste comes from the presence of certain impurities in the water. Raindrops falling through the atmosphere absorb some of the gases through which they pass.

Most important of these gases is oxygen, which makes it possible for living things to exist under water. Carbon dioxide is another important gas in water. Its presence in a water solution (carbonic acid) makes water capable of eroding limestone rocks and forming caves and sinkholes.

The action of this carbonic acid in water dissolves lime and magnesium carbonates, and this is what makes water "hard." Hard water does not produce a soap lather easily. If boiled, it leaves a lime coating on the inside of kettles.

Besides gases, natural waters contain dissolved salts. And river and lake water is also likely to contain inorganic particles that simply float in the water.

Water is distributed over the earth in a great "energy cycle." The sun draws up water into the air by evaporation from the seas and oceans. In the air, water vapor gathers into clouds and falls as rain, hail, snow, or dew, and works its way back to the sea.

WHERE DOES IT RAIN THE MOST?

Many things determine how much rain or snow any area of the world receives. These include temperature, height above sea level, location of mountain ranges, and so on.

Probably the rainiest place in the world is Mount Waialeale, Hawaii, on the island of Kauai. It has an average yearly rainfall of 471.68 inches. Cherrapunji, India, might be the next rainiest place, with its yearly average of 425 to 450 inches. At one time 150 inches of rain fell on Cherrapunji in a period of 5 days. And in one year, 1861, its rainfall added up to 905 inches.

To give you an idea of how much rain this is, let's note the rainfall in a number of cities around the world. New York City gets about 40 inches a year; San Francisco, about 20 inches; Boston, 42 inches; Chicago gets 30 inches; Ottawa in Canada gets 34 inches; Madrid, about 17 inches; and Paris, 22 inches. So you see what a contrast 450 inches in Cherrapunji is.

The driest place in the world is probably Arica, Chile. It averages only 0.02 inches of rain a year! The driest area in the United States is Greenland Ranch, Death Valley. There the average yearly rainfall is less than 1.5 inches.

Some large regions of the earth have heavy rainfall throughout the year. For example, almost every point along the Equator receives 60 inches or more of rain every year. The Equator is the meeting point of two large streams of air. All along the Equator, air moving down from the north meets air moving up from the south. There is a general upward movement of hot air laden with water vapor. As the air rises to colder heights, large amounts of water vapor condense and fall as rain.

A great deal of rain falls on the windward side of mountain ranges. The other side, called the lee, receives much less rain. An example is the Cascade Range of California. Westerly winds laden with water vapor sweep in from the Pacific Ocean. After striking the coast, the air rides up the western slopes of the mountains, cooling as it climbs higher. The cooling causes the water vapor to condense and fall as rain or snow.

WHAT IS A QUARRY?

Quarrying is the process by which rock materials are removed from the ground. The rocks may be quarried as solid blocks or slabs, or as crushed and broken stone. The block or slab rock is usually used for building. Crushed rock is most often used for roadbeds.

There are different types of quarries. In some, the rock is in a huge, solid mass. In others, the rock forms layers of different thicknesses. A pit quarry is actually a big hole in the ground. Sometimes it's wide and shallow, and sometimes it's a deep, narrow hole. Workers in pit quarries have to use ladders or stairs, or they may have to be lowered into the quarry by mechanical devices.

In pit quarries, there is often a water problem. This is because the quarry is like a big stone bowl, collecting and holding all the rainwater that pours into it. When this happens, the water has to be pumped out.

Sometimes rock suitable for quarrying is found above the ground. This is called a shelf quarry. In such a quarry, machines can be moved right up to the face of the quarry, and the rock can be hauled away directly.

How is it decided where to establish a quarry? Tests must be made first. Geologists can tell where the chances of finding a high grade of rock are good. Then the rock itself must be tested.

In testing, a number of holes are drilled at various spots in the area. Special drills are used that can cut a core of rock about two inches in diameter. This core is brought up to the surface and analyzed. Some drills can go down as far as two thousand eight hundred feet, or more than half a mile. The test indicates whether there is enough good stone available to make quarrying profitable.

HOW MANY TYPES OF CLIMATE ARE THERE?

There are many different types of climate on earth. Climate, by the way, is the combination of temperature, moisture, wind, and sunshine at a place over a period of many years. Climates of the world can be classified according to their latitudes and the plants that grow there. Different kinds of plants need different amounts of moisture and heat to grow. So the vegetation of a place tells us about temperature and rainfall conditions over a long period of time.

Basically, there are five major classifications of climates, with many subdivisions in each class. There are tropical climates, subtropical climates, mid-latitude climates, high-latitude climates, and high-altitude climates.

Tropical climates are found in regions between 350° North and 350° South latitude. In the tropical rain forests (nearest the Equator), conditions are warm and rainy all year long, and there is a thick cover of trees. In this tropical area there are also tropical wet-and-dry climates; tropical savannas, where the climate is too dry for forests; tropical steppes (still drier); and the tropical desert climate.

Subtropical climates prevail in 30° and 40° North and South latitudes. In these areas there is a Mediterranean climate of hot, dry summers and mild, wet winters and a humid subtropical climate of hot summers and mild winters, with enough rainfall in all seasons to sustain forests.

Mid-latitude climates occur between 40° and 60° North and South latitudes. Included in this area are a marine west coast climate (west coast of North America); cool steppe or cool desert climates; and humid continental climates—each with different vegetation and rainfall patterns.

High-latitude climates are characteristic of from 60° North and South latitudes to the Poles. Here temperatures are very cold in winter and cool in summer. Within this area is a taiga climate (very cold in winter); a tundra climate, where only grasses, mosses and lichens can grow; and the polar climate, where great ice caps exist.

High-altitude climates, or highland climates, are found on the high mountains of the world, even at the Equator.

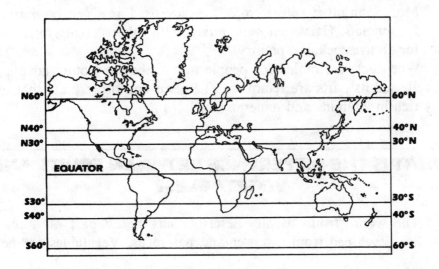

WHAT ARE OATS?

Oats are the seeds of a plant belonging to the grass family. When you think of oats, you probably think of the breakfast cereal called oatmeal or of oatmeal cookies. These are the only forms in which most people eat oats. What happens to the rest of the huge crop of oats? Most of it is used for animal food.

The first oats probably originated in the cool, moist areas of eastern Europe. For centuries men considered oats to be a weed. Some experts believe that the early Greeks and Romans cultivated oats for animal food. But it wasn't until the thirteenth century that peasants began to depend on oats as one of the most important foods for people.

Oats were brought to some small islands off New England in 1602 and spread rapidly as a crop in North America during the next fifty years. Today the United States is the biggest producer of oats, with Canada, the Soviet Union, and countries of northern Europe also producing great quantities.

Oat plants grow from two to five feet tall. The leaves are long and slender. Each stem has a head with many small, delicate branches. The branches end with little spikes on which the flowers blossom and the grains later form.

The plants grow in cool, moist climates. Oats do not need special soils, and as long as the land is not too wet, will often grow in places where other crops cannot be grown at all.

More than other cereal crops, oats are used as a general-purpose feed for animals. Harvested oats, mixed with other cereal grains, are used for all livestock and poultry.

When oats are milled for people to eat, the hard outer covering, or hull, and its parts are removed. The germ and other parts that are very rich in vitamins and minerals are left in.

WHAT IS THE DIFFERENCE BETWEEN FRUITS AND VEGETABLES?

The word "fruit" usually describes any fleshy part of a plant that has developed from a flower and has seeds. Vegetables are herbaceous plants. An herbaceous plant is one that has a soft stem and little or no woody tissue.

According to botanists, the part of a plant that carries seeds is its fruit. They divide fruits into three main classes: fleshy fruits with seeds in the flesh, such as oranges, melons, berries, and apples; fruits containing pits or stones, such as cherries, plums, and peaches; and dry fruits, such as nuts, grains, beans, and peas.

If it surprises you to learn that botanists consider beans and peas fruits (because they contain seeds), you will be even more surprised to learn that cucumbers and squash can be called fruits also! It all depends on how technical we want to be. In addition, because eating customs vary in different parts of the world, the same edible part of a plant may be considered a fruit in one place and a vegetable in another.

Just as there are "families" of related creatures in the animal kingdom, so many vegetables are related. Did you know, for example, that the cabbage, turnip, radish, broccoli, and cauliflower all belong to one family of vegetables?

Lettuce, chicory, and artichokes belong to another vegetable family. The gourd family includes cucumbers, melons, pumpkins, and squash. The pea family consists of peas, all kinds of beans, peanuts, and soybeans.

Asparagus is related to the common onion, leek, garlic, chive and shallot. Beets, spinach, and Swiss chard all belong to one family. And here is an interesting one: the nightshade family. It includes potatoes, eggplants, peppers, and tobacco!

Fruits and vegetables are alike in that they supply us with the vitamins and minerals that help to keep us healthy.

IS THE TOMATO A FRUIT OR A VEGETABLE?

Of course, it doesn't really matter very much which it is, since we use it in this country as a vegetable. A fascinating thing about this question is that the Supreme Court of the United States actually had to decide what the tomato is!

Botanically, the tomato is a fruit. There can be no question about that. But it is used in soups, sauces, ketchup, and in many other ways in the main part of the meal. So, for purposes of trade, the Supreme Court in 1893 classified the tomato as a vegetable!

The tomato originated in its wild form in South America in Peru, Ecuador, and Bolivia. Long before Columbus came to the new world, cultivated forms of the tomato had already been developed in Mexico. And it is probable that tomatoes from Mexico were the first ones ever seen by people in Europe.

The first definite description of the tomato in Europe was in Italy in 1554, where it was called *pomi d'oro,* or "apple of gold." This means that a yellow type of tomato was the first kind known in Europe. Before the end of the sixteenth century, tomatoes were being grown in the gardens of England, Spain, Italy, France and the countries of mid-Europe. But they were considered a sort of curiosity.

By the mid-1700's people in several countries of Europe were using the tomato as food, and the first person to grow it in the United States was Thomas Jefferson, in 1781. But a great many people considered the tomato to be poisonous. It wasn't until about 1900 that it became popular for eating.

The tomato plant is a relative of the potato and tobacco plants. It needs a long growing season and light, rich, well-drained soil. In northern Europe and the northern United States it is often grown in hothouses during the winter. It is also grown in Florida, Texas, and Mexico during the winter. Winter tomatoes are picked while green and shipped to northern markets. They ripen on the way to market.

HOW IS TOBACCO GROWN?

The tobacco plant usually grows four to six feet high. The leaves are large, about two or three feet in length. They are covered with many long, soft hairs that hold a gummy juice.

There are many ways in which this plant is grown, but all commercial tobacco needs a lot of care. Tobacco seed is mixed with fertilizer and corn or cottonseed meal before it is sown. In warm areas, the seedbeds are covered with cotton cloth. In colder areas the covering is usually glass.

In six to ten weeks in most areas, the plants grow six to eight inches. They develop four to six leaves, and are now ready to be set into fields that have been carefully prepared and fertilized.

As the plants begin to flower, each is topped, which means that the budding seed head is removed. This is done so that the leaves will be stronger and have a deeper color.

Three or four months after the seedlings have been placed in the growing field, the plants are ready for harvesting. Two methods are used: priming and stalk cutting.

In priming tobacco, each leaf is pulled separately as it ripens. Two to four leaves are removed from a plant each week. This process takes five to eight weeks. In stalk-cut tobacco, the whole plant is cut down.

After harvesting, the tobacco must be cured. The purpose of this is to dry the leaf and bring out the proper color. A tobacco leaf is cured by heat, air, or sun. In flue-curing, green leaves are hung in small insulated barns that are heated by flues. Stalk-cut tobacco is air cured. Other types of tobacco are strung together on sticks and hung in the sun.

The final stage in the care of tobacco is aging. This is done to mellow the leaf and improve its flavor.

WHAT IS PAPRIKA?

True pepper is made from the pepper plant, which has the scientific name of *Piper nigrum*. But a great many other kinds of pepper are obtained from plants of entirely different families.

For example, there are the red pepper or chilies. They belong to the genus *capsicum*. There are also cayenne peppers and tabasco peppers. Still another kind, bell peppers, are called pimientos when canned in oil. Pimientos is the Spanish name for the pepper plant. And finally there is paprika, which is a red pepper produced from the bell pepper. When these are ripe, they are red and hot, but are milder than many other kinds. That's why paprika can be used more freely than other kinds of pepper.

Pepper is considered to be the most important of all the spices in the world. After salt, it is the seasoning most used for food. In ancient times, and during the middle ages, only the rich could afford to use pepper. It had to be carried by caravan from the Far East, and this made it so expensive that a pound of pepper was considered a fitting present for a king!

In some ways pepper was like gold. People could pay taxes with pepper, and it was given as tribute to rulers by their subjects. When an army conquered an enemy and soldiers were given a share of the spoils, pepper would be one of the great rewards they would receive.

The Portuguese were so anxious to find a way of getting pepper at lower cost that they tried to find a sea route to India. After they found the way around the Cape of Good Hope, the cost of pepper in Europe dropped a great deal. Today, of course, pepper costs so little that we don't even think twice when we buy it. In the United States, more than fifteen thousand tons of pepper are used a year!

Pepper comes from the fruit or seeds of a climbing shrub. Black pepper is made by picking unripe berries and drying them until black. White pepper is made by removing the outer coat before grinding.

WHAT IS A HYBRID PLANT?

First of all, what is a hybrid? A hybrid is a crossbreed of a plant or animal. This means that it is the result of the union of the male of one species, race, etc., with the female of another.

This can happen in nature or among people without any deliberate plan. But in plants this is often done deliberately and for very good reasons.

Probably the best example of the advantages of hybrid plants is the case of corn. In the early days in the United States, farmers took particular care in the selection of seed ears for the next year's crop. By constant selection many varieties and strains of corn thus came into existence. These were selected because of their adaptability to different soils and climates.

But beginning about 1905, plant scientists started a new method of producing different kinds of corn. It was discovered that when the plant was self-pollinated—that is, the pollen in the tassels was applied by hand to the silks on the ear of the same plant—widely different kinds of corn plants appeared. By repeating this process and saving only the best plants for seed strains, "inbred lines" were established.

Many of these inbred lines had certain special, desirable characteristics, but all of them were lower in yield. Now came the next step. When such inbred lines were cross-pollinated, by applying the pollen of one strain to the silks of another, the kernels thus formed often gave rise to very productive hybrid plants.

And these hybrid plants were very good indeed! In many cases they were superior in disease resistance and in strength of stalks, and were very high in yield. Thus by first purifying or sorting out the most desirable characters of the old varieties, and then recombining these, very superior types of corn have been produced. In other plants, too, the same process of producing hybrids has had wonderful results!

WHAT IS A SPORE?

A flowering plant makes a new plant by means of a seed. Plants that don't have flowers make a new plant by means of a spore.

A spore is a one-celled organism. It is invisible to the eye and can only be seen under a microscope. There are spores in the air all around us. That's why when food is left exposed, and molds and mildews form on it, we know where they came from. Some types of spores that were in the air settled on the food and began to grow.

Some of the plants that reproduce by means of spores are mushrooms, ferns, and mosses. The algae that live in water also produce spores.

A plant carries its spores in cases that are called sporangia. In a mushroom, the sporangium is inside the gills beneath the mushroom cap. In mosses, the spores are carried in a capsule at the top of the stalk.

When the spore case is ripe, it opens, and the ripe spores are released. Since they are finer than dust, the wind scatters them far and wide. In the case of water plants, such as the algae, the spores can actually swim away. They have tiny tails called cilia. These spores are called zoospores, and when the ripe case opens, the zoospores swim away quickly. After a short time they come to rest and lose their tails. Then they begin to grow into new plants.

Some spores reproduce by cell division. They grow by pushing out a germ tube through a thin place in the cell wall. The germ tube branches into a mass of threads out of which the new plant grows. This is called asexual reproduction, because differentiated male and female cells are not needed for reproduction to take place.

Other spores are specialized male and female cells. In order to start a new plant, one male and one female cell must join to form a fertilized egg. Some plants alternate in the kind of spores they produce, asexual in one generation and sexual spores in the next.

DO CACTI HAVE LEAVES?

A cactus (plural: cacti) is able to exist under extreme conditions because it is a plant that has adapted itself to those conditions.

Cacti have the same basic structures and processes as other plants. But the work that is done by leaves in most other plants is done by the stems and branches of the cacti. In fact, the absence of leaves and the presence of spine-covered branches and stems enable them to survive in hot, dry regions.

The leaves of other plants are thin structures and are filled with pores through which the plant breathes. During the cell-making process carried on by the plants, water is given off to the air through these pores.

A cactus plant must guard every drop of water. So the work of the leaves is taken over by the stems and branches. Their thick skins have very few pores, and the water in the cactus is retained.

The roots of cacti are spread out, close to the surface of the ground. That's why cacti can quickly absorb water from the earth after

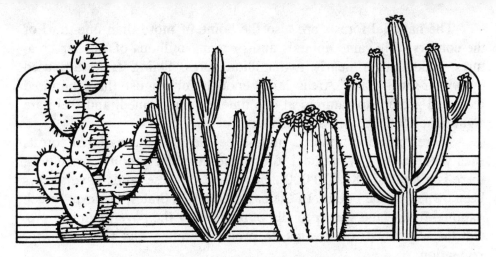

a rainfall. This water, which is taken in through the roots, is stored in the spongy or hollow stems of a cactus. The outer layer of the plant is thick and waxy, and this also prevents the escape of water.

The outer skin of a cactus is ribbed. Some cacti have ribs that fold and expand like an accordion. They expand as they fill up with water and fold together as the water in the stem is used up.

There are some members of the cactus family that do have leaves, such as the lemon vine of the West Indies. But in most cacti the leaves have developed into spines, needles, or hairs. These help protect the cacti from animals that would otherwise eat them, since they may be the only green plants in the area.

WHAT IS A NATIONAL FOREST?

National forests are areas that belong to all the people of the United States. They are protected and managed, along with the national grasslands, by the Forest Service of the United States Department of Agriculture.

To most people the word "forest" means trees. And it is true that the national forests are the source of much of the nation's timber. But they are much more than this. Many of them contain grazing lands that have few trees. Some parts of the national-forest system have been set aside as wilderness areas. No cutting of trees is allowed there, there are no structures to spoil the scenery, and no machines are allowed to disturb the peace and quiet.

The national forests are also the home of more than one-third of the country's big-game animals and of many millions of smaller creatures. Lakes cover nearly two million acres. Skiing areas are used by winter-sports fans. Areas large enough for almost three hundred thousand persons to camp in at one time are maintained, and there are eighty-one thousand miles of fishing streams.

More than one hundred million people visit the national forests each year. In the 154 national forests and nineteen national grasslands, there is a total of 186,000,000 acres. Most of these lands have always been owned by the public. In the eastern United States, however, much national-forest land was specially purchased by the government to protect the watersheds of streams, to produce timber, and to provide for recreation.

National forests differ from national parks. National parks have been set aside to preserve in a natural state some outstanding examples of America's scenic and scientific treasures. In the national parks no hunting, cutting of timber, or other removal of resources is permitted.

WHAT ARE HARDWOODS AND SOFTWOODS?

Trees, and the woods that come from them, have been divided into two main classes. The common name for one class of trees and lumber is softwoods, and the other class is called hardwoods. The difference between them is supposed to be in their hardness or softness of texture. A harder wood, as you might imagine, doesn't scratch as easily and stands up better under wear and tear.

The most important North American softwoods are the cedar, southern cypress, Douglas fir, true fir, hemlock, western larch, northern white pine, ponderosa pine, southern pine, sugar pine, western white pine, redwood, and spruce. Softwoods are also described in terms of being evergreens, cone-bearing trees, or needle-leaved trees.

Hardwood trees generally have broad leaves and shed them in the autumn or in the spring, as some oaks do. The important North American hardwoods are the ash, aspen, basswood, beech, birch, cottonwood, elm, gum, hickory, maple, oak, black walnut, and yellow poplar.

But the terms "softwoods" and "hardwoods" are really used as names for a class of woods or trees. Some of the softwoods are really hard in texture, and some of the hardwoods are soft—softer than some of the so-called softwoods!

The "basic wood substance" of which the cell walls of all woods are made weighs about the same in all kinds of woods. But because the cells have cavities of various sizes, a greater or lesser portion of the wooden block is taken up by these cavities. The size and proportions of the openings and walls of the wood cells vary greatly. This is why there is so much difference in the weight of various woods. Oak, for example, weighs more than twice as much as basswood. The greater the weight, the stronger the wood.

WHAT IS JADE?

Jade is a gemstone that almost glows. It has been prized by man for thousands of years.

The Chinese language uses the same word to mean both "jade" and "precious stone." The English word "jade" comes from the Spanish *piedra de ijada,* which means "colic stone." The Spanish called it this because they believed jade cured stomach pains!

Jade can be either of two separate minerals, jadeite or nephrite. These look so much alike that only an expert can tell them apart. Jadeite is slightly harder than nephrite. It also has a translucent glow and comes in more colors.

Jade is white in its pure state, but enough mineral impurities are usually present to make jade bright yellow, red, or one of the many shades of green. The most desired shade of jade is an emerald-green, or "Imperial" jade, which may be almost transparent. This type comes from Burma.

Because jade is a tough and hard stone, primitive men used it to make axes, hammers, knives, and other useful tools. Later, men used it for bowls, carvings, jewelry, and charms.

Jade is so tough that it is very difficult to carve. Steel chisels will not work. So instead, gritty materials are rubbed over the surface until it wears away. Making a simple vase may take two or three years of work.

Carved jade pieces have been found in Mexico that are at least three thousand five hundred years old. The early men of Central America used some jade in tools, but used it mostly for religious purposes. The Aztecs considered jade to be worth many times its weight in gold.

China is the country where jade has been of the greatest importance. For three thousand years the Chinese have been making lovely jade carvings. The Chinese admire jade so much that those who can afford it always carry small pieces with them. They believe that when jade is fingered, some of its secret virtues rub off.

WHAT IS A FUEL?

A fuel is a material that is burned in order to get heat and light, and also to generate power. The process of burning, or combustion, is a chemical reaction. A material combines with oxygen from the air and gives off energy. The energy is given off in the form of heat and light.

The energy in fuels came originally from the sun. The plants from which fuels come trap energy from the sun's rays and use it to build their tissues. Burning wood and charcoal releases energy that has been stored up by plants in this way. When we burn coal or oil, we use energy stored up by plants that lived millions of years ago.

There are many different types of fuels, and actually anything that burns can be called a fuel. But the most common fuels are wood, coal, natural gas, and gasoline.

Fuels can also be classified as solid, liquid, or gaseous. Or they can be classified according to their origin—natural, chemical, or metal based.

Wood was one of the first fuels used by man, and was his most important one for many centuries. It was the easiest to get, and the cheapest. But during the sixteenth century, wood started to become scarce in Europe, and coal began to replace it.

Coal contains a high percentage of carbon. Carbon is the most important part of most fuels. Fuels with a high percentage of carbon burn evenly and with a hot flame. Hard coal, or anthracite, has a higher percentage of carbon than other types of coal, and so makes less smoke and ash.

The most important liquid fuels come from petroleum. They include kerosene, gasoline, and heating oils.

WHAT IS NATURAL GAS?

In certain parts of Iran and India, where natural gas issued from crevices in the rocks, the natives thought their fire god was responsible for it. So they kept it burning as a tribute to him.

The curious thing is that in the United States, which seems to have the greatest accumulation of natural gas, people didn't know what it was either for a long time, and didn't know what to do with it. Since natural gas sometimes escapes from rocks or crevices without any drilling, these places were called "burning springs" in the United States as early as 1775. The first discovery of gas by drilling was made in the nineteenth century. It wasn't collected and piped on a commercial scale until 1872.

Natural gas is a mixture of combustible gases and vapors, chiefly methane. Sometimes it is found alone; sometimes it is found mixed with oil and must be extracted. At other places it is found with oil but is not mixed with it.

In nearly every oil field there is natural gas. It gathers in porous rock with a covering of heavy shale that keeps the gas in and keeps the air out. It accumulates in a kind of arched section of the stone, and sometimes there are gas beds above the oil.

When drilling is carried on at oil fields and oil is brought in, it sometimes happens that a gas bed is tapped, too, and gas begins to escape in a great flame. At one oil field in Oklahoma, about $25,000 worth of oil a day was collected, but at the same time $75,000 worth of gas escaped every day for a whole year!

Natural gas is clean and convenient to use for cooking and heating, but because of the problem of transportation it costs more than coal in most places. Today there are great pipeline systems that carry natural gas from its source to far distant places in a network that covers the country. In some cases the natural gas is carried through these pipes for more than one thousand miles!

WHAT IS A CORAL REEF?

Let's start by finding out what coral is. A chunk of coral is made of the skeletons of tiny marine animals called coral polyps.

The polyp's skeleton grows outside its body. It is cup-shaped, and it protects and supports the polyp's body and grows as the animal grows. When the polyp dies, the skeleton is left. Coral reefs and islands are formed of billions upon billions of these tiny skeletons.

A coral colony consists of living corals. Each is attached to a solid base, such as a rock or the skeletons of earlier generations of corals. Coral colonies are found in all the seas, but reef-building coral polyps are found only in warm, shallow waters. A depth of about 150 feet is best for them. Yet in some parts of the world coral reefs rise from great ocean depths.

The mystery of how coral reefs were formed was solved by Charles Darwin, the famous naturalist. Darwin knew that the earth's surface changes. Mountains are forced up in one place; in another, the crust of the earth sinks.

When he was studying coral reefs, he noticed that there were three kinds: fringing reefs, barrier reefs, and atolls (rings of coral). Putting all this information together, he worked out the following theory:

A volcanic island forms where an undersea volcano rises above the surface of the water. In the shallow waters of the island shores, corals build a fringing reef. As time passes, the volcano becomes cold and dead; it begins to sink back into the sea. As a result the fringing reef now becomes separated from the island by a wider channel of water, and it goes on growing. It has become a barrier reef.

If the volcano sinks completely and vanishes, only the coral reef is left; it has become an atoll, a ring of coral surrounding a lagoon. In addition, we know today that island shores may rise or sink, and ocean levels may rise or fall. All these changes help explain the building of coral reefs.

HOW ARE SEASHELLS FORMED?

If you've ever walked along a beach, you've probably seen a seashell lying on the sand where it has been washed in by the waves. The shell will nearly always be empty, for it is the home of some sea animal that has died.

By the way, shells are also found in woodlands, rivers, and ponds as well as the sea. When people speak of shells, they usually mean those of soft-bodied animals known as mollusks.

Most mollusks have shells outside their soft bodies. The shell is a mollusk's skeleton. It is part of the animal and the mollusk is attached to it by muscles. The soft animal inside can never leave its shell and return to it. As the mollusk grows bigger, its shell increases in size and strength.

The shell is made of a form of limestone and is built by the mollusk itself. Certain glands in the mollusk are able to take limestone from the water and deposit it in tiny particles at the edge of, and along the inside of, the shell. As a mollusk grows in size, its shell increases in thickness and size. You can see the lines of growth that are marked by ridges that run parallel to the outer edge. You've probably noticed these growth lines in the shells of oysters and clams. The other ridges are caused by ridges in the "mantle" of the mollusk, or by muscles in its body.

The shell of a mollusk consists of three layers. The outside is covered with a thin layer of hornlike material that contains no lime. Under this is a layer of carbonate of lime. The inside layer is the "mother-of-pearl," or nacre. It is made up of very thin alternate layers of carbonate of lime and a horny substance.

The coloring of the shell comes from some glands of the mollusk that contain coloring matter. So a shell may be spotted, all one color, or marked with lines. Some shells are so tiny they can only be seen with a magnifying glass, while the giant clam has a shell that can be four feet long.

DOES SEAWEED HAVE ANY USE?

All over the world wherever there is a body of sea water, there seaweed may be found. Seaweed occurs in many varieties. It belongs to a large group of water plants called algae—plants without true leaves, stems, roots, or flowers.

But they do contain a green pigment called chlorophyll. Therefore, they are capable of making their own food. The reason these plants don't look green is that the chlorophyll is often concealed by other pigments. So some seaweed looks brown or red.

In the Temperate Zone, the most common seaweeds belong to the brown algae. This is the seaweed that grows between the high and low-tide lines. It has bubblelike floats that children enjoy crackling open between their fingers. The plants are attached to rocks by means of rootlike holdfasts.

Another well-known form of seaweed is the kelp. It has various forms. Most commonly they are long, flat, tough, bladelike forms that fasten to rocks by means of leathery stalks. Some of these seaweeds along the Atlantic Coast grow as long as twenty feet, and the giant kelp of the Pacific Ocean is even longer!

These kelp are among the seaweeds that are useful to man. They are often used as fertilizer because they have a high concentration of potash. They are also a source of iodine.

Another useful kind of seaweed is called Irish moss. It is rather rough and leathery in form. It produces a great deal of agar, which is a colorless substance resembling jelly. In the Orient, tons of seaweed belonging to the red-algae group are dried and used as food! They are not very nourishing, but contain a great deal of agar. They are used in thickening soups and providing bulk in other foods.

Seaweed is also a primary source of food for ocean life. Smaller sea creatures feed on it, and they in turn become food for the larger ones. Seaweed gives off oxygen, and this helps to keep the water pure. So you see why seaweed is considered quite useful to man.

WHAT IS THE CONTINENTAL SHELF?

When you think of the Atlantic Ocean, you think of the top surface of the water. But what is under the water, at the bottom of the ocean floor? Let's imagine that we are making a voyage out of New York, due east across the Atlantic Ocean. Here is a picture of the bottom as we move across the ocean.

For about two hundred miles, the bottom gradually slopes down. It is generally flat, but occasionally there is a V-shaped valley or canyon. This is the continental shelf. The continental shelf is part of the North American continent. It just happens to be too low to stand out of the sea.

At the depth of about one thousand two hundred feet, the shelf suddenly comes to an end. It is no longer gently sloping but there is a steep incline. This is the continental edge or slope, and it goes down to the full depth of the ocean.

Moving along past the slope, the ocean depth is about two-and-a-half miles. We are now crossing the deep ocean. Here the ocean bottom is very flat. It is called an abyssal plain. Abyssal plains cover about a third of the sea floor and are among the flattest places found on earth.

As we keep on moving across the ocean, we reach an area where there are humps on the sea floor. Some are the size of hills. This is called the Mid-Atlantic ridge. Near the center of the ridge the hills are higher and steeper, and some rise like mountains to within five thousand feet of the surface.

Between the mountains are deep valleys with flat floors. Right in the middle of the ridge lies the largest valley of all. It is called the mid-ocean rift. The rift is like a crack between the two halves of the ridge.

As we continue eastward, we again cross an abyssal plain. The plain slopes gently upward to the continental shelf off Portugal. And this is a picture of the bottom of the Atlantic Ocean.

WHAT IS A MARINE BIOLOGIST?

A marine biologist studies the creatures that live in the sea. To do this he has to catch fishes and study them when they are dead. Or else he must go down in the water and watch them while they are alive.

One of the most important tools of the biologist is the pickling bottle, containing alcohol or formalin. Without it he would have very little time to look at a creature he has collected, for the animal would soon decay.

Besides the pickling bottle the marine biologist uses a trawl net to catch fishes and other sea creatures. The trawl net is cone-shaped and looks something like a butterfly net. Its mouth is sewn to a hoop, and the rest trails behind. A towline from a ship is attached to the hoop. A heavy weight pulls down the line as the ship sails along.

Water and fishes flow in through the mouth of the net. The water escapes, but the fishes are caught. To catch bigger and fast-swimming fishes, the net is made with large meshes so that the water can flow through easily and the trawl can be towed very fast. To catch smaller fishes, the meshes are made finer.

When the biologist feels that enough has been caught, the net is hauled in. It is tipped out onto a canvas. The various kinds of creatures are counted, and the ones to be kept are popped into their bottles. What is left is thrown back or sent to the ship's galley.

Sometimes color pictures are taken of the specimens minutes after they die. This is done because many dead fish lose their color very quickly, even when they are preserved.

Back in the laboratory, the specimens are dissected. This means that they are carefully taken apart in order to examine every part of their bodies. The biologist dissects to learn how creatures are built. Then he can determine their differences and similarities.

WHAT IS ANTHROPOLOGY?

Like most sciences, the name of this one tells you what it is about. The name anthropology comes from two Greek words: *anthropos,* meaning "man," and *logos,* meaning "science." So anthropology should mean the study of man.

In a large sense, that is what anthropology is concerned with: man's physical structure, his customs and habits, his languages, arts and religions, and his civilizations. This means that a great many other studies are very closely linked with anthropology—for example, anatomy, physiology, psychology, ethics, sociology, and so on.

But, in actual practice, anthropology limits itself to a much narrower field. You might say that for practical purposes, three studies make up anthropology. The first is the study of man's place in nature. What separates man from other animals? What characteristics of his body set him apart from monkeys and other animals? How does his skull compare with that of a chimpanzee? The purpose of such studies is to trace the connection between man's physical qualities and his development and civilization.

The next study anthropology is concerned with is the various races of man and their classification. This is called ethnology. This science deals with the physical differences between the various human races. It compares the skeletons and skulls of prehistoric man with those of modern man. It also deals with the customs and religions of various tribes and peoples to find out how races differ and how they develop.

There is a third, a special branch of anthropology, called anthropometry. This is the science that deals with the physical measurements of man, the height and weight of various races, the shape of their bones, and so on.

WHAT IS THE SPHINX?

Of course, the sphinx most of us think of is the Great Sphinx that stands at Giza, Egypt, near the pyramids. Actually, a sphinx is a monster that was common in the myths of ancient peoples. The Greeks thought of it as having the head of a woman, the body of a lion, and wings. The Egyptians thought of it as a wingless lion with the head and breast of a man.

The Great Sphinx of Egypt was once a hill of rock left over from the building of the Great Pyramid. Later it was carved into a huge lion with the head of a man. It stands 66 feet high with a length of 240 feet. It was probably carved to resemble the face of a king called Chephren, a king of the fourth Egyptian dynasty.

In ancient times, lions lived in the desert just beyond the valley of the Nile. Because they were strong and beautiful, Egyptian sculptors carved statues of them to guard the entrances to temples. Later on, instead of a lion's head, they carved the head of a king.

In ancient Egypt the kings were considered to be descended from the sun god, who was called Ra. When a king died, he himself was supposed to become the sun god. So the Great Sphinx represents the king as the sun god guarding the pyramids.

Although there is no other sphinx as large as the Great Sphinx at Giza, many kings had their likenesses carved as sphinxes. In one case, a sphinx was made with the face of a woman, Queen Hatshepsut, who seized the throne and ruled the country. This sphinx was given a beard to represent Queen Hatshepsut's power.

WHY IS A FOUR-LEAF CLOVER LUCKY?

The desire of man to protect himself from unknown forces, or to create good fortune for himself, has led to thousands upon thousands of superstitions the world over. In fact, we can roughly divide superstitions into those that are supposed to bring good luck and those that are supposed to bring bad luck.

The four-leaf clover is believed by people all over the world to be a sign of coming good fortune and happiness. It is such an old superstition that no one can say exactly how or where it began. But there is an old legend about it that some people believe. The legend is that when Eve was sent away from Paradise, she took a four-leaf clover with her. Because the clover was a bit of green from the Garden of Paradise, it came to be considered an omen of good luck if found in one's own garden!

Just as widespread, and just as hard to explain, is the common belief that a horseshoe is lucky. Almost every country has a different legend or tradition concerning the horseshoe. The Irish say that the horse was in the stable where Christ was born, and therefore the horseshoe has magical power. In Russia, the blacksmith used to be considered a kind of magician, and it is claimed he used the horseshoe as a charm in performing his magic. Even the ancient Romans believed

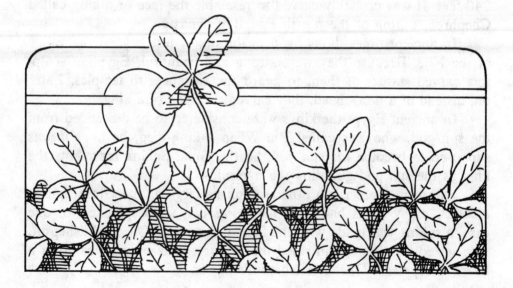

that finding a cast-off horseshoe in the road would protect one from illness. This may be because iron at one time was regarded as a good-luck charm.

When it comes to bad-luck omens, the fear of a black cat is one of the oldest. In the Middle Ages, when people believed in witches, it was assumed that witches and evil spirits took the form of the black cat. Today, many people are still uneasy to see a black cat cross their path!

The broken mirror is another bad-luck superstition that goes back to ancient times. In ancient Greece it was believed that one saw the will of the gods in the mirror. Therefore, if a mirror was broken accidentally, it meant that the gods didn't want the person to see the future because it held unpleasant things!

The Romans believed that a person's health changed every seven years. Since the mirror reflected the health of a person, they thought that breaking a mirror meant that the health of a person would be broken for seven years!

WHAT IS THE ROSETTA STONE?

As you know, one of the greatest civilizations of all time was the one of ancient Egypt. A long time ago, man had already begun to unearth monuments and buildings and treasures of all sorts going back to ancient Egypt. There was a strange kind of writing found with many of these objects and buildings, but no one could read it. And there seemed to be no way to figure out what it meant.

The early Greeks believed that Egyptian priests produced these writings for sacred purposes, so they called them *hieroglyphs,* which meant "sacred carvings." And this type of writing came to be known as hieroglyphics.

After the Greeks, no big effort was made to understand these writings until the seventeenth century, when many scholars worked on the problem. But they had no success. Then in 1799, a wonderful discovery was made. A black slab of basalt was found, which had lain for centuries near one of the mouths of the river Nile. It was named the Rosetta stone after the town where it was found.

Now what made the Rosetta stone so valuable was that it had a message written in three different languages. One was Greek; a second, hieroglyphics; and the third, a late form of Egyptian writing called demotic, a sort of abbreviated hieroglyphic.

Many years of study of these writings now began. The Greek text could be read and understood, and by comparing it to the others the long-lost secret of hieroglyphic writing was finally revealed. The man who accomplished this in 1822 was a brilliant young Frenchman called Jean François Champollion.

As a result of his discovery, it has been possible for historians to trace the life, customs, and religion of the Egyptians as far back as 3500 B.C. This was because hieroglyphics were the earliest form of Egyptian writing and one of the oldest-known systems of writing.

Basically it is picture writing. Each picture represents an object. But this writing developed as time went on, and later Egyptians wrote down words and ideas and sounds.

WHO WERE THE KNIGHTS?

Knights were the highest class of fighting men in Europe during the Middle Ages. The knights, who fought on horseback, were the aristocrats of the battlefield.

Their whole way of life was based on warfare, and they were the great heroes of that time. The high position of the knights was partly due to the fact that during the early Middle Ages kings and governments had very little real authority. Power belonged to the best fighters. The man who had horses and heavy arms and knew how to use them had a great advantage.

From their walled and moated castles the more powerful knights ruled the nearby countryside. They honored no law but their own, and they freely made war against their neighbors. A knight did as he wished, because no one else was powerful enough to stop him. Many knights did keep some sort of order in their land and protected their people from bandits. But many a knight was no better than a bandit himself.

The warfare of the knights was like a game, and their games were like war. The sport that was most like battle was the tournament. In time, tournaments became mock battles in which knights fought with flattened lances and blunted swords. The object of a tournament was about the same as that of a battle—to capture an enemy and collect ransom.

Knights had rules of behavior, called the code of chivalry. A knight was supposed to treat his captive as an honored guest, even if they had been bitter enemies. One knight was not supposed to attack another without warning.

Knights observed this chivalry among themselves because it was a matter of mutual advantage. A knight might be captured by another knight someday.

Knights could be attacked without warning, so no knight left his castle without wearing his heavy, uncomfortable armor for protection.

HOW OLD WAS JOAN OF ARC?

Saint Joan of Arc is honored by the people of France as one of their greatest heroines. She was born on January 6, 1412, and was burned at the stake on May 30, 1431. So she was only nineteen years old when she died.

When Joan was very young, much of France was ruled by the Burgundians, a powerful group of nobles who had joined with the English to gain control of the country.

When Joan was about thirteen years old, she began to hear "voices," which she said were those of Saints Catherine and Margaret, and of Michael the Archangel. She said the voices told her that she must bring peace to France by having the Dauphin Charles, who was heir to the throne, crowned king.

In time, Joan convinced Charles that she could lead his troops to victory. Joan inspired the French soldiers; they defeated the English, and the Dauphin was crowned Charles VII.

Later on, the king didn't give her full support in her efforts to continue the fight, the French troops began to suffer losses, and Joan was captured by the Burgundians.

She was accused of being a witch. Her judges were French clergymen who supported the Burgundians and English. During her trial, Joan behaved with great bravery. But she was found guilty and sentenced to death.

In 1455 a new court judged that she had been wrongly executed. The Catholic Church declared Joan a saint in 1920, and celebrates her feast on the anniversary of her death, May 30.

The story of Joan of Arc has become one of the most inspiring in history, and many books, plays, and ballads have been written about her.

WHO WAS NAPOLEON?

Few men in history have had as great an influence on the world and the times in which they lived as Napoleon Bonaparte.

He was born on August 15, 1769, in Ajaccio on the island of Corsica. When he was a boy, he identified himself with the great heroes of ancient history whom he read about. He was barely sixteen years old when he graduated from the military academy in Paris.

When he was just twenty-four years old, he was promoted to brigadier general for helping recapture the city of Toulon from the British. Later he led armies to victory over Austria, and won a war in Egypt.

Napoleon became the first consul, the ruler of France. He reformed the whole structure of government, enacting the Code Napoleon, which became the basis of modern French law.

In 1804, Napoleon was proclaimed emperor of France. During the ten years of the French Empire under Napoleon, there was almost continuous war. But his victories enabled him to dominate Europe from Spain to the borders of Russia.

In 1812 he decided to invade Russia with an army of more than six hundred thousand men. Even though he captured Moscow, his army didn't have enough supplies, so had to retreat. Only about one hundred thousand men survived the march home.

After several other defeats, Napoleon abdicated and was sent into exile on the island of Elba. He escaped from Elba and gathered a new army, but lost the battle at Waterloo to an allied army.

Napoleon surrendered to the British, who sent him as a prisoner to the barren island of St. Helena. There he remained until his death on May 5, 1821. While he led France to new greatness and power, it can also be said he caused great suffering and ruined the lives of whole nations of people.

WHO WAS LEONARDO DA VINCI?

Leonardo da Vinci was one of the most remarkable human beings who ever lived. Probably no one in history achieved so much in so many different fields as this man did.

Leonardo lived from 1452 to 1519. He was an outstanding painter, sculptor, and architect; he also designed bridges, highways, weapons, costumes, and scientific instruments. He invented the diving bell and tank and designed flying machines, though they could not be built with the materials of the time. He made important discoveries about the structure of the human body.

Leonardo approached science and art in the same methodical manner: After studying a problem, he made many sketches to help him find a solution. He saw no difference between planning a machine and a painting, and he became an expert in every field that interested him.

By the time Leonardo was twenty years old, he was listed as a master of the painters' guild. His work had a great influence on other painters, because he was always trying new things, such as the use of chiaroscuro, a technique which creates contrasts of light and dark.

One of Leonardo's greatest works, *The Last Supper,* was painted in Milan. Even though it is one of the world's masterpieces, it was actually an unsuccessful experiment. Because he worked slowly, Leonardo painted in oil on a damp wall. As a result, the painting began to peel, and today it is quite badly damaged.

Leonardo was interested in studying the human body, and he dissected corpses to find out how the body was put together. He also made many discoveries about plant growth.

Probably the single most famous painting in the world, the *Mona Lisa,* was painted by Leonardo in Florence.

WHO WAS SIR WALTER RALEIGH?

Almost everybody has heard the name of this man, but few people seem to know much about him. In the age of Elizabeth I, there were many great men, but Raleigh was probably the most varied in his genius and talents. He was soldier, sailor, courtier, poet, colonizer, historian, and scientist.

Raleigh was born about 1554 in Devonshire, England. As a youth he fought in the wars in France and later in Ireland. He won the favor of Queen Elizabeth I and was knighted and given various posts in the government.

Then Raleigh decided to do an interesting thing with the money he got from the Queen. He used it to start settlements in America. He sent out the first colony in 1585, a group of about one hundred men who lived on Roanoke Island, off the coast of North Carolina, for a year. This was the first English colony to experience life in the New World. All the later colonies flowed from this first attempt.

Much of our early knowledge of the Indians and of the geography of America and its plant and animal life we owe to Raleigh's efforts. In 1587 he sent out a second colony, but the colonists were all lost in the forests.

Raleigh knew many of the great poets and writers of his time, and he himself was one of the leading poets of his age. In 1595 he made his first voyage to Guiana in South America, where he hoped to find gold.

When King James I came to the throne, he accused Raleigh of being in a conspiracy against him and condemned him to death. Though the sentence was suspended, he spent most of the rest of his life in the Tower of London.

There he wrote a great book, *History of the World,* and made experiments in chemistry. In 1616 he was allowed out of prison and sailed again to Guiana. Instead of finding gold he clashed with the Spaniards and he was executed for this in 1618.

Raleigh was the man who introduced the potato from the New World to Ireland and was also the man who made smoking tobacco popular in Europe.

WHO WAS GEORGE WASHINGTON CARVER?

George Washington Carver was one of America's greatest agricultural scientists. His parents were the black slaves of a man called Moses Carver, who lived in Missouri. Soon after George was born, his father died. A few months later the baby and his mother were kidnapped by bandits. Moses Carver was able to buy George back, but his mother was never found, so the Carvers raised George themselves.

George showed a love for growing things at a very early age. He used to care for and cure sick plants, and the neighbors called him the plant doctor. He wandered about the United States seeking an education, doing all kinds of work to pay for his schooling. Finally he entered Iowa State College. He was the first black person to graduate from the college, and he became their first black teacher.

In 1896, he joined the staff of Tuskegee Institute, a new black college in Alabama. He was appointed to head the school's agriculture department. With the aid of his students, Carver built a homemade laboratory, using for equipment pots, kettles, and whatever else he could find that might be useful.

For nearly fifty years Carver taught at Tuskegee. In his laboratory he worked long hours, seeking ways to help the poor southern farmers. He introduced the peanut, pecan, and sweet potato to the cotton farmers, and showed them how these crops would enrich soil worn out by years of cotton planting.

In his laboratory he discovered new uses for these plants. From peanuts he made butter, coffee, ink, and soap. From sweet potatoes he made flour, cereals, glue, dyes, and rubber. He also made synthetic marble from wood shavings, rope from cornstalk fibers, and paint from Alabama clay.

Carver gave his discoveries to the world, asking no profit for himself. He gave advice freely to all who consulted him. He received offers of many high-paying jobs, but he preferred to remain at Tuskegee and teach. Today his great work is carried on through the George Washington Carver Foundation, which he set up with money from his savings. It provides scholarships for black students in agricultural research.

WHO WAS BOOKER T. WASHINGTON?

Booker Taliaferro Washington was one of America's great educators. He was born on a Virginia plantation on April 5, 1856. His mother was a slave who served as cook for the master's family.

After the Emancipation Proclamation was signed by Lincoln in 1863 freeing the slaves, Booker's mother left the plantation and moved with her children to Malden, West Virginia. There Booker entered a school for black children. To help support the family, he worked mornings in salt furnaces and coal mines before going to school.

At the age of seventeen, Booker entered the Hampton Normal and Agricultural Institute for black students in Virginia, and studied there for three years. After graduation he taught school and for awhile served as secretary to General Samuel Armstrong, principal of Hampton.

General Armstrong suggested Washington as organizer of a new industrial and teacher-training school for blacks in Tuskegee, Alabama. The school was very poor; no money was provided for buildings and land, and the first classes met in a run-down old church.

It was at Tuskegee that Washington did his great work as organizer and teacher. For years he traveled widely, sometimes by mule and buggy, to raise funds for the school. He was a stirring orator and made many speeches for the school. Washington was soon recognized as a leader in the field of Negro education.

During Washington's lifetime his school in Tuskegee grew until its campus consisted of over one hundred buildings, and its student body numbered almost one thousand six hundred. When he died in 1915, the school, now called Tuskegee Institute, remained as a monument to his life's work.

He was the author of several books. One of his best known is *Up From Slavery.*

WHAT IS THE DIFFERENCE BETWEEN A DEMOCRACY AND A REPUBLIC?

We in the United States live in both a democracy and a republic. A republic is a form of government that has no hereditary ruler, such as a king. But a republic need not be a democracy. A republic might have a dictator at the head of the government who holds all power, disregards the will of the people and doesn't allow the people to express their free choice.

On the other hand, a democracy might be a monarchy with a royal family, such as England has. England is one of the world's oldest and greatest democracies, even though it isn't a republic.

The word "democracy" comes from Greek and means the rule of the people. No nation can be considered democratic unless it gives protection to various human liberties. Among the democratic liberties are freedom of speech, movement, and association. The people must be free to express themselves on all issues and questions, and to move about as they please and associate with whom they choose.

Freedom of the press, religious freedom, and equality before the law are other democratic rights. It is very important in a democracy that life, liberty, and property be free from arbitrary and unlawful controls. Men of all races, religions, and degrees of wealth must be treated as equal before the law.

Such liberties are guaranteed by many nations in their constitutions. But such guarantees are not always upheld, and not every nation that claims it is a democracy really is.

Today, all over the world, the idea of democracy is being greatly expanded. It is believed by many that democracy should also include economic democracy, which means more equality in the wealth of men, and social equality, which means equality of opportunity to enjoy all the benefits of society, such as housing, health, and recreation.

HOW DID LAFAYETTE HELP THE UNITED STATES?

The Marquis de Lafayette, who was a brilliant leader in the French Revolution, also was a great fighter for the freedom of the American colonies.

He was born on September 6, 1757. At the age of thirteen he inherited a fortune so large that, in terms of today's money, he had an income of two million dollars a year. He was married at the age of sixteen.

In 1776 Lafayette decided to go to America to fight for the freedom of the colonies. Benjamin Franklin and other Americans in France encouraged his sympathy. Lafayette and a few companions reached Georgetown, South Carolina, on June 13, 1777. From Georgetown, Lafayette and his party traveled nine hundred miles overland, by coach and on horseback, to Philadelphia. There the Continental Congress gave him a commission as major general.

He first saw action at the battle of Brandywine, where he was wounded in the leg. He also went through the hardships of Valley Forge and fought at the Battle of Monmouth.

Lafayette then went back to France where he was able to arrange for six thousand French troops to be sent to America. He returned to bring General George Washington the good news.

Washington entrusted him with the defense of Virginia against the British. Lafayette successfully laid seige to the British Army under Lord Cornwallis. The British general had promised that he would capture "the boy." Instead, Lafayette was present at Yorktown on October 19, 1781, when Cornwallis surrendered. Then Lafayette, who knew that American independence was assured, returned to France. He was barely twenty-four years old.

When Lafayette died in Paris on May 20, 1834, flags in the United States were flown at half-mast, and the Army went into mourning for six months, as it had after George Washington's death.

WHAT IS A CATHEDRAL?

During the Middle Ages all of Western Europe was Roman Catholic. Each community had its own church. These churches were grouped into districts called dioceses. Each diocese was under the jurisdiction of a bishop.

The principal church of the diocese contained the throne of the bishop. In Latin the name of this church was *ecclesia cathedralis,* or "cathedral church." In English it has been shortened to "cathedral."

Most European cathedrals were constructed with the floor plan in the general shape of a cross. The long part of the cross is the nave and serves as the assembly room for the congregation.

The two arms of the cross are the transepts, and the fourth part, containing the altar and choir, is the apse. The section where the four parts meet is the crossing. Towers or domes were often built over the crossing.

Cathedrals have been built in nearly every style of architecture. But most of the very famous European cathedrals were either Byzantine, Romanesque, Gothic, or Renaissance.

Most of the very famous European cathedrals, such as Notre Dame of Paris, are in the Gothic style of the twelfth and thirteenth centuries. Strangely enough, the world's largest Gothic cathedral, St. John the Divine, was built in the nineteenth and twentieth centuries in New York City, and is not Roman Catholic, but Episcopal.

St. Peter's in Rome is not officially a cathedral, since it is not the seat of a bishop. It is an outstanding example of a Renaissance building. The dome was designed by the great Michelangelo, and is considered to be a masterpiece in itself.

WHAT WAS THE MONROE DOCTRINE?

Before and during the crisis over Cuba, there was much discussion of the Monroe Doctrine. The American Government said it had a right to keep European powers from trying to run the affairs of countries in the Western Hemisphere.

The Monroe Doctrine is a statement on foreign policy issued by President James Monroe. In December, 1823, he delivered a message to Congress, and part of it was devoted to foreign policy. This part came to be known as the Monroe Doctrine, and the foreign policy of the United States has been guided by it ever since. Here are the four main points included in this famous statement:

1. The American continents are not to be considered open to future colonization by any European powers.

2. The European political system is different from that of America. Any attempt to extend the European system to the Western Hemisphere will be considered dangerous to the peace and safety of the United States.

3. The United States will not interfere with any existing colonies or dependencies of European powers.

4. The United States has never taken any part in the internal affairs of European nations, nor will it do so in the future.

But for a long time the United States was not strong enough to enforce the Monroe Doctrine. For example, Napoleon III of France used French troops to place Archduke Maximilian of Austria upon the Mexican throne. But, in 1904, Theodore Roosevelt said that the United States could interfere in the affairs of Latin America to keep Europeans out, and United States Marines were sent into several countries during the next twenty years to restore order and protect the property of United States citizens.

Today the United States tries to uphold the Monroe Doctrine, but without interfering in the internal affairs of other American nations.

WHAT IS FASCISM?

Fascism is the name of a political movement founded by Benito Mussolini in Italy in 1919. Led by Mussolini, the Italian Fascists took over the government in 1922 and set up a one-party and one-man dictatorship that ruled Italy until 1943.

Similar movements in other countries, such as Hitler's Nazis in Germany, copied Mussolini's methods. The word "fascist" is used to describe all of these movements in general.

The fascists hated democracy. They believed ordinary people should not have the right to elect a government. Under fascism the "weak" were forced to obey the "strong." There was no political party but the fascist party.

The fascists had no use for justice or the rights of man. There were police and courts of law, but they were not there to protect the ordinary citizen. They were used to carry out the orders of the men in power.

The fascists had no use for freedom. People were forced to do what the state (which meant the fascists in control of the state) wanted them to do. The schools taught young people to obey and not to ask questions.

The fascist party controlled newspapers, books, and radio. They told editors and writers what to say and write. Nobody was allowed to write or say anything the fascists disliked.

The fascists had no use for peace. They wanted the nation to be strong and united so that it could go to war. They declared that a nation was only great if it made itself feared by others.

When Germany and Italy were defeated in World War II, fascism as a political philosophy and form of government was completely discredited.

WHAT IS EASTER?

Easter celebrates the Resurrection of Jesus Christ. It is the most important feast in the Christian calendar.

Easter Sunday does not come on the same date every year, but falls sometime between March 22 and April 25. It falls on the first Sunday after the first full moon following March 21, the vernal equinox (the time in spring when day and night are of equal length). The date of Easter Sunday was established by the church council of Nicaea in 325 A.D.

Easter Sunday ends a period of preparing for the feast of Easter. This forty-day period of prayer and fasting, called Lent, begins on Ash Wednesday and ends on Holy Saturday, the day before Easter. The Lenten fast commemorates Christ's forty-day fast in the desert.

The week from Palm Sunday to Easter Sunday is known as Holy Week. During Holy Week, church services remind one of the last days of Christ's life on earth. Palm Sunday marks Christ's entry into Jerusalem. Holy Thursday, also called Maundy Thursday, marks the Last Supper. Good Friday marks Christ's crucifixion, and Easter Sunday, his resurrection.

There are many customs that have developed around Easter. The custom of a sunrise service on Easter Sunday can be traced to ancient spring festivals that celebrated the rising sun. The new clothes worn on Easter Sunday are a symbol of new life. The custom comes from the baptism on Easter Sunday of early Christians, who were led into the church wearing new robes of white linen.

The familiar Easter parade goes back to the Middle Ages, when people walked about the countryside on Easter, stopping along the way to pray. Now, of course, it presents an opportunity for people to see and show their new spring clothes.

The egg is an Easter symbol, because it is a symbol of life. The Persians and Egyptians also colored eggs and ate them during their new year's celebration, which came in the spring.

IS NEW YEAR'S DAY THE SAME AROUND THE WORLD?

Welcoming the new year is one of the oldest and gayest customs celebrated the world over. But no festival has been observed on so many different dates or in so many different ways.

The ancient Greeks began their new year with the new moon after June 21. Before the time of Julius Caesar, the Roman new year started on March 1. In most European countries during the Middle Ages, the new year began on March 25.

What about today? In most Christian countries the new year begins on January 1. But other countries and religions observe New Year's Day on different dates, according to the calendars they use.

The Chinese celebrate two New Year's Days. One is on January 1, and the other takes place on the New Year's Day reckoned according to the Chinese lunar calendar. This may occur any time between January 21 and February 19.

Indonesia also has two New Year celebrations, one on January 1 and another on the Islamic New Year, a date that varies from year to year. The Russian Orthodox Church observes the New Year according to the Julian calendar, which places the day on January 14.

The Jewish New Year, Rosh Hashanah, is celebrated about the time of the autumnal equinox at the end of September or the beginning of October. In Vietnam the New Year usually begins in February.

Iran celebrates New Year's Day on March 21. Each of the religious groups in India has its own date for the beginning of the year. One Hindu New Year comes sometime in April or May.

The people in Morocco observe the beginning of the year on the tenth day of Muharram, the first month of the Islamic year. The Koreans celebrate their New Year during the first three days in January.

By the way, the custom of sending New Year's cards is a very old one. The Chinese have been doing it for more than one thousand years. Their cards carried the name of the visitor who came to call, but no greeting or message.

WHAT IS ESPERANTO?

Man for a long time has been trying to create a universal language that would serve all men all over the world as a common means of communication.

Since the seventeenth century, more than seven hundred such languages have been constructed. There are two kinds of such languages. The "a priori" kind have no connection with any existing language. The "a posteriori" kind use a mixture of existing languages. The most popular of the constructed languages is Esperanto.

It was invented by Ludwik Zamenhof, who lived in the town of Bialystok, Poland. As a young man, he saw that there was a great deal of enmity between the four groups of people who lived there— the Russians, Poles, Germans, and Jews. He felt that a common language would help these people get along better. When he was still in school, he had already worked out the beginnings of his international language.

In 1887, he published a brochure describing his language, and he used the pen name of Dr. Esperanto (one who hopes). Soon people in various parts of the world became interested in this language, which came to be called "Esperanto."

Today, Esperanto is spoken by about eight million people throughout the world. Even governments and international organizations recognize it in many ways. For example, you can send an international telegram in Esperanto. It is often used on radio broadcasts from official government stations.

There are many rules of grammar for this language, and here are a few. The definite article is "la" and does not change. All nouns end in "o," all adjectives in "a," all adverbs in "e," and all infinitives in "i." The plural of nouns and adjectives is formed by adding "j."

Here is the beginning of the Lord's Prayer in Esperanto: "Patro nia, kiu estas en la cielo, snkta estu via nomo; venu regeco via; esto volo via, kiel en la cielo, tiel ankau sur la tero."

WHAT IS THE DIFFERENCE BETWEEN A COLLEGE AND A UNIVERSITY?

Someday you may be preparing to enter a college or a university, and then you will become very interested in what each place has to offer and why you should try to go to one rather than another.

The chief difference between a college and a university is that the university usually includes a number of colleges. Many institutions pretend to be universities when they are not. On the other hand, some colleges are more like universities.

Here is one definition of a university given by the National Education Association: "an institution of higher education, having as a nucleus a college in which the so-called liberal arts are taught in a course of three or four years for a degree . . . and in addition one or more departments for the learned professions, medicine, law, or divinity."

The term "college" originally meant any society or union of persons engaged in common activity or granted certain powers and rights to carry on a common work. That's why the cardinals who elect the Pope at Rome are called the "College of Cardinals." And the United States has an "electoral college" that chooses the President and Vice-President. But in the United States, when we say college, we usually mean an institution attended after graduation from high school, and one that gives general, rather than highly specialized or technical training.

There are many "colleges" in the United States, however, that really should not be considered colleges. For example, any institution of higher education that has but one faculty (teachers in only one field of knowledge) and offers a single course of study is likely to be known as a college.

A college and a university differ in that the university includes several special colleges or schools. These special schools give instruction in professions such as law, medicine, forestry, and so on. Sometimes students go to college first, and then take graduate work at a university.

WHAT IS DONE WITH OLD MONEY?

Most of us would say: "If they don't know what to do with it, let them send it to me!" But the Government does know what to do with it. In fact, if old money weren't taken out of circulation at a regular rate, we'd find it a big nuisance, for torn and wrinkled paper money is inconvenient to handle.

The average life of a paper bill is only about a year, and for a dollar bill it's even less! So every day, the Treasury receives from banks and other sources worn and dirty bills to replace. How much? From four to five tons of paper money a day!

The old money is cancelled; that is, taken out of circulation. Then the bills are destroyed in a machine called a macerator, which does away with a million dollars a minute.

If you have damaged paper money, this doesn't make it worthless. If three-fifths of the note is preserved, you can send it to the Treasury and redeem it at full value. If more than two-fifths but less than three-fifths is sent in, you will get half of its value.

The paper on which the notes are printed is specially made for the Government. It has in it a mixture of linen and cotton. In the paper are embedded colored fibers of silk, nylon, or other synthetic material. When you hold a bill up to the light, you can see some of these fibers.

United States money used to be of various sizes. From 1861 to 1928 it was 7 and 7/16 inches by 3 and 1/8 inches. But in 1928 it was made smaller, and the new size is what we have today—6 and 5/16 inches by 2 and 11/16 inches.

All United States money is coined or printed by the Treasury Department. Paper money is printed by the Bureau of Engraving and Printing at Washington.

WHY DID RUSSIA SELL ALASKA?

Today Alaska is our forty-ninth state. But at one time the tremendous potential and importance of this area were recognized by very few people. In fact, when it was bought by the United States in 1867 for $7,200,000 from Russia, it was called Seward's Folly.

William Seward was Secretary of State under Lincoln, and he had urged that we buy it. We obtained an area about twice the size of Texas, 586,400 square miles, at a price a little less than two cents an acre! Most Americans at the time thought it was too much to pay for such a barren, far-off place.

Alaska was one of the last areas of the world to be discovered and explored by white men. In the early eighteenth century, under Peter the Great, Russia extended its empire through Siberia and into the Pacific. In 1741, Vitus Bering, a Dane in the service of the Russian Navy, led an expedition of two small ships (his second expedition) that finally succeeded in reaching Alaska.

Throughout the rest of the eighteenth and much of the nineteenth century, Russia explored its Alaskan territory, then known as Russian America. It governed Alaska through the Russian America Company. But during this time also, sea captains of Spain, France, and Great

Britain explored the Alaska coast. The first United States vessels reached Alaska in 1788.

In 1821 Russia declared other nations were not to be allowed to trade or fish or do business north of a certain line. But in 1824 and 1825 Russia signed treaties with England and the United States giving them trading rights.

When the Crimean War broke out in 1854, the Russians felt that they had too much trouble at home to bother with Alaska. They also felt that Alaska was too exposed and too far away for Russia to be able to protect it. Negotiations were started in 1859 to sell Alaska to the United States. The Civil War temporarily halted negotiations, but in 1867 the sale was made.

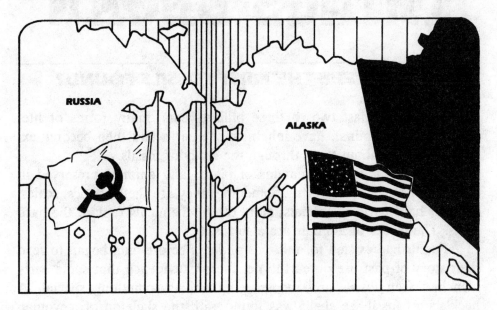

CHAPTER 2
HOW THINGS BEGAN

WHERE WERE THE FIRST FOSSILS FOUND?

During the past two to three billion years, many forms of life, both plant and animal, have inhabited the earth and then become extinct. We know about them through the study of fossils.

Most fossils are the remains of plants and animals preserved in rock. Fossils take many forms. Sometimes they are shells, bones, scales, or other hard parts of animals; more often, chemicals replace the hard parts. The tracks of animals are also fossils.

Fossils had existed for millions of years before man began to read their story of past life on earth. Yet there is evidence that some early men had seen fossils and recognized them as something special. A necklace of fossil sea shells was found with the skeleton of a woman who died thirty thousand years ago.

The scholars of ancient Greece and Rome found fossil sea shells far up in the mountains. They realized that these shells were the remains of animals that had once lived in the sea. And so they reasoned that in past ages these mountains had been under the sea.

Scientists did not really begin to study fossils until the late 1700's. One of the first men to do so was Baron Georges Cuvier, a great French naturalist. In the rocks along the river banks near Paris, Cuvier found the bones of elephants, hippopotamuses, and many other animals no longer seen in that region. He realized that the climate around

Paris must once have been very different, something like the climate of India and Africa today.

Then an Englishman named William Smith began to study fossils all over England. He discovered that each kind of rock had its own group of fossils. Older rocks would generally contain simpler fossils than newer rocks. From this he was able to tell the relative age of the rocks. Charles Darwin later used evidence from fossils to show how living forms developed from past forms, and how higher forms might have developed from simpler ones.

WHEN DID CIVILIZATION BEGIN?

It took man a long, long time to reach what we call a state of civilization. At first he lived in a state of savagery, much like animals. He had no language, and obtained food wherever he could find it.

Later on he had a family organization, learned to make fire, and still later, how to make tools and hunt for food. He invented pottery so that he could cook his food, began to live in tribes, and was able to move to new places.

The next stage of man, which is called barbarism, saw him learn how to raise food from seeds and how to tame animals. Then he began to smelt metals, such as copper and iron, so that he could make better weapons. He also began to build houses. When he invented a system of picture writing, it marked the end of barbarism and the beginning of civilization.

The invention of writing is considered the beginning of civilization, because it enabled man to keep records of past happenings. In this way, people could learn from the experience of others. This happened about five thousand or six thousand years ago.

By the time man reached this stage, he had developed in other ways, too. He had built up agriculture and industry to the point where people could live in villages and even in cities. There was government, there was trade, there were laws, and there were migrations of people.

The earliest civilizations that are known to us in history are those of the Egyptians and the Babylonians. The Egyptians had a form of writing four thousand five hundred years ago. They had a system of government and an understanding of mathematics (used in building the pyramids); they had a calendar, employed architects, and knew how to use various machines.

There was also a civilization on the island of Crete about four thousand years ago; and the Sumerian people, who lived along the Tigris and Euphrates rivers, had a civilization as far back as four thousand five hundred years ago.

DID PEOPLE ALWAYS LIVE IN FAMILIES?

No one knows how the first family started. Excavations in ancient caves show that men, women, and children lived together in small groups. It is not certain that the groups separated at first into units of father, mother, and children that we think of as a family, although the women probably cared for their own children. The "family" kept warm with fire and protected themselves against wild animals with simple weapons.

A family kind of life is more necessary among human beings than among other creatures. This is because the most helpless creature on earth is the human baby. Most insects and other members of the lower forms of life can move about and get their own food as soon as they are hatched. But the young of the higher forms of life—human infants, baby bears, and other animals—must be fed and protected.

The father (human or animal) usually brings the food for the mother and protects the young against enemies. The mother is most important, for she provides the milk for the baby. Thus the family is formed because it is necessary for the young and adults to stay together.

During the hundreds of thousands of years that family life has existed, different forms of family organization have developed among different peoples. In some tribes, the mother's brother was head of the family. The father had little to do with the children.

The pharaohs in ancient Egypt married their sisters. During Biblical times and earlier, a man might have two or more wives. Among some peoples a woman might have several husbands. The marriage of a man or woman to more than one mate is called polygamy.

There are still families in Africa and the Near East with more than one wife, but the practice seems to be dying out.

HOW DID ANIMALS GET THEIR NAMES?

Not all the English names of animals came about the same way. Some are just the English word for a name that already existed in another language. Others are combinations of words that describe the animal. Let's consider the names of some animals and see how they originated.

Hippopotamus is the Greek for river horse. *Hippos* meant horse, and *potamos* meant river. Rhinoceros is a Latin term derived from two Greek words. *Rinos* meant the "nose," and *keras* was a "horn." And the rhinoceros has a horn on its nose!

Leopard comes from the Latin *leopardus,* which meant a spotted lion. Lion comes from the Latin *leon.* Camel comes from the Arabic *gamel,* which was *camelos* in Latin.

Wolf is a modern spelling of the Anglo-Saxon *wulf,* which goes back to the Latin *vulpes,* and which meant fox. Our name fox comes from the Icelandic *fax,* which meant a hair-mane. The name opossum comes from *opassum,* which is what the Indians of Virginia called this animal.

Bull comes from the Anglo-Saxon *belkan,* which meant to roar. Deer was originally *deor* in Anglo-Saxon, and meant a wild animal. Porcupine comes from two Latin words: *porcus,* a swine, and *spina,* a thorn. So it's a pig with thorns.

When we call a cat a puss it goes back to the Egyptians. They called a cat *pasht,* which meant the moon, because cats were active at night. This became shortened to *pas,* and that's how we got puss.

The name poodle comes from the German *pudel,* which meant a puddle. This was because it was a water dog. And the word dog itself is a contraction of the Icelandic *doggr.* These are only a few names of animals, but you can see how they originated in many different ways.

WHO BUILT THE FIRST CASTLE?

The idea of a castle is connected with defense. In fact, the word "castle" comes from a Latin word meaning *fort.* So a castle was a home of a ruler or lord that could be defended.

Even in ancient Egypt, the royal palaces were fortified with towers and parapets, and so were like castles. In ancient Greece, too, the chieftains fortified their palaces. But the castle as we think of it really came into its own during the Middle Ages in western Europe, from A.D. 1000 to A.D. 1500.

The reason for this was the feudal system. Individual nobles controlled their own sections of the country and their people. They would often attack or take advantage of neighboring areas in order to strengthen their power. And, of course, they would be attacked in return. So they had to make their own homes into strong forts, and thus built what we call castles.

Since the conditions were pretty much alike in most of Europe, the castles that were built were quite similar, whether they were in France, Germany, Spain, or England. One of the first such structures was the Tower of London, begun in 1078 by William the Conqueror. It was several stories high, had double walls, small windows, and spiral staircases in the corners of the tower. The lord and his garrison of troops lived there.

Another early castle, Hedingham Castle, in Essex, England, was built in 1130. It had double walls of stone twenty feet thick, and its corners were even thicker. There was a great center hall, two stories high. The only light came from a few small windows high up in the wall. It was planned this way for reasons of defense; few and small windows were good protection.

Later on, castles were built around inner courtyards, so that there would be more room for the people living in them, and more comfortable facilities could be set up.

WHO INVENTED THE FIRST PLOW?

Before a farmer can plant his seeds, he must prepare the ground by plowing. The plow breaks up the hard ground and turns the soil over.

The plow is a very ancient invention, and no one knows who made the first plow. The earliest plows that have been found are about five thousand years old. The main purpose of all plows is to stir up the soil by dragging or raking something through it. At first the plow was just a forked stick or log, pulled by men or women. Later, men learned to use animals to pull plows.

Gradually the shape of the plowing stick was changed so that it would work better. The bottom of the stick was shaped into a pointed blade called the plowshare. This helped the plow cut through the ground more easily.

Then curved sides were added to the plow. These sides turn the soil over as it is plowed up and break it up more thoroughly. The sides are called moldboards. Together the plowshare and moldboards are called the plow bottom. The type of plow that is most commonly used today is called a moldboard plow.

The plowshare was made much stronger and sharper by cutting it out of metal. In the eighteenth century the British began making cast-iron plowshares. In 1797 Charles Newbold, an American inventor, patented the first American cast-iron plow. Modern plows are made of cast iron or steel, depending on what kind of soil the plow is to be used in.

Did you know that Thomas Jefferson used mathematics to find the best shape for a plow bottom (the plowshare plus the moldboards) and helped make the cast-iron plow popular?

In dry, hard soils, disk plows are used instead of moldboard plows. Instead of pointed blades on the bottom, disk plows have sharp-edged steel disks. Disk plows are good for rocky soil because they can roll over rocks that might stop or damage a moldboard plow. Disk plows are also very good for plowing old plants into the soil to enrich it.

WHERE DID CORN ORIGINATE?

Corn, or maize, is one of the most useful plants known to man. Today it is an important crop in southern Europe, Africa, parts of Asia, and, of course, the United States.

Scientists believe that it originated somewhere in Central or South America. Prehistoric Indians probably selected seeds year after year from wild grasses. After several centuries they had developed a plant very much like the corn we know today. Corn is a plant that cannot survive unless man cares for it. No wild plants closely resembling corn are now known.

Indians had their own stories about the origin of corn. In one tale a young girl turned herself into a corn plant to give mankind a new grain. She left her hair on the plant as corn silks to remind people to take good care of her gift.

The Indians liked corn with blue, red, and black kernels. They gave their colorful corn to the Pilgrims to feed them during the first cold winter in America. The next year the Pilgrims shared their own harvest with the Indians. This was the first Thanksgiving.

Corn was first introduced to the Old World as maize by Christopher Columbus. Maize was the Indian name for the grain. It has kept this name, spelled in a variety of ways, in most countries. Since the word "corn" in England meant any kind of grain, the Pilgrims called this new grain "Indian corn."

Today there are six chief types of corn. Dent corn is the most widely grown. It has a notch at the top of the kernel. Flint corn has hard kernels and withstands cold and disease.

The corn we eat is usually sweet corn, flour corn, or popcorn. Sweet corn is high in sugar. Flour corn is used to make flour. Popcorn is corn that bursts from its small, hard-shelled kernels when heated.

WHERE DID ORANGES ORIGINATE?

There are records that show that in China the orange was known at least four thousand years ago!

There are two kinds of orange tree, the sweet and the sour. The sour orange was the first orange grown in Europe. It was introduced by the Moors who invaded southern Spain and Sicily around the ninth century.

By the eleventh century the Moors were quite strongly in control of the conquered countries, and they planted sour orange and other trees. Sour oranges were widely grown in southern Europe until the fifteenth century, when increased trade with the Orient brought sweet oranges to Europe. Although some sour oranges are still grown and eaten, they are now used mainly as rootstocks for sweet oranges.

Sweet oranges were at first a luxury that only very rich people could afford. Kings and nobles paid great prices to obtain orange trees, which they planted in their gardens.

In the colder countries the delicate trees would be killed during a cold winter, so special greenhouses, called orangeries, were built. The orange trees were planted in tubs. During the summer they were moved outside, but in winter they were kept safe behind glass in the orangeries, where they could bloom despite the cold outside.

Did you know that when Christopher Columbus sailed for the New World he carried seeds of oranges and many other citrus fruits with him? The seeds were planted on the island of Hispaniola. Citrus trees flourished in the tropical climate of the West Indies and what is now Florida.

The Indians ate the oranges and, as they traveled about, they dropped the seeds. Planted in this way, groves of citrus trees were soon growing wild.

Today the United States leads the world in the production of oranges. The state of Florida has the greatest number of orange trees and produces more sweet oranges than any other state—or country!

WHERE DID WATERMELONS ORIGINATE?

On a hot summer day is there anything that tastes as good as a cold, juicy watermelon? It's no wonder then that this fruit has been enjoyed by man for thousands of years.

The watermelon originated in tropical Africa and spread from there to every possible place where the soil and climate were right. In ancient Sanskrit there is a word for watermelon, and there are early Egyptian drawings that show watermelons. So we know that it has been cultivated for more than four thousand years!

The watermelon is one of several types of melons, all of which belong to the gourd family. Like cucumbers, they are trailing annual vines with flat, lobed leaves and bell-shaped flowers.

Muskmelons are another ancient type of melon, which grew originally in southern Asia. All muskmelons have a faint, musky perfume, which gives them their name. Muskmelons are often called cantaloupes.

The Casaba and the honeydew melons ripen late in the season and keep better than other melons. Casaba melons are large, with smooth, yellowish-green rinds. Their flavor is delicate and their flesh is pale green. Honeydew melons have an even smoother rind, and their flesh is deeper green than that of Casaba melons.

Watermelons are considerably larger than muskmelons, and much juicier. Some watermelons weigh more than fifty pounds, but most of them are smaller. The rind is hard and green, often mottled or striped with lighter green. The flesh is pinkish, yellowish, or red.

Watermelons need a long growing season and a hot climate. They are planted after the ground is warm and there is no danger of frost. Watermelons are usually eaten fresh, but they can be pickled and the rind made into a preserve. In Oriental countries their seeds are considered a delicacy.

WHEN WAS WINE FIRST MADE?

Wine is the fermented juice of grapes. It has been enjoyed by man for thousands of years.

Probably the first people to make wine were Persian farmers living near the Caspian Sea. The Egyptians learned how to make wine from them as long ago as 3000 B.C. Pictures on the walls of tombs in the pyramids show the ancient Egyptians making wine.

Wine was common in the everyday life of the early Greeks and Romans. It was important to their religious ceremonies. The god of wine was called Bacchus by the Romans and Dionysus by the Greeks.

In the fourth century B.C., the Greek conqueror Alexander the Great carried grapevines and the knowledge of wine-making to Central Asia. The Greeks also took vines to southern France. Roman invaders probably took vines to northern France and Germany in later centuries.

When Leif Ericson landed on the eastern coast of North America in about 1000 A.D. he found so many wild grapevines growing there that he called the place Vinland. Later, Spanish explorers and missionaries brought grapevines from Europe to California.

Wine was used ceremonially in many ancient religions. And it is used today in many Christian and Jewish religious ceremonies. In times when pure water was scarce, wine was considered safe and healthful to drink.

Wine can be made from many fruits and plants that contain natural sugar. But most wine is made from grapes. When we say "wine," without using a descriptive name, such as "peach wine" or "blackberry wine," we always mean grape wine.

There are more than eight thousand varieties of grapes that can be used to make wine.

WHO MADE THE FIRST TABLE?

Can you imagine a house without a table in it? A table fills so many needs—eating, writing, playing games, holding lamps, and so on—that tables seem to have existed since the beginning of civilization.

A small table, made of metal or wood, was known to the Sumerians, and theirs is the first civilization of which we have any records. The Babylonians and Assyrians got the idea from them, as did the Egyptians. The Egyptians produced small, low tables that were beautifully designed and had fine workmanship.

The Greeks, who adapted many things from the Egyptian civilization, developed all kinds of furniture, including tables. Their tables were made of marble, metals, and inlaid woods.

Then the Romans carried the development of furniture to an even higher level. They not only had tables made entirely of metal or wood, but they also made costly ornamental tables that were delicately carved and inlaid with ivory and precious metals. The legs were carved into sphinxes, fluted columns, or to resemble the legs of rams or lions.

It was the custom among them to recline rather than sit at the dining table, so the tables were low in height. By the way, in ancient times, tables of any kind were owned only by the rich.

During the Middle Ages, tables appeared in all kinds of shapes: circular, oval, and oblong. But they were made quite simply—just boards supported by a fixed or folding trestle. They were covered with tablecloths that reached to the floor in order to hide the supports. After a meal, they were cleared out of the way.

During the sixteenth century, in the castles of the rich, there would be a fixed table in the great hall. This was reserved for the nobility, and ordinary people sat at smaller, separate tables or boards.

WHY DO MEN RAISE THEIR HATS TO LADIES?

This custom, like so many others that we practice today, passed through many stages of development before it came down to us.

Long, long ago, uncovering one's body in the presence of another person was considered a sign of respect and deference. Usually, it was

the upper part of the body that was uncovered. In time, instead of uncovering the body, it was considered enough to uncover one's head. And gradually, the mere raising of the hat was all that was necessary to show respect.

During the age of knights, it was the custom for a knight to wear his full armor in public. But when a knight came among friends, he would remove his helmet. This was a symbol of the fact that he felt safe among friends and didn't need the protection of his helmet.

This custom, combined with the already existing custom of uncovering one's head as a sign of respect, created the tradition of raising the hat as a mark of courtesy. In our civilization, of course, it is men who are expected to show signs of courtesy to women, so the custom of raising the hat is still practiced by men today!

WHEN DID PEOPLE FIRST FREEZE FOOD?

We think of frozen food as a new invention, but it is actually one of the oldest methods known for preserving food. From the days when man first inhabited cold regions, he froze fish, game, and other meats for future use.

The first known patent for freezing food was granted as early as 1852 in England. The method used was to immerse the food in an ice-

and-salt brine. Many other patents were granted for freezing food at that time, all using ice-and-salt mixtures.

But frozen foods could not be used extensively until the development of mechanical refrigeration. This made it possible to freeze and transport meats over long distances.

Early in the twentieth century, attempts were made to preserve foods other than meats and fish by freezing. A man called H. S. Baker froze fruits in Colorado as early as 1908. The purpose of this was to freeze the part of the fruit crop that couldn't be marketed and sell it for use later.

Only certain fruits were frozen at first, chiefly strawberries and cherries. They were frozen by what is known as the cold-pack method. This means placing barrels or containers of the fruit in large storage rooms where the temperature is maintained at 10 and 15 degrees below zero fahrenheit.

In 1916, experiments in Germany showed that foods could be frozen by the quick-freeze method, which meant freezing the food in a few hours instead of in several days. In 1917 a man called Clarence Birdseye began to work on methods for freezing food in small containers for sale in stores. It wasn't until 1919 that the first commercial pack of this type was put on the market.

As the result of his experiments and the work of others, it was found that many vegetables could also be preserved in this manner, and the frozen-food industry was on its way.

WHEN WAS COAL FIRST USED?

Coal has been used by man since very ancient times. Probably the first people to use it were the Chinese. There are records to show the Chinese used coal to smelt copper and iron perhaps as far back in time as three thousand years ago.

Coal is mentioned in the Bible. In the Book of Proverbs we read: "As coals are to burning coals, and wood to fire, so is a contentious man to kindle strife." The Greek philosopher Aristotle, who lived from 384 to 322 B.C., mentions coal in his writings.

During the period when the Romans occupied Britain, which began about 50 B.C., coal was used. We know this because in the ruins of Roman villas in Britain both coal and cinders have been found.

Here is an interesting fact about a certain coal mine. There are records that show that coal was mined in the Dutch province of Limburg in the year 1113. This mine, now known as the Domaniale Mine, is still being used and produces the most coal in the Netherlands!

During the mid-thirteenth century, women and children gathered what was known as sea coal along the English coast, and there were already several mines in England. Blacksmiths needed the coal for heating the iron for their smithies. Owners of small shops kept their places warm with coal. And poor people preferred coal to wood for heating purposes because it was cheaper.

By the way, the nobility at that time refused to have anything to do with coal. They wouldn't enter a house in which coal was burned or eat food that had been cooked over coal fires. They believed the smoke poisoned the food. And, of course, since houses at that time didn't have chimneys, smoke used to fill the rooms, which is what made people suspicious of coal.

After the invention of the steam engine, which made it possible to transport coal from the mines, the use of coal finally became common.

WHEN WAS METAL FIRST USED?

About six thousand years ago man lived in what we call the Stone Age. This is because he made most of his tools and weapons out of stone. He had not yet learned how to use metals.

Probably the first metals man learned how to use were copper and gold. The reason is that these metals occur in nature in a free state as well as in ores. Man found nuggets of copper and gold and was able to hammer them into various shapes without having to melt them. We don't know the date when man discovered how to use these metals, but we do know that copper was used as long ago as 5000 B.C. Gold was first used some time before 4000 B.C.

By about 3000 B.C., man had learned some of the most important things about using metals. By this time the metals silver and lead had been discovered, too, but copper was the one used most since it was the strongest and most plentiful.

Man first learned to beat metal into useful shapes, such as bowls, tools, and weapons. Once he began using metals, he discovered the processes of annealing (making a metal soft and tough by heating and then slowly cooling it), melting, casting, and smelting. Also, he could get copper from its ore, which was more plentiful than the nuggets.

Later man discovered tin and learned to mix copper and tin, which made bronze. From about 3500 B.C. to about 1200 B.C., bronze was the most important material for making tools and weapons. This period is called the Bronze Age.

Man knew about iron from meteorites he found, long before he discovered how to smelt it from its ore. By about 1200 B.C., man had learned how to work iron, and this knowledge spread all over the world. Iron replaced bronze for most uses. This was the beginning of the Iron Age.

By the time of the Romans, seven metals were known: gold, copper, silver, lead, tin, iron, and mercury.

WHO MADE THE FIRST TIMEPIECE?

When we talk of a timepiece, we mean an instrument to measure time. But man found ways of measuring time long before he invented any instruments to do so.

The rising and setting of the sun were man's first units of time. The lengthening and shortening of shadows made by sticks, stones,

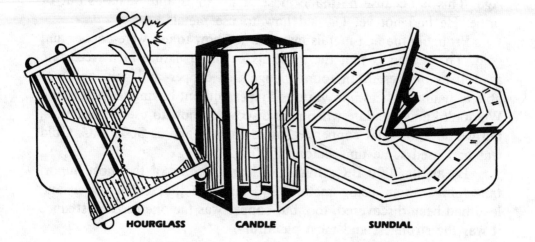

HOURGLASS   CANDLE   SUNDIAL

and trees also gave him an idea of the general time of the day. And the movements of the stars furnished him with a kind of gigantic clock. Man noticed that as the night passed, different stars became visible.

The ancient Egyptians divided the night into twelve time periods, corresponding to the rising of twelve stars. They divided the day into twelve periods also, and our twenty-four-hour day is based on the Egyptian division of day and night. The Egyptians also made shadow clocks—blocks of wood with pointers. Eventually these shadow clocks, or sundials, had twelve periods of time to divide the day—so they were the first timepieces.

The next kind of timepiece developed by man used fire and water. A candle with notches cut in the side will measure time as it burns from notch to notch. A dish with a small hole in the bottom can be set on water. After a certain period of time the floating dish will fill with water and sink.

About two thousand years ago, man developed still another kind of timepiece—the hourglass. This consisted of two hollow glass containers connected so that sand could flow from one to the other. The top container was filled with enough sand to flow through the hole for one hour.

About 140 B.C. the Greeks and Romans used the toothed wheel to improve the water clock. A float placed in a container rose as water trickled into the container. The float was connected to a toothed wheel. The wheel turned a pointer that gradually moved from one hour-mark to another.

The first true mechanical clock was invented about fourteen hundred years later. A weight was attached to a cord wound on a spool. As the cord unwound, it turned the spool, which moved a series of toothed wheels, or gears. The wheels turned a hand on a dial.

WHEN WAS THE WASHING MACHINE INVENTED?

Everybody knows about washing machines, but in many homes they are still a luxury. Before any kind of mechanical washers were invented, home washing was done in a wooden or galvanized tub. The wash was rubbed on a corrugated washboard to force the water through and the dirt out. Then the wash was put through a wringer to squeeze out the excess water, and finally it was hung out on a line to dry.

One of the first home washing machines was made in 1858 by Hamilton Smith of Pittsburgh, Pennsylvania. This home washer was operated by turning a crank at the side that rotated paddles that were inside the tub. There was another early washing machine that imitated the scrubbing action of a washboard.

But these first machines were not successful. The clothes often became tangled, knotted, or torn. It wasn't until 1907 that a practical washing machine was developed that operated by motor. By 1912 nearly all makers of home washing machines were making them to be driven by electric power.

The tubs of the first washing machines were made of wood. Gradually, the manufacturers turned to metal: copper, galvanized steel, aluminum, and zinc. By 1961 practically all tubs were made of porcelain enamel, because such machines could resist the strong washing powders and all temperatures of water.

The agitator was developed in 1922. Most agitators consist of a cone with several fins at its lower end. The agitator moves the wash up and down and side to side. The fully automatic washing machine first appeared in 1937.

Most washing machines hold between eight and ten pounds of wash. They generally use between thirty-five and forty-five gallons of water per wash, and the water temperature is usually kept between 135 and 165 degrees fahrenheit.

The first successful home dryer was built in 1930. A combination washer-dryer was first put on the market in 1953.

WHEN WERE WHEELS INVENTED?

The wheel was one of man's greatest inventions. Before men had wheels, they moved heavy loads on sleds pulled by men or oxen.

The earliest known wheels were made in ancient Mesopotamia (modern Iraq) between 3500 and 3000 B.C. They were of two kinds: the cart wheel and the potter's wheel. The potter's wheel was the ancestor of our pulleys, water wheels, gear wheels, clockwork, and other wheeled machinery.

The first carts were simply sleds mounted on wheels. The idea of mounting a sled on wheels probably came from the practice of putting logs under a sled to act as rollers. As the sled rolled forward, the rollers were picked up behind it and laid down again in front of the sled.

The earliest wheels were probably fastened solidly to their axles. Wheel and axle turned together. When a cart with wheels of this kind rounded a corner, the outer wheel traveled farther than the inner wheel. So one wheel or the other had to skid or drag.

A later invention—fastening the axle to the vehicle and letting the wheels spin freely—made turning much easier.

The first wheeled vehicles were farm carts, war chariots, royal hearses, and the sacred wagons of the gods.

Early carts and chariots were made with two wheels or with four. But the early four-wheeled vehicles were not practical. Both the front and rear axles were fastened to the body. Since neither axle could swing, the vehicle could not make sharp turns. About two thousand years ago someone developed a front axle that was pivotal so it could turn right and left.

The spoked wheel was invented in southwestern Asia about 2000 B.C.

WHAT WAS THE SANTA FE TRAIL?

The Santa Fe Trail was a traders' path. It was never an actual road, but rather a broad route that followed rivers and wagon ruts. It led from the Missouri River to Santa Fe, New Mexico.

The people of Santa Fe, which was a Mexican mission town, wanted to trade with Americans, but Mexico's rulers forbade this. When Mexico rebelled against Spain in 1820, Santa Fe was opened to American trade.

The first man to reach Mexico after trade was opened was William Becknell, who is called the "Father of the Sante Fe Trail." On his return trip, snow clogged the northern trail he had planned to follow, so he took a shortcut across the Cimarron Desert. This Cimarron Cutoff became part of the Santa Fe Trail.

When Becknell returned to his home in Franklin, Missouri in January, 1822, he poured out the Mexican silver dollars he had received for his goods onto the sidewalk, to the amazement of his neighbors. People became interested in carrying on such profitable trade, so Becknell organized a trading party. They planned to take wagons where wagons had never gone before.

Becknell and his party crossed the Missouri, struck out across the Great Plains to the Arkansas River, and followed its course. Often they had to float or drag wagons across the river to avoid steep cliffs. Going through the Cimarron Cutoff meant crossing fifty miles of dry, hot wasteland without a landmark to help them find their way.

Finally they reached the Cimarron River and crossed it. They were safely past the desert. Over three hundred miles of rough travel through foothills brought them to Sante Fe. They had proved men could take wagons over the Trail.

When they returned and showed their rich profits, others flocked to the trade. From 1822 to 1843, caravans headed west each spring over the Sante Fe Trail. Trouble with Mexico stopped the trade in 1843, but after the Mexican War ended, Sante Fe was in American territory. The Trail became one of the roads serving California gold hunters.

WHY WERE COVERED BRIDGES BUILT?

There are not many covered bridges left in America today, and those that still stand have become tourist attractions. This is not only because they are rare, but many are quite beautiful and quaint.

At one time, covered bridges dotted the American countryside from the Atlantic coast to the Ohio River. The bridges looked like square tunnels with peaked roofs. Why were these bridges built with covers?

Some people claim that the bridges were covered so that horses would not be frightened by the water underneath. Others say that they were built as a shelter for travelers in bad weather.

Actually the coverings were designed to protect the wooden framework and flooring of the bridges and keep them from rotting. Some of these covered bridges still standing today are more than one hundred years old!

Many of these bridges have been destroyed to make room for modern highways. To protect the bridges that are left, the National Society for the Preservation of Covered Bridges has been established. Many states also try to protect the bridges by making them historical landmarks.

When it comes to unusual bridges, two of the most interesting are London Bridge and the Ponte Vecchio in Florence, Italy. London Bridge was the first one over the Thames River to be built entirely of masonry. Houses were gradually erected on the bridge until it was covered with buildings. The old London Bridge was replaced by the new London Bridge about 1830.

The Ponte Vecchio was another bridge on which people lived. It was built in 1345, and is still lined with houses. Most of these houses are now used for shops.

WHO MADE THE FIRST BOAT?

If you lived near a body of water and had never seen or heard of a boat before, what would you do? You'd probably want to get across the water or move down it in some way, and you'd look for something that would hold you up on the water.

In very much this way, primitive man probably discovered that if he tied some brush or tree trunks together, and if he used a stick or a branch as a pole or paddle, he could get across a river or lake. And thus the idea of a boat was born.

This kind of boat, consisting of objects that float being tied together, was really a raft. But the problem with a raft is that it doesn't move very fast, and water washes over it and through it.

So in looking for some kind of faster and drier boat, primitive man thought of hollowing out a tree trunk. It was faster and fairly watertight. But you couldn't carry as much in this kind of boat as on a raft, and it could easily tip over.

So primitive man tried to improve the "dug-out" kind of boat. He shaped the bow and stern for greater speed; he bulged out the sides for more stability; he flattened out the bottom. Then he invented the keel, and he tried to raise the sides by building them up with planks.

Meanwhile, those who were still using the raft began to make improvements on it, too. They put a floor on the raft composed of timbers that were squared and shaped. They built a platform on it for greater comfort and protection (which was the beginning of the deck). They built up the sides and turned up the ends. And they had a kind of boat that later on was to become an ark, or punt, or junk—all types of flat-bottomed boats.

In time, the raft and the dug-out boats began to have many features in common. From then on it was a question of combining the best features of each, depending on what kind of boat was needed. So we can say that boats as we know them today began with both these ideas first thought of by primitive man.

WHO WERE THE FIRST PEOPLE TO USE SAILS?

A long, long time ago man made an important discovery, though nobody knows exactly when it happened. The discovery was that it was easy to move a boat along in the same direction as the wind.

All that was needed was to hoist up a section of skins, cloth, or something like it on a stick. With such a crude sail the boat would move along easily and it wouldn't be necessary to row it.

Of course, a real sailing vessel has another advantage: it can also sail against the wind. For this, it is necessary to know how to tack, or to approach by zigzags. It was a long time before ships and sails and this kind of know-how were developed.

On the way to this kind of use of sails, there were many steps. The ancient Egyptians had ships that used both oars and huge sails. At first, their ships were used only on the Nile River, but later they went out to sea. But the sails were only used with a following wind.

The Greeks and Romans developed a kind of ship called a galley. It used slaves to do the rowing, and it also had a sail that was used only with a following wind.

Another kind of ship they developed, called "round" ships, were used to carry cargoes. At first, these ships had only one mast with one great sail. But around the time of Christ these ships already had an additional small mast and sail in the bow, and sometimes also a small topsail.

These ships were still not able to head into the wind, but some of them could operate with the wind coming in on the side.

The Vikings also developed ships with sails, and by 800 A.D. had ships with large square sails.

WHAT WERE THE FIRST OCEAN LINERS?

Today most travel across oceans is done by air, though ocean liners are still in use. Ocean-liner service across the Atlantic started in 1816. The first line to run ships on a regular schedule was the Black Ball Line of New York. Its ships sailed between New York and Liverpool, England. Soon afterward other ship lines began operating.

The early liners were sailing ships. They were called packet ships because they carried packets of mail as well as passengers. The ships were not very comfortable. First-class passengers had only small cabins. Travelers in the cheapest class, called the steerage, had no cabins at all. They slept on bunks of rough boards, stacked three deep in low, narrow spaces below decks.

On some ship lines the steerage passengers had to bring their own food. Each passenger had to show his supply of food before he was allowed aboard. The required supply included quantities of biscuits, flour, potatoes, tea, sugar, molasses, two hams, a tin pot, frying pan, mug, teapot, knife, fork and spoon. To help provide milk and food for other passengers, most packet ships had a cow and a flock of chickens on board!

The first steam-powered ship to cross the Atlantic was the American vessel *Savannah*. In 1819 she made the trip from Savannah, Georgia, to Liverpool in twenty-nine days. The *Savannah* used her sails most of the way, running on steam power only when the winds died down.

Sails were carried on the early steamships because seamen didn't trust the new steam power. They were afraid that the steam engine might break down in mid-ocean or that the fuel might run out.

One of the famous early steamships had paddle wheels and screw propellers. This was the *Great Eastern*. She was 692 feet long and 83 feet wide, and remained the world's largest ship for forty years.

HOW DID NAVIES ORIGINATE?

Did you know that originally the navy of a country meant all of its ships, whether used for war, the carrying of merchandise, or fishing? Today, of course, the word "navy" has come to mean a country's fighting ships and those that help in warfare.

The first navies were created when the armed men of a tribe or town went to sea in the largest ships they had in order to give battle to their enemies or raid territory from the sea. The ships used were ordinary fishing or commercial ships. Only later on were ships especially designed for purposes of war.

At the time of the ancient Greeks and Romans, the very first long ships were built for speed in war, instead of round ones to carry merchandise. When the Persians threatened to attack Athens in 483 B.C., the Greeks increased their navy from fifty to one hundred long ships. By the end of the fifth century B.C. this fleet of long ships had increased to 300 and later even to 360, which makes it quite a navy! In times of peace these warships were kept on slips and under cover in sheds.

The most ancient warships were many-oared galleys, each requiring a great number of rowers. These great rowing galleys were used to ram other ships or as a means of boarding the enemy ships.

In both the ancient Greek and Roman navies there were many similarities to the organization of a modern navy. The Greeks had a captain, a sailing master, a number of petty officers, seamen and oarsmen, and soldiers or marines who did the fighting. The Romans always had a body of soldiers, called the *classici,* who were especially assigned to service in the navy.

Today, of course, a navy is a very complicated organization with dozens of types of ships and units organized to maintain them.

WHEN DID MEN BEGIN UNDERWATER EXPLORATION?

The first underwater explorer was probably looking for something to eat.

Hundreds of thousands of years ago, people knew how to get fish from the water. These early fishermen lived on the shores of lakes in Africa, and they probably waded in to make the catch with their hands.

Wading led to swimming. Then swimmers learned how to hold their breath and became divers. The first dives were along lakeshores and seacoasts where the water was deep and clear. Gradually divers learned to explore at greater and greater depths.

They found all sorts of interesting and useful things to bring back. There were shellfish to eat, and there were beautiful colored corals and shells that people used for beads or for money. As far back as four thousand years ago, Indians did deep diving off the coast of Peru to obtain mussels, a kind of shellfish, which was one of their favorite foods.

At the same time—thousands of years ago —on the other side of the world, men were bringing up oysters from the Arabian Gulf, but not to eat. These divers wanted the pearls that sometimes grew inside the shell in the soft part of the oyster's body. The pearls were made into jewelry, just as they are now.

The men of ancient Greece and Turkey are sometimes called the fathers of modern diving. They began exploring for sponges in the Aegean Sea more than two thousand years ago, and what they learned is still useful today.

They discovered that the more air they could take down with them, the longer they could stay underwater. One of them finally thought of carrying extra air down in a device called a water bladder.

This was made from the skin of a goat, sheep, or pig. It was oiled and made waterproof. All but one opening was sewn up tightly. The diver would blow the skin full of air, and with a heavy stone to keep himself underwater, would go down into the water. He could work for some time, getting air from the inflated skin as he needed it.

HOW DID SWIMMING START?

Man does not swim naturally, as certain animals do. He has had to learn how to swim.

Originally, man must have learned to swim by watching animals that swim by instinct. Early man probably had to learn how to swim in order to survive under certain conditions.

The first effort man made to swim imitated a dog. Such a stroke has always been known as the "dog paddle." But then man wanted to find a way of swimming that gave him more buoyancy and an opportunity to coordinate the motions of the arms and legs. So more than two thousand years ago he developed the method of swimming known as the breast stroke. This stroke is still used by many people

86

for restful distance swimming in rough open water.

The next stroke that man developed in swimming was the side stroke. In this stroke the "scissors kick" was used. After that came the "over-arm" side stroke. In this, the upper arm was extended out of water. It allowed a longer arm pull and produced greater speed.

The next stroke to be developed is called the Trudgen, after John Trudgen, an Englishman who introduced it in 1783. This consists of an alternate over-arm stroke and a scissors kick. He broke so many records with this stroke that many people adopted it.

Next we come to the crawl stroke. It is called that because in its original form it resembled a man crawling. It was brought to England in 1902 by Richard Cavill, who had learned it in Australia, where the natives used it. It was first called the Australian crawl. People using the crawl stroke broke so many swimming records that it was adopted as the speediest of all strokes.

By the way, swimming was rated highly in the ancient days of Greece and Rome and was used as part of the training of warriors.

WHO WAS THE FIRST TO GO UP IN A BALLOON?

Why does a balloon go up? Air itself is made up of gases, the chief ones being oxygen and nitrogen. Certain other gases are lighter than air. One of these is helium, and that is why a balloon filled with helium rises. Hot air will also make a balloon rise, because it is lighter than cold air.

Man sent balloons up into the air before he went up with them. The first big balloon was built by two French brothers called Montgolfier. On June 5, 1783, they launched their balloon by building a fire under it. When hot air from the fire filled the balloon, the brothers released it and it floated hundreds of feet into the air.

The first live passengers in a balloon were a rooster, a duck, and a young sheep. The Montgolfier brothers put them in a basket carrier and filled a huge balloon with hot air from a fire.

This inspired two brave men to risk their lives by being the first humans to leave the ground and fly in the air. One man was the Marquis d'Arlandes; the other was Jean de Rozier, a French doctor.

In a Paris park they tied a basket to the bottom of their beautifully decorated balloon. A roaring fire filled the balloon with hot air.

The two men jumped into the basket and released the ropes. They rose above the heads of the people on the ground for the first human flight. The year was still 1783.

That same year, a French scientist, Jacques Charles, filled a balloon with hydrogen and sent it up into the air. This was to avoid the danger of fire when hot air was used to fill balloons.

Later that year, Charles and a friend, Jean Robert, went up in a balloon that was filled with hydrogen. They also invented a valve that enabled them to come down by letting hydrogen escape from inside the balloon.

WHEN DID AUTOMOBILE RACING BEGIN?

Did you know that the best-attended sporting event in the whole world is the Indianapolis 500 (500-mile race) held each Memorial Day at Speedway, Indiana? Millions of people all over the world watch automobile races every year.

Quite soon after the automobile was developed, different manufacturers became involved in arguments as to who was making the fastest and most durable automobile. This led to the first international auto race in history. It was run in France in 1895, and was a 732-mile race from Paris to Bordeaux and back. The race was won by a French Panhard, traveling at an average speed of 15 miles per hour!

In 1900, James Gordon Bennett put up a trophy for a series of races. The cars that competed had to be entirely the products of the country they represented. This really started international automobile racing.

In 1906, the Automobile Club of France decided to run its own race, the Grand Prix. The cars in this contest took two days to complete 12 laps on a 64-mile course near Le Mans. Grand Prix racing developed from this and there are now such international races in Monaco, Belgium, Holland, France, England, Germany, Italy, Mexico, South Africa, and the United States.

The first important automobile race in the United States was spurred by the success of the race in France from Paris to Bordeaux. It was held in Chicago on November 28, 1895. The object was to test the speed and the stamina of American-made cars. J. Frank Duryea, one of America's leading auto manufacturing pioneers, won in a Duryea car at a speed of 7½ miles per hour.

Today, automobile racing is divided into many groups. There is stock car racing, in which a car must not be over three years old, must resemble a showroom automobile, and must use a stock production engine. There are also sports-car racing and drag racing. In drag racing, the object is to cover a prescribed straightaway distance, usually ¼ of a mile, as quickly as possible. Even drag racing has over 75 classes of cars.

HOW DID KINDERGARTENS START?

Most children start first grade when they are five, six, or seven years old. But many children start going to school before first grade. They attend kindergarten or nursery school.

In the public school system of the United States, kindergarten is the class in elementary school that comes before the first grade. Children in kindergarten are at play most of their day, but they are constantly learning through their play. They learn to plan activities, to follow simple directions, and to adjust to school life.

The idea of schools for the very young began in Europe in the late 1700's and early 1800's. Industry was growing, and many mothers who went to work had to take their youngest children into the factories with them.

One answer to this problem was the development of the infant school. The first infant school was started in Scotland in 1816 by a man called Robert Owen. He set up a system of schools for all the children in a mill town who were under twelve. The very youngest children were placed in an infant school as soon as they had learned to walk.

But even before this, educators had been concerned with the training of young children, and had many theories about this. A German teacher called Friedrich Froebel developed his own theory and method of teaching young children. He opened a school in Blankenburg, Germany, in 1837, and named his school *Kindergarten,* or "children's garden." This was the first kindergarten.

Froebel believed that children expressed their interests through their play. He developed a set of play materials, which he called gifts, for use in the kindergarten. The gifts included six soft, colored balls, and several wooden spheres, cubes, and cylinders. In addition to using the gifts, children in Froebel's kindergarten sang songs, played games, and listened to stories.

Other educators later developed other ways of helping very young children start learning in kindergarten.

WHEN DID FREE EDUCATION START IN AMERICA?

It is hard for today's student to realize how difficult it was to get free schooling for everyone, and to make sure that all children went to school.

Many people thought that poor children did not need to be educated. They insisted that the government had no right to take tax money from one man to educate another man's children. And poor families wanted their children to work, because they needed the money.

In 1647, the colony of Massachusetts passed a school law that required every town with at least fifty families to have an elementary school, and every town with one hundred families to have a Latin grammar school (these were schools that taught reading, writing and Latin, but no science, history, mathematics, or English).

This law marked the beginning of American public education. Other New England colonies passed similar laws. The New Englanders who settled the West took this idea with them.

The New England elementary schools were public schools open to all children. They were built by the town, and some tax money was used to run them. But parents who could afford it had to pay a fee for each child.

Sometimes there was not enough money to keep these schools going. Then parents had to pay if they wanted their children in school. In 1827 Massachusetts passed a law saying that the schools would have to be paid for entirely out of tax money. Most of the other New England states soon followed.

The struggle for tax money to pay for schools went on, state by state. It was not completely won in New York until 1867, and in Pennsylvania until 1868. Public schools in New Jersey were not free until 1871. Delaware, Maryland, and the southern states did not have free education until after the Civil War.

The midwestern states did better, because the Federal Government helped start their school systems. It gave the states free, unsettled land that could be sold for money to start school funds. Before the end of the nineteenth century, there was free education in all the states.

WHERE DID HUMMINGBIRDS ORIGINATE?

Sometimes we hear about strange and interesting creatures that are found far off in exotic lands. Well, one of the most remarkable creatures of all is found right here—a native of North and South America. This is the hummingbird, the smallest and most brilliant of birds.

There are about five hundred different kinds of hummingbirds in South America and sixteen species in western North America. The only hummingbird found east of the Mississippi River is the ruby-throated hummingbird.

The hummingbird gets its name from the humming sound made by its vibrating wings. A hummingbird doesn't fly the way other birds do. Its wings move so rapidly that they cannot be seen clearly by the eye, so that when you look at a hummingbird hovering over a flower, it seems to be suspended in mid-air as if by magic!

A hummingbird has a long tongue that can be folded lengthwise to form a sucking tube. It sticks this tongue into flowers and sucks up the nectar, somewhat the way butterflies do. It eats spiders and insects it finds on plants, and sometimes it captures them on the wing!

The bill of the hummingbird varies with the species. In some cases, the slender bill is shorter than the rest of the head, as with most birds. But some hummingbirds have a bill that is actually longer than the rest of the body. One kind, the sicklebill hummingbird, has a bill that curves downward like a hook.

The ruby-throated hummingbird, which is found in the eastern part of the United States, is only about three-and-a-half inches long, including the bill. It builds a nest shaped like a cup that is only an inch and a half wide! This delicate little nest is made of fine fibers, plant down, and bits of lichens, and is fastened in place with spider webs.

The way the hummingbird feeds its young is interesting, too. After swallowing soft insects and partly digesting them, the mother bird puts her bill into the open beak of the nestling and squirts the food into the young bird's mouth!

HOW DID NATIONAL ANTHEMS ORIGINATE?

A national anthem is a patriotic song that is sung or played on official occasions as a special sign of respect for a country. National anthems and patriotic songs serve to unite a people in their common hopes and ideals.

The origin of many national anthems is unknown. Often a melody was already popular as a folk song when someone set a patriotic text to it. Only a few melodies were actually written to be national anthems. The most famous of these is the anthem of West Germany, which was originally composed for Austria by the great composer Franz Joseph Haydn.

Several older national anthems and patriotic songs have the same melodies but different words. Some of them have even been sung as war songs by opposing armies in the same battle. The British anthem, "God Save the Queen," has provided the melody for patriotic songs in Denmark, Germany, Russia, Switzerland, and all English-

FRANCIS SCOTT KEY

speaking areas of the world. In the United States the words of "America" are sung to this same melody.

"God Save the Queen" first appeared as a tune in 1619. It was written by the English composer John Bull. The first public performance of the anthem took place on September 28, 1745.

The national anthem of the United States was written during the War of 1812. Francis Scott Key, a Baltimore lawyer, was aboard one of the British ships that attacked Fort McHenry. All night long, Key watched the attack. When he saw the American flag at dawn, still flying over the fort, he was so moved that he wrote the words of "The Star-Spangled Banner" on the back of an envelope. For the tune, he had in mind an old English song called "To Anacreon in Heaven."

The "Marseillaise," the French national anthem, was the battle song of the French revolutionary period (1789–1815). The words and music were written by Claude Joseph Rouget de Lisle, a captain in the French Army. It was declared the official national anthem of France in July, 1795.

HOW DID NATIONAL PARKS START?

One of the greatest pleasures in traveling through the United States is to visit a national park or national monument. Just think what a loss it would be to us if these lovely or historic places weren't preserved and guarded and kept up in good condition.

National parks and monuments are areas of great scenic, historic, and scientific importance that have been set aside by the United States Government for the use and enjoyment of the people. Every year millions of people visit the parks, monuments, and other areas that make up the National Park System. The national parks in Canada are also popular with tourists.

The National Park System had its beginning in 1870. A small group of men had just completed a month-long exploration of the Yellowstone region. They were gathered around a campfire, and after hours of discussion the men decided that they should not claim this wonderland for themselves. They felt that it should be set aside for the use and enjoyment of all the people.

So they started a campaign, and two years later, in 1872, an Act of Congress, signed by President Ulysses S. Grant, made the Yellowstone region a "public park or pleasuring ground." This was the first national park in the whole world!

In the years that followed, other beautiful regions of the country were set aside for the people. To manage these parks, the National Park Service was set up by Act of Congress on August 25, 1916.

In a national park, park rangers are on duty at all times to answer questions and to help visitors in any difficulty. Nature walks, guided tours, and campfire talks are offered by specially-trained staff members. The park service also protects the animals and plants within the parks.

WHEN WAS THE CAPITOL IN WASHINGTON BUILT?

In the Capitol Building in Washington, D.C., the Congress of the United States meets to debate bills and make laws. The Capitol is also the site of the Presidential Inauguration.

This huge, impressive building dominates the skyline of Washington. Wide avenues radiate from the Capitol like spokes of a great wheel.

The cornerstone of the Capitol was laid in 1793 by George Washington. The main portion of the building, made of Virginia sandstone, was constructed between 1793 and 1827. The House and Senate wings, built of Massachusetts white marble, were added between 1851 and 1865.

The Capitol's iron dome, which rises to a height of 288 feet, is capped by the Statue of Freedom. This statue, made by the American sculptor Thomas Crawford, was set onto the dome during the Civil War in 1862. Abraham Lincoln watched as it was placed in position and 35 cannons roared in salute. Encircling the base of the dome are 36 columns, representing the states in the Union when the dome was completed.

The Capitol has had several renovations. It was burned by the British in the War of 1812. The fire destroyed the original wooden roofing, much of the Capitol's interior, and many marble columns. Then in 1961 the East Front of the Capitol was remodeled. It is on the steps of the East Front that the President takes his oath on Inauguration Day.

Near the Capitol are the Supreme Court and the Library of Congress. The Court, of white marble, symbolizes the prestige and solemnity of the law. Here, in the highest court of the land, the nine justices of the Supreme Court meet.

WHO DISCOVERED MEDICINE?

A doctor practices medicine—and so the first man who could help someone feel better was really, in a way, the first doctor. For example, a caveman who pulled a thorn out of somebody's finger was doing what a doctor does.

Primitive people practiced a kind of medicine that we would call magic. They used chants or songs, or a stew of herbs and leaves. Or, by accident, they may have discovered that the warmth of a fire eased a sprained shoulder, or an herb drink helped a stomach-ache. Many primitive peoples of today can set and splint a broken bone, or use plants that are laxatives or that will put people to sleep.

But doctors as such seem to have existed from the earliest civilizations. The Babylonians left medical writings describing various diseases so clearly that doctors today can recognize them. The ancient Egyptians had medical treatments, and these included pills and ointments containing drugs. They even performed surgical operations on the outer surfaces of the body.

A man called Aesculapius was the earliest physician in Greek history. He practiced a kind of magic medicine. But gradually true medicine began to develop. A man called Hippocrates, who lived about 400 B.C., did so much to rescue medicine from such magic and superstition that he is called the "Father of Medicine."

In his writings he taught that the physician should observe the patient closely and accurately. He should use gentle treatment and try to encourage the natural healing process. The physician should never risk harming the patient. He should keep the patient's secrets.

Hippocrates also recognized and described many diseases. Some of the medical facts he observed are as true today as they were over two thousand years ago. So perhaps we can call him the world's first doctor in terms of what we mean by that today.

WHO DISCOVERED INSULIN?

Insulin is used for the treatment of a disease called diabetes. When a person has this disease, some fault in his body chemistry keeps it from using starches and sugar to make energy.

A large gland called the pancreas makes a substance called insulin that the body needs to use starches and sugar. The body of a person with diabetes either does not make enough insulin or does not use its insulin. If this disease goes untreated, he suffers from extreme thirst, loses weight, feels weak, and may eventually become unconscious and die.

However, these things need not happen to a person with diabetes now that insulin is manufactured. The diabetic patient can take it by daily injection. With this manufactured insulin and a regular diet, he can lead a normal life.

Doctors had known for some time that a person suffering from diabetes could not make use of the sugar in his body. The problem was how to provide diabetics with insulin. Scientists thought they knew the answer: give a diabetic insulin taken from the pancreas of a healthy animal. But no one had been able to extract insulin.

This was the achievement of Frederick Grant Banting, a Canadian doctor and scientist who was born in 1891 near Alliston, Ontario. He was teaching in London, Ontario, and one evening, while preparing a lecture on the pancreas, he suddenly realized how he might extract insulin. He went to the University of Toronto and asked Professor John Macleod, director of a large laboratory, for help. Macleod agreed to let him use the laboratory for a few weeks.

In May, 1921, with the help of Charles Best, a young graduate student, he set to work. They worked day and night, and within several weeks obtained the first insulin from the pancreas of a dog. By January, 1922, after many tests, they were able to give insulin to a diabetic, a young boy near death. He showed immediate improvement. Other patients given insulin improved, too. An important step forward in medical history had been made.

WHO STARTED THE BOY SCOUTS OF AMERICA?

Many years ago, an American businessman called W. D. Boyce was in London. In the fog, he couldn't find the house of a friend he was looking for, so he stopped a boy who was passing and asked for directions.

The boy not only gave him directions, but guided Mr. Boyce to the house. When the American offered the boy a coin, it was refused. "I am a Boy Scout," the boy said. "Helping you was my daily good turn—Boy Scouts do not accept tips."

Mr. Boyce was so interested by this explanation that he wanted to learn more about Boy Scouts. He went to the London Scout headquarters, where he was told the history of the movement and provided with pamphlets and other printed matter.

He learned that the Boy Scout movement had been founded in England by Lord Baden-Powell when he returned to England after the Boer War. Baden-Powell had become interested in various boys' organizations and had combined their best features with ideas of his own, finally developing the Boy Scout program.

Mr. Boyce was so impressed with what he learned that on February 8, 1910, he incorporated the Boy Scouts of America. Scouts observe this anniversary with much ceremony every year. In 1916 the

Boy Scouts of America were granted a federal charter, because Boy Scouts had been so helpful in many ways in their various communities. The charter gives protection to the name and insignia of scouting and authorizes the members to wear an official uniform.

From the time the Boy Scout movement started in the United States, more than seventeen million boys and leaders have been registered members. There are three age groups in scouting, with programs and activities adapted to the interests of boys at each level. The Cub Scouts are boys eight through ten years of age; the Boy Scouts, eleven through thirteen; and the Explorers, fourteen and up.

HOW DID THE SALVATION ARMY START?

Today there are very few countries in the world where the Salvation Army and its work are not known. Yet this great organization began in the mind of a single man. This man was William Booth.

In 1865 Booth was a young Methodist revivalist who walked the dreariest streets in London's East End. There he prayed for the men and women who gathered around him, though they usually jeered at him and even threw stones.

But Booth refused to be discouraged. Day after day, he went into the streets with his wife and a few followers. Day after day, this small group invited people to come to meetings held in a tent, a dance hall or an old warehouse. During these meetings they tried to bring religion to the poor and to do whatever they could to relieve their misery.

At first the group called themselves the Christian Mission, but in 1878 they organized themselves as the Salvation Army. The organization adopted a kind of "military" system. Its founder, William Booth, was called General, and its workers wore uniforms. It grew with amazing speed.

The Army as a whole is divided into territories, which are made up of divisions, which in turn consist of corps and outposts (mission stations). The General and other international officers operate from the international headquarters in London.

The Salvation Army has set up about eighteen thousand posts throughout the world. At these posts it carries on its social work. Its services include hotels with inexpensive food and lodging, factories, farm colonies, orphanages, rescue homes, day nurseries, insurance societies, and so on.

The Salvation Army was organized in the United States by George Scott Railton in 1880. Evangeline Booth, daughter of William Booth, became the Commander in the United States in 1904, and in 1934 she became the first woman General of the Salvation Army.

WHEN WERE THE FIRST FIRE FIGHTERS ORGANIZED?

Man has always known that fire can be his friend and servant, and can also be a great destroyer. Primitive man, however, didn't have the problem of fighting fires as we have, simply because he didn't live in houses that were grouped together—in other words, in villages, towns, and cities.

But when men began to live together in large groups, they had to concern themselves with the problem of fighting fires. And so, long before Christ (in fact, many centuries before), fire brigades were organized. They existed in many cities throughout the world. The ancient Romans had fire brigades to protect the city, and used slaves for this work.

By the way, the Romans also developed the first means of throwing a continuous stream of water. Roman firemen used axes, blankets, buckets, ladders, and poles! In the Middle Ages there was some organized fire fighting here and there, but it was not very efficient.

Fire fighting as we know it was started in England. It came about because fire-insurance companies were organized, and they, of course, were interested in cutting down the loss from fires and preventing their spread. The officials of London hadn't done much about this problem, so the insurance companies organized fire brigades of their own.

Probably the first such brigade was organized in 1722, and then others followed. These insurance companies would place fire marks on the buildings they insured, and probably didn't bother too much with other buildings. In 1833 the first organized fire fighting system for the city of London was set up.

In the United States, as in most parts of the world, before the local authorities (of the city or town) set up fire brigades, the citizens themselves would organize volunteer fire fighters. In fact, the job of fighting fires is still done mostly by volunteers. There are about one million fire fighters in the United States—and only one out of ten is a paid fireman working full time!

WHEN DID LABOR UNIONS BEGIN?

In ancient Greece and Rome slaves did much of the labor. Food and shelter were provided by their masters in return. During the Middle Ages, serfs were required to work for the lord of the manor in return for protection. Laborers were tillers of the soil, not wage earners.

As trade increased, the town replaced the feudal manor as the principal place where people worked. Merchants and artisans organized into associations, or guilds, for each craft. These artisans and craftsmen worked at home or in small shops, and there were a few factories with many workers laboring together.

This was all changed toward the end of the eighteenth century with the coming of the Industrial Revolution. As machines were developed that could produce more goods faster than the individual worker, factories were built to house the machines. Handwork and small shops all but disappeared. The worker had to seek a job from an employer, and he was paid in wages for his services. And when workers had problems, they had no one who would listen to them.

Conditions in the early English cotton mills were particularly bad. So the workers began to organize into unions. They felt that if they stood together, their grievances and complaints had a better chance of a fair hearing.

These trade unions were founded in the towns as small clubs of skilled craftsmen. In 1868 the Trades Union Congress, the first big and successful union organization, was formed in Manchester, England.

There was a great need for unions in the early days of the American Republic, but they were hard to organize and public opinion was against them. The first union in the United States was formed in 1792 by eight shoemakers in Philadelphia. It did not last a year.

During the early years of the nineteenth century, unions began to form city-wide trade associations. The first was the Mechanics' Union of Trade Associations. It was founded in Philadelphia in 1828. The first important national labor federation was formed in 1866.

HOW OLD IS WEAVING?

Weaving is the method by which threads are interlaced to make cloth. The principles of weaving have not changed through the ages. Modern textile mills do quickly on machines what ancient peoples did slowly by hand.

Cavemen, who lived about thirty thousand years ago, learned how to weave. They used straw, stalks of reed, or other materials to weave baskets. Nets for fishing and the capture of game were also woven by man in prehistoric times.

What these ancient peoples didn't realize was that cords, which are really yarns, could be interlaced to make soft fabrics or cloths. The idea of weaving cloth seems to have developed in certain particular places and then spread all over the world.

The most ancient woven cloths that we have records of are these: the Near East, about 5000 B.C.; Egypt, about 4000 B.C.; central Europe, about 2500 B.C.; China, about 1200 B.C.; and the Peruvian coast of South America, about 1500 B.C.

The use of different fibers for weaving developed in various places according to what was available. Wool was first used when the sheep was domesticated, about 1600 B.C. Cotton was first used in India and spread from there through Asia and finally to Europe.

Silk fibers were first used in China. On the other side of the world, in ancient Peru, the cotton plant and llamas and alpacas were providing material for making cloth. And since man has always liked to have colorful clothing, it is interesting to know that the ancient Peruvians had already found ways to have more than 150 tints and shades in their cloth.

Today, of course, most weaving is done in mills. But in many cases the weaving of rugs and tapestries is still done by hand by skillful artists.

WHEN WAS THE FIRST POTTERY MADE?

Wet clay can be modeled into almost any shape. After a few days the clay becomes dry and hard. If the clay is baked, or fired, the nature of the clay changes. It can no longer be made soft and workable. Objects made of baked clay are called ceramics. Ceramic vessels (containers) are called pottery.

The first pottery was made about ten thousand years ago. To keep grain from spilling through the holes in baskets, the insides were smeared with wet clay. Perhaps one day a basket of this kind fell unnoticed on a campfire. The reeds burned away, and the first piece of pottery had been made.

There are three kinds of pottery—earthenware, stoneware, and porcelain. The simplest kind of pottery is made from clay and then fired. It is called earthenware. It is porous, and water will slowly leak out of it.

As time passed, people learned that certain rocks could be melted into a kind of glass. The rocks were crushed to a fine powder and mixed with clay. The pottery made from this clay is called stoneware. Stoneware, which does not leak, can be used over a fire for cooking.

During the Tang dynasty (618–906 A.D.) the Chinese began to make another kind of pottery. It was made from a special white clay mixed with powdered rock. This pottery, called porcelain, was fired in a kiln almost hot enough to melt iron. Porcelain is translucent (light can be seen through it) and hard.

About 3300 B.C., the potter's wheel came into use. The potter puts a ball of wet clay onto the center of the wheel. As the wheel spins, the potter shapes the clay by pressing it with his fingers. Pots made on wheels are always round.

All the ancient civilizations—Egyptians, Persians, Mesopotamians—made beautiful pottery. The Egyptians used glazes of many colors. The Persians painted on their pottery as far back as 4000 B.C. The ancient Greeks and Romans also made large pottery vases. But it was the Chinese who made the most beautiful pottery in ancient times.

WHO PAINTED THE FIRST PICTURES?

The first artists on earth were the cavemen. On the walls of caves in southern France and Spain there are colored drawings of animals that were made from 30,000 to 10,000 B.C.

Many of these drawings are amazingly well-preserved, because the caves were sealed up for many centuries. Early man drew the wild animals that he saw all around him. Very crude human figures, drawn in lifelike positions, have been found in Africa and eastern Spain.

The cave artists filled the cave walls with drawings in rich, bright colors. The pigments used were earth ochers (iron oxides varying in color from light yellow to deep orange) and manganese (a metallic element). These were crushed into a fine powder, mixed with grease, like animal fat, and put on with some sort of brush.

Sometimes the pigments were used in sticks, like crayons. The grease mixed with the powdered pigments made the paint fluid and the pigment particles stuck together. The cavemen must have made brushes out of animal hairs or plants, and sharp tools out of flint for drawing and scratching lines.

One of the first civilizations was developed in Egypt, and they had artists who painted pictures. Much Egyptian art was created for the pyramids and tombs of kings and other important people. Artists recorded scenes from the life of the person in wall paintings in the burial chamber. They used watercolor paints and washes.

Another early civilization, the Aegean, also developed the art of painting to a surprising degree. Their artists had a free and graceful style, and they painted sea life, animals, flowers, athletic games, and processionals. Their paintings were made on wet plaster walls, a kind of painting we now call fresco.

So you see that painting goes back to the very earliest times of man and civilization.

WHEN WAS SCULPTURE FIRST CREATED?

It may be that sculpture is the oldest of the arts. People carved before they painted or even designed homes.

Only a few objects survive to show what sculpture was like thousands of years ago. But people living today in primitive societies often carve things that may be similar to prehistoric sculpture.

Prehistoric sculpture was never made to be beautiful. It was always made to be used in rituals. Figures of men, women, and animals were made to honor the forces of nature, which were worshipped as evil or good spirits.

The earliest civilizations of man also used sculpture to express their beliefs. The ancient Egyptians believed in life after death, and they carved life-size and even larger statues of their rulers, nobles, and gods. They were placed in tombs, and the Egyptians believed the spirit of the dead person would return to these images.

One of the greatest periods in the history of sculpture came with the Greek civilization that started about 600 B.C. For the Greeks, sculpture became one of their most important forms of expression.

The Greeks made the human figure the principal object of their art. Sculptors in Greece were always looking for better ways to represent the human figure.

During the first one thousand years of Christianity, very little sculpture was produced. But after the year 1000, and for the next three centuries, some of the most impressive Christian churches were built and much great sculpture was created for these churches.

Later on, during the Renaissance, the human figure was again glorified and great sculptors produced masterpieces that are among the world's greatest treasures.

HOW DID POETRY ORIGINATE?

First of all, what is poetry? Poetry is language that is deeply felt and deeply moving, written or spoken in a special form. The rhythm of a poem is what makes it different from prose.

From this we can get an idea of how poetry began. Of course, we can never know who first created it or where. But because we know something of the way primitive people acted, we can guess at the beginnings of poetry.

Man had some sort of rhythmic dance even before he had a language. He made sounds and gestures and uttered grunts and cries at special times, such as before a battle or a hunt. Also, he created a drum on which he could beat in many ways. And soon he was using sounds and the drums to send magic words to his gods.

Primitive man then began to develop the dance, and it became more and more complicated as it advanced. Soon the words of the chant to the gods became more important than just sounds from the drum. The words could be understood. In time, the leading performer of such a ceremony was actually a kind of poet, or bard.

WHERE WAS THE FIRST THEATER?

The theater as we know it took a long time to develop. The idea of drama itself had its beginnings in religion.

The Chinese first performed dramalike dances in their temples. Later a playhouse was used. It was just a platform without curtains or changes of lights that had a roof decorated like the roof of a temple.

The Japanese also developed a form of theater in ancient times. One type of drama was called *No,* and a popular form of drama was called *Kabuki.* They were performed on a platform with a temple roof.

In ancient India, dramatic performances were given on specially-built raised platforms, with draperies as background.

The ancient Greeks developed a very great form of drama. The audience was seated on a hillside. The action of the play took place in a grassy circle. There was a building called the *skene,* which was used for the entrances of the actors, for dressing, and for scenic background.

During the Middle Ages, the Christian church condemned all forms of drama, but later religious drama became an important part of church life. Priests in the Middle Ages acted out bible stories as part of the church services.

During the reign of Elizabeth I, the theater in England took a great step forward. In 1576 an actor, James Burbage, built the first playhouse. It was known simply as "the Theatre" and was patterned after the stages that used to be set up in inn courtyards.

Soon other theaters were built, and these included the Globe, where many of Shakespeare's plays were performed; the Red Bull; and the Blackfriars. The audience stood in the pit, in front or around the sides of the stage, or were seated in boxes around and above the stage. Our modern theater had its beginnings with these early English theaters.

HOW DID THE ORCHESTRA DEVELOP?

An orchestra is a large group of musicians playing many kinds of instruments. The standard orchestra has at least seventy-five to one hundred players. Of these, more than half play stringed instruments, which form the foundation of an orchestra. The rest play woodwind, brass, and percussion instruments.

An orchestra such as this is called a symphony orchestra. An orchestra that has fifteen to thirty players is called a chamber orchestra. It is small enough to play in a small hall or "chamber." A string orchestra is made up of only the stringed instruments of the symphony orchestra.

The modern symphony orchestra developed over hundreds of years. There were many experiments and changes, and it was actually the composers of music who had a great deal to do with shaping the orchestra.

The first great pioneer in writing for the orchestra was the Italian, Claudio Monteverdi (1567–1643). He was also the first great composer of opera. In one of his works he used an orchestra of thirty-five musicians playing violas, guitars, harpsichords, organs, trumpets, trombones, and flutes.

When the violin was perfected in the seventeenth century, the strings became the leading instruments of the orchestra. The great French opera composer Rameau (1683–1764) was one of the first composers to use clarinets in the orchestra. He also used bassoons and horns regularly.

Turkish bands traveling in Europe introduced several new percussion instruments. These included the bass drum, triangle, cymbals, and others in this family. So we see how the orchestra grew in terms of the kinds and the number of instruments composers could use. And composers wrote music designed to get new sounds and tone color from the orchestra.

The first orchestra in the United States, still in existence, was the New York Philharmonic, founded in 1842. The Boston Symphony was founded in 1881.

WHEN DID BALLET DANCING BEGIN?

What is a ballet? It is a kind of theatrical entertainment that combines several things: dancing, stage design, and music. Some ballets tell a story, but others just depict an idea or mood.

When you see a ballet, you see the human body performing in the most elegant and harmonious way possible. And it takes strict and strenuous training to enable the dancers to look natural and beautiful as they perform.

Ballet is nearly five hundred years old. It began in Italy about the time Columbus discovered America. It was quite different then from what it is today. At that time ballet was a form of court entertainment. Italian noblemen amused themselves and their guests by combining dancing, music, pantomime, poetry and drama.

So the first ballet dancers were the royalty and nobles of the court, since there were no professional dancers. The steps were modeled on the elegant and rather simple court dances of the day, and the dancers didn't wear toe slippers. However, dancing of this kind was not called ballet until almost one hundred years later at the court of King Henry III of France.

In 1581 Queen Catherine de Médicis ordered a grand entertainment to celebrate a royal wedding. The result was a spectacular ballet. There were hundreds of dancers, singers, and actors. The Italian musician de Beaujoyeulx organized it. He was probably the first choreographer, or maker of dances, as we know the word today. He called his work *The Queen's Comic Ballet,* and ever since performances of this kind have been called ballets.

The leading lady in a ballet company is called a prima ballerina. The first of these was a woman called Lafontaine, who danced in 1681. Later on, various individuals introduced changes and improvements in ballet.

CHAPTER 3
THE
HUMAN BODY

WHAT IS LIFE?

This is probably one of the deepest questions man can ask and one of the greatest mysteries facing him.

Scientists have discovered that all living things are made of a material called protoplasm. They can make a chemical formula for protoplasm, and they can take molecules of various elements and compounds and put them together and make materials like protoplasm. But the materials they make are not alive!

All man can do is examine the living creatures on earth, in all sizes and shapes and wherever they live, and find what it is they have in common. Then we can say that these common qualities make up life.

Let's see what these qualities are. All living things must be able to grow. They grow to a fairly definite size and shape. A kitten becomes a cat; an acorn becomes an oak tree. For some living things it takes a short time to grow to full size; a redwood tree may take thousands of years. But all living things grow.

All living things can replace and repair parts of themselves. A lobster can grow a new claw, human beings can grow new skin or bones, trees grow new leaves.

Another characteristic shared by living things, and living things only, is the ability to reproduce. If this ability didn't exist, living things would disappear from the earth as they grew old and died. Animals, fish, birds, insects, plants—all produce offspring.

110

Living things are able to adapt to their environment. Man can do this better than any other creatures because of his brain. But plants can do this only to a limited extent.

Living things can also respond to stimuli. This means if something outside of themselves affects them they can react. When you smell food, you respond, and flowers grow toward the light.

This doesn't tell you what life is, but it does describe the qualities that things must have to be considered "alive."

WHY MUST WE BREATHE?

We all know instinctively that we must breathe. But why is it necessary for all living plants and animals to breathe? The reason is a very simple one. By breathing we take in air that provides oxygen. Without this gas, no life can exist.

When we exhale the air, it has changed. As it made its way through our system, some of the oxygen was used up, while the amounts of carbon dioxide and water were increased.

Nature keeps up a constant supply of oxygen for our breathing. In fact, from year to year, there is little change in the amounts of oxygen and carbon dioxide found in the air. This is because the carbon dioxide we breathe out into the air is taken in by plants. They breathe out oxygen, which we need.

Breathing, or respiration, is made up of two parts: external and internal breathing. External breathing is what most of us think of when we refer to breathing. It consists of inhaling and exhaling, or inspiration and expiration. Inspiration means taking in air through the mouth, the nose, or both. Expiration means sending out air through those same channels, but air that has had about one-fifth of its oxygen exchanged for an equal amount of carbon dioxide. This happens in the lungs.

Internal breathing is the opposite of external. The oxygen taken from the air in the lungs is carried to the tissues of the body by the red cells in the blood. In the tissues this oxygen burns certain food products, making them available for use by the body. The blood takes away the waste products, including water and carbon dioxide. These are returned in the blood to the lungs for exhaling.

Since an exchange of gases (oxygen and carbon dioxide) takes place both in the lungs and in the tissues, a large surface is needed to make this possible. The linings of the lungs of an adult, for example, are equal to a space about 36 feet square. This is larger than the ceiling space of one floor of an average house! Much of this area is kept in reserve, since we might need 8 or 10 times as much oxygen during work as we need at rest. If we need more oxygen, we breathe more deeply or more quickly.

Different creatures breathe at different rates, depending on the oxygen they need.

A newborn baby breathes about once a second, but at the age of 15, breathing is about 20 times a minute. An elephant breathes 10 times a minute; a dog, 25 times a minute.

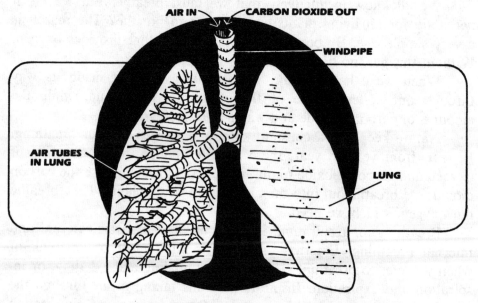

WHAT KEEPS THE HEART BEATING?

As most of us know, the heart is a pump. It drives the blood through the body, thus making life possible.

But what an amazing pump it is! With each beat of the heart, it sends out about one hundred cubic centimeters of blood. In the course of a day this amounts to about 10,567 quarts of blood that are pumped through the blood vessels. In an average lifetime, a heart pumps about 264,175,000 quarts of blood!

Each beat of the human heart lasts about eight-tenths of a second. The heart beats about one hundred thousand times a day, and rests an equal number of times between beats. So it rests about six hours total per day.

Now, what we call the "beat" of the heart is a contracting and a relaxing. During the contracting the blood is pumped out; during the relaxing new blood enters. But this doesn't take place in a simple way as, for example, you might open and close your fist. The contraction takes place in a kind of wave that starts at the bottom of the heart and moves up toward the top.

What keeps the heart beating? Does this impulse to contract and relax come from somewhere else? Is it self-starting? It is one of the most fascinating questions in biology, and much about it still remains a mystery. Let me tell you about an interesting experiment that has been known about for hundreds of years.

Suppose you take a chicken egg and incubate it about twenty-six hours. Now you open it and with a magnifying glass study those cells in the egg from which the chick's heart will later develop. You will see those cells beating! Even before those cells have become a heart, they are already beating!

Now suppose you remove this mass of cells and allow them to grow in a medium. If you cut the growing heart into six pieces, each piece continues to contract for some time! What is the explanation? We don't know. All we can say, it seems, is that the heart has a certain characteristic of automatically contracting. And one of the secrets of life—why it keeps beating—remains a riddle!

WHAT IS HEREDITY?

Every new organism, whether it is a plant, fish, animal, or human, resembles its parents—and yet it differs from them. For example, children may look like one parent or the other, but usually they have some features of each parent. What has happened is that the parents have passed down to the children certain characteristics. The children have "inherited" them. So heredity is the study of how offspring resemble their parents.

The unit of heredity is called the "gene." Genes are large molecules found in the nuclei of both sperm cells and egg cells. Within the nucleus of each cell are long, thin strands, or threads. They are called "chromosomes," and they carry the genes.

Since chromosomes occur in pairs, their genes are also paired. The chromosomes of a cell may contain hundreds of thousands of pairs of genes. Each gene pair controls one or more features of the organism, such as color of hair, shape of nose, size of body, and so on.

There are many "laws" of heredity, which means that the process takes place in certain ways. For example, every trait that is inherited depends on a single "factor," and each factor behaves independently. Because a certain trait is inherited from the parents, it doesn't mean that any other trait will also necessarily be inherited. In other words, the factors, or genes, have nothing to do with each other.

Some genes carry traits that are "dominant," and others carry traits that are "recessive." For example, the gene for curly hair seems to be dominant to the gene for straight hair. When both parents are curly-haired, they usually have curly-haired children. But if each parent carries a recessive gene for straight hair, some children may be straight-haired.

Scientists have studied such human traits as color of eyes, hair, and skin, so that they usually can tell how they will be inherited by people whose family history is known for several generations.

WHY ARE SOME PEOPLE SMARTER THAN OTHERS?

One thing everybody seems to realize is that some people seem to be bright and intelligent, and others seem to be backward and learn slowly. But not everybody agrees as to why this is so.

We do know that many cases of low mental ability are the result of injuries at birth, glandular disorders occurring before or after birth, or diseases that have caused damage to the brain. In many cases the causes of retarded mental development cannot be determined.

There is a great deal of disagreement among experts as to the influence of heredity on intelligence. Some believe that in most cases a child inherits his intelligence. Others think that a child's intelligence is a result of the experiences he has had and the kind of environment in which he has lived.

Probably both of these opinions are partially true. The most common belief is that a child inherits a capacity for mental growth. But the degree to which he develops within that capacity depends upon a great many factors in his environment. There are perhaps many people who could have developed higher mental abilities if during childhood they had had better opportunities.

How is intelligence measured? What is really measured is "mental age." This is done through a series of mental tests. For example, most children of six years can do the problems and perform the tasks required in a certain test. A few four and five-year-olds can also do them. On the other hand, there may be children of ten or twelve years of age, or even adults, for whom they are too difficult.

The first group are "average," the second group are "superior," and the third, "retarded." If a child passes enough tests so that his average is that of a six-year-old, his mental age is said to be six years.

If a six-year-old has a mental age of six years, his intelligence quotient (IQ) is 100. If a five-year-old has a mental age of six, his IQ is 120. IQ's above 110 are generally considered superior.

HOW DOES THE BRAIN STORE INFORMATION?

Storing information is remembering, and remembering is closely linked to learning.

Psychologists have tried to explain how people remember and why they forget many of the things they learn. No one has yet found all the answers. It is believed, according to one theory, that when a person learns something, a physical change of some kind takes place. A trace, or pattern, is left in the brain. And it is believed that memories, or the traces memory may leave in the brain, simply fade away in the course of time.

The way you feel about a particular experience may also determine whether you remember or forget it. In general, people are apt to forget things that are unpleasant or upsetting and remember things that are pleasant.

Brains can learn different kinds of tasks. Better-developed brains can learn more complicated tasks. In the simplest brains, learning is very crude. Humans show the greatest learning abilities.

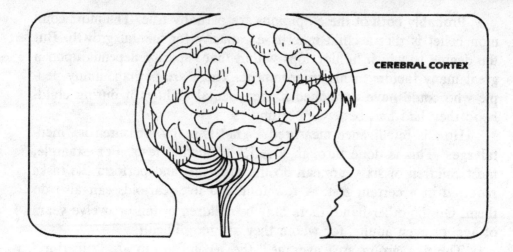

CEREBRAL CORTEX

But how and where does the brain store the information that we call memory? As we said, scientists are not yet able to fully explain it. In the human brain, areas of the cortex appear to be involved. The cortex is the twisted, wrinkled, and knotted surface of the largest part of the brain (the cerebrum).

When these areas are excited by weak electrical currents, a person "relives" past experiences. These stimuli force the brain to reproduce experiences that are stored within it from the past. And it is known that injury to certain areas of the brain will result in loss of memory.

But are these the places in the brain where the information is stored? We don't know. Nor do we know how the information is stored. Some scientists think that storing information is a chemical process—the individual nerve cells have chemically-coded information within them. Other scientists believe that memory is the result of some permanent change in the structure of the nerve. So memory is still a mystery!

WHAT IS MULTIPLE SCLEROSIS?

It is always unpleasant to read about diseases that afflict people, but they are part of our knowledge of man and how he lives.

Multiple sclerosis is a disorder of the brain and nervous system. It usually develops early in adult life, and it seems to attack people who are otherwise healthy. The disease often stops and then reappears again, and it may last over a period of years.

What happens in this disease is that certain matter in the nervous system, in the spinal cord, and in the brain is destroyed. This happens in tiny spots scattered through the nervous system.

Because this disease shows up in many different symptoms and fluctuates so much, it is hard to diagnose. Often, at the beginning of multiple sclerosis there is a temporary mistiness of vision. There may be no pain, and the person doesn't become blind. In fact, this symptom may be so mild that the person may let it pass without going to a doctor.

Then later the person begins to have double vision and a tingling or burning sensation in the skin. The patient may also not be able to coordinate his movements, and he may feel weak and may shake or even begin to stammer. In some cases, the person starts to talk in a strange way, slurring his speech, or talking monotonously.

Eventually, the muscles of the legs become stiff or have spasms. In some patients there are also mental symptoms. The mind doesn't seem able to work well. And a person may be very depressed or very elated.

When a case is far advanced, the patient may become very aggressive. A curious thing is that the most common symptom is that the person feels everything is fine; he is very optimistic even though he has severe symptoms. He might smile or giggle frequently.

At present there is no known cure for multiple sclerosis.

WHAT IS A PHOBIA?

Did you ever know anybody who was afraid of high places, or someone who was afraid of closed places? There are people who are afraid of crowds, or of being touched by others. There is a name for behaving this way: it is called a "phobic reaction," and we say the person has a "phobia."

Is something "wrong" with such people? Are they "sick" in some way? No—but we might say they are suffering from some emotional disturbance. Something upsets them—or has upset them in the past—

very strongly. And such a person is trying to deal with this emotional disturbance—it can be called "emotional pain"—just as you would try to deal with physical pain.

We all react to emotional upsets. We cry, we blush, we might break out in a sweat. But some people, who feel this emotional stress more strongly, or whose power of resistance is weaker, try to deal with this emotional pain in an unnatural, unusual way. This kind of reaction is sometimes called "neurotic."

One such way of reacting is to develop a phobia, which is unreasonable fear of a specific thing, such as fear of high places, or closed-in places. An interesting thing about a phobia is that the thing the person is afraid of is usually a thing or situation he can avoid. After all, nobody forces people to climb to high places or get into closed places. And as long as a person can avoid these things, he feels fine. He doesn't have what is called "anxiety."

But why should a particular person have a fear of high places, to take an example? The truth is, he is really afraid of something else, or perhaps felt afraid of something else when he was a child. It might have been his father whom he loved and feared at the same time. He didn't want to admit he was afraid of his father, so he substituted a fear of high places, which is a symbol of his father. And since he can avoid high places, he can avoid facing the fact that he is afraid of his father. All of this seems very complicated, doesn't it? But then the human being and how he behaves is a very complicated matter!

WHAT HAPPENS TO THE WATER WE DRINK?

You may think that when you drink a glass of water it goes bubbling through your body and out as if it were going through a pipe. But water and your body are involved in a much more complicated way.

An adult man takes in about two quarts of water a day as fluids, and he takes in another quart from what we call "solid" foods. Fruit, vegetables, bread, and meat are really 30 to 90 percent water! Besides these three quarts he takes in from the outside, in his body about ten quarts of water pass back and forth between the different systems and

organs. For example, every time you swallow, you swallow some saliva. In the next few moments, a quantity of water equal to that saliva will pass from the blood vessels into the salivary glands to replace the water you swallowed! The swallowed water returns from the stomach and the intestines to the blood. And so the ten quarts of water in your body are circulating between the blood and the organs every day!

A man has about five quarts of blood in his blood vessels, and three of them are water. His blood vessels will continue to have these three quarts of water no matter what he does. He may be "dried out" after a long hike, or he may have drunk four quarts of beer at a party —there will still be three quarts of water in his blood! And even if a man could drink ten quarts of water at a time, he could not dilute his blood; it keeps that balance of water and solids all the time.

What happens when you drink a certain quantity of water? One-fourth of it goes to the intestine; one-fourth goes into the liver; one-fourth goes into the muscles; and the last fourth goes to the kidneys and bladder. The muscles are the largest water reservoir you have in your body. In a grown man, the muscles can take in and hold up to thirty quarts of water!

When the liver gives up water to the blood, it stimulates the kidney to excrete water. This fills up the bladder, and we get rid of the excess water.

WHAT MAKES YOUR VOICE CHANGE?

The kind of voice you have depends chiefly on your vocal cords. These vocal cords are made of elastic fibers. You might compare them to the very best violin strings.

The vocal cords can be made tense or slack. In fact, your vocal cords can be in any of about 170 different positions. When a column of air (which you push upward) strikes the vocal cords, they begin to vibrate. This vibration produces sound waves.

If the vocal cords are slack, they may vibrate about eighty times per second and the result is deep tones. If they are tensed, they vibrate rapidly, perhaps one thousand times a second, and produce short sound waves or high tones.

A child has short vocal cords. So they produce short air waves and a child has a high-pitched voice. As a child grows, the vocal cords become longer. As they become longer, the voice becomes deeper. The average length of a man's vocal cords is greater than that of a woman's, which is why men's voices are deeper.

In boys, growth often takes place so quickly, and the whole larynx changes so quickly, that they can't get used to it and can't control it perfectly. That's why we often have "the breaking of the voice" with young boys.

While the general pitch of an adult's voice depends on the length of the vocal cords, each voice has a certain range. It is this range that determines what kind of voice the person has. Voices can be divided into six groups: bass, baritone, and tenor for men, and alto, mezzo-soprano, and soprano for women.

The quality of a human voice, however, depends on many other things as well, especially the resonating spaces such as windpipe, lungs, nasal cavities, and so on. People with beautiful voices have resonating spaces shaped a certain way and know how to control them.

HOW ARE DEAF-MUTES TAUGHT TO SPEAK?

Until the sixteenth century, deaf-mutes were treated very cruelly. They were regarded as idiots, incapable of intelligence, and were locked up in asylums or even killed. But in the sixteenth century, an Italian doctor named Jerome Cardan got the idea of teaching deaf-mutes through written characters.

As the result of his work, about a hundred years later a finger alphabet was developed, similar to the finger alphabet used today. With the finger alphabet, a deaf-mute makes the letters with his fingers and spells out words. He also depends on sign language. For example, sweeping the forefinger across the lips means "You are not telling me the truth." A tap on the chin with three fingers means "My uncle." With this alphabet some deaf-mutes can spell out as many as 130 words a minute!

But many teachers of deaf-mutes believe that the use of sign language and the finger alphabet is not the best method. It forces the deaf-mute to communicate only with other people in the same condition. So these teachers use a method known as "oral instruction." In this method the deaf are taught to understand what is spoken to them, and even to speak themselves.

Nowadays many of the deaf and hard-of-hearing learn to interpret what is said by watching the lips of the speaker. They learn to speak themselves by observing and feeling the lips and vocal organs of the teacher and then imitating the motions.

Hearing aids are being used more and more. In schools and classes for deaf and hard-of-hearing children, group hearing aids are used. The group hearing aids have individual earphones for each child so that the volume and tone can be adjusted. The teacher speaks through a microphone, and the children hear her in the same manner as if they were listening to a radio with earphones.

WHY DO HUMANS HAVE HAIR ON THEIR BODIES?

Birds have feathers, and mammals, such as man, have hair. It is believed that feathers and hair enabled birds and mammals to develop far beyond their common ancestors, the reptiles.

In human beings, there are only two parts of the body where there is no hair: the palms of the hand and the soles of the feet. The hair on the rest of the body is believed to be a leftover from the coat of heavy hair that our prehistoric ancestors had.

When a human baby is about a hundred days old in the mother's body, a thick coat of hair sprouts from the skin. After another hundred days, these hairs are shed. This is called the embryonal hair.

This hair is replaced by the delicate hair of a newborn baby. Then this hair is transformed at the time of puberty (about fourteen years in boys and twelve years in girls) into the final coat of hair that the person will have.

The development of the adult coat of hair is regulated by the sex glands. In males, certain hormones promote the development of hair on the face and body, and keep down the growth of hair on the head. The female hormones act in just the opposite way.

Why we need this hair is not quite understood by science. We can say that the hair of the eyebrows, lashes, ears, and nose, are probably there to protect us against dust and insects. A man's beard, in prehistoric times, probably helped set men apart from women—even at a distance—and helped give the man an appearance of power. According to Charles Darwin, the fine hairs of the body help us to shed perspiration and water.

An adult male has from three hundred thousand to five hundred thousand hairs in his skin. Blond persons with finer hair have the most hair; red-haired people, who have the coarsest hair, have the fewest hairs on their bodies.

WHAT MAKES OUR MUSCLES TIRED?

Muscles are the "movers" of the body. For every bone that can move, there are muscles to move it. Muscles are firmly anchored to the bones.

They move a bone by pulling it. A muscle pulls because it has the ability to contract; that is, to make itself shorter and fatter. When it contracts, it pulls.

When a muscle contracts, or pulls, it produces lactic acid. This acid is like a fatigue poison—it is the chief reason the muscles feel tired. For example, when lactic acid is removed from a tired muscle, that muscle is able to go to work again. So in the course of a day, by using our muscles, we "poison" ourselves with lactic acid. We become tired.

There are other substances in the body that make us feel tired. They are called fatigue toxins, and they are created in the body when we carry on muscular activity. The blood carries these toxins through the body so that not just the muscles feel tired, but the whole body does, especially the brain.

An interesting experiment shows how the lactic acid and toxins are involved with tiredness. A dog is made to work until it is so tired it falls asleep from exhaustion. The blood from that dog is then transfused into a dog that is feeling perky and fresh. The second dog will become tired and fall asleep right in the middle of the transfusion! And it works the opposite way—blood from a wide-awake dog will wake up a tired, sleeping dog.

Why does all this tiredness occur in the body? Because the cells of the body need rest. When we are tired and resting, damages to cells are repaired, nerve cells of the brain recharge their batteries, the joints are lubricated by fluids, and so on.

Sometimes a person who is involved in some athletic activity suddenly seems about to collapse. He feels weak and can hardly breathe. This is exhaustion, and is really almost like a kind of paralysis. The cause of such exhaustion is not known, but it may be produced by an excess of the lactic acid and other fatigue toxins.

WHAT ARE SPRAINS, STRAINS, AND BRUISES?

If you were to play in a rough football game, or get into a fight, you might emerge with sprains, strains, and bruises. What causes them, and what should be done about them?

A sprain is an injury to a joint, such as the ankle, knee, or wrist. In a sprain, the ligaments are stretched or torn. This is usually caused by stretching, twisting, or pressure at the joint. One symptom of a sprain is swelling over the joint, which appears very quickly. You also can't use the joint without increasing pain, and it may look discolored. Since a joint may also be fractured, it shouldn't be used until it has been properly examined. Sometimes it takes longer for a sprain to heal than a simple break in a bone!

A strain is a different kind of injury. In a strain it is the muscle or tendon that is injured. This usually comes from some severe exertion, such as lifting a heavy object from an awkward position.

The symptoms of a strain are stiffness and pain in the part that is affected. The first thing to do for a person who has received a strain is to make him comfortable so that the injured muscles are relaxed. In some cases, heat application and gentle massage will provide some relief by stimulating the circulation. Always rub the affected part in an upward direction. Rubbing alcohol may help in the gentle massage to "loosen up" the tightened muscles.

A bruise is still another kind of injury. It is caused by a blow to some part of the body that breaks the small blood vessels under the skin. As the blood collects in the tissues, it causes swelling and discoloration. A cold cloth may help to prevent discoloration, reduce the swelling, and relieve pain. But usually no treatment is needed for minor bruises. If the skin is broken, a bruise should be treated as any other open wound.

Maybe the best idea of all is simply to be careful when you play or exercise so that you can avoid sprains, strains, and bruises!

WHAT IS ARTHRITIS?

The word arthritis is used to describe a great variety of diseases, all of which affect adversely the joints of the body.

The two most common types of arthritis are degenerative arthritis and rheumatoid arthritis. In degenerative arthritis the aging process of the body is involved. In rheumatoid arthritis there is inflammation, and usually some crippling of the body occurs.

In degenerative arthritis there is no fever, no loss of weight, no general stiffening of the joints or deformity of the body. The joint does not become inflamed. It is a disease of advancing years, and usually begins after forty. The cartilage of the bones becomes worn away and broken, so that surfaces of the bone come in direct contact with each other. This is because cartilage acts as a sort of shock absorber of the joints.

The symptoms are either stiffness or pain when there is movement. Knobs begin to appear at the end joints of the first and second fingers. There is also usually pain and stiffness of the knee.

Rheumatoid arthritis is popularly known as rheumatism. What happens here is that the joints become inflamed. The membrane that lines the joint becomes enlarged, and this eats into the cartilage underneath.

At the same time, the bone below the cartilage begins to change. It loses its mineral substances, and the joint becomes stiff. In time, this can end in loss of motion altogether in the joint, so that the person becomes crippled.

What brings on this type of arthritis is still not fully understood by medical science. There are many theories about it, and one is that it is caused by infection. Victims of arthritis have long been hoping for some cure or magic "pill" that would end their suffering. But none has yet been found. Medical authorities want people to realize that the cause of this arthritis is still unknown, and that even some of the drugs that seem to help only give relief while the drugs are being used. When they are stopped, the symptoms return. And the damaged tissue is not repaired.

CAN WE CONTROL OUR HUNGER AND THIRST?

When you feel thirsty, you have a dry sensation in your throat. And when you feel hungry, you may have the sensation that your stomach is empty. But the truth is that neither that feeling in your throat, nor the one in your stomach, is responsible for your hunger or thirst.

Your blood should normally contain a certain amount of water and salt. This is also true of the tissues. Now, suppose this balance is upset for some reason. Your blood draws water from the tissues of your body in order to keep its balance constant. As this water is being removed, it registers in a "thirst center" in your brain. The thirst center sends an impulse to the pharynx, or throat, making it contract. This contraction makes you feel your throat is "dry," and you experience thirst.

The feeling of hunger originates in the brain, too. There is a hunger center that acts as a sort of brake on the activities of the stomach and intestines. When there is enough food in the blood, the hunger center slows up the action of the stomach and intestines. But if the blood doesn't have enough nourishment, the hunger center responds by releasing the brakes. The intestines become active, and we experience a feeling of hunger. Our stomach "growls."

To a certain degree we can control hunger by controlling the rate at which we use up our food supplies. In nature, the smaller and more active animals use up their food supply fastest. For example, a small bird may starve to death in five days, but it may take a dog twenty. When a person is calm, the protein stores of the body last longer than when he is excited or afraid.

There are people who can train themselves to go without food for long periods of time. They do this by a deliberate form of concentration, just as people can make themselves perform some exceptional athletic feat. It seems to be more difficult to control thirst, but people can make themselves able to endure it better by conscious efforts.

WHAT IS PROTEIN?

All living cells contain protein. This would suggest that protein is a substance necessary to life. And, in fact, we get our word "protein" from a Greek word meaning "first," because proteins are thought to be the most important part of living matter.

Each kind of cell has its own protein. The proteins are made up of combinations of substances called "amino acids." There are more than twenty-one different amino acids. Each amino acid group contains the chemical element nitrogen, in addition to carbon, hydrogen, and oxygen. The different amino acids can combine in different ways to form different proteins, and there are thousands of different proteins. For example, we all know that meat contains protein, but did you know that it is made up of at least twelve to fifteen different proteins?

Many of the foods that are considered important for us to eat are so because of the proteins they contain. These include milk, eggs, lean meats, fish, peas, beans, peanuts, and certain grains. They are important to man because they provide him with the amino acids that his body cannot make for itself. He must get the amino acids from the protein in the food he eats. In fact, they are called the "essential amino acids," which means the body cannot get along without them.

Certain kinds of amino acids, and definite amounts of them, are necessary so that the body tissues can use what they need. Plant proteins, such as those in peas, beans, and cereals, do not contain all the essential amino acids. But they are valuable in the diet when they are combined with some of the animal proteins.

Man cannot store amino acids in his body for later use. This means that the different kinds he needs have to be taken into the body at the same time. Bread and milk have to be eaten at the same meal, so the amino acids they provide can be used together to form new body tissue.

Moderate amounts of different kinds of protein foods should be eaten at each meal. In this way, you are sure of getting enough of the essential amino acids to meet the body's protein needs.

DO WE NEED TO TAKE EXTRA VITAMINS?

Vitamins are a group of substances found in food. The body needs them for life and health. So, naturally, a great many people are concerned with the question: Am I getting enough vitamins, and am I getting the right kind?

Even though very small amounts of each vitamin are enough for the needs of the body, the worry that people have about vitamins has some basis. And this has to do with their diet—the food they take in. A person eating a good variety of foods gets all the vitamins now known to be needed (with the possible exception of vitamin D).

The problem is that there are many people who don't choose foods wisely, don't get enough variety, and don't eat the basic foods they need to get their vitamins. So the answer to this question is: No, extra vitamins are not needed, providing you eat proper foods. In fact, many of the vitamins cannot be stored in the body, so when extra vitamins are taken in, the body simply gets rid of them.

It is even harmful to put too much of certain vitamins into the body. This has been found to be true of vitamins A and D, when large amounts are taken in capsules and liquids.

What foods supply what vitamins? Here is a quick, general idea. Vitamin A, for the health of the eyes, skin, teeth, and bones, is found in green, leafy vegetables, yellow vegetables, fruits, eggs, liver, and butter. B-1, which helps the nervous and digestive system and prevents certain diseases, is found in whole-grain bread, cereals, pork, and liver. B-2 is found in milk, eggs, greens, and lean meats.

Vitamin C, which helps tissues, bones, and teeth, is found in citrus fruits, tomatoes, and raw cabbage. Vitamin D is found in fortified milk and sunshine. These are only a few of the most important vitamins the body needs. The best thing to do is to get from your doctor a proper diet that includes the basic foods, and to be sure that you follow it.

WHAT IS PELLAGRA?

Pellagra is a disease that results when a person doesn't have enough of a certain vitamin. The vitamin is nicotinic acid, or niacin, which is one of the B-complex vitamins. Most persons with pellagra also suffer from deficiencies of riboflavin and other vitamins.

Pellagra occurs in most parts of the world, but it has been especially prevalent in the southeastern United States and in South Africa. The reason for this in the United States was that many people in this area lived chiefly on a diet of corn. With better diets and the addition of vitamins to many foods, pellagra has now become less common. Drug addiction and alcoholism can also lead to pellagra, because people who are addicted to alcohol or the use of drugs often fail to follow the proper diet and generally neglect their health and physical well-being.

Among the first symptoms of the disease are loss of appetite, loss of weight and strength, headache, and stomach upset. A person is also likely to get diarrhea and outbreaks of the skin.

The sores on the skin are deep-red areas that gradually turn brown and become large, thickened, and scaly. They are strongest about the neck and backs of hands and forearms. There is also an inflammation of the gums and lining of the stomach.

An even worse sign of this disease can be a kind of mental unbalance that takes the form of sleeplessness, depression, or even violent behavior. So you see, pellagra is a rather unpleasant disease. At one time, about 65 percent of all patients who had it died from it.

But when it was discovered that nicotinic acid could cure pellagra, the death rate dropped to a low level. Usually, the giving of this vitamin must be accompanied by other vitamins, too. And the person must go on a well-rounded diet.

Following this kind of treatment, the symptoms begin to disappear within a few hours, and a person can feel complete relief within a few days. In fact, even the most severe mental symptoms of this disease disappear quickly after treatment with nicotinic acid.

WHAT IS A GOITER?

In the front of your neck there is a very important gland of the body called the thyroid gland. It needs iodine in order to function.

While the body needs only a tiny amount of iodine, having this amount is essential. It helps in the formation of hormones, it is important in controlling the process of metabolism, and it has an effect on the nervous system.

The thyroid gland is subject to many different diseases, and the most common one is goiter. Goiter means an enlargement of the thyroid gland. The commonest form of goiter occurs in those parts of the world where the supply of iodine in the soil is low.

In mountainous areas, for example, iodine is often washed out of the soil, so the plants that grow there contain very little of it. Plant life is, directly or indirectly, the major source of food. So people in such areas soon become deficient in iodine.

What happens then is that the thyroid gland becomes enlarged in an effort to make up for the lack of iodine by producing more hormones. This enlarged gland is called a goiter. Sometimes such effort works, and sometimes not. It depends on the amount of iodine that reaches the thyroid. If there is no iodine at all reaching the body, then the enlargement of the gland doesn't solve the problem.

The amazing thing about this is the very tiny amount of iodine that is needed. The entire human body only contains about one fifteen-hundredth of an ounce of iodine. This is about two drops. And the daily requirement is even less, since iodine is used over and over again. By the way, this is why laws have been passed in many places requiring that iodine be added to table salt. Look at the box of salt in your home. It will probably have the word "Iodized" on it.

The addition of iodine to salt has done away with a good part of the goiter problem in the United States.

IS ALL HUMAN BLOOD THE SAME?

All human blood is made up of basically the same plasma, cells, and other chemical materials. But individuals differ in some of the arrangements and proportions of the chemicals in their cells and plasma.

There are four main groups, or types, of blood, and every human being can be classified under one of them. The groups are called A, B, O, and AB, based on the presence or absence of certain protein molecules in the blood.

When blood from two different groups is mixed and the blood

clumps, it is because of a reaction between the protein molecules in the red cells and the plasma. Such chemical reactions make it dangerous for a person to receive a transfusion of whole blood from someone whose blood group is unknown. But if the cells are removed from blood, then the remaining plasma can be given to anyone, no matter what his blood group.

Blood can be exchanged among human beings whose groups and subgroups have been matched. However, certain large populations may have more of one particular group than another. Anthropologists who study man's physical development use blood groups as one of the ways of showing relationships among individuals and population groups.

So although human blood has many different groups and subgroups, it is basically all the same. In fact, each species of animal has its own kind of blood. For example, all cats have the same kind of blood, just as all dogs have the same kind of blood. The blood of one species cannot be exchanged for the blood of another.

WHAT IS THE RH FACTOR?

When a person loses a great deal of blood for one reason or another, his life can often be saved by a blood transfusion. The blood of another person is put into the circulatory system and replaces his lost blood.

The first recorded blood transfusion was performed in 1677, when the blood of a lamb was injected into the veins of a dying boy. That boy was lucky and recovered. We now know that the blood of lower animals is different from human blood and cannot be used for transfusions with safety.

In 1940, it was found that there was still another way of dividing blood into groups, and this was according to the Rh factor. This discovery was made in the course of experiments on rhesus monkeys, and that's why it came to have the name "Rh."

It was found that when certain combinations of blood were made, the red blood cells broke apart. The cause was traced to certain differences in the Rh factor.

The blood of human beings in this case is divided into Rh positive and Rh negative. When blood from an Rh-positive person is transfused to a person who is Rh negative, the latter will develop a blood disease when he receives Rh-positive blood again.

In rare cases (one in forty or fifty), an Rh-positive father and Rh-negative mother will produce an infant with a blood disease if certain other conditions exist.

HOW DO BLOOD BANKS WORK?

Many hospitals have blood banks. In these banks, blood of all types is stored. When a unit of blood is needed, it is taken from the bank. Healthy people then give blood to the bank to replace the blood that is used. Blood can be kept refrigerated for about three weeks. A chemical such as sodium citrate is added to prevent clotting of the blood.

Transfusions are given mainly to replace blood that has been lost through severe bleeding. Such bleeding may occur as the result of illness, surgery, or accident.

Sometimes only a part of the blood is used for transfusions. Plasma, the liquid part of the blood, may be given alone. Transfusions of plasma are often given when people have been badly burned. In cases of severe burns, large amounts of plasma are lost from the bloodstream.

Transfusions of red blood cells alone may be used to treat certain cases of anemia. Anemia is a condition in which a person has too few red blood cells or his red blood cells contain too little hemoglobin.

When a person gets a transfusion, he gets blood of the same type as his. Otherwise there may be a bad reaction. For additional safety, the blood that is to be used in a transfusion is tested with the blood of the person who is to receive it. This testing is called cross matching of the blood.

Giving transfusions of blood that had been stored for some time was started by an American doctor, Oswald Robertson. He used it to treat wounded soldiers in 1918 in World War I.

WHAT IS HEMOPHILIA?

Did you know that you carry about an invisible first-aid kit in your blood? When a blood vessel is ruptured, nature applies "absorbent cotton" to stop the flow of blood. It isn't really absorbent cotton, of course, but it's something very much like it. It is a process known as clotting of the blood, and what makes it possible is the appearance of firm and very elastic fibrin threads that act as a sort of plug to stop the blood flow.

In every person's body the speed with which the blood clots form is different. There are some people whose blood clots very slowly or not at all. They are known as "bleeders," and their condition is called hemophilia.

Luckily, hemophilia is very rare. But, unfortunately, it is a condition that is inherited. It is transmitted in a peculiar way. Hemophilia appears only in men, but it is never transmitted directly from father to son.

It is transmitted from a father to a daughter, who herself remains healthy. She in turn gives it to her son, the grandchild of the sick father. So the rule for this disease goes like this: The son of a bleeder is always healthy and does not transmit the disease. The daughters of a bleeder are also healthy. Among their sons, however, the grandfather's disease reappears!

When the tragedy of this disease strikes it may be in a rich family or a poor one. In fact, this disease appeared in three of the most famous families in the world: in the Spanish royal family, in the Russian royal family, and in the children of Queen Victoria of England. In two of these cases, that of the Russian and the Spanish, the uncrowned successors to the throne were bleeders.

WHAT GIVES OUR EYES THEIR COLOR?

The eye is one of the most remarkable organs in our body. It is really a form of camera, with an adjustable opening to admit light, a lens that focuses the light waves to form an image, and a sensitive film on which the image is recorded.

Here we are not going to discuss "how we see," but rather the structure of the eye itself. The shape of the eye is round, except for a little bulge that sticks out in front where the light enters. This bulge, which curves outward in front, is called the cornea. The cornea is transparent. It helps bend the light rays as they enter the eye, and since it guards the opening into the eye, it is very sensitive. Any dust or dirt that alights on it is quickly felt so it can be removed.

The "camera film" of the eye is the retina. It is made up of ten very thin layers of cells and lines the entire inside of the eye. So now we have the opening to the eye, and the "film" which the light must reach inside.

To regulate the light coming in, we have the iris and the pupil of the eye. The iris is the circle of color, and the pupil is the little black dot in the center. By the way, the reason the pupil appears black is because it opens into the dark interior of the eye.

The size of the pupil is regulated by the iris, which closes the opening to a pinhole in bright light and expands the opening in dim light. Directly behind the iris and the pupil lies the lens, which is just like the lens of a magnifying glass. The lens is elastic and adjusts itself to long- or short-distance vision. It is the lens that bends the waves of light so that they will all come to a focus on the retina.

When we look into someone's eyes, the color we see is in the iris. The reason for this is that the fibers of the iris have pigments in them to protect the iris against light. The back part of the iris has most of the pigments, the front part almost none. Since the front part is very transparent and absorbs the red and yellow light waves as they pass through it, the light reflected from the pigmented part appears blue. The blue color is just a reflection of pigments from the back part of the iris.

If pigments don't develop in the front part of the iris in later years, the iris continues to look blue all through life. But if pigments do develop in the front of the iris, then it becomes brown.

WHY CAN'T WE SEE COLORS IN THE DARK?

Light from the sun or from any very hot source is called white light. But, as Newton was the first to show, white light is really a mixture of light of all colors.

When a beam of light is made to go through a glass prism, we see all the colors of the rainbow—red, orange, yellow, green, blue, and violet. Each shade blends gradually into the next without a break. This spread of color is called a spectrum.

These colors are present in sunlight to begin with, but show up only after being spread out by refraction in the prism. Each color is refracted a slightly different amount, red least and violet most. This spreading out is called dispersion. Without dispersion, the mixture gives the appearance of white to the eye.

Color is determined by the wavelength of the light (like the distance between one crest and the next in a wave traveling on water). The shortest visible light waves are violet; the longest are red.

Most of the colors we see in our surroundings are not of a single wavelength, but are mixtures of many wavelengths. When white light falls on an object, some wavelengths are reflected, and the rest are absorbed by the material. A piece of red cloth, for example, absorbs almost all wavelengths except a certain range of red ones. These are the only ones that are reflected to your eye, so you see the cloth as red.

So color is a quality of light. It does not exist apart from light. All our color sensations are caused by light rays entering our eyes. All objects are seen by reflected light, and the colors that they show exist in the light and not in the object.

DO DREAMS FORETELL THE FUTURE?

If we tried to assemble all the superstitious beliefs that have existed about dreams since the beginning of time, we could fill a library! Most of these superstitions have to do with the "meaning" of dreams, and the "meaning" usually has something to do with the future.

It isn't just primitive peoples who believed that dreams foretold the future. In Europe there were soothsayers who claimed they could read a person's future from his dreams. In fact, divining the future from dreams was a recognized art in ancient times and was called "oneiromancy." This is taken from the Greek word *oneiros,* which means "dream."

Of course, we are all familiar with the story in the Old Testament of how Joseph interpreted the Pharaoh's dreams. And we know that even today there are people who buy "dream books" that are supposed to help them foretell their futures from their dreams.

What does science today believe about the content of our dreams? Why do we dream what we dream, and what does it mean? For one thing, science does not accept the idea that dreams are a "message" to us from any source, foretelling the future.

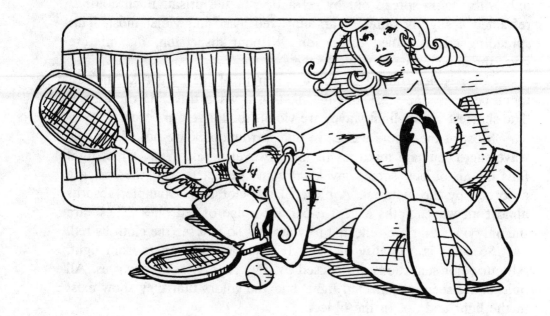

The subject of our dreams comes from any of several sources. It may come from some stimulus that affects us at the very moment we are dreaming, such as a sound, or the fact that our feet are cold, or a breeze blowing over us.

The subject may also come from our store of past experiences, or something we are interested in, or some strong urge we feel. Sometimes in the dream we repeat past experiences almost exactly as they happened. At other times the events are rearranged in our dream. But the subject of our dream is a result of our past experience, and not a foreshadowing of the future.

WHAT CAUSES BLINDNESS?

Did you know that there are at least fourteen million blind people in the world? There are many degrees of blindness, so it is hard to define blindness. Some people cannot even see light. Others can only tell light from dark. Still others have a small amount of vision.

Of all the blind people in the world, only a small percentage were born blind. Blindness at birth is called congenital blindness. The causes of it are not all known.

Blindness that occurs after birth is caused mainly by diseases of the eyes. A general disease of the body, such as diabetes or meningitis, rather than a disease of the eye itself, may also cause blindness. Accidents and explosions are two other causes of blindness.

In countries where people live longer because of good medical care and a high standard of living, old age often brings on certain eye conditions. Two of these eye conditions are cataracts and glaucoma. Cataracts are the leading cause of blindness in the United States.

A cataract is a clouding of the lens of the eye. The lens, the transparent part of the eye through which light rays pass, becomes cloudy, and only strong light rays can pass through it. There is consequently a loss of vision. Cataracts can be removed by surgery.

With glaucoma, there is a hardening of the eyeball and great pressure inside the eye. Today there are medicines to control glaucoma if it is discovered in time.

The greatest single cause of loss of sight is trachoma. It is a contagious disease of the eyes caused by a virus. It affects the inner linings of the eyelids. Also, blood vessels grow over the cornea. This can destroy the vision.

Antibiotics can now control trachoma, but it is still common in some parts of Europe, Africa, and Asia.

WHAT IS CHICKEN POX?

The word "pox" means a disease with eruptions, and in chicken pox there are eruptions on the skin that may sometimes make it look like the skin of a chicken.

Chicken pox is also called "varicella," and is a contagious disease. While it is considered a childhood disease, adults may get it, too.

The specific organism that causes chicken pox has not yet been identified by medical science, but it is agreed that it is a virus. Chicken pox is passed on from one person to another by direct contact. It is rarely, if ever, passed on by contact with clothing or other articles touched by the infected person.

Here are the symptoms of chicken pox: a slight rise in temperature, loss of appetite, headache, and backache. Quite often, before any of these symptoms appear, a person breaks out in a rash or there are skin eruptions. The first skin eruptions are reddened spots about the size of a pinhead. They first show up in patches on the trunk of the body.

A few hours later, they enlarge and form blisters (vesicles) in the center of each spot. There is a clear fluid in the blister that later turns yellow, and then a crust or scab forms.

Most of the patches of eruptions appear on the back and chest. In severe cases almost all of the body may be covered.

Chicken pox is not considered a serious disease and usually requires little special treatment. But a doctor should be called to diagnose it and make sure there will be no complications.

The patient is usually made to stay in bed as long as new eruptions appear or there is some fever. Scratching the skin must be avoided to prevent infection or scars. One attack of chicken pox usually makes the person immune to the disease.

WHAT IS PLAGUE?

The first definite record we have of an outbreak of the plague is in the Old Testament. The Philistines were overcome by plague after they defeated the Israelites.

Plague is an acute infection that first attacks rats and other rodents, and then man. It is caused by an organism called *Bacillus pestis*. Fleas that live as parasites on the rodents transmit the disease by biting human beings.

When a person has plague, he has fever, chills, and swollen nodes in the groin. Spots also appear on the skin, and because these spots have a dark color, and because many people die of this disease, it was called the Black Death in the Middle Ages. It has also been called bubonic plague, and here is the reason: The swelling of nodes in the groin has been called a bubo, which comes from the Greek word *boubon*, meaning "groin." A serious epidemic of any kind is sometimes called a plague; but there is a definite disease called the plague.

One of the greatest outbreaks of the plague in history was the Black Death of the fourteenth century. It originated in Central Asia, reached the shores of the Black Sea, was brought into many European ports, and within five years had spread over the whole continent.

When plague appeared, the first reaction was usually panic, and people would try to leave the region. But not everyone could. All kinds of steps were taken to prevent the spread of the disease. People were isolated in their homes and couldn't leave, and no one could visit them. Food was provided by special messengers. When a plague patient died, everything he owned was burned.

Bubonic plague returned to Europe in the seventeenth century. Almost half the population of Lyons, France, died. Some eighty-six thousand people died in Milan, and almost five hundred thousand perished in the Venetian Republic.

Today all kinds of preventive measures are taken to stop the rise and spread of plague, and most of them deal with the control of rats.

CHAPTER 4
HOW OTHER CREATURES LIVE

WHAT IS THE WORLD'S LARGEST ANIMAL?

In prehistoric times there were gigantic creatures living on land and in the sea that were far larger than any animals alive today. The largest animal in existence today is the blue or sulphur-bottom whale. It may be over a hundred feet long and weigh 125 tons. And interestingly enough, about one-third of the length of this animal is taken up by its head!

Perhaps the most amazing thing about the whale is not its size, but the fact that it is a mammal and not a fish. Like all water mammals (such as dolphins and porpoises), whales are descended from ancestors that lived on land. There is evidence for this in the structure of their bodies. The skin and flesh of their paddlelike flippers cover the bones of a five-fingered "hand." Some whales even have the bones of hind legs embedded in their flesh.

Since the whale is a mammal, the baby whale is fed on its mother's milk like other little mammals. It is not hatched from an egg but is born alive, and for sometime after it is born it stays with its mother.

Whales have no gills, and breathe air through their lungs. They have horizontal tails, or flukes, which enable them to rise easily to the top of the water for air. The internal organs of the whale and the skeleton, circulatory system, and brain are also quite unlike those of the fish.

As whales developed and adapted themselves to life in the water, many changes took place; among them was the development of blubber. Mammals are warm-blooded animals, and it is very important for them to keep their body temperature within certain limits. Whales have a layer of fibrous tissue under their skin that is filled with oil and retains heat. On a larger whale, this layer of blubber may be from fourteen to twenty inches thick.

On the top of the whale's head are one or two blowholes; this makes it easier for them to breathe at the surface of the water. Underwater these nostrils are closed by little valves, and the air passages are shut off from the mouth, so there is no danger of taking water into the lungs. Whales can remain underwater for three-quarters of an hour!

WHAT IS A NARWHAL?

A narwhal is a type of whale, one of the most interesting of this fascinating family of creatures. Most of us think a whale is a whale, but there are actually quite a few varieties.

Toothed whales generally live on various types of fish that they chase and capture. Sperm whales are the largest of the toothed whales. They may be sixty-five feet long, and their heads are huge. Another toothed whale is the bottle-nosed whale, which has strange bony crests on either side of its head.

The narwhal is one of the toothed whales. It is found chiefly in Arctic waters and has something that cannot be found on any other whale: the male narwhal has a long ivory tusk on the left side of its mouth that sticks out in front like a sword!

WHAT ARE PINNIPEDS?

Pinnipeds are fin-footed mammals with limbs that they use as paddles or flippers. The three main kinds of pinnipeds are the walrus, the sea lion, and the seal.

They are all carnivores, or flesh eaters. They are aquatic (water) carnivores with the same distant ancestors as land carnivores such as dogs, cats, and bears.

These early ancestors lived on land many millions of years ago. Eventually one branch of these early carnivores took to the sea and became adapted to life in the water. These were the ancestors of our seal, sea lion, and walrus.

Today about thirty different kinds of pinnipeds live in the world's oceans. Most of them live in the cold waters of the Arctic and Antarctic oceans and in the nearby areas of the Atlantic and the Pacific. A few kinds range into warmer waters, and several forms live in freshwater lakes.

Since pinnipeds spend most of their lives in the water, they have become very well adapted for this kind of existence. All are expert swimmers. Their bodies are tapered and streamlined, with a thick layer of blubber that gives them added buoyancy in the water and helps them keep warm. The blubber also serves as a reserve of food when needed.

Pinnipeds are expert divers. They can go two hundred or three hundred feet down in search of food. Many of them have big eyes that are useful for seeing in the dim depths. When they are underwater, their nostrils close. Most of them have sharp, backward-pointing teeth, so that they can seize prey and direct it down the throat.

Pinnipeds are sociable animals and live together much of the time in large herds. This is especially true during the mating season or when pups are born. All of them must return to land, or at least be on a cake of ice, before bearing their young. The young seals, sea lions, and walruses are born with their eyes open and with full coats of hair or fur.

WHAT IS A SEA ELEPHANT?

The sea elephant might be considered a fourth kind of pinniped, but it is really a giant seal.

There are two species of the giant elephant seals, or sea elephants. One, the southern elephant seal, lives in waters around Antarctica. The other, the northern elephant seal, lives in waters off the coast of lower California, and breeds in Guadaloupe and other small islands.

Both species look very much alike and grow to about the same size. Big adult males may measure nearly twenty feet long and weigh up to eight thousand pounds! The females are much smaller, usually not more than nine or ten feet long. A single ninety to one hundred-pound pup is born about fifty weeks after the mating season.

The enormous male elephant seal has a long, dangling snout. When danger threatens, a male inflates his snout and roars loudly.

Because they were hunted for their hides and oil, the northern elephant seals were almost extinct by 1890. But the Mexican government stepped in and protected the herds, which slowly increased. Now, each year at the breeding grounds, as many as eight thousand to ten thousand of these huge creatures can be seen.

WHAT ARE OTTERS?

Otters belong to another group of animals, the mustelids. This word comes from the Latin, and means "weasel." Other members of this family of animals include weasels, skunks, and badgers. They are all short-legged, have thick coats of fur and sharp, tearing teeth, and are meat-eating mammals.

Otters love water, and their webbed feet, thick tails, and dense fur make them well suited for life in the water. Two kinds of otters are found in and around North America. One is a fresh-water otter; the other is a sea otter.

The fresh-water otter is found in streams and lakes from Mexico to Alaska. Its coat is a rich, dark brown. This otter is a restless animal, always on the move; a male sometimes wanders fifty or sixty miles during the winter. It is a very shy animal and is seldom seen by people.

The home of the fresh-water otter is usually a hole dug into the bank of a stream or lake. The hole leads to a den lined with leaves. Here the young, usually two or three to a litter, are born in late winter or early spring. Before the young can swim, the mother sometimes carries them about on her back in the water.

But the young learn very quickly to swim themselves. Their parents teach them to dive and to catch the fish on which they feed. Soon the cubs are able to stay underwater for as long as four minutes.

The sea otter is found off the western coast of North America, from California to Alaska, and in other northern waters. Sea otters are larger and heavier than fresh-water otters. Their thick fur is dark brown and has a frosted appearance. They have white whiskers from which they get the nickname, the "old men of the sea."

When they are not in a hurry, sea otters often swim and float on their backs. They use their stomachs as tables from which they eat crabs, sea urchins, mollusks, and other sea creatures.

Sea otters were widely hunted for their valuable fur, and they almost became extinct. But they are now protected by international treaty and are coming back in great numbers.

WHAT IS A NEWT?

Newts are a certain kind of salamander. They belong to the class of animals known as amphibians, which includes frogs and toads as well as salamanders. Most amphibians spend part of their lives in water and part on land.

Today there are only three main groups of amphibians: frogs and toads, which have no tails as adults; salamanders and newts, which do have tails; and caecilians, which have tails but no legs.

Because newts have long bodies, people sometimes mistake them for lizards. But there is a way to tell them from lizards: lizards have scales, salamanders do not; lizards have claws, and salamanders do not.

Newts like to keep their bodies cool. Most of them live in the temperate zones of North America and Europe, where the winters are cold. Here they have adapted in various ways to the world around them. They may live entirely in the water or in underground caves. They may live in rotting trees or in cracks in rocks. On land they crawl or walk on small, weak legs. In water a salamander or newt swims or wriggles, helped by its long tail.

Newts are usually smaller than most other salamanders and have a thicker, drier skin. They are found in Asia, North Africa, Europe, and North America.

One kind of newt common in the United States leads a triple life. The eastern or red-spotted newt starts life in the water. In two or three months the tiny, light-green tadpole completes its metamorphosis and is ready for life on land. The newt turns coral-red, with two rows of black-bordered red spots on its back. It is now about one-and-a-half to three inches long, and is called the red eft.

After two or three years on land, the eft returns to water to lay its eggs. Its skin changes again, turning olive green on top. The skin becomes smooth. The round tail grows new fins. And the newt lives the third stage of its life in the water.

WHAT ARE LIZARDS?

Lizards are reptiles, a class of animals that also includes crocodiles, turtles, and snakes. There are about three thousand kinds of lizards.

A typical lizard is four-legged, short-bodied, and long-tailed. All lizards shed their scaly skins. They may do this several times a year. Lizards are found in all parts of the world except the polar regions. They thrive in tropical regions, but are also found in the temperate regions. Lizards of the temperate regions must hibernate in the winter.

Most lizards are small, usually less than two feet in length. The largest lizards are the Komodo monitors of Indonesia, which may grow to ten feet in length and weigh three hundred pounds. A lizard like that looks pretty much like the dragons of fairy tales.

As a rule, lizards have short life spans. Some live only two or three years. The record for a lizard in captivity is about twenty-five years.

Most lizards eat insects that they catch with their tongues or snap out of the air. They usually eat food that can be swallowed whole. Lizards have teeth that help hold their food, but they rarely use these teeth to bite off food.

Some lizards have quite specialized diets. The horned lizard usually eats only ants. Other lizards eat plants or perhaps only fruit. The large monitor lizard is one of the few meat-eating lizards. It eats dead animals and sometimes catches small wild pigs, which it swallows whole.

Most kinds of lizards are hatched from eggs, although many are born alive. The eggs are buried in the soil or hidden in decaying logs. Often the female guards the eggs against animals that might feed on them. The young have a special "egg tooth" that grows up from the tip of the upper jaw. The tooth is used to cut through the eggshell at the time of hatching, and then the tooth disappears.

Many lizards live in deserts. They can withstand the heat and dryness that make it impossible for most other animals to stay alive there.

WHAT IS A HORSESHOE CRAB?

A horseshoe crab is a rather fascinating creature. To begin with, it isn't a crab, and it doesn't look much like a horseshoe. It is, however, related to crabs and spiders.

Its scientific name, *Limulus polyphemus*, describes its eyes. The animal has four eyes. One pair bulges from the sides; the other two are set close together at the front of the head and look like one eye.

A horseshoe crab is what scientists call a living fossil. Its body form has changed very little during millions of years. In fact, it has existed in its present form for almost 200 million years!

The entire body is armored by a thick shell. The tail is sword-shaped, long and pointed. It is also barbed. If the horseshoe crab is overturned by a wave, it uses the tail to right itself.

A horseshoe crab has six pairs of legs. Four pairs are used for walking along the sandy bottom of the ocean. A stronger back pair is used in pushing and swimming. A short front pair helps hold and push food toward the mouth. This mouth is practically hidden by the walking legs, so it's hard to find when you look for it.

The "shoulders," or inner joints, bear spikes. These grind and tear food and stuff it into the mouth. A horseshoe crab eats almost anything, from small clams, worms, and fish eggs to seaweed and decaying matter.

A horseshoe crab breathes by means of gill books. Each gill book has about 150 thin leaves, which take oxygen from the water. As long as these leaves stay moist, the animal can breathe.

Baby horseshoe crabs hatch from very tiny eggs. They are born without a tail and with a very soft shell. In about four weeks it is too large for its shell. The shell does not grow, so the animal must shed its shell, or molt.

Before a horseshoe crab reaches its full length of one to two feet, it may molt as many as twenty times!

WHAT IS THE DIFFERENCE BETWEEN OYSTERS AND CLAMS?

There is a large group of animals that scientists call mollusks. The name comes from a Latin word meaning "soft." All mollusks are alike in that they have soft bodies that are covered by a thin envelope of flesh. The envelope is called a mantle. Oysters and clams belong to the mollusk family of animals.

Some mollusks have two shells. They are called bivalves (meaning "two shells"). Oysters, mussels, clams, and scallops are bivalves.

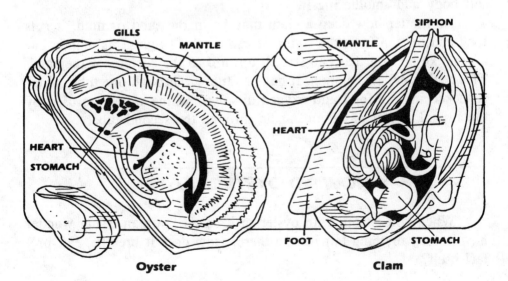

Oyster

Clam

Oysters generally live in shallow waters, where they may be found cemented to rocks and shells near river mouths or along shores. The shells of an oyster open a little when it is feeding and close tightly when it is disturbed. An oyster withdraws into its shell when an enemy approaches or when the tide goes down.

The main body parts of an oyster—including heart, stomach, kidneys, and gills—lie inside the mantle. An oyster has no head, but it does have a mouth. It feeds by straining food out of the water. Food particles are drawn into a space between the soft body and the mantle. They stick to mucus that is produced by the gills. Then the food is passed along from the gills to the mouth folds and, finally, into the mouth.

Clams are usually found buried in sand or mud anywhere from just below the level of low tide out to depths of several hundred feet. Clams burrow into the sand or mud to protect themselves from various enemies and to secure firm anchorage.

A clam has a large foot that it uses for burrowing and for withdrawing quickly into the sand. When the clam wants to move from place to place, the first thing it does is extend this foot. There is a cavity in the foot, and when the clam extends it, blood rushes into the cavity. This makes the tip of the foot swell up, and it provides a kind of anchor. Then the clam contracts the muscles in the foot. Since the foot is anchored, it stays in place, and the clam's body moves forward. The clam's tough shell prevents sand or mud from pressing in on the soft body and smothering it.

No matter how deep a clam may be in the sand or mud, it gets food and oxygen from the water. It can do this because its mantle has a necklike portion that can stretch upward to the surface of the sand. This neck is called a siphon. It has two tubes. Through one tube, water is sucked in, and food and oxygen dissolved in the water are used by the animal. Water passes out again through the second tube.

HOW DO OYSTERS EAT?

When you examine an oyster in its shell you can easily wonder how it does anything but just lie there! How does it breathe, eat, protect itself?

The oyster, however, is not just a glob of living matter; it is quite a complicated creature that carries on many complex activities. It has various organs, blood, a nervous system, and so on. But here we will only concern ourselves with how the oyster eats.

First of all, what does it eat? The food of an oyster consists of tiny algae and other micro-organisms. This means organisms so small that they can only be seen under a microscope. These tiny food particles enter into the body of the oyster with the water that constantly "flows" through the oyster when its shell is open.

The food is strained from the water and becomes entangled in the mucus secreted by the gills of the oyster. The oyster actually selects certain food and rejects other organisms that are unsuitable or too big or the wrong shape, but we don't know how it is able to do this.

The oyster has an alimentary canal that begins at its mouth, and four feelers that guard the mouth's opening. These feelers receive and sort out the food.

There is a narrow esophagus that opens into the stomach, which is a large, saclike structure. A sort of rod about half an inch long projects into the stomach. This rod rotates in the stomach, mixing and grinding the small food particles. This rod also contains the enzymes that digest the food. There is also a large digestive gland surrounding the stomach.

In this gland there are blood cells that surround the food and digest it inside their bodies. Of course, this is only a rough idea of the whole eating process—but you can see that an oyster does eat!

HOW DOES A SPONGE EAT?

It may seem hard to believe, but sponges are animals! They are among the strangest members of the animal kingdom, and they look much more like plants than animals.

There are more than five thousand different kinds of sponges. They range in color from green, brown, yellow, red, and orange to white. They may be shaped like fans, domes, vases, bowls, or trumpets.

Some sponges branch out like trees. Others are flattened masses of spongy tissue spread out on the surface of underwater rocks, shells, or wood. Some are small, less than an inch long. Others are big, measuring two or three feet in height or width.

Adult sponges never move about. And even though a sponge is a living animal, when you touch one it doesn't react. A sponge does not have a head or mouth. It has no eyes, ears, feelers, or other sense organs. And a sponge has no heart, stomach, muscles, or nervous system. If a living sponge is cut in two, all you see is a slimy mass with holes or channels running through it.

This doesn't make it seem much like an animal, does it? And you can understand why even scientists didn't realize for a long time that sponges actually were animals.

Then what does make a sponge an animal?—The way it feeds, chiefly. A sponge captures its food. It does not make its own food, as green plants do. It captures tiny plants and animals from the water around it.

How does it do this? The tube wall of a sponge is like a sieve, or filter, that strains tiny plants and animals out of the water. Water is forced in and out of the sponge by the beating action of tiny, whip-like threads (called flagella). The cells with flagella capture the food. Around the bottom of the flagella, there is a sticky surface that catches the food. Some of the food is digested there and some is passed on to the rest of the sponge by cells that wander through the sponge.

WHAT DO TURTLES EAT?

Turtles have many very interesting and unusual attributes, but their food habits are rather ordinary. The fact is, most turtles eat just about anything.

It depends, of course, on the particular kind of turtle. The snapping turtle, which is not a very pleasant creature to meet, is quite a good hunter. It feeds under water chiefly on fish, frogs, and even ducks!

The terrapin turtle, which people themselves like to eat, can eat its food best under water. It eats insects, tadpoles, and fish. The box turtle, which is a sort of connecting link between the land and the water turtles, likes to spend most of its time on land. But in the hot summer months it enjoys cooling off in the water. When it is on land, it likes to wander through the woods in search of berries and fungi.

Gopher turtles dig burrows in dry, barren places in which they rest during the day. In the early evening they come out and search for their favorite foods—fruit and vegetation.

And what do turtles do in the winter, when their food supply disappears? Like all reptiles, turtles who live in temperate climates go to sleep during the winter months. The length of their sleep depends on the climate. But many turtles can go without food and sleep away the time from October until March! Turtles that live in the water usually bury themselves in the bottoms of rivers and ponds. Land turtles hide themselves in the ground to spend the winter.

Land turtles breathe air through lungs, and have shells made up of a "bony box" covered with horny plates or with soft skin. These shells are divided into two parts. One part covers the back; the other covers the underpart of the turtle's body. Through the openings between the two parts the turtle can thrust out its head, neck, tail, and legs.

Turtles have a good sense of sight, taste, and touch, but their hearing is poorly developed.

HOW DO FROGS CROAK?

If you've ever lived near a pond, then you were sure to wonder about the croaking of frogs. The noises they sometimes make at night can be enough to keep you from sleeping!

While some female frogs may make certain sounds when they are injured, the familiar singing or croaking we hear is limited to the male. The chief reason he sings his throaty song is to attract the female. But he doesn't limit his croaking to the mating season. His voice can be heard at night long after the mating season is past.

This is the way a frog makes that croaking sound. He inhales, closes his nostrils and mouth, and forces the air back and forth between the mouth and lungs. The sound is produced when the air passes over the vocal cords and causes them to vibrate.

Many kinds of frogs have vocal sacs that open into the mouth. When the frog is singing, these sacs become filled with air and enlarge. These enlarged sacs act as resonators and help give the frog's croaking that peculiar sound. By the way, the American bullfrog's voice may sometimes be heard from a distance of a mile or more!

While the adult frog has lungs, it does not breathe air into them as we do. It sucks air into its mouth through two nostrils, at the same time lowering its throat. Then the nostrils are closed, and the frog lifts its throat and pushes the air into its lungs.

Did you know that the frog uses its eyes in swallowing food? As you know, frogs catch their prey with sticky tongues. When an insect sticks to the tongue, it is folded back into the mouth. The large, bulging eyes of the frog are separated from the mouth cavity by only a thin skin. When closed, they bulge inward. So the frog closes its eyes when it has an insect in its mouth, and the inner bulging helps to push the food down its throat! Frogs are useful to man because they are insect eaters and help keep the insect population down.

HOW MANY KINDS OF INSECTS ARE THERE?

What do most people think of when you mention "insects"? Well, they may think of pests, such as flies, mosquitos, moths, and beetles.

Or, they may think of ants and bees and wasps; and attractive insects like butterflies. And then if you ask if they can think of any more insects, they might be able to think of a few more.

But do you know how many different kinds of insects there actually are? Get ready for a surprise. There are somewhere between two and four million different kinds of insects! Scientists have actually described in scientific language as many as 625,000 different kinds. They practically have no hope of ever being able to classify every single kind of insect that exists. There is no other class of animals on earth that even comes close to having as many kinds as do insects.

When it comes to trying to estimate how many insects are living in the world today, the number is so vast that the human mind cannot even imagine it! The only way scientists can even begin to count the insect population in any one area is to count all the insects that can be found in and on a square yard of rich, moist soil. That can be anywhere from five hundred to two thousand. So it can be said that in a single acre of good soil, about four million insects live in cozy comfort!

Remember that if you, who are untrained in observing insects, were to go over this same acre and count insects, you would see only an occasional butterfly, bumblebee, or beetle. But the majority of insects are so small that the human eye does not readily notice them. Many are microscopic. And there are only a few thousand insects of all those that exist that become annoying enough to man for him to try to control them.

When you think of it this way, you realize that man really moves about in a world of insects—but he has no idea that most of them exist or how many there are!

By the way, there are two things most insects have in common: Their body is divided into three parts; and they usually have six legs. This is true of most, but not all of them.

WHAT ARE FLEAS?

Most of us think of fleas as the tiny creatures that live on dogs and cause them to be constantly scratching. But did you know that there are more than nine hundred different species of fleas?

Fleas are parasitic insects, which means they live on other creatures. They live on all mammals (including man), as well as on birds and many other animals. In fact, next to flies, fleas are the insects with which people all over the world are most familiar. This is because they infect domestic animals and man, and have done so since the earliest times.

The bite of a flea can cause quite a bit of discomfort, but that is not the chief reason they are troublesome. Fleas can carry serious diseases, like typhus fever and bubonic plague, which may result in death.

Fleas lay their tiny eggs right on the host animal on whom they are living, or in the places where the host sleeps. The eggs are scattered widely by the movement of the host.

Larvae come out of the eggs, and when these are mature, they spin a tiny cocoon, and out of this the adult flea eventually comes. It only takes twenty-eight to forty-eight days for the human flea to develop from an egg stage to an adult. The rat flea in the tropics takes only twenty-one days.

An adult flea has no wings. But it has well-developed legs that it uses for leaping, and some species of fleas are quite remarkable leapers. Some can jump as high as eight inches straight up and thirteen inches horizontally!

The mouth parts of a flea are adapted to pierce the skin of other animals and to suck blood, on which they live. The body itself is flat.

Fleas are most abundant in the tropics and warmer regions, but they also exist in the polar regions and in deserts. In North America, the most important species of fleas are the human flea, the dog flea, and the cat flea. All three kinds, however, attack humans, dogs, and cats, among other animals.

DO ANTS HAVE A SENSE OF SMELL?

Ants are such amazing insects that it would take much more space than we have here to tell their fascinating story. So let's just consider a few facts about them for now.

To begin with, you'll find ants in desert sands, prairies, seashores, mountain slopes, forests—practically anywhere in the world, except perhaps on the very summit of the highest mountains! They can endure almost all kinds of climates.

There are thousands of different species of ants, but they all are related to bees and wasps; that is, they belong to the same order of insects. All ants are social. This means that ants live in colonies. Each colony has three sorts of ants: the males; the females, or queens; and the workers.

The males and the queens of most species of ants have wings, but the workers are wingless. The queen gets rid of her wings after her mating flight. The colonies of ants vary greatly in size. Some may have only a few dozen ants living together; others may have hundreds of thousands of busy ants in the same colony!

Although ants vary greatly in size, they are all more or less alike in appearance. A pair of long feelers, or antennae, wave from the ant's head. These are constantly moving, and they serve not only as feelers, but also as organs of smell. So while the ant doesn't have a "nose" for smelling, it does have a sense of smell. The antennae also help the ant to distinguish other ants and to communicate with them.

The head of the ant also contains the brain, a pair of compound eyes, and its powerful jaws and mouth. In addition to the compound eyes, most ants have other seeing organs called simple eyes, or stemmata.

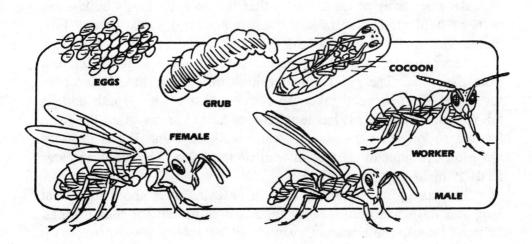

EGGS

GRUB

COCOON

FEMALE

WORKER

MALE

The life cycle of the ant is a fascinating one. The females of a colony fly high into the air, and the males follow them. After this mating flight, the males die almost at once, and each female, or queen, goes off by herself and starts a new colony. She digs a nest and lays some eggs. After these eggs hatch into little legless grubs, the queen mother helps each spin a cocoon. When the young ant has grown, she cracks open one end of the cocoon and pulls the ant out of its shell. Almost at once, these newborn worker ants begin their life of devotion to their mother and to the rest of the colony.

WHAT IS AN ANTEATER?

The anteater is an animal that feeds on white ants, the kind of ants we usually call termites. The anteater probably chooses ants rather than other foods because it has no teeth. Its very long jawbone is almost entirely covered with skin.

The anteater has a very small mouth and a wormlike tongue that is more than a foot long and is covered with a sticky substance. When the anteater sees a termite, it pushes out its tongue. The termite is trapped on the sticky substance until the anteater swallows down its prey.

Because many of the termites that the anteater hunts build large nests of hard mud, Nature has given it powerful forearms and long claws. The anteater uses its long claws to tear open the termite nest.

There are three kinds of anteaters, and each is quite different from the other. The giant anteater lives on the ground. It is about seven feet long; its head takes up about a foot of this length and its tail measures two feet. It has long, coarse hair. The claws on the front feet are so long that the anteater can't walk on them. It has to move along on the sides of its feet instead of the soles. The giant anteater feeds at night and sleeps all day.

The tamandua is another kind of anteater. It is about three feet long and has short hair. The tamandua uses its tail for many things. Without its tail, the tamandua would not be able to live in trees as it does.

The silky anteater is the smallest anteater of all. It is about a foot and a half long, half of which is the tail. So it can also live in trees. In fact, it spends the day curled up on a branch. The silky anteater lives in the area between southern Mexico and Brazil.

WHAT DO MOTHS EAT?

Most of us worry about moths in terms of destruction to our clothes. While clothes moths—in their caterpillar stage—do eat articles made from wool, fur, and other animal matter, they are not the only destructive moths in existence. Let's just go down the list of some other moths and see what they eat, or destroy.

The clearwing moth eats woody plants. There are peach, currant, and squash borers and you can guess their favorite foods. Then there is a species of moth that eats grain and potatoes. The pink bollworm, a very destructive type, eats cotton.

There are also pea moths, strawberry leaf folder moths, grapeberry moths, and bud moths. The species known as Pyralidae includes eight families of moths, all of them very destructive, including the European corn borer, the melon worm, the celery leaf tier, the meal moth (which feeds on cereals and other seeds), the oriental rice borer, and the sugarcane borer.

The larvae of the wax moth feed on wax, even going into beehives where they often cause serious damage. The Indian-meal moth is one of the worst destroyers of such foods as cereals, flour, nuts, and dried fruits.

Many of the tiger moths eat cultivated crops and trees. Some hawk moths feed on tobacco, tomatoes, grapes, and apples. The coddling moth is the chief pest in the apple orchard.

But, remember, adult moths eat only nectar from flowers. It is when the moth is in the caterpillar stage that it eats all these other things.

By the way, the caterpillars of some moths have actually been used as food by some primitive peoples. For example, Indians in certain parts of the western United States ate the caterpillars of the Coloradia pandora moth.

DO INSECTS HAVE BLOOD?

As we look at living creatures much smaller than ourselves, many of us imagine that they must lack the organs and functions that we have. How can something as tiny as an insect have a heart? How can it have a circulatory system and blood in its tiny body?

But the miracle of life is not only that these creatures have organs, but that these organs are perfect for each insect's way of life.

Adult insects have bodies with three sections: head, thorax, and abdomen. The head has a pair of antennae in front that are feelers, and that usually have some tiny organs of smell. The eyes and mouth are part of the head, too.

Not only does an insect have a heart, but it also has blood and a circulatory system. The blood passes into the heart by means of holes equipped with valves. When the heart contracts, these holes close, and the blood is driven out through the arteries. Insects don't have a system of capillaries and veins as we do.

The reason their circulatory system is not greatly developed is that they don't depend on the circulation of the blood for their supply of oxygen. In our bodies, as you know, the blood carries oxygen to every part and enables it to function.

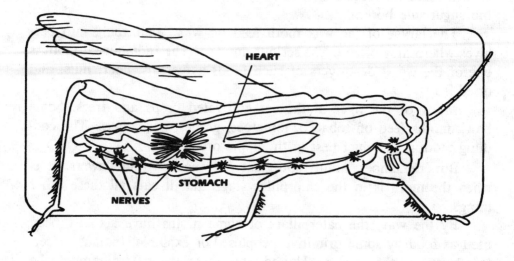

But insects have a different system of breathing. They have tiny branching tubes that end in little air holes in the sides of the body. The air comes in right from the surface of the body and goes directly to the cells.

A more complicated system would be too much for their size. On the other hand, a simple system like theirs wouldn't be enough for larger animals. It's not too bad a system, though, considering that more than half of all living animals have it!

Did you know that one name for an insect is hexapod? The term is from two Greek words meaning "six" and "foot." If you count the feet of an insect, you can see why hexapod is a good way to describe most insects. The legs are usually in three pairs, and are attached to the thorax.

There are thousands and thousands of different species of insects, among them some of man's best friends as well as some of his worst enemies.

WHERE DO SNAKES GET THEIR VENOM?

Scientists think there are about two thousand four hundred different kinds of snakes now living. Of these, only about 8 percent are poisonous kinds that stun or kill their prey with venom. In many poisonous snakes the venom is not strong enough or plentiful enough to be dangerous to man.

All snakes have a large amount of saliva that helps them swallow and digest prey. In the venomous snakes one of the saliva glands produces a substance that is poisonous to the snakes' prey. This substance is the snakes' venom.

Some snakes have venom that is strong enough to kill an elephant. Others have venom so mild that they can kill only small lizards. Probably only two hundred species of venomous snakes can be considered dangerous to man.

Among the venomous species of snakes known, the cobras and their relatives make up one family; the vipers, a second. And there are some venomous snakes among a kind known as the colubrids, the largest family of snakes.

The cobras and their relatives have fangs at the front of the mouth, one on each side of the upper jaw. The fangs are grooved, but in most cobras the groove is closed over, forming a hollow tube. A muscle surrounds the venom gland. When the snake bites, the muscle presses on the gland. This forces the venom down into the fang and out through the fang tip directly into the prey.

There is a spitting cobra that can spray venom from its fangs. The cobra aims at the eyes of a threatening animal, such as an antelope or buffalo. The spray reaches about eight feet and causes almost instant blindness.

In general, cobra venom affects the nervous system of the victim and makes him unable to move. When the venom reaches the nerve centers that control breathing or heartbeat, the victim dies.

Vipers have very long fangs. Their venom affects mainly the blood cells and blood vessels of the victims. It may cause great swelling and bleeding.

WHAT DO SNAKES EAT?

There are no "vegetarian" snakes. They are all carnivores and eat animals of some kind.

Snakes have powerful digestive juices—and they need them, for snakes always eat their meal whole. They do not have teeth that can cut up food, such as cats have, for example. Birds and turtles have sharp beaks. All that snakes have are slender, needlelike teeth with which they can catch their prey and pull it into their mouth. But they can't chew it up.

One of the most unusual things about snakes and their eating is the construction of their jaws. The jaws are very loosely attached to the other bones of the skull. They are edged with teeth, and most snakes also have two rows of teeth in the roof of the mouth. All these rows of teeth are on bones moved by special muscles.

A snake eats by pushing one jaw over the food while the teeth of the rest of the jaw hold the prey. Then another jawbone is pushed over the food. In this way the food is pulled down into the throat of the snake.

Because of the arrangement of the jaws, a snake can eat animals that are surprisingly big. For example, pythons sometimes eat animals that are as large as deer and leopards! Of course, small snakes eat small animals. Most snakes eat animals of moderate size: grasshoppers, frogs, fish, mice, rats, and birds. Some tiny blind snakes eat only termites. And there are some snakes that eat other snakes!

Snakes tend to be particular about what they eat. A green snake may eat spiders, fish, birds and caterpillars, but not lizards or mice. And a water snake may eat fish and frogs, but not insects or mice. Garter snakes, however, seem able to eat a variety of animals, including worms, fish, frogs, rodents, and birds.

HOW DO WOLVES HUNT?

The wolf has always had a bad reputation. It is cast as the villain of many of Aesop's fables and countless nursery rhymes and fairy tales. Little Red Riding Hood was pursued by a greedy wolf, and so were the three little pigs.

How does this creature go about getting its food? When searching for food, wolves travel regular hunting trails that may extend for a hundred miles or more. Sometimes several weeks pass before the wolves cover the entire circuit. From time to time the wolves fan out—eyes, ears, and noses alert for possible prey.

At intervals along the trail, the wolves have "scent posts." These are stumps, trees, rocks, or other landmarks upon which they urinate, just as dogs do on fireplugs or shrubbery. Each time a wolf comes to a scent post, he sniffs it carefully. In this way he learns what other wolves have passed that way.

The main food of wolves is meat, and the kind depends on what prey is most readily available. Wolves will attack and eat deer, moose, and many other large, hoofed animals. In Canada and Alaska, wolves follow herds of caribou and prey on the calves and stragglers.

In the Arctic, they sometimes attack musk oxen. And whenever domestic stock is left unguarded in wild country, it is likely to be killed and eaten. Rabbits and rodents are hunted when no easier prey is around. If wolves can't find any meat, they will eat fruit, such as berries.

Sometimes wolves track their prey for many hours. They keep up a tireless pace that is not swift, but that they can continue for mile after mile. Finally the prey is brought to bay. Several wolves may attack from the rear, others from the front. When the quarry finally goes down, the pack swarms all over it, slashing and biting until the victim is dead.

Then all the members of the pack gorge themselves, sometimes eating as much as fifteen pounds of meat each. The remainder of the meat may be hidden or buried as a supply for future meals.

HOW DO ELEPHANTS LIVE IN HERDS?

An elephant herd may vary from ten or twenty animals to fifty or more, most of whom are related.

The leader of the herd is usually a wise old cow, or female elephant. Most of her followers are females with young in various stages of growth. Young males also travel with the herd, but adult bulls often travel alone. Many live apart from the herd, but visit it often.

When two or more bulls join the herd at the same time, they are likely to fight each other. When one of them gains the upper hand, he may gore the other, drive him away, or even kill him.

The herd wanders far and wide, visiting favorite food areas at different times of the year. During the dry season they migrate into forests or stay close to a good supply of water. In the rainy season they wander out onto grassy plains.

The daily life of an elephant herd often follows a routine. In the early morning hours the animals may travel to a nearby river. There they drink and bathe—snorting and rolling and squirting water over themselves. Elephants are good swimmers and can cross broad rivers.

After bathing, the elephants feed on trees and other plants for several hours. Then they pause in some shady area for a midday rest. As evening comes on they sometimes go back to the river to drink again.

They may feed far into the night before taking another rest period. Some elephants lie down to sleep, but many adults—especially among the African elephants—sleep standing up.

All the adult elephants in a herd are constantly on the alert for danger. They have poor eyesight and only fair hearing, but they have a keen sense of smell. When a youngster in a herd is attacked— possibly by a lion or tiger—the rest of the herd rallies to its defense. In Asia, tigers kill about one of every four elephant calves. Adult elephants are rarely attacked by any other animal.

WHAT IS A GAZELLE?

A gazelle is a kind of antelope. There are about a hundred species of antelopes, which are members of the cattle family and which are characterized by their graceful build and upward-sweeping horns.

The graceful horns of some gazelles look like a lyre. These horns may be heavy, streamlined, or bent, varying in shape from a V or U to a bracket, depending on the species.

A gazelle is about twenty-six inches high.

The expression "swift as a gazelle" comes from the fact that they can move with great speed. A gazelle can run faster than a greyhound.

Antelopes as a whole are most abundant in Africa, where there are about ninety species. Ten species are found in India. At one time antelopes lived over most of Europe and Asia.

All male antelopes have horns, and in half the species, females have horns, too. Some kinds have only one-inch spikes, while the giant sable antelope has tremendous sixty-four-inch half-circles.

Most antelopes are graceful and shy, but certain species, such as the wildebeest, sable, roan, eland, and oryx, are dangerous when approached or wounded. The wildebeest, or gnu, looks like a horse with a beard and buffalo horns, and is especially savage. It has such great endurance and speed that it can easily outdistance a horse.

Many antelopes live on open plains, often in herds of hundreds. Others live singly or in small herds. Some live in marshes, near riverbanks, on cliffs, or in deserts.

Antelopes are usually tawny, reddish, or gray, often with white belly, rump, and face markings. Some are beautifully marked and colored. Antelopes walk on two-toed hoofs and, like other cattle, ruminate, or chew the cud.

IS THE DUCKBILL A MAMMAL OR A BIRD?

It would be hard to find a stranger creature in all the world than the duckbill, or platypus. The chances are that you will never see a live duckbill, because it dies in captivity. What makes this creature so odd?

For one thing, the duckbill is like a fish, like a fowl, and like a reptile, yet it is not any of them! It's a kind of in-between animal that came about by evolution.

Mammals nurse their young, and so does the duckbill. Fowl and birds lay eggs, and so does the duckbill. The body temperature of a reptile changes with the heat or cold of its surroundings, and this also happens to the duckbill! Actually, however, the duckbill is a mammal, one of the only two mammals that lay eggs (the other is the anteater).

The duckbill has webbed feet and a ducklike bill instead of a mouth. It swims in the water somewhat like a fish. It is found only in the eastern portion of Australia and in Tasmania.

The males are about twenty-one inches long, and the females, about eighteen inches. The body is covered with a fine underfur hidden by a coat of long, coarse guard hairs, whose ends turn in toward the body. It has a flat tail, somewhat like a beaver's. The duckbill can hear quite well, even though it looks as if it has no ears. It hears with a set of internal ears.

The duckbill can't breathe underwater, so it must keep its bill in the air while it swims. But since the nostrils are about one-third of the distance from the tip of the bill, it has to keep only the end of its bill out of water.

On the heel of each hind foot of the male is a horny organ connected with poison glands, so this creature can take pretty good care of itself. This peculiar animal makes its home in burrows in the banks of quiet, deep pools in rivers. The duckbills stay in the burrow most of the day and come out only at night to feed in the water. They eat water insects, worms, and shellfish.

The duckbill builds a special burrow for nesting purposes, which it fills with leaves, grass, and reeds. The female lays her eggs in the nest and lies curled around them to incubate them. The young are born blind and helpless, and remain in the burrow for some time, feeding upon the mother's milk.

WHAT IS THE BALD EAGLE?

The bald eagle is an American bird. Despite its name, it is not what we think of as bald.

The bald eagle was named at a time when "bald" meant "white" or "streaked with white." The adult bald eagle has white feathers on its head. Its tail is white, too. Its body and wings are dark brown, and its eyes, beak, and feet are yellow.

The bald eagle is fond of fish and likes to live near water. It feeds mainly on dead or dying fish. Sometimes the eagle steals its catch from the osprey, another large fishing bird. The bald eagle also eats small animals, such as rabbits or birds.

The bald eagle is the national emblem of the United States. Like all the other eagles in North America, it is becoming rare. But eagles are among the most interesting birds known to man.

Some eagles are more than three feet long from head to tail, and their wingspread may be more than seven feet. An eagle's beak is large and hooked. Its toes end in talons, which are strong claws. An eagle has far keener eyesight than a human being.

An eagle is a bird of prey; that is, a hunter. The eagle swoops down, picks up the prey in its talons, and flies off. An eagle, which weighs eight to twelve pounds, may be able to carry off an animal weighing as much as seven-and-one-half pounds! With its beak, it tears the food to pieces. Eagles, by the way, hunt only in the daytime.

An eagle keeps the same mate for many years, perhaps for life —no one is sure. A pair of eagles build their nest at the top of a very tall tree or on a rocky ledge. The nest, called an aerie, is built of sticks. The largest aerie on record is nine-and-one-half feet wide and twenty feet deep. Many eagles use the same nests year after year. An eagle may live as long as thirty years.

DO ANY BIRDS HIBERNATE?

When the cold of winter comes, we can tuck ourselves into a warm house, sit by the fire, and stay indoors until we want to go out. But even though we are a warm-blooded animal, we can't hibernate. If man did hibernate, do you know he'd be able to prolong his life by surviving freezing temperatures?

Birds, alas, cannot hibernate either. They can, however, endure very cold temperatures. Even a little canary such as you might keep in a cage could survive outdoor temperatures of minus thirty degrees, or even minus fifty degrees, providing it could obtain enough food. For birds who can obtain food and who don't migrate to warmer climates, hibernation is not necessary.

The process of hibernation is controlled by a temperature-regulating center in the brain. When it becomes cold, warm-blooded animals react by sending blood from the skin to the interior of the body, by erecting their fur or feathers to improve the insulation against cold, and then by shivering, which increases the heat production.

Hibernating animals simply "turn down" this heat regulator in their bodies when it comes time to hibernate. They become practically cold-blooded animals. The process is triggered by cold temperature, a lack of food, shorter days, and other conditions.

As an animal enters hibernation, its temperature regulator becomes poor; when the body temperature falls, it doesn't respond as it normally would to keep the animal warm. Instead, the body temperature drops to conform with that of the air. Breathing becomes slow and irregular, the heart beats irregularly and slowly, and various nervous reflexes stop functioning.

If the air temperature drops to freezing, however, many hibernators begin to breathe faster and raise their heat production a bit. Some wake up. Those that don't respond at all may freeze to death.

HOW CAN PARROTS TALK?

People are amazed and delighted to hear parrots talk. But it seems that no one can yet explain how these birds are able to imitate human speech so well!

Some people think parrots can talk because of the structure of their tongue, which is large and thick. It may be that this kind of tongue does help it to talk, but it certainly isn't necessary in order for a bird to be able to talk. Other "talking" birds, such as mynas, crows, and ravens, don't have large, thick tongues. Hawks and eagles do have such tongues—and can't talk!

Is it because parrots are more intelligent than other birds? This doesn't seem to be the reason either. As a matter of fact, most biologists think that parrots and other talking birds do not realize the meaning of their own words. They do, however, seem to form definite associations between certain expressions and actions.

It may be that parrots can "talk" because their voice mechanism and hearing work more slowly than those of other birds. And probably the sounds made by human beings resemble the sounds naturally made by parrots, so it is easy for them to imitate them.

Parrots are rather remarkable birds in other ways, too. They can adapt themselves to practically any kind of living condition. This is why, for example, sailors have long taken parrots along on their trips. And even though a parrot is a tropical bird, when it is in captivity it can get along quite comfortably in temperate and even in cold climates.

Parrots are very brave birds and loyal to their kind. If a common danger threatens a group of them, the whole flock will stand by. When searching for food, they swing from one limb of a tree to another like monkeys, using their bill as well as their feet. In fact, they can use their feet at times almost like hands, especially when eating.

DO DOGS DREAM?

If you have a dog in your house, you may have noticed that when he is asleep he makes little noises and moves or twitches his legs, as though chasing something. Most dog owners who have had this experience believe this to be a sign that their dog is dreaming. While they cannot say positively that dogs do not dream, scientists will tell you that dogs probably do not dream.

To understand these scientists' theory, we must remember that men and animals are the products of evolution. This means that over millions of years gradual changes have been taking place. While men and animals are alike in some ways, the mental make-up and senses of animals have evolved in ways different from ours. As a result, animals live in worlds that are different from ours.

If the senses and the working of the minds of animals are different, we cannot expect their organs and brains to produce what our organs and brains produce. The intelligence and personality of animals are not a "miniature" of the human model.

We cannot know what thoughts animals have. So when we see what we think is a dog dreaming—moving its legs or making noises in its sleep—we cannot assume we are right. The brain cells might just be repeating their messages to the muscles, and the dog might not have any vision of a dream at all.

Those animals that have brains built something like our own may have thoughts like ours, but they will be far simpler.

WHERE DID THE RAT ORIGINATE?

Nobody likes to talk about rats, since they are unpleasant creatures. But they have had a very important effect on the life of man. In fact, the brown rat carries fleas that can spread a very dread disease: bubonic plague, or the Black Death. More people have died from this disease than from all the wars of history!

The brown rat, which is the common house rat, was originally a native of Asia. It came into Europe at about the time of the Crusades. It came partly by land, and partly on the ships that brought the Crusaders back. In a short time the brown rat was everywhere in Europe.

It came to the United States during the American Revolution, and soon spread out everywhere as the pioneers moved westward.

Why has man had such a difficult time fighting against this creature? The reason is that the rat has amazing powers of adaptation. The more prosperous man gets, the better this rat lives. Because the more food there is around, the more food it gets. When times are bad for man—and we are speaking in terms of history over the centuries—rats have a way of taking care of themselves: they become cannibals and begin to eat one another.

The brown rat is also unusually cunning. It is not fooled by the same trick twice. If poison is mixed with a food, it may kill a few rats the first time, but then the other rats learn to avoid it.

Common house rats weigh about three-quarters of a pound. They vary in color from pure gray to reddish or black-brown. Their total length is sixteen to nineteen inches. When there are other types of rats around, the brown rats drive them away and take over. They are found wherever man lives, except in the Far North and in very dry lands. Most cats, by the way, are not too good as rat-catchers.

WHAT IS A HAMSTER?

Many young people enjoy having hamsters and guinea pigs as pets. They are gentle and inquisitive rodents, easy to raise.

The golden hamster is five to six inches long and weighs four to five ounces. Its home is Europe and Asia. The name comes from the German word *hamstern,* which means "to hoard."

This is because when the hamster is wild it does just that. It stuffs its large cheek pouches with food, which it then hoards in burrows, or underground holes.

The cheek pouches can carry up to half the animal's weight in food. To empty its cheeks, the hamster presses on them with its forefeet and blows. It has a plump body and short limbs. The thick, soft fur is reddish-gold on its back and grayish-white on its belly.

The hamster is one of the fastest-reproducing mammals. It has four or five litters a year. Sometimes there are more than a dozen babies in each litter. The mother nurses the young for about four weeks.

An interesting thing about keeping hamsters as pets is that it is necessary to make it possible for them to exercise, or they will get a form of paralysis. So a hamster cage should be equipped with an exercise wheel. If the cage does not have a wheel, the hamster should be allowed out of the cage often to run and get its exercise.

WHAT IS A PARAMECIUM?

If you examine a drop of pond water under a microscope, one of the smallest creatures you may see will be longish and shaped like a slipper, rounded at one end and thin at the other. It may be hard to believe, but this tiny living thing can be classified as an animal. This is because, like all other animals, it gets food by eating plants and other organisms (plants make their own food), and it must move about to get food (plants stay in one place).

This creature is a paramecium. Its body is almost completely covered with thin, hairlike threads, which are called cilia. The cilia beat rhythmically, like thousands of tiny oars, driving the body forward or backward or in turns.

The paramecium lives in fresh water, feeding on bacteria, yeasts, and other protozoans (tiny animal-like microbes). And it seems able to control the beating of its cilia, for it can change direction rapidly to get food or avoid danger.

Like all living organisms, the paramecium can reproduce, or multiply. When it is fully grown, it may divide in two and form two new individuals. A paramecium can also reproduce by exchanging body materials with another paramecium.

The remarkable thing about the paramecium is that while it carries out many of the same living activities that humans and large animals do, it does so in a single cell. In the human body, for example, there are billions of cells, and they are organized into groups to do specific tasks.

There is a kind of specialization even in the one-celled paramecium. Inside the cell, there are two ball-shaped masses, one larger than the other. These are the nuclei. The small nucleus controls reproduction. The large one controls the other activities of the cell.

Paramecia are one of the more than one hundred thousand different kinds of micro-organisms that man has discovered and studied. (Micro-organisms are too small to be studied without a magnifying glass or microscope.) The first animals on earth may have been something like these tiny animal-like microbes.

WHAT ARE NITROGEN-FIXING BACTERIA?

Can you imagine something that is absolutely necessary to life, that is all about you, and yet that has to be "captured" to be used? This is nitrogen.

About four-fifths of the air we breathe consists of nitrogen, which is a gas. But we breathe it right out again unchanged! We only use the nitrogen to dilute the oxygen of the air so that we won't get too much at one time. Protoplasm, the substance inside all living cells, requires oxygen to be formed, and proteins, the essential food materials, are built around nitrogen compounds.

So it's pretty important for us to be able to capture nitrogen from the air. The process of doing this is called nitrogen-fixation. And a good deal of this is done for us by bacteria.

There are two kinds of nitrogen-fixing bacteria. One kind lives on the roots of plants, and the other lives free in the soil. How do they "fix" nitrogen? These bacteria take nitrogen directly from the air, combine it with oxygen, and then use this combination to build proteins.

Those that live on roots live only on the roots of plants such as beans, clover, alfalfa, and peas. But they fix more nitrogen than these plants need. The plants store the surplus in their roots. When these plants die or are harvested, the surplus nitrogen passes into the soil.

When a soil area has been used continuously for long periods of time and the plants all harvested, nitrogen is not being returned to the soil. The soil is then not able to nourish new crops. This is why farmers must use fertilizers.

The fertilizers that replace nitrogen in the soil include sodium nitrate, ammonium sulphate, and the waste products of animals and birds, such as manure. Today there are also artificial methods of nitrogen-fixation to replenish the soil.

CHAPTER 5
HOW THINGS ARE MADE

HOW IS THE CORRECT TIME DECIDED?

The two main units of time that we have are the day and the year. They are both determined by the movement of the earth. The spinning of the earth on its axis gives us the solar (sun) day. The journey of the earth around the sun gives us the solar year.

The solar day is divided into twenty-four hours. The hour is divided into sixty minutes, and the minute into sixty seconds. Actually, the length of a solar day varies. One reason for this is changes in the earth's speed around the sun. But even though each solar day is sometimes longer or sometimes shorter than exactly twenty-four hours, we say that the mean (average) solar day is twenty-four hours.

For convenience in locating places, man has marked off the earth into meridians—circles that run through the poles. Places that are on the same meridian have the same solar time. Places that are east or west of each other have different solar times. The difference in solar time is one hour for each meridian.

There is a meridian that runs through Greenwich, England, that is numbered 0. It is called the prime meridian. This is the starting point, and all other meridians are marked off east and west of Greenwich.

Clock time the whole world over is based on mean solar time at Greenwich. Astronomers at Greenwich Observatory check their clocks against the sun or a particular star. They check the exact time when the sun or the star crosses the meridian.

Observatories in other countries also keep track of the correct time. They broadcast time signals by radio. In the United States, the Naval Observatory in Washington, D.C., determines the correct time. Special clocks are used to keep the correct time. The United States Naval Observatory uses quartz-crystal controlled clocks. The electric motors in such clocks are controlled by the vibrations of the quartz crystals. The clocks keep time to within 1/500 second per day!

WHAT DO A.M. AND P.M. MEAN?

Everybody uses the expressions A.M. and P.M. to indicate before noon and after noon. But do you know exactly what they mean, and how these terms came into being?

As you know, the turning of the earth makes the sun and the stars seem to move across the sky. Daylight, of course, begins when the sun rises in the east and ends when it sets in the west. When the sun is high in the sky, between these two positions, half of the daylight hours have been spent.

Therefore, by noticing where the sun stood in the sky, early man knew he could tell the time of day. At night, the motion of the stars served the same purpose.

The important thing in keeping time is to know the exact moment of noon. For each of us, wherever we are, noon is when the sun is directly overhead. Think of an imaginary line, a meridian, drawn across the sky, stretching from the north point of your horizon down to the south point.

When the sun crosses your meridian, it is noon for you. While the sun is still east of this line or meridian, it is morning. After the sun has crossed this meridian, it is afternoon.

The Latin word for "midday" is *meridies,* from which comes our word meridian. So A.M. is an abbreviation for *ante meridiem,* or before midday. And P.M. is the abbreviation for *post meridiem,* or after midday.

Each of the world's time zones is about fifteen degrees wide in longitude, which is about the distance the sun moves through the sky in an hour. Everyone who lives in the same time zone observes noon at the same moment. In this way, the time differs by one hour as you move through each time zone.

WHY DO WATCHES HAVE JEWELS?

When a watch is advertised, the number of jewels it has is often mentioned as an indication of its quality. What exactly is a "jewel" in a watch, and why is it there?

A watch (or clock) is only useful to us if it is accurate, and if it doesn't constantly break down. The average watch contains about 211 different pieces, so obviously it's quite a complicated mechanism. Let's see what makes a watch go and the part that jewels play in this.

A watch gets its power from the mainspring, which is a coiled wire about two feet long when straightened out. When you wind the watch, you tighten the coil of the mainspring.

From the mainspring, the power travels through a series of four wheels, called the train, to the balance wheel. The train moves the hands on the dial. The balance wheel acts like the pendulum on a clock. It is the heart of the watch and regulates its movement.

Inside the balance wheel is the hairspring, a coiled steel wire no thicker than a hair. One pound of the right steel will produce eight miles of this wire!

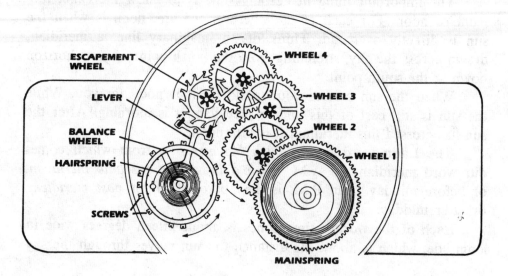

Around the edge of the balance wheel are adjusted tiny screws of steel or gold. Their position and weight control the speed of the watch. They are so small that an ordinary thimble will hold twenty thousand of them! Then there is the escapement wheel, which catches the balance wheel and lets it go. This regulates the movement and this is the sound that we call the "ticking" of a watch.

We've mentioned various wheels that constantly move in a watch. These wheels rest on pivots, and the constant motion creates friction. To withstand this friction, the pivots rest on tiny pieces of precious stones, such as ruby, sapphire, or garnet. These are the jewels of a watch. The more jewels, the less likely is friction to wear out or slow up the moving parts in your watch!

WHAT ARE THE PRIMARY COLORS?

If you hold up a glass prism to a beam of sunlight, you'll see the light form a rainbow of colors. This is called the spectrum. It consists of all the colors that make up "white" light.

Now, although you might be able to see six or seven colors in the spectrum, the white light is really made up of three basic colors. These are called the primary colors, because they cannot be made from any other colors. The primary colors of light are orange-red, green, and violet-blue. The other colors you see in the rainbow or spectrum are made by a mixture of the primary colors.

When the naked eye looks at the spectrum, it can see three mixed colors, which are called secondary colors. The secondary colors in light are green-blue, yellow, and magenta-red. You can produce these colors by mixing the primary colors in certain combinations.

But remember, we are talking about light. Paint colors are substances, and are exactly the opposite from light colors! The secondary colors in light are the primary colors in paint. This means that in paint the primary colors are yellow, green-blue, and magenta-red. And with these three colors, you can mix any colors in paint.

There are many other ways we classify colors. A color that is brilliant and has no black or white paint in it is called a hue. Yellow, red, blue, and green are hues. A color that is mixed from a hue and black is called a shade. Deep brown is a shade. A color that is made with a hue and white is a tint. Pink and ivory are tints. A color that is a mixture of pure hue, black, and white is a tone. Tan, beige, and gray are tones.

Here is an interesting fact about color. How do you think red paint looks before the can is opened? It doesn't look red. It actually looks black! That's because where there is no light, there is no color. In a dark room, there is no such thing as color.

The color of an object depends on the material of the object and the light in which the object is seen. For instance, an orange-red sweater looks orange-red because the dye in the wool reflects the orange-red part of the light. The violet-blue and green parts of light are absorbed by the sweater. Only the orange-red is reflected for you to see.

WHAT MAKES HOT AND COLD?

Some things are hot to the touch, other things are cold. Sometimes the air feels hot, other times it feels cool. What makes the difference?

According to present theories, heat consists of the motion of atoms and molecules. For example, the atoms and molecules in the air are able to move about freely, bumping into each other and into objects in their path. Now, these tiny particles may move rapidly or slowly. If they move rapidly, we say the temperature of the air is high, or that the air is hot. If they move slowly (as on a cold day), we feel the air to be cool.

When it comes to liquids and solids, the atoms and molecules cannot move so freely—but they are still able to move rapidly. For example, in a block of hot iron the atoms vibrate perhaps a million times each second—and that's rapidly! If you were to touch the tip of your finger to such a block, you would feel pain because of the sudden and violent motion imparted to the molecules in your skin when they come near the fast-moving particles of the iron.

Do molecules really move about? Countless experiments prove that the molecules actually do move constantly. In fact, under the microscope tiny particles of matter in water can be seen being knocked around by millions of invisible molecules in motion.

At the temperature of melting ice, on the average, an oxygen molecule moves with a speed of about one thousand four hundred feet per second; and a hydrogen molecule about four times as fast. Even in a cubic inch of air a thousand million million collisions per second take place among the molecules!

Heat and temperature are not the same thing. The heat energy a body contains depends upon the energy of motion of its atoms and molecules. The quantity of heat may be measured in "calories." A calorie is the amount of heat energy required to raise the temperature of one gram of water one degree centigrade. But the temperature of a body indicates the level or "degree" to which the heat energy that it contains brings it. The coldest temperature possible is 273 degrees below zero centigrade. Scientists believe that at that temperature the molecules are at rest.

HOW DO FIREWORKS GET THEIR COLORS?

Fireworks have been making people say "Ahh!" and "Ohh!" for thousands of years. The magnificent displays of the Chinese delighted their people hundreds of years before fireworks appeared in western Europe.

The Greeks had some sort of fireworks known as "Greek fire," and Roman emperors put on elaborate exhibitions of fireworks to amuse the people. But fireworks didn't really develop as we know them until gunpowder came into general use and the science of chemistry had made certain advances.

In the nineteenth century the art of making fireworks was really perfected, and amazingly elaborate displays were created. For instance, certain fireworks were shot into the sky in which beautiful colored designs served as a backdrop. Other pieces were attached to frameworks against this background. When these fireworks were lit, unbelievable patterns were produced, such as waving flags, rushing trains and steamboats, and even mock battles between famous people!

The basic materials used in making fireworks are saltpeter, sulfur and charcoal. These ingredients are ground together into a fine powder and then nitrates of lead, barium, and aluminum are sometimes added in various combinations to obtain spectacular effects.

The colors in fireworks are produced by the addition of various salts of metals. Strontium produces red, barium creates green, sodium is for yellow, and copper for blue. The showers of dazzling sparks are made by using iron filings. So you see it takes quite a knowledge of chemistry to produce our modern fireworks.

Of course, there is a serious side to fireworks, too. In warfare, rockets are used for signaling, and flares can light up whole battlefields or convey messages. At sea, various colored flares and rockets have often been the means for saving hundreds of lives. And pilots in airplanes have often been able to make emergency landings, thanks to flares dropped from the plane.

CAN A THERMOMETER BE MADE WITHOUT MERCURY?

We are so accustomed to thinking of a thermometer as having mercury in a thin tube that we tend to forget exactly how a thermometer works.

A thermometer is simply an instrument that measures heat. The way we measure heat is by observing what heat does to certain materials. Heat causes many materials to change. We look at what kind of change has taken place in the material, and we can say that this kind of change was caused by a certain amount of heat.

The reason mercury is used so commonly in thermometers is simply because mercury reacts quickly to a rise in temperature. It expands evenly, and it is easily seen. So in the modern mercury-in-glass thermometer, heat causes the mercury to expand; it moves up the narrow tube, and a scale on the thermometer tells us how high it has moved.

Alcohol, for example, can also be used in thermometers. But alcohol presents certain problems. It boils easily. So alcohol is not very useful for high temperatures. But alcohol makes an excellent thermometer for measuring extremely low temperatures.

There are other kinds of thermometers that use no liquid at all. Instead, two metals are used. A strip of iron and a strip of brass are fastened together in the form of a coil. One end of this coil is fastened, while the other end is connected to a pointer and is free to move.

The metals expand and contract at different rates. When heated, the free end of the coil winds or unwinds, as the case may be, and this movement positions a pointer on a dial with degrees on it.

By placing a pen on the pointer and by providing a rotating chart, we have a recording thermometer that keeps a record of the temperature for as long as we want it to!

WHAT IS THE LAW OF FALLING BODIES?

A falling body is an unsupported object that is being pulled toward the earth's surface by the force of gravity. Gravity is the earth's force of attraction for other objects.

When there is no air resistance, all bodies fall according to a definite law. It is known as the law of falling bodies, and was first discovered by the famous Italian scientist Galileo in the 1500's.

Galileo experimented with falling bodies in his laboratory. Out of these experiments came this new law: In the absence of air, the speed of a falling body depends only on the length of the fall. The speed of the body does not depend on the body's weight.

The longer a body falls, the faster and faster it moves. When anything picks up speed, we say it accelerates. A freely-falling body has an acceleration of thirty-two feet a second during each second that it falls. This means that for each second a body falls, it gains thirty-two feet a second in downward speed.

A falling body has a speed of thirty-two feet a second after falling for just one second. It has a speed of thirty-two plus thirty-two, or sixty-four feet a second after falling for two seconds, and so on.

However, a body falling through the air does not continue to gain speed at this rate. It reaches a certain top speed. Because of air resistance, there is a limit to how fast an object falls.

This is true of even the heaviest objects. They accelerate as they begin to fall, but air resistance builds up. Soon the air resistance becomes equal to the pull of gravity on the object. Then the object can fall no faster. It has reached its final or "terminal speed," and keeps this speed as it continues to fall.

WHAT MAKES A BALLOON RISE?

A balloon is really the simplest form of aircraft. It usually consists of a light spherical or cylindrical bag made of paper, rubber, silk, or rubberized fabric, containing hot air, hydrogen, or helium. To the bag may be attached (by cords or netting) a basket, or car, or gondola to carry passengers and cargo.

A balloon floats in the air for exactly the same reason that a fish floats in water. Each displaces, by its bulk, more than its own weight of the air or water that surrounds it.

As long as a balloon and all the equipment attached to it weigh less than the volume of air displaced, it will rise. If it loses some of its lifting gas, so that its volume decreases, it will sink. Hot air, hydrogen, or helium are used as lifting gases because all three are lighter than ordinary atmospheric air.

Once released, a balloon will ascend to a level where the weight of the displaced air is exactly equal to its own weight. To change flight altitude, a balloon pilot must either reduce his buoyancy to go down, or reduce his weight to go up. To go down, he must allow some of his lifting gas to escape through a valve in the top of the balloon. To go up, he must throw weights (ballasts) overboard.

Since neither gas nor ballasts can be replaced in flight, it is easy to see that the amount of control available to a balloon pilot is quite limited. At best, he can go up or down for a short time only, depending on the size of the balloon.

Once aloft, he is entirely at the mercy of the winds. A balloon cannot be steered in flight. It can only drift with the wind, and for this reason has very little use as a means of getting from place to place.

Balloons are now generally used for upper-air exploration. In warfare they are commonly used as elevated observation posts. They may form balloon barrages (like aerial fences) to protect cities from bombers.

WHAT MAKES AN AIRPLANE STALL IN THE AIR?

To understand this, we must first understand what enables an airplane to stay up in the air. Because an airplane weighs more than the same volume of air, it needs some force to hold it up. This force is called lift.

An airplane develops lift by moving forward against the air swiftly. How does this motion create lift? It has to do with the flow of air past the wings. The air flows over and under the wings as the plane moves forward. The air under the wings pushes up against the wings. The air over the wings is forced into a slight upward curve over the wings, which creates an area of decreased pressure. So we have two effects working together: the air under the wings pushes up; the decreased pressure above the wings helps draw the wings up. The result is lift.

In order for the plane to move forward, it uses engine power. The propellers screw forward into the air just as a wood screw does in wood. This is possible because when air moves swiftly, or something moves swiftly into it, the air begins to act like a solid. This forward pull of the plane is called thrust. The thrust overcomes the "drag" exerted by the plane, the lift overcomes gravity, and the plane is able to stay in the air.

As long as the upward lift and the pull of gravity downward are exactly equal, the plane flies level and straight. If the speed is increased, the plane will climb because there is more lift, so the pilot must turn the plane's nose down.

When the speed is reduced, the pilot must bring the nose up. If the speed is reduced and the nose is not brought up, the air becomes "burly," and the lift is lost. The nose drops, the plane stalls, and may go into a spin.

When a stall takes place high above the ground, there is enough altitude to enable the plane to recover and regain speed, but a stall near the ground may result in a crash.

WHAT IS A SEXTANT?

When you travel by land, you can usually find your way because you know where a road leads. And if you travel by ship and can see the shore, you can also find your location easily. You can recognize hills, mountains, forests, beaches, and so on.

In the earliest times, therefore, sailors kept their ships within two or three miles of the coast, so that they were never out of sight of land. The men who did venture out into the ocean were taking a great risk because there was no sure way of knowing their location.

Later, a way was found to pinpoint the location of ships at sea. This was done by finding the latitude and longitude of the place. Latitude is distance north or south of the Equator. Longitude tells how far east or west a place is, and it is measured by degrees east or west of an imaginary line that goes through Greenwich, England.

To find latitude and longitude at sea, the navigator observes the position of the stars and the sun. In the daytime, the navigator can find the latitude of his ship by measuring how high the sun is at noon. At night, he does this by measuring how high in the sky the stars seem to be. Longitude is measured by comparing the time on board the ship with the time at Greenwich, England. If his time is earlier, he is west of Greenwich; if later, he is east of Greenwich. Each hour's difference equals fifteen degrees east or west.

The sextant is an instrument used by navigators to measure the position of the sun, moon, planets, and certain stars. The sextant is shaped like the wedge of a pie, with a scale marked on its rounded edge.

One end of a swinging arm is attached to the point of the sextant. A movable mirror is fixed at that end of the arm. The other end extends to the scale. A telescope is mounted on the sextant, and a glass mirror is mounted in front of the telescope. By looking at the horizon through the telescope and a clear glass, and then moving the mirror until the reflection seems to touch the horizon, the scale end shows the height of the body observed.

HOW DO WE KNOW THE HEIGHT OF A MOUNTAIN?

When we read of high mountains in newspapers or books, we are often told their exact height in terms of feet. How do we know exactly how high a mountain is, especially in the case of mountains that may never have been climbed by man?

It is done by means of one of the oldest techniques on earth—surveying. The science of surveying is a branch of civil engineering. It is concerned with determining the shape and size of any part of the earth's surface.

There are various kinds of surveying, but they are all based on a method known as "triangulation." When you study geometry, you will learn that if you know one side and two angles of any triangle (or two sides and one angle), you can find out the rest of its measurements.

Whether the land you want to measure is one acre, or a thousand acres, the method of measuring it is the same. You begin by measuring one distance very accurately with a chain, steel rod, or wire.

This now becomes the side of the first triangle, and is usually a level piece of ground between two landmarks. Now you select a third landmark, and make this the apex of the triangle. You then measure the angles it makes with each end of the first line you measured. You now have the requirements for measuring the area of the triangle as described above (one side and two angles of a triangle).

The instrument for measuring those angles is called a transit. Now that you have the area of one triangle, you keep on dividing the land to be measured into triangles until you have the area of the entire piece of land.

The transit doesn't just work horizontally; it also works vertically. This is called leveling, because there is a spirit level at the base of the instrument that indicates when it is level. By raising the sight to any landmark on a mountain, the same process of measuring angles can be done, and the length of one side (the height) can be measured!

HOW DOES AN AQUALUNG WORK?

The aqualung is a modern aid to diving. It makes it possible for a diver to go on breathing underwater without an air supply from a ship. He carries his own air supply with him, strapped to his back. He is a free diver.

For air supply the aqualung has two or more sturdy steel bottles filled with compressed air. A special valve gradually lets the air out of the bottles. A hose from the valve goes to a mouthpiece. This is made so that the diver can grip it with his teeth. Because the diver's nose is covered with his faceplate, he has to breathe through his mouth.

With the aqualung strapped to his back and a heavy belt to keep him down, a man can swim almost as freely as a fish. He uses big flippers on his feet, so he doesn't need his hands for swimming. He can hold a camera or perhaps a fishing spear. In shallow water he may be able to stay down for a half-hour or more.

But even the best free-diving outfit will not let a diver go down more than three hundred feet. At this depth the weight of the water above presses on everything ten times as heavily as on the surface. The air in the diver's bottles is used up ten times as fast. So even big bottles will let him stay there for only one minute or so.

There is another problem in deep diving. The compressed air in the aqualung bottles is about four-fifths nitrogen and about one-fifth oxygen, like ordinary air. We need the oxygen to stay alive. Ordinarily the nitrogen we breathe in is breathed right out again. But as the pressure of air increases, some of the nitrogen dissolves in the blood and tissues.

As the diver comes up, the nitrogen must leave his blood and tissues. If it cannot come out fast enough through his lungs, it turns into tiny bubbles inside his body. The bubbles squeeze nerves and block blood vessels, and the diver gets what is called the bends. The diver feels great pain. A bad case of the bends may kill him or cripple him for life.

This is why a diver must come up quite slowly when he is down to a depth of two hundred or three hundred feet. And he must stop often on the way up.

HOW IS WATER MADE DRINKABLE?

First of all, why does water have to be made drinkable? Why can't we drink it just as we find it? The reason is that we can almost never obtain pure water.

Probably the purest natural source of water is snow. The next purest is rain water, but rain contains dissolved gases of the air and traces of carbon dioxide, chlorides, sulfates, nitrates, and ammonia. Even the water from streams and lakes that are found in the mountains may contain dissolved inorganic salts. Water from rivers and lakes in low regions is usually quite polluted. Water from springs and wells has filtered through the ground, so it is quite pure, but it may also contain inorganic salts.

So it seems that all water we drink needs to be purified to some degree. There are many methods for doing this. One is simply by storage. When water is stored in a reservoir, certain things take place. Solid impurities settle at the bottom, a process known as sedimentation. Many bacteria lose their power when water is kept in a storage reservoir.

But this method does not give complete protection. So chemicals may be added to provide better sedimentation. In addition, the water may be aerated to remove tastes and odors and dissolved gases.

Many years ago it was discovered that if water could be filtered through sand, many of the impurities and most of the bacteria could be removed. So various methods for sand-filtering were set up, including a method that forced the water through mechanically at great speed.

A commonly used method for purifying water is chlorination. This is a very cheap, quick, and effective method. From two to eight pounds of chlorine are added to a million gallons of water. This is enough to destroy most of the dangerous bacteria that may be in the water.

HOW IS FASHION DECIDED?

The French word *couturier* means "dressmaker." In the world of fashion, the word has come to describe a designer of high fashion or *haute couture*. It is these designers who begin trends and create new silhouettes. The work of famous couturiers of different countries is copied all over the world.

Paris has always been the traditional center of world fashion. But recently Italian designers have had great influence in setting new styles, and so have certain designers in London.

French designers guard the secrets of their new designs until their collections are shown to the public. Then pictures of the styles are published in newspapers and magazines all over the world.

People from many countries travel to Paris to buy the clothes and to copy the newest ideas. In January they come to see the spring clothes; in July, to see the fall designs.

Many dress manufacturers from other countries buy the original clothes of the famous French designers. They take them back to their own design rooms, where the clothes are copied line-for-line to be made in great numbers. That's why you may be able to buy in your town the clothing that is in the latest style without paying a very high price for it.

Some manufacturers use the Paris styles only as a starting point for their own ideas. Others may adapt only a part of the French design into their own styles.

The United States has become one of the most important fashion centers in the world. In New York City, there are American designers who create new fashions and show their collections. Buyers from stores all over the world come to New York to buy the clothes.

After the buyers choose the designs, the dress manufacturers add up the store orders, buy fabrics, and have the dresses sewn by machines. They are then shipped to cities all over the United States and the world.

WHAT IS LIPSTICK?

Like so many other cosmetics in use today, lipstick is a product of the chemist's laboratory. Every ingredient that goes into it has a definite purpose, and the combination makes quite a complicated formula.

The chief ingredients in a lipstick are castor oil and a mixture of various waxes. In addition there are cacao butter, lanolin, mineral oil, petrolatum, and different chemicals. Coloring matter to obtain the exact shade is, of course, a very important ingredient.

The oils and waxes are melted together and the colors mixed in by grinding. The whole mass is then remelted and poured into molds, where it is allowed to harden. Lipsticks are made so that they will soften under pressure, which makes it possible to apply them to the lips evenly.

The use of cosmetics by women goes back to very early times. They probably originated in the East, but in ancient times they reached their greatest development in Egypt. Almost six thousand years ago various kinds of cosmetics were already being used in Egypt.

Cleopatra carried the use of cosmetics to new heights. At that time, it was the eyes that received the most attention. Women of the court painted the under side of the eye green, and the lid, lashes, and eyebrows black! Henna was also used to dye the fingernails, palms, and soles of the feet.

In the Bible there are many references to the use of cosmetics by women—for example, "When Jehu was come to Jezreel, Jezebel heard of it; and she painted her face. . . ."

In Rome, at the time of Nero, cosmetics and perfumes were widely used. Here are some of the cosmetics they had then: white lead and chalk to whiten the skin; paint for the eyelids and lashes; a rouge for the cheeks and lips, which may be the ancestor of our lipstick;

barley flour and butter as a cure for blemishes; and pumice stone for whitening the teeth. They also had a kind of soap for bleaching the hair.

In England, about four hundred years ago, women used to take all kinds of baths to make their skin beautiful. It is said that Mary, Queen of Scots, actually bathed in wine, and other women of the time took milk baths!

WHAT IS LACE?

Lace is an airy and delicate fabric made of fine threads stitched into patterns. Lace is used to add beauty to many of the things we wear and use. It may be made by hand or by machine.

The first true hand-made lace was probably made in Italy in the middle of the 1500's. Very soon afterward, laces were being made in France. Today hand-made lace is made chiefly in Italy and Belgium. Machine-made lace is produced in England, France, and the United States.

Hand-made lace is usually made by one of two methods: needlepoint or bobbin. Needlepoint lace is made by drawing the design on a thick piece of paper backed by linen. The outline of the pattern is stitched onto the paper. The stitching is used as a framework on which the lacemaker works with a needle and single thread, building up the pattern with looped stitches. When the work is completed, the framework stitches are clipped and the lace is lifted off the pattern.

Bobbin lace is made with a large number of threads, each fastened to a bobbin (spool). The pattern is drawn on paper, and the paper is fastened onto a cushion. Then pins are stuck into the cushion to keep the threads in position while the lace is being made. The lace is made with a pair of bobbins in each hand. These are moved from side to side to twist or interlace the threads. As the work progresses, the pins are moved farther along.

Chantilly lace is a bobbin lace that has vine or spray patterns on a mesh ground; it is often used on evening dresses and bridal veils. Cluny lace is a fairly coarse bobbin lace; it is often used to trim children's dresses and household linens.

WHAT IS EMBROIDERY?

Embroidery is the art of sewing decorative stitches on cloth. It is a very old art. Evidences of embroidered clothing have been found by archaeologists digging among ancient Assyrian and Persian ruins. The Old Testament describes the beauty of the embroidery done by the Jews in Biblical times.

In the Middle Ages embroidery reached a high point. Great Italian and Dutch painters designed needlework tapestries illustrating religious subjects. Noblewomen spent many hours in their castles embroidering gowns to be worn on state occasions, or altar cloths and hangings for the church.

One of the most famous medieval embroideries is the Bayeux tapestry, which illustrates the Battle of Hastings. Its warriors and horses, griffins, phoenixes, and monsters are worked in eight shades of wool on a linen strip measuring 230 feet long and nearly 20 inches wide.

During the eighteenth century embroideries became so valuable that they were worth more than their weight in gold! In the 1700's and 1800's, little girls in America had to spend a certain amount of time each day learning to embroider. They practiced different stitches on a piece of linen that was called a sampler. Houses, animals, numbers, the letters of the alphabet, and sometimes verses were embroidered on the sampler. When the stitching was finished, the little girl added her name, her age, and the date.

Each country has its own style of embroidery. The Chinese and Japanese use silk and gold threads on fine damask to embroider dragons, birds, flowers, and landscapes. Warm countries, such as Spain and Italy, produce embroideries that are gay in color and pattern.

France and Switzerland are noted for the most delicate kind of needlework, often embroidered in plain white. In the Balkan countries embroidery of fine stitches in vivid colors decorates clothing and linens that are passed on from generation to generation.

WHAT IS KAPOK?

Today, chemists are able to create all kinds of wonderful products in their laboratories. So many of them appear on the market under various names that we sometimes forget that Nature herself is able to turn out some pretty interesting products, too! Kapok is one of these.

Kapok is the product of a tree of the bombax family that is cultivated in Java, the Philippines, Malay, and Ceylon. The tree is native to the West Indies and other parts of tropical America.

Since this tree can be grown under widely different conditions, many varieties of it have been developed. In fact, there are now at least fifty-four different trees that produce what we call kapok, and some of these trees yield crops for fifty years or longer.

What is kapok? It looks like fine, yellowish, shiny cotton. It grows in fat pods on these tall trees. The growing kapok fibers are not attached to the seeds, so ginning (as with cotton) is not necessary.

The cleaned kapok fiber, which is called floss, is springy, slick, and odorless. It sheds water like a duck's back, and resists the passage of sound and heat. It is half as heavy as wool and just as warm. High-quality floss supports as much as thirty-eight times its own weight in water.

Each kapok fiber is a smooth closed tube coated with wax. Not having the twist that grows in cotton fibers or the hooks found in sheep's wool, kapok won't mat or felt, and cannot be spun into threads.

Kapok-stuffed life preservers support six times as much weight as those filled with cork. They last three to five times as long without getting waterlogged. In wartime, kapok is used to line tanks, trench coats, and sleeping bags. In peacetime, it is used to insulate refrigerators and airplanes, and in softballs, boxing gloves, mattresses, and upholstery. The seeds of the kapok tree yield an oil that is used in food and in making soap.

WHAT IS ORIGAMI?

You have probably enjoyed many, many times just sitting around and folding pieces of paper to make them look like a bird, a ship, or some animal. What you probably didn't realize is that you were practicing a very ancient "art," the art of paper folding, or origami.

The Chinese invented paper almost two thousand years ago, and origami is just as old as paper itself. It is possible that the art developed from an ancient custom: the Chinese funeral rite of making paper houses, furniture, vehicles, and servants, as well as paper money. In fact, at Buddhist funerals colored-paper symbols of all kinds of things are burned. The idea is that the dead person will enjoy all the comforts that are symbolized by the paper objects in the next world.

In the seventh century paper folding was brought to Japan. The Japanese developed many of China's arts and crafts into their own forms of expression. They found new methods of folding paper into pretty forms and images, and made origami a highly creative art.

From a few simple folds the Japanese make things of great beauty and realism. Some decorate the shrines and temples as religious symbols. Others, such as the crane, tortoise, and lobster, are good-luck symbols. These are fastened to gifts as ornaments or used as festive decorations.

Japanese magicians, traveling in Europe, introduced paper folding to the western world. The magicians were so expert that with a few quick movements they could make a bird, animal, or insect to surprise and delight the audience.

Did you know that many great men of the past not only enjoyed origami, but also became very good at it? Among these people were Leonardo da Vinci, the poet Shelley, and the writer Lewis Carroll, the author of *Alice in Wonderland*.

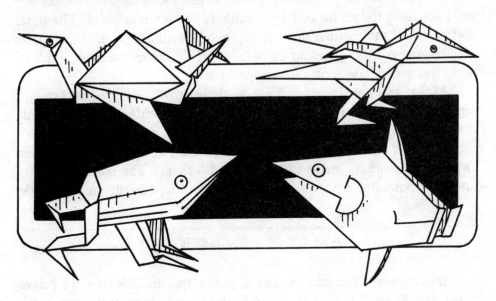

WHAT ARE DIES AND MOLDS?

Many of the things we see and use every day are made with dies or molds.

Dies are special tools that shape and cut metal and plastic by pressure. If you have ever watched as star-shaped cookies were punched out of a sheet of dough by a cookie cutter, you have seen a very simple type of die in action.

Molds are special tools used to shape materials in liquid form. Metal, plastic, or whatever other material is used is poured or forced into the cavity of the mold and is allowed to solidify. A mold of gelatin is an example of a very simple type of mold.

Dies are used in industry to make parts with shapes that are hard to produce with other machine tools. Examples are automobile parts, such as hoods and fenders.

Molds are also used in industry to make parts, such as refrigerator-door handles, radio casings, and some automobile radiator grilles.

To make parts like these by regular machine operations of cutting, grinding, and drilling would take a great deal of time and much material would be wasted. With dies they can be stamped out like cookies. The same holds true for molds.

In addition to producing difficult shapes, dies and molds are good for fast production of large numbers of identical parts. The parts that dies and molds turn out usually need no finishing. Difficult parts may require a little grinding or polishing to remove seams on molded parts and rough edges on die-stamped parts.

Molds and dies in general are made in two halves. When brought together they will make the shape of the part. Molds form the outside shape only. Dies can form both the inside and outside shapes.

Did you know that dies were used as long ago as 650 B.C., when Greek metalworkers made silver coins with them? The coins were produced by pounding metal into a pattern cut into a harder metal block.

WHAT IS CERAMICS?

In a museum you can see vases, jars, cups, and dishes—all pieces of pottery. Pottery is clay that has been shaped when soft, then hardened by heat. The art of making such products is called ceramics.

The word "ceramics" is sometimes used for enamel and glass, as well as pottery. In all three cases the work involves applying heat to earthy materials—clay, sand, or ground rock.

Ceramics is one of the oldest of man's arts. Clay is found almost everywhere. Pieces of ceramic work have been found that date from before the beginning of recorded history. A well-hardened piece of pottery is very durable. It may break, but it will not rot or rust away.

The outstanding early potters were the Chinese. They made a very hard and translucent type of pottery known as porcelain. In the West, porcelain became known as china, after the country that first produced it.

There are six main groups of clay that are used in ceramics. The first is called common clay, and is not used for making fine pottery. The pottery made from common clay is called earthenware.

The purest type of clay is called kaolin, or china clay. It is used to make Chinese porcelain. When fired, it turns a pure white.

Many years ago, before refrigeration was developed, ceramic jugs (called "crockery") were used to keep liquids cool. This is because crockery is a coarse type of ceramics that permits liquids to seep through its tiny pores. The liquid then evaporates on the outside. And the constant evaporation of the moisture keeps the jug and its contents cool.

Today, however, most crockery is glazed and has a shiny surface; this doesn't allow this kind of evaporation to take place.

WHAT IS CONCRETE?

Concrete is one of the most useful building materials ever developed by man. It is strong, long-lasting, fairly cheap to use, and easy to handle. It is not harmed by fire, water, weather, or heavy pressures. Huge dams, bridges, and skyscrapers, as well as highways, homes, and airport runways, are built of concrete.

Concrete is made from Portland cement, water, and sand, gravel, or crushed stone. The materials are measured and mixed together to make concrete. After mixing, the concrete can be given any shape that is wanted by placing it in molds that are called forms.

The mixing turns the water and cement into a paste that coats the pieces of sand and gravel. When this paste hardens, it holds the pieces together in a solid, rock-like mass. Keeping the concrete moist after putting it in the forms makes it even harder. Because of a chemical reaction between the cement and the water, the concrete keeps getting harder as it ages.

Concrete is treated in various ways to make it suitable for special purposes. For example, when concrete is used in long, slender parts, it may snap or be pulled apart. To make concrete structures hold up under forces that would bend them or pull them apart, steel rods or mesh can be set in the concrete. This is called reinforced concrete.

Concrete can also be strengthened by casting (pouring) it around high-tension steel wires. When these wires are tightened—before the concrete hardens—they place the concrete in a squeeze that makes it stronger. Such concrete is called prestressed concrete.

A kind of concrete is now made that contains billions of tiny air bubbles in each cubic inch. It is called air-entrained concrete. Highways built of this concrete are not harmed by freezing and thawing.

So you can see how much can be done with concrete to make it serve special needs in construction.

HOW MANY KINDS OF NAILS ARE THERE?

Nails are usually used for joining pieces of wood or for fastening other materials to wood. Nails are simply hammered into place and are held there by friction. Some nails have roughened shanks so that they will hold better.

Most nails are made by machine from heavy steel wire. These machines can make hundreds of nails per minute. First the machine cuts the wire to the correct length. Then it flattens one end of the wire to make the head. And finally, it cuts the point at the other end.

Some types of nails, called cut nails, are stamped, or cut, from sheets of metal. Cut nails are rectangular, rather than round.

There is a tremendous variety of nails, since they are used for so many different purposes. The ordinary all-purpose nails most of us use are called common nails. Finishing nails, used in furniture and cabinetwork, have very small heads that do not show on the finished work.

Roofing nails have very large heads. They are used for nailing shingles or tar paper to a roof. The large head holds the thin material and keeps it from tearing loose.

Some nails have two heads, one above the other. The nail is driven only as far as the first head. The top head of the nail remains above the surface of the work, to make it easy to pull the nail out. Two-headed nails are used to hold scaffolding and other temporary structures together.

Most nails are made of steel. Masonry nails, used on concrete or masonry, are made of specially hardened steel. Some nails, such as roofing nails, are galvanized. That means they are coated with zinc to prevent rusting.

Nails used on boats must be extra rustproof. They are usually made of brass or bronze. Large nails are called spikes, and are usually over six inches long.

WHAT IS A DREDGE?

The water in harbors, rivers, and lakes often contains a large amount of mud and silt, which settle on the bottom. If enough of this material builds up, the water becomes too shallow for ships to use. To keep the waterways open, the mud and silt must be scooped up and removed from time to time. The machines used for this are called dredges.

Some of these dredges are mounted on ship hulls and can sail about under their own power. Others are mounted on floating platforms that have to be towed about in the water.

Dredges use several different kinds of power. Suction dredges, which suck up mud and silt like a vacuum cleaner, are usually driven by steam turbines or diesel engines. Some dredges use electric power supplied from the shore. Dipper dredges operate by means of steam or diesel power.

A dipper dredge is a seagoing version of the common steam shovel. A dipper on the end of a dipper stick is attached to a long boom that can be raised and lowered. The steel cutting teeth of the dipper bite into the mud. When the boom is raised and swung over a barge, the hinged bottom of the dipper opens and dumps its load into the barge.

A kind of dredge known as a grab dredge has two types of buckets: the "clamshell" and the "orange peel." The clamshell bucket has two hinged parts that open to scoop up the mud. The orange-peel bucket has three hinged parts.

The ladder-type bucket dredge scoops up mud and silt with an endless chain of buckets. The buckets are mounted on a long steel frame, which is lowered to the bottom. As each bucket reaches the bottom, it fills with mud and silt. It travels back to the surface, and at the top of the frame it up-ends, spilling its load onto a barge.

Ladder bucket dredges are also used in mining operations in swampy areas in Alaska, California, South America, and many other places. They dig up the earth and feed it into huge washing cylinders that separate out the ore.

HOW DOES AN OIL DERRICK WORK?

When you think about drilling for oil, you may imagine a tall steel structure with black oil gushing out of it. But gushers are a thing of the past. Modern drilling methods have practically eliminated them.

Many kinds of oil derricks are used. Some are as tall as a twenty-story office building, others are attached to trucks, and still others are located on platforms and barges for offshore drilling.

Rotary drilling accounts for about 85 percent of the wells in the United States. Rotary drilling uses a rapidly-turning bit that bores into the earth. Different kinds of bits are used for different kinds of rock. Attached to the bit is a drilling pipe in thirty-foot sections called joints, each weighing about five hundred pounds.

A flat steel turntable grips and turns the pipe, which extends through it into the earth. As the pipe turns, the bit attached to it cuts into the earth. Section after section of pipe is added as the drill chews its way downward.

During the drilling, "drilling mud" is pumped down inside the pipe, which cools and lubricates the bit. As the hole deepens, a long steel pipe, called casing, is added from time to time.

Cutting through rock dulls the bit, so it must be replaced often. This means all the drill pipe must be pulled out of the hole. There is a lot of work involved in this, and it may take four to six hours to replace the bit and put the pipe down again.

When a well has reached a certain depth, the bit and drill are pulled up, and casing is run all the way down and filled with chemical mud. A small gun is lowered to make holes in the casing and start the oil flowing. Later, water is pumped in to get rid of the mud. Pressure begins to rise from the well, and finally oil begins to bubble out of valves into an open tank.

HOW DOES A GEIGER COUNTER WORK?

You've probably read about a modern type of "prospector" who goes out looking for precious metals with a Geiger counter. Or perhaps, when people are talking about the danger of atom bombs, there is mention of using Geiger counters as a safety measure.

In both cases, what is involved is the matter of radiation. Certain radioactive substances give off rays, and a Geiger counter is a simple way of detecting and measuring these rays. The Geiger counter was invented by Hans Geiger, and later perfected by a man called Müller.

It is really a kind of vacuum tube. In simple terms, the tube consists of a very thin glass envelope, much like an ordinary radio tube. Inside are two metal plates and a small amount of gas, such as argon.

You're familiar with another kind of tube that contains a gas—the neon tube. In the neon tube or lamp, the gas can be made to glow by connecting the plates to a source of electrical voltage, providing this voltage is high enough. The high voltage breaks the gas down and allows a large flow of electrons to take place between the plates. And when this flow takes place, the gas inside the tube begins to glow.

In a Geiger counter, the voltage is deliberately kept too low so that the glow of the gas won't take place under normal conditions. Now, let's assume there is some radioactive substance nearby. A ray from this radioactive substance enters the tube and collides with the gas molecules. This gives them enough energy (just as higher voltage would) to cause the gas to glow.

So now there is a current surging through the tube. This current can be put through an indicating meter so that you can read the amount of radiation that has entered the tube. Or, it can be made to produce that familiar ticking sound that is associated with Geiger counters.

Since a Geiger counter is a means of detecting radiation, it obviously can't detect anything that doesn't emit rays. So its use is limited in searching for precious metals.

HOW DO ESCALATORS WORK?

An escalator is basically a set of moving stairs.

Each step is loosely connected to the next step by two very heavy roller chains. This is so that the steps can rise and sink easily. Each step has axles with wheels or rollers on them. The wheels rest on metal tracks inside a steel frame called a truss. The truss rests between two floors like a steeply slanted ladder. In fact, the word "escalator" was made up from a Latin word meaning ladder.

The steps lie flat at each end of the escalator. This is to make it easier for passengers to get on and off. As the steps travel up or down the escalator, they automatically rise so that they look like steps in a staircase. As the steps approach the end of the ride, they automatically flatten out again.

Under the floor at the top end of the escalator is a set of sprockets. A sprocket is a wheel with projecting teeth, like the gear wheel of a bicycle.

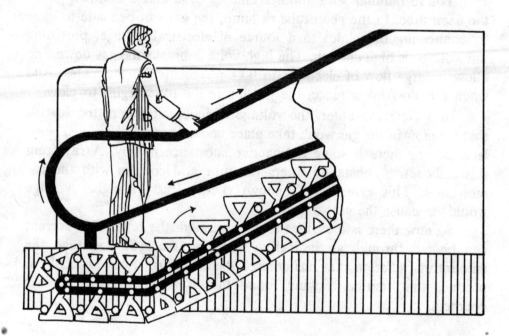

The teeth of the sprocket catch the links of the roller chain and drive it around and around, pulling the steps along their rails. The sprocket at the top end of the escalator is driven by an electric motor beneath the floor. The chains run over pulleys at the bottom. These pulleys steer the chains properly and keep them tight.

At each side of the moving steps is a protective wall called a balustrade to keep passengers from falling off the sides of the steps. On top of the balustrade is a moving endless belt of rubber or metal, which is the handrail passengers hold onto to keep their balance.

The first escalator was patented in the United States in 1859, but it wasn't used commercially. The first practical escalator was built in 1891.

HOW ARE BELLS RUNG?

For hundreds of years bells in church towers have been rung for a variety of purposes. Bells reminded Christians of the relation of the church to their daily lives. They would be rung at daybreak to wake people up and call them to morning prayers. Through the day the bells counted the hours, the half-hours, and the quarters. They pealed for weddings and tolled for funerals, and were heard at Easter and Christmas.

A bell may be rung in two ways: the bell may be swung to hit the clapper; or the bell may be struck by the clapper or by some outside object. In the Far East some big stationary bells are rung by striking them with a log in the manner of a battering ram. One such bell in Burma weighs about ninety tons.

The Russians once cast a giant bell that weighed twice as much, but it cracked. To ring such a bell requires several men pulling a rope attached to the clapper.

In England a different method of bell-ringing was developed, called change-ringing. In change-ringing, the bells swing in complete circles in a definite order. The bells sound variations, or changes, on a descending scale. There is no melody, only a rhythmic pattern, and it can go on for hours.

There are over five thousand towers in England, each containing a set of bells for change-ringing. A set can number from three to twelve bells, and each bell is swung by one ringer using a rope and wheel.

A bell known as a clock-bell originated in the monasteries of Europe. This was because the monastic day was divided into devotional periods called canonical hours. In some monasteries the bell had to be rung seven times in twenty-four hours.

Since the first clock-bells could not ring by themselves, a man was hired for the job of striking them at the proper times of day. But in time he was replaced by machinery. With machinery it was possible to ring many bells, and it became customary to ring a short tune as a warning that the hour bell was about to strike.

HOW DOES A SATELLITE TRANSMIT TV PROGRAMS?

An artificial satellite is a man-made spacecraft circling the earth. Such satellites are sent into space for many purposes.

Satellites can be any size—from a tiny package of instruments to a huge balloon. They can weigh a few pounds or many tons. They can be any shape—balls, hatboxes, tin cans, bell buoys, and cigar boxes.

Some satellites have orbits around the earth as near as 110 miles away. Some travel 22,300 miles from earth. A satellite's orbit is chosen by scientists in advance, according to the task the satellite must perform.

All satellites need electrical power to operate their equipment. The main source of this power is the sun. Satellites carry many solar cells on their outside surface. A solar cell is a device that uses sunlight to generate electricity; this electricity keeps the satellite's batteries charged.

Radio and television signals can be sent from one continent to another by means of communications satellites. Most communications satellites have receivers and transmitters. The receivers pick up radio and television broadcasts from a ground station.

Electronic devices then increase the strength of the broadcast signals. The transmitters send the broadcasts to a distant ground station, which may be on another continent.

An example of such a satellite is Telstar. Telstar I was launched by the United States in July, 1962. Direct television transmission between the United States and Europe was first made possible by Telstar I.

One type of communications satellite has a "stationary" orbit around the earth. It is at a distance of 22,300 miles above the earth and completes one orbit in 24 hours, the same time it takes the earth to rotate on its axis. Thus the satellite is always in the same place above the earth. The Early Bird satellite is this kind of satellite. Because its orbit is so high, it can transmit signals over very great distances.

WHAT ARE RADIO WAVES?

Did you know that the space around you is filled at all times with radio waves from nearby broadcasting stations? These waves cause minute vibrations in all the metal objects in the room. You cannot hear the vibrations until they become sound waves, and they become sound waves only when you turn on your radio.

A radio wave might be called a disturbance that moves out into space. When electrons move back and forth rapidly, we have a radio wave. Heat and light also travel through space in the form of waves. The difference is that radio waves have a much longer wavelength than either heat or light waves.

Radio waves travel through space in much the same way that waves travel when a pebble is dropped into water. The waves radiate in all directions from their source. Although all radio waves travel at a speed of about 186,000 miles a second, the number of radio waves that travel past a point in one second can vary greatly. This number is called the frequency.

One complete wavelength is called a cycle. So frequency is the number of complete cycles that take place in a second. If wavelength is short, the waves are close together; the crests are close together and follow each other quickly. If wavelength is long, crests are far apart and follow one another slowly. So long waves are of low frequency, because crests do not come as frequently as those of short waves.

High-frequency waves are measured in kilocycles, or thousands of cycles per second. On your radio, from left to right, are the numbers 540, 550, 560, and so on to 1600 kilocycles. Each number refers to a wave frequency. A radio program broadcasts its programs only on its own wave frequency.

The existence of radio waves was predicted long before they were actually discovered. The prediction was made in 1864 by James Maxwell. In 1888 a German physicist, Heinrich Hertz, demonstrated that the waves actually do exist, and travel through space.

WHAT IS A RADIO TELESCOPE?

When we look at stars and planets through a telescope, we see light waves that they send out. Light is a form of radiation. But stars send out other forms of radiation besides light.

Part of the radiation from stars is sent out as radio waves. Some of these waves can be detected by special radio receivers here on earth. The radio receivers collect and magnify the radio waves, just as ordinary telescopes collect and magnify the picture the light waves give. These radio receivers are called radio telescopes.

There are many kinds of radio telescopes, but all of them consist of two parts—an antenna and a radio receiver. The antenna is often a huge, spectacular-looking metal dish. It may be fitted on a movable stand or mounting, so that it can be pointed to any part of the sky.

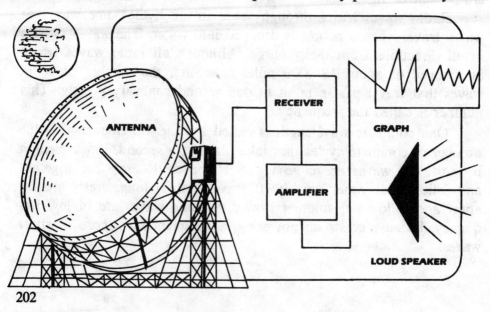

ANTENNA

RECEIVER

GRAPH

AMPLIFIER

LOUD SPEAKER

The large metal dish is what people usually think of when they think of a radio telescope. But the radio receiver is an equally important part. Without the receiver the huge antenna would be of no use.

Special kinds of radio receivers are needed to magnify, or amplify, the incoming waves. This is because the waves are often very weak. After the radio signals are amplified, they may be sent to a loudspeaker that lets the astronomer hear their hissing noise. Usually, however, a record of the radio waves is made on paper. The signals are written down in the form of a wavy line on a strip of paper.

Radio telescopes can operate in all kinds of weather, because radio waves are not affected by mist or fog or other kinds of bad weather. They can also be built in any place that is convenient, and don't have to be built on high ground or on mountains as optical telescopes must be.

Radio telescopes help astronomers learn facts about the universe that could not be learned in any other way we now have.

WHAT IS RADIO ASTRONOMY?

In 1931, a communications engineer working for Bell Laboratories was exploring radio frequency disturbances in the atmosphere that might interfere with a transoceanic telephone. He noticed that he was picking up a noise that didn't come from thunderstorms—but from somewhere in outer space! He discovered that he was able to pick up radiation from far away in our galaxy; and a new branch of astronomy was born—radio astronomy.

Radio astronomy works in two ways. By using special types of antennae, it picks up radiations sent out by objects in space. Some of these are "thermal" radiations, the radiations that any heated body emits in radio frequency waves. But there is also noise, or "cosmic static," which is picked up from outer space and is not thermal in origin.

Another way radio astronomy works is in sending signals out to such objects as meteors and the moon, and obtaining the reflection. This is the way radar works.

So far radio astronomy has been most useful in the study of meteors, the moon, the sun, and other planets. By bouncing back beams from meteors, we learn much about their orbits. By studying the moon with radio astronomy, we learn something about its surface. For example, even before men landed on the moon, radio astronomy led scientists to believe that its surface layers consisted of powdered rocks.

Perhaps the most exciting use of radio astronomy is about to begin—the search for messages from other worlds! A radio telescope has been developed that can detect a signal almost 50 trillion miles away. What kind of signal do scientists hope to pick up? They believe that if there is some civilization somewhere in outer space, and it wants to make its presence known, it would probably send out some very simple signal such as a series of numbers. It is also thought that the signals would be of the radio frequency of 1,420 megacycles, the frequency at which natural hydrogen emits radio energy in outer space.

INDEX

205

TELL ME WHY #5

BY ARKADY LEOKUM

ILLUSTRATIONS BY KATHIE KELLEHER

CONTENTS

Chapter 3

The Human Body

Chapter 4

How Things Are Made

Chapter 5

How Other Creatures Live

Chapter 6

Love, Families, and Babies

CHAPTER 1
HOW THINGS BEGAN

WHEN DID HORSE RACING BEGIN?

Using horses for racing seems to be one of the oldest sports enjoyed by man. Races between horses were run in very ancient times. They were held in Egypt, Babylonia, and Syria. Homer described a Greek chariot race that took place about eight centuries before the birth of Christ.

But modern horse racing as we know it originated in England, and it had to do with the development in England of the thoroughbred horse. There were horse races in England as early as the 12th century, but it was in the late 17th and early 18th centuries that the breeding of horses for sport really began.

Eastern horses were brought to England from Arabia, Turkey, and Persia. Stallions from these countries were bred to English mares. Three of these stallions were very important. They were called the Darley Arabian, the Godolphin Arabian, and the Byerly Turk. The lineage of every modern registered thoroughbred traces back to all three in the male line!

During the 18th century horse racing became an important English sport. The Jockey Club was established in 1751. And in 1793 the first issue of the "General Stud Book," which lists the lineage of thoroughbreds, was issued.

Horse racing has long been known as the "sport of kings." This is because English royalty has owned and raced champion horses, and because royalty and wealthy people in other countries have been involved with the sport.

In the United States, horse races were held in the early 17th century, even before the development of the thoroughbred.

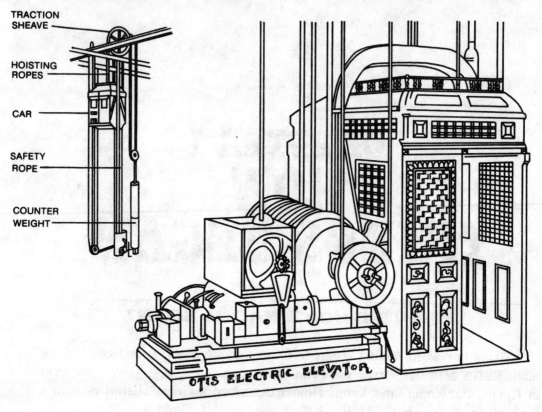

TRACTION
SHEAVE

HOISTING
ROPES

CAR

SAFETY
ROPE

COUNTER
WEIGHT

OTIS ELECTRIC ELEVATOR

TRACTION ELEVATOR

WHO INVENTED THE ELEVATOR?

The idea of the elevator was invented by no one man; it was developed over a long period of time. This is because the mechanical principles of elevators had been in use for centuries.

The ancient Greeks knew how to lift objects, using pulleys and winches. A pulley is a grooved wheel that a rope can slide over. A winch is a machine that has a broad wheel, or drum, with a rope fastened to it. By turning the drum with a crank, the rope can be wound up on the drum or let out. By running the rope over a pulley, it can be made to raise or lower a load.

In the 17th century, a "flying chair" was invented. It was designed to carry people to the top floors of buildings and was operated by a system of weights and pulleys. The chair and its machinery were outside the building. The "flying chair" never became popular.

During the first half of the 19th century, elevators were already in existence, but they were mostly used for freight. Steam power was used to turn the hoisting drums of these elevators.

What people were afraid of was that the rope holding the elevator might snap and the elevator would go crashing down. Then Elisha Otis invented a safety device that prevented this from happening, and elevators became popular. Also, at this time hydraulic power (fluid under pressure) began to be used to raise and lower elevators.

The electric elevator, which is what is used today, was developed by the German engineer, Werner von Siemens.

WHEN DID THE FIRST FIRE DEPARTMENT BEGIN?

Long ago there were no regular firemen. If a house caught fire, everybody became a fire fighter. People formed bucket brigades to fight fires. They stood in line to make a human chain from the burning house to the river or well. They passed buckets of water along from hand to hand for those up front to pour on the flames.

In 1666 London had a fire that burned down 13,000 buildings, including St. Paul's Cathedral. The English then began to develop hand-operated pumps so fire fighters could spray water through a hose. Citizens began to join together in volunteer fire companies. These volunteers promised to drop everything and rush to fight fire whenever it broke out.

The first paid fire department was established in Boston in 1679. There had been a series of big fires there in 1653 and 1676. Boston ordered a hand-operated fire engine from England and appointed 13 men to man it.

The first volunteer fire department in the United States was founded in 1736 in Philadelphia by Benjamin Franklin. It replaced the bucket brigades that had existed up to then.

In 1835, New York City established its first paid fire patrol. There were four members who were paid $250 a year. The following year there were 40 members, who were known as Fire Police. The first firehouse was organized in 1855 in New York City.

Today, in the United States, there are about one thousand fire departments manned by fully paid professional firemen, and more than fifteen thousand other departments that are part-paid and volunteer. There are more than eighty thousand professional firemen in the United States and over eight hundred thousand volunteer firemen.

WHERE WAS THE FIRST THEATER?

Theater as we know it first developed in Greece as part of religious observance. The stage was simply a circle of turf on which the worshipers danced around the altar of Dionysus. The spot was usually at the foot of a hill so that the spectators on the slopes could watch the dancing.

This started the tradition of Greek theaters—semicircles of seats built into a hillside. In fact, the word "theater" is of Greek origin and means "a place for seeing."

A theater built in Athens about 500 B.C. had a circular place, called the orchestra, where the performance was given. Erected behind the circle of the orchestra was a dignified-looking stage building. It was used as a dressing place for the performers. This "skene" (from which comes the word "scene") served as a background for the action of the play. Very little scenery was used by the Greeks, and no artificial lighting was needed, because the plays were presented in the daytime.

The first permanent stone theater was built in Rome in 52 B.C. The theaters of the Romans were similar to those of the Greeks, except that they were built on level ground. The Romans were the first to fill the orchestra with seats and present the play on a raised stage behind which was the "skene."

After the Roman world turned Christian, no theaters were built for about a thousand years. The first modern theater was the Teatro Farnese at Parma, Italy. It was built in 1618 or 1619. Its stage, instead of projecting far out into the orchestra, was built into one of the walls. A curtain was used to separate the stage from the auditorium, so that changes of scenery could be made out of sight of the audience.

WHO WERE THE FIRST BARBERS?

There have been barbers since very ancient times—so long ago, in fact, that we can't possibly know who the first barbers were. The first records of barbers in history go back to ancient Egypt. Later on, in ancient Greece and Rome, barbershops were favorite meeting places where men discussed affairs of the day.

Everybody knows what the barber's pole looks like. Those red-and-white stripes have something to do with work that barbers did in olden days. In ancient times, doctors didn't want to have anything to do with surgery. So it was the barbers who performed surgery on patients. They did bloodletting (letting a patient bleed so that the "bad blood" or "sick blood" would leave the body). They treated wounds, and some of them even extracted teeth.

The barber's pole of red-and-white stripes goes back to those days. The red stands for blood, and the white for bandages.

In England the barbers were chartered as a guild as far back as 1462. In 1540, their guild was merged with the guild of surgeons. But about this time, the king of England forbade the barbers who cut hair and gave shaves to practice surgery.

In the next two hundred years, the work of the barber was separated more and more from that of the surgeon, and in time all they were allowed to do was give haircuts.

By the way, the word "barber" comes from the Latin word "barba," which meant "beard." So their work of trimming beards may have been more important than cutting hair.

WHY ARE LONDON POLICEMEN CALLED "BOBBIES"?

The idea of a police system to protect a city originated in London. In 1737 a law was passed creating a police system with 68 men. But as the city grew and poverty increased, looting and rioting were soon out of control in London.

In 1829 Sir Robert Peel formed the London Metropolitan Police, with headquarters in Scotland Yard. The new recruits wore top hats and tailcoats. But this new force that Peel had created was much larger, better trained, and more highly disciplined than any other police force had ever been.

The rioting in London was soon controlled, but before long it spread to other areas. As a result, in 1835 all towns and cities in England were empowered to form their own police departments. From Sir Robert Peel's name came the familiar nickname "bobby" for the English policeman.

In the 1830's a group of people from New York City made a study of the British police system. As a result, in 1844 New York became the first city in the United States to establish a day-and-night police force similar to Peel's.

Before long other cities followed New York's example.

Why are American policemen known as "cops" or "coppers"? Some people believe that the name comes from the eight-pointed copper star once worn by New York policemen. Others believe that the name was taken from the initial letters of the words "constable on patrol."

WHO FIRST MADE BREAD WITH YEAST?

The action of yeast in moist, warm dough is called leavening. The yeast cells convert the starch of the dough into sugar, which they then digest. As they do this they give off carbon dioxide as a waste product. The gas is trapped in the dough, forms larger and larger bubbles, and makes the dough rise.

Wild yeast spores are almost always present in the air and will land naturally on the dough. The first people to discover the value of yeast were the Egyptians. They tried baking with fermented dough and liked the lighter, tastier bread. Bread that rises with the aid of wild yeast, however, may turn out differently each time. This is because different kinds of yeast may fall on it.

The Egyptians discovered a way to control this. Each time they baked they set aside some of the leavened dough to mix with the next batch. In this way they could be sure of using the same kind of yeast.

Around 1000 B.C. Phoenician traders carried the art of making leavened bread to the Greeks, who became the master bakers of antiquity. The Greeks had over 70 different recipes for bread.

The Romans turned baking into a large-scale industry and passed many laws governing the quality of bread. The bakers were so proud of the superior taste of their bread that each baker marked his loaves with his name, just as bakeries put their brand name on the wrappers today.

WHEN DID THE SPORT OF SURFING BEGIN?

Surfing is the sport of riding ocean waves on a long, narrow surfboard. The sport is enjoyed at beaches all over the world and has become so popular that we tend to think of it as a new thing.

But surfing is actually quite old. It apparently originated in the Pacific islands hundreds of years ago. When Captain James Cook discovered Hawaii in 1788, surfing was already a very popular sport among the Hawaiians.

The Hawaiians held surfing contests and the winners who won prizes were acclaimed by the people. The islanders used boards 14 to 18 feet long which were about 150 pounds in weight.

About 1957 a big change took place in surfing that helped make it popular. Lightweight boards began to be used. These boards, which are about 10 feet long and weigh as little as 22 pounds, have made it possible for women and even children to take up surfing. The new boards are generally made of foam plastic, coated with fiberglass and resin. A surfboard is the only special equipment the sport requires.

When riding a wave, surfers stand on the board and maneuver right and left. The surfer must first take his board out past the surf line—the point where the waves begin to break. Kneeling or lying prone on his board, he waits for a set, or series of swells, to form. When the wave he wants to ride comes up behind him, he paddles quickly toward shore with his hands. As the wave moves beneath him, the board first rises with it, then slides down the unbroken front of the wave. Having "caught" the wave, the surfer stands, one foot forward, and steers away from the breaking part of the wave.

HOW DID THE WORDS IN THE ENGLISH LANGUAGE ORIGINATE?

The words of the English language originated in many different ways from many different sources, but Greek and Latin supplied most of the words used in English today. A single Latin word like "manus" ("hand"), for example, is the source of "manufacture," "manicure," "manipulate," "emancipate," and so on.

The Latin word "scribere" ("to write") gives us "scribble," "scripture," "subscription," and many others. The Greek word "autos," meaning "self," gives us "autobiography," "automobile," "autograph," "automatic," and so on.

Many words are formed simply by putting part of a word in front of the root (called a prefix) or adding to the end of a root (a suffix). For example: bi- ("two") makes "bicycle" and "bisect." And: -able ("fitness for") makes "lovable" and "peaceable."

The English language includes words borrowed from many other languages. The English language began early in the Christian era with the dialects of such tribes as the Angles, Jutes, and Saxons. Viking invaders from Scandinavia added to it. And at the time of the Norman Conquest (1066) William the Conqueror's invaders brought many thousands of French and Latin terms into the language.

Later, as English explorers and traders ranged over the world, they borrowed many words from the peoples with whom they traded. For example, from India came such words as "madras," "bungalow," "punch," and "faker." From the Dutch came "freight," "schooner," and "landscape." From Spain and Latin America came "potato," "cargo," "tobacco," and "hurricane." And our language has continued to grow with words from dialects, different peoples, and from new developments in science, sports, and all kinds of activities.

HOW DID WE LEARN TO WRITE?

Nobody knows exactly where and when writing originated. But we do have an idea of how it developed from earliest times.

Man began by making pictures to serve as records of his hunting, wars, and tribal life. Pictures could also be used for messages. A picture of the sun meant a day. Two marks next to the sun meant two days. Such signs are called pictographs.

When civilization developed, this method of writing was speeded up by simplifying the pictures. The Egyptians used a wavy line to mean a body of water. The Chinese used an ear between two doors to mean ''listen.'' Such signs are called ideographs or ideograms.

The ancient Egyptians used a system of signs that we call hieroglyphics. At first it was entirely ideographic. But over the centuries the Egyptians developed a phonetic system as well. This is writing where the signs represent sounds rather than objects or ideas.

As civilization further developed, men needed more and more signs. So they developed a method of spelling words according to sound. For example, in English we would write the ''belief'' by drawing a bee and a leaf. Such signs are called phonograms, and the writing is syllabic because it uses syllables.

The next stage in the development of writing was the idea of using an alphabet of single letters. Both the ancient Egyptians and the Babylonians knew how to write in the alphabetic way. From their method came the Greek and Latin alphabets which are used today by most people outside of Asia.

WHO INVENTED COMIC BOOKS?

The comic strip is usually found in daily newspapers. It is made up of three or four picture panels telling a story with one or more characters. Comic books are extensions of comic strips into magazines. Each magazine is about one set of characters and the pictures tell a complete story.

While the first newspaper comic strip appeared in 1892, it was not until 1911 that an entire publication was devoted to comics—a comic book. That year the *Chicago American* offered reprints of Bud Fisher's ''Mutt and Jeff'' in pamphlet form.

The pattern for present-day comics was set much later. In 1935, *New Fun* appeared. It was a 64-page collection of original material in four colors, and was sold at newsstands. In 1938, *Action Comics* appeared, and the *Superman Quarterly Magazine* came out in 1939.

Comic books are not all humorous stories. The types of comic books issued include: adventure, animal, biography, detective, fantasy-mystery, history, humor, military, religion, romance, satire, science-fiction, teen-age, and western.

Some types, such as adventure and humor, sell better, so there are more of them. The popularity of comic books, however, has led all kinds of groups to use comic books to tell a story. Many companies use comic books to tell the story behind a product or the history of their company. Comic books are also published to explain complicated subjects, to dramatize public needs, or to give the history of a particular event. So "comic books" can be as varied as the subject matter and the purpose behind them.

WHAT IS THE ORIGIN OF THE DOG?

All living members of the dog family are descended from a wolflike creature called "Tomarctus." This ancient canine, called "the father of dogs," roamed the earth's forests about 15,000,000 years ago.

Tomarctus itself was descended from a small, weasel-like creature called "Miacis"; it lived some 40,000,000 years ago. This creature was also the distant ancestor of the bears and raccoons. They are the dog's closest living relatives today.

While man admires and lives with the domestic dog, he usually hates and fears such animals as wolves, coyotes, jackals, and foxes. But these are called "wild dogs." Domestic dogs are brothers under the skin to wolves, coyotes, and jackals—the typical wild dogs. All belong to the foremost branch of the dog family, the genus *anis*. All are so closely related that domestic dogs can mate with wolves, coyotes, or jackals, and produce fertile offspring. But they cannot interbreed with foxes. Foxes belong to another branch of the canine family tree.

At some time long ago early man tamed a few wild dogs. These dogs may have been wolf cubs. Or they may have been jackals or some other member of the wild dog family. Man found that these animals could be useful.

As man became more civilized he found that the dog was a good friend and a helpful guard for his home and cattle. In time, different breeds of dogs were developed for special purposes. Dogs with long noses were bred to scent game. Keen-sighted, fast dogs were bred to chase animals. Strong, heavy dogs pulled carts. Other dogs were bred for guard work. In this way the different breeds of dogs we have were developed.

WHEN WERE THE FIRST KEYS MADE?

The ancient Egyptians were the first to use a kind of key to open a door. They had a lock that was made up of a wooden bolt that fitted into a slot. Movable wooden pins known as tumblers were fastened in the top of the slot. When the bolt slid into place, the wooden tumblers dropped into holes cut in the bolt. The bolt was held fast until the tumblers were lifted up with a key.

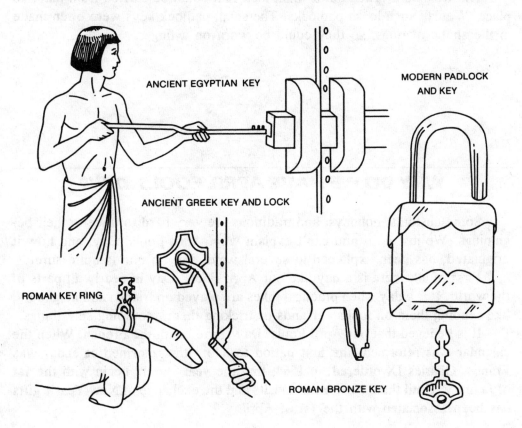

ANCIENT EGYPTIAN KEY

MODERN PADLOCK AND KEY

ANCIENT GREEK KEY AND LOCK

ROMAN KEY RING

ROMAN BRONZE KEY

This first key did not look at all like a key as we know it today. It looked more like a giant-sized toothbrush with pegs instead of bristles on one end. When the key was put in the slot, the pegs went under the tumblers. By raising the key, the tumblers were forced out of the bolt, which was then easily drawn back.

The Egyptian key could only be used on that side of the door where the bolt was placed. The Greeks discovered a way to slide back the bolt from the other side of the door. They slid their key through a hole in the door above the bolt until its tip touched a notch in the bolt on the inside. The Greek key was a curved bar, in shape and size much like a farmer's sickle. Some of these keys were over three feet long and were carried over the shoulder.

The Romans later became the most skillful lockmakers of the ancient world. They made a great improvement in the key. The pegs on the end of the Roman keys were cut in many different shapes. Now a thief had to make a key with pins not only in the right position and of the right length but also of the right shape.

The Romans worked out a small lock that could be carried from place to place. We call such locks padlocks. The small padlock keys were often made in the shape of rings, so they could be worn on a finger.

WHY DO WE HAVE APRIL FOOLS' DAY?

Some customs, holidays, and traditions are very hard to trace to their beginnings. We just do it and can't explain why. April Fools' Day, and how it originated, has been explained in several ways, but no one is quite sure.

First of all, there is a day like our April Fools' Day in nearly all parts of the world. It is a day when practical jokes are played on friends and neighbors, like sending them on foolish errands or tricking them into doing silly things.

It is believed that our April Fools' Day started with the French. When the calendar was reformed, the first nation to adopt the reformed calendar was France. Charles IX ordered, in 1564, that the year should begin with the 1st of January. Until then, New Year's visits and the exchange of New Year's gifts has been associated with the 1st of April.

Now, after Charles issued his decree, all this became associated with the 1st of January. But there were many people who objected to the change and refused to go along with it. The other people made fun of them for this.

They did it this way: they sent them mock gifts, they pretended to be visiting them, they invited them to mock New Year's celebrations—all on the 1st of April. In other words, they were April Fools—people who still felt April 1st was the beginning of the new year. Also, the custom of fooling somebody on this day started with the mock gifts and celebration they had with these people.

WHO SET UP THE ARRANGEMENT OF TYPEWRITER KEYS?

The modern typewriter is a complicated piece of machinery. Development to its present form took many years, and many people contributed to it.

Inventors had been thinking about a machine for writing since early in the 18th century. But it was not until 1867 that the first practical model was built, by Christopher Sholes of Milwaukee, Wisconsin.

Shole's machine was called the Type-Writer. People did not seem too interested in typewriting at first. The popularity of typewriters began to grow, however, in the early 1880's. And changes and improvements kept being introduced all the time.

But the odd arrangement of the typewriter keys has never been improved. This arrangement was the one used by the typewriter's original designer. Some typewriter designers believe that the keys could be arranged more efficiently. They have tried to make such changes in typewriters, but they have not been successful. It seems that the public is used to the keyboard the way it is and wants no change.

The arrangement of the keys is practically the same on all makes of typewriters. This common arrangement of the letters of the alphabet is known as the "universal" keyboard.

Some experts claim that this arrangement is actually a very good one. They say that the letters which occur together most often are placed so that the operator's fingers reach them successively in the most natural way.

WHEN WERE GEMS DISCOVERED?

Nobody knows when man first discovered gems, but he has been fascinated by them since the earliest times. For many thousands of years gems were worn as charms, or amulets, to protect people from demons and diseases. Even today there are people who believe gems have this power.

One of the first written records about gems is found in the Bible. The 28th chapter of Exodus tells of the breastplate worn by the high priest, Aaron. The breastplate was adorned by 12 precious stones.

The ancient Egyptians used gems as ornaments and charms. They were highly skilled in the art of gem engraving, and their writings on precious stones still exist. The Egyptians wore curious amulets, known as scarabs. These were precious stones engraved with the figure of the sacred beetle of Egypt. Those who wore scarabs were believed to have charmed lives.

In ancient times, the various gems were distinguished only by their colors. The name "ruby" was given to all precious stones of a red hue. All green stones were called emeralds. All blue ones were called sapphires.

Later on it was seen that some of the gems were harder than others and endured longer. So it came about that the value of a gem depended not only on its color, brilliance, and rarity, but also on its hardness. For example, diamonds are today considered the most precious of gems because, besides their beauty, they are the hardest of all stones.

All the gems are called precious stones, but in its strict meaning the term "precious" is given only to the four most valuable stones—the diamond, the ruby, the emerald, and the sapphire.

HOW WERE TIME ZONES DECIDED?

Before time zones were set up, there was a great deal of confusion, especially when people had to use railroad timetables. To end this confusion the United States in 1883 began using a system of standard time zones.

In 1884 an international conference was held in Washington, D.C., to set up a system to fit the whole world. The earth was divided into 24 zones, each covering 15 degrees of longitude. This is a natural division, for the earth rotates at the rate of 15 degrees each hour.

Within each zone the time is the same, and the difference between one zone and the next is exactly one hour. Greenwich (London), England, was selected as the starting point. Thus, when it is noon in Greenwich, the time in the next zone eastward is 1 P.M. The time in the next zone westward is 11 A.M. In New York, five zones west of Greenwich, the time is 7 A.M.

The United States is divided into four zones based on the 75th, 90th, 105th, and 120th meridians. The times in these zones are called Eastern, Central, Mountain, and Pacific Standard Time.

On the opposite side of the world from Greenwich is another dividing line, the International Date Line. This line is approximately the 180th meridian. When it is noon at Greenwich it is midnight at the International Date Line. Crossing the line, a person gains or loses a day, depending on whether he is moving east or west.

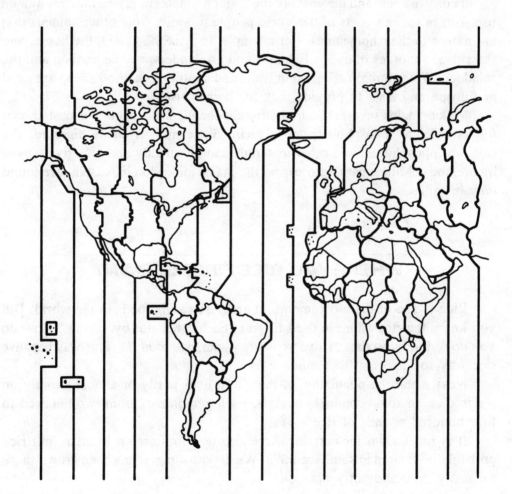

WHEN WERE COWS FIRST USED FOR MILK?

Early records often mention man's use of milk and milk products, and cows were used for milk long before any records were kept.

A temple that was discovered near Babylon has a scene on one of the walls that shows a cow being milked. This temple is thought to be five thousand years old!

Instead of milking cows from the right side, as is done today, the man is milking the cows from behind. The milker sits on a milking stool. Other men are straining the milk into a container on the ground. A third group collects the strained milk in large stone jars. So it seems that the business of getting milk from cows was pretty well organized five thousand years ago.

Today the cow and the goat are the major animals supplying milk for human use. But in various parts of the world people use milk from other animals that are native to their homelands. For example, in Asia the camel, the horse, and the yak are sources of milk. Eskimos and Laplanders use the caribou and the reindeer. Water buffalo are used in India and central Asia. And sheep are used in Europe and Asia to provide milk for human use.

Milk contains several hundred different chemical parts, but it is best known for its calcium, phosphorus, and protein. Since milk is easily digested, the calcium, phosphorus, and other materials can be quickly and effectively used by the body. Milk sugar (lactose) and the major milk protein, casein, are found only in milk.

WHERE WAS RICE FIRST GROWN?

Rice is one of the most important and fascinating foods in the world. Did you know that the Chinese used to greet each other not by saying "How do you do?" but by saying "Have you eaten your rice today?" This was because rice was so important to them.

Nearly half the population of the world lives partly or almost entirely on a rice diet. In some countries of Asia, each person eats from two hundred to four hundred pounds of rice a year.

It is not known for certain where rice was first grown by man, but rice probably originated in southern India. We do know that it has been grown there for many thousands of years.

Rice spread from there eastward to China more than five thousand years ago. It spread westward into Persia and Egypt soon afterward. Rice was not introduced to North America until the 17th century. Although North Americans eat some rice, most of them prefer wheat. At the present time in the United States only about five pounds of rice per person is eaten every year.

Rice with the hulls removed is called brown rice. Brown rice is covered with a brownish outer skin called the bran, in which most of the vitamins and minerals of the rice grain are stored.

Brown rice does not keep as long as white rice, however. Also, most people prefer white, well-milled, polished rice to brown rice. In some countries polished rice is enriched by adding vitamins and minerals.

Rice is used in many ways besides food. Rice flour is used for making glue, starch and in face powders. Wine is made from rice in Japan, China, and India.

WHY WAS THE METRIC SYSTEM INVENTED?

As science began to develop a few hundred years ago, scientists had trouble with measurements. Standards varied from nation to nation and even within one country. So during the 1700's scientists argued for a sensible system of measurement that could be accepted all over the world.

Such a system was invented in France in 1791. The French had other reasons for doing it, too. They were in the middle of a revolution at the time. The leaders of the revolution wanted to get away from all reminders of their hated past. They were therefore willing to set up a new system of measurement.

They began with length. They decided to establish the "meter" (from a Latin word meaning "measure") as a standard. Because of this, the entire system of measurement is called the metric system. Originally they tried to make the meter exactly 1/40,000,000 of the circumference of the earth. But when calculations turned out to be wrong about the earth's circumference, the meter was taken to be the distance between two marks on a platinum-iridium bar. All units of measurement in this system—length, capacity, mass—are linked in some way to the meter.

Actually, the metric system is easy to remember and easy to use. At first, though, people didn't want to change over. In 1840 the French Government had to insist that the people use the metric system or be punished.

Other nations gradually adopted the metric system, and today almost the whole world uses it. The United States is "phasing in" the system today.

WHO INVENTED TRAFFIC SIGNALS?

After the coming of the automobile, the first traffic controllers were foot patrolmen, directing traffic by hand. Then they were given hand-operated traffic lights. It was not until the early 1920's that automatic traffic lights were first used.

But these lights left an important problem unsolved. The amount of traffic passing through an intersection changes at different times of the day.

In 1927 two men patented "traffic-actuated" controllers. These were traffic lights designed to adjust to the amount of traffic passing through an intersection at a given time. One of these lights, invented by Harry Haugh of Yale University, was first installed in New Haven, Connecticut, in April, 1928.

This device worked by means of pressure detectors in the road pavement. A car passing over a detector signaled the "call box" on the light pole, which caused the light to turn green for the approaching vehicle. This type of traffic light, with some changes, is still widely used today.

Charles Adler, also in 1928, invented a traffic light that used a microphone to activate the call box. When a motorist, facing a red light, blew his horn, the microphone transmitted the sound to the call box, which caused the light to change. Today, there are other types of traffic controllers that use sound to change the light.

WHY IS SPEED AT SEA MEASURED IN KNOTS?

When ships first ventured out to sea, they had no sure way of knowing their location. Eventually, this was done by finding the latitude and longitude of the place. Latitude is distance north or south of the equator. Longitude tells how far east or west a place is. It was decided that zero degrees longitude would be the longitude line that goes through Greenwich, England.

To get an idea of their longitude, early ships first calculated how far they had traveled in a certain period of time. They used a "log" to find this out. It was a log of wood, weighted at one end, with the other end fixed to a long piece of rope. The log, thrown over the stern of the ship, floated, and the rope was let out as the ship sailed on. The speed of the ship could be calculated by seeing how much rope had been let out in a given time.

In later years, knots were tied at equal distances along the rope. A sailor counted how many knots passed through his hands in a certain time. This gave the speed of the ship. Sailors came to use the word "knots" to mean the speed of a ship.

Today, a knot has come to mean one nautical, or sea, mile per hour. A nautical mile equals 6076.1 feet, a little more than a land mile. Suppose a ship is sailing at a speed of 15 knots. This means that it is sailing at a speed of 15 nautical miles an hour.

Logs are still used to show how fast a ship is traveling. But today the logs are special metal rods with flat blades around them. As the ship sails through the water, the metal rod rotates and twists the rope round and round. The spinning rope works a device back on the ship that shows the actual speed.

WHEN DID PEOPLE BEGIN TO PIERCE THEIR EARS?

Piercing the ears to wear earrings goes back to prehistoric times. The ancient East Indians, Medes, Persians, Egyptians, Arabians, and Hebrews wore earrings.

Earrings became expensive and artistic ornaments in ancient times. The Etruscans, for example, made gold earrings that took the form of flowers, fruits, vases, shields, rosettes, crescents, peacocks, swans, and so on. The Greeks made beautiful gold earrings, and even put them on statues of the goddesses. In those days, Greek men wore earrings until they reached the age of adolescence.

The ancient Romans copied the Greeks in wearing earrings, and some of the Roman women had very expensive ones made with pearls and jewels. Roman men began to pierce their ears to wear earrings, and this became so popular that in the 3rd century A.D. the Roman emperor issued an edict forbidding men from doing so.

After the Middle Ages, men began to wear earrings in the left ear only. Then the hair styles for men and women changed; and when hair was worn long and over the ears, earrings went out of style. But they came into vogue again in the 15th and 16th centuries.

Earrings for women have been popular ever since that time. At one time, doctors said that it was good for ears to be pierced, but they no longer believe that it helps the ear.

WHO WERE THE FIRST PEOPLE TO MAKE MUMMIES?

The ancient Egyptians believed in life after death. They thought of the soul as a bird with a human face that could fly around by day but must return to the tomb at night for fear of evil spirits. The body was therefore preserved so that the soul could recognize it and know which tomb to enter. This is where the word "mummy" comes from. It is Arabic and means a body preserved by wax or tar.

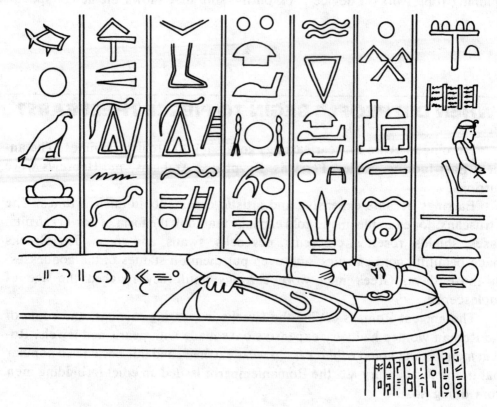

Most mummies were not made using wax or tar. The body was treated with salts. Salts, put inside the body, together with the dryness of the desert air, took out the moisture. When the body had been dried out, it was bathed, rubbed with resin from pine trees, and wrapped in hundreds of yards of linen.

Before about 3000 B.C. the Egyptians buried their dead in a curled-up position in the hot sand of the desert. The sand preserved the bodies. Later, important persons were buried in tombs cut from rock and in magnificent pyramids. But the pyramids and rock tombs were not so dry as the desert sand. This made it necessary to develop the art of mummification.

About 1500 B.C., mummies were given a plaster covering, shaped like a body and elaborately painted. Soon the coffins took the same shape and were decorated. Beards were added to some of the mummy cases. The beard in ancient Egypt was the sign of a god or king. Adding a beard showed that the dead man expected to live in very high company in the afterworld.

The Egyptians also believed that certain animals were sacred. These animals were also mummified and buried in animal cemeteries.

WHY DO WE HAVE CHRISTMAS TREES?

The custom came from Germany and dates to a time when primitive people revered trees—particularly evergreens. These trees did not die or fade in winter and seemed to be a sign of immortality. The Christians changed the custom into one honoring Christ.

The northern peoples of Denmark, Sweden, and Norway, where the forests are plentiful, adopted the custom of bringing small trees into their homes at Christmastime.

Trees were not used in English homes until a German prince, Albert of Saxe-Coburg-Gotha, married Queen Victoria. Prince Albert had the first decorated Christmas tree set up at Windsor Castle in 1841.

The first Christmas trees in the New World were introduced by Hessian soldiers in 1776, during the American Revolution. Later on, German immigrants brought the tradition into wider use in the United States.

Many other Christmas decorations used today were once pagan symbols. The Romans used flowers and leafy boughs in their rites. Records show that the Saxons used holly, ivy, and bay in their religious observances. The Druids gave the world the tradition of hanging mistletoe in the house. (Ancient Celtic priests believed the plant to be a sign of hope and peace.)

WHY WAS WASHINGTON D.C. MADE THE CAPITAL OF THE UNITED STATES?

After the American Revolution the United States needed a capital city. The selection of the site resulted from a compromise. Various cities and sections of the country wanted the honor of being the nation's capital.

It was finally decided to create a new city. Congress passed a bill in 1790 giving permission for a site to be chosen. It was to be somewhere near the Potomac River and not over ten miles square. The ten-mile square section of the land was to be called the District of Columbia, after Christopher Columbus; and the city to be built on it was to be named Washington, in honor of the country's first president.

In 1791 George Washington chose the place where the city now stands. He thought it was a good location because the Potomac River was deep enough for ships to come as far as the city.

The land was given to the federal government by the states of Maryland and Virginia. About 64 square miles were given by Maryland and about 36 square miles by Virginia. Later, in 1846, the land given by Virginia was returned to the state at her request.

President Washington chose a brilliant French engineer and architect, Major Pierre L'Enfant, to design the new city. The plan called for broad avenues lined with trees, beautiful government buildings, and monuments to honor great men.

By 1800 the president's house was nearly completed. The Capitol was built on a hill, renamed Capitol Hill, for the building in which Congress was to meet. In 1800 President John Adams and other members of the government moved to the new federal city, Washington, D.C.

HOW DID THE NAME "UNCLE SAM" ORIGINATE?

"Uncle Sam," of course, stands for the United States. What is hard to believe is that this nickname arose quite by accident, and there actually was a man called "Uncle Sam"—and that most people never heard of him!

There was a man called "Uncle Sam" Wilson. He was born in Arlington, Mass., Sept. 13, 1766. His father and older brothers fought in the American

Revolution. Sam himself enlisted at the age of 14 and served until the end of the war. He moved to Troy, N. Y., and began a meat-packing business.

On Oct. 2, 1812, a group of visitors came to his plant. One of them, Governor Daniel D. Tompkins of New York, asked what the initials "EA-US" on the barrels of meat stood for. A workman replied the "EA" stood for the contractor for whom Wilson worked, Elbert Anderson. And he added jokingly that the "US" (actually an abbreviation for United States) stood for "Uncle Sam" Wilson.

A story of this incident appeared in the May 12, 1830 issue of the New York *Gazette and General Advertiser*. Since Wilson was a popular man, and was an example of a hard-working and patriotic American, the idea of "Uncle Sam" as a name for this kind of man caught on quickly.

By the end of the War of 1812, "Uncle Sam" had come to symbolize the character of the nation and the government. In 1961 Congress adopted a resolution saluting "Uncle Sam" Wilson of Troy, N. Y., as the "progenitor of America's national symbol."

HOW OLD IS THE GAME OF CHECKERS?

Two of the oldest games played by man are chess and checkers. They are related in some ways, but since checkers is simpler in form it is assumed that it came first.

Checkers was played in the early history of Egypt, which means it's at least five thousand years old. Plato and Homer mentioned the game of checkers in their works, so it was known in ancient Greece. The Romans are believed to have taken the game from the Greeks.

The earliest records of the game seem to indicate that the kind of board used was similar to what we use today, and that it was played with twelve men on each side.

The first book on checkers was published in Spain in 1547. In 1620 another book of checkers was published in Spain that contained sample games and traps that would still be useful to know today. It is believed that the Spaniards may have learned about checkers from the Moors, who brought it from Arabia.

In England (where it is called "draughts"), the first book on checkers appeared in 1756. In 1800 another book by a man called Joshua Sturges became a guidebook for playing checkers that everyone followed for more than 50 years.

Today, checkers is played by millions of people all over the world. It is also recognized by educators as a good way to help people develop foresight, judgment, and concentration.

WHEN WERE THE FIRST MUSEUMS OPENED?

Museums are places where collections of objects are preserved and displayed. The objects may be anything found in nature or made by man. There are museums devoted to art, science, history, industry, and technology.

The word "museum" comes from the Greek word *mousion,* meaning "temple of the Muses." The Muses were goddesses of the arts. One of the first institutions to be called a mouseion was founded in Alexandria, Egypt, in the 3rd century B.C.

The aim of the Museum of Alexandria, as it was known, was to collect information from everywhere that could be of interest to scholars. Scholars lived and did their research there. The museum displayed a collection of objects of art and curiosities that included statues, instruments used in astronomy and surgery, elephant tusks, and hides of unusual animals.

There were many collections that might be called museums between that time and the 19th century, but they belonged to princes and noble families and were not established for the benefit of the people. Even the British Museum, which was founded in the middle of the 18th century, admitted few people.

It took the French Revolution to open the doors of French museums to everyone. In 1793, during the Revolution, the Republican Government made the Louvre in Paris a national museum.

In the 19th century, for the first time, buildings were specially designed as museums. One of the first buildings in Europe planned as a museum was the Altes Museum in Berlin, Germany. It was constructed in 1830.

WHO INVENTED THE VIOLIN?

The violin is known as the queen of instruments. Of the more than one hundred musicians in a great orchestra, over thirty are violinists. The violin's high rank is due to the beauty of its tone and its wide range of expression.

The violin took many centuries to develop. Its history begins in India, where the use of a bow to play stringed instruments was probably invented. During the early Middle Ages in Europe various stringed instruments were played with a bow.

One of these was the vielle, which was probably introduced to Europe through the Balkan Peninsula in the 10th century. Like the violin, the vielle was held against the player's shoulder.

Later the vielle was changed through the influence of the rebec. This was an Arabic instrument that spread from Spain to the rest of Europe. By combining the sturdy body of the vielle with the clever arrangement of the pegs in the rebec, a new group of instruments was born.

The violin received its basic form between 1550 and 1600. Since that time it has changed only in small ways. The most successful violins were made in the 17th and 18th centuries.

Italy produced outstanding families of violin-makers. Probably the greatest of these was Antonio Stradivari (1644-1737). Stradivari is called the master of all masters. He developed a larger, flatter type of violin than had been made before, which gave it more tone power.

Stradivari is said to have built 1,116 instruments. Of these, 540 "Strad" violins are known to us. Most of them have nicknames, such as the Viotti or the Vieuxtemps, after the famous violinists who played them.

WHO INVENTED MUSICAL NOTES?

For a very long time music was not written down. It was sung or played from memory. As it was passed on from person to person, many changes crept into the tunes. A way of writing music down was needed so that it would be sung or played exactly as it had been composed. The method that man developed for writing music is called notation.

The system of musical notation generally used today in the Western world is the result of centuries of development—from about the end of the 9th century to the early 1700's. This development began in the cathedrals and monasteries of the Roman Catholic Church.

Since many of the Church's services were sung, they were sung from memory. Toward the end of the 9th century dots and dashes and little squiggles were written over the words in the service books. These signs, called neumes, showed the direction in which the melody should go. But they were still very vague.

About A.D. 900 the music was made a little easier to read. The neumes were written at certain distances above or below the horizontal red line (representing the note F) to show how high or low the note should be sung.

Then the staff was invented by a monk called Guido d'Arezzo. This was made of four lines. A method of notation that made it possible to show the length of each note was developed in the 13th and 14th centuries. Notes took new shapes and stems were added to some notes according to their length. By the 1600's the notes had become round and musical notation began to look the way it does today.

WHY DO SOLDIERS SALUTE?

What is a salute? It is a gesture of respect to a person of superior rank. It is formalized, that is, it is done in a certain way every time.

Salutes of all kinds have existed in all periods of history and in all cultures. The form of salute has varied. In some cases it meant bowing, in others it meant kneeling, or lying on the ground, or various gestures of the hand and arm. The individual military salute that a soldier gives—raising the right hand to the forehead or to the hat brim or visor—was developed quite recently in history.

Until the end of the 18th century the way junior officers saluted superiors and soldiers saluted officers was to doff the hat. In fact, civilians still do this as a gesture of respect. And this custom probably goes back to the days when a knight would raise his helmet's visor or uncover his head before a lord.

The change from taking off the hat to just raising the hand in a salute, took place for a very practical reason. When soldiers fired their muskets, black powder would settle on their hands and make them very grimy. If they then had to use their grimy hands to take off their hats in a salute, it would ruin the hats. So at the end of the 18th century the change was made to the hand salute.

An officer or soldier carrying a sword or saber at the shoulder, whether mounted or on foot, salutes by bringing the hilt to his mouth, then extending the point to the right and downward. This form of salute dates back to the Middle Ages when knights, in a religious gesture, kissed the hilts of their swords as symbolic of the cross of Christ. It was then a form of oath-taking.

WHEN DID ATHLETICS BEGIN?

If we go back far enough, athletics probably began with religion. Primitive men worshipped their gods by performing certain dances. These dances imitated the actions of fighting and hunting. Later on, these dances were performed simply for the pleasure they gave—and they were actually a form of athletics.

The Egyptians had some form of athletic sports about four thousand years ago. But athletics as we know it really began with the Greeks. The first recorded Olympic games of the Greeks took place in the year 776 B.C.

Today, we imagine that sports activities play an important part in our lives. But it cannot compare to how important athletics were to the ancient Greeks. Every boy was trained in running, jumping, and wrestling, while he was still at school. A man was supposed to be good at athletics until he was well past middle age.

The ideal of the Greeks was to have a sound mind in a healthy body. So they didn't admire men who were just athletes, nor men who were just brilliant but couldn't participate in sports. But they also had professional athletes, especially in boxing and wrestling.

The Greeks had many athletic festivals, but the oldest and most important were the Olympic games. Only young men of pure Greek descent who had undergone ten months' training could compete. At first the games were just contests in running and jumping. But later on they added wrestling, boxing, discus and javelin throwing, and chariot races.

WHO INVENTED INDOOR PLUMBING?

By indoor plumbing we generally mean a system that consists of two parts. There is a system of pipes and valves that brings the water from a large pipe (water main) under the street into the house and to the various rooms. There is also a drainage system of pipes through which waste liquids are taken from the house and fed into a sewer pipe in the street.

The first "plumbing" system that we know about goes back about 4,000 years. Archeologists doing excavations on Crete, an island in the Mediterranean Sea, uncovered a 4,000-year-old palace that had a water and drainage system.

The water system was formed by conduits—stone channels through which water flows. The cisterns of the conduits collected water that fell as rain or flowed down from the hills. The water was carried by the conduits into vertical shafts and from the shafts to bathrooms and toilets.

Waste water was carried away by pipes made of terra-cotta, a form of baked clay. Amazingly enough, these terra-cotta pipes were designed so that they could be installed easily. One end of each pipe was made so it would fit into the next, and the pipes were fastened together with cementing clay.

The first people to use pipes made of lead were the Romans. They called the craftsman who installed pipes a "plumbarius," meaning "worker in lead." This is the origin of the English words "plumber" and "plumbing."

While lead is still used in some kinds of pipes today, other materials used are steel, copper, brass, cast iron, concrete, and plastic.

WHEN WAS JEWELRY FIRST WORN?

Jewelry can be made from many different kinds of materials. But we usually think of it as precious jewelry, made of the rarest and most beautiful metals and gemstones.

Gold is the oldest precious metal used in jewelry. The use of it dates back to the earliest Egyptians. In fact, more than four thousand years ago, the Egyp-

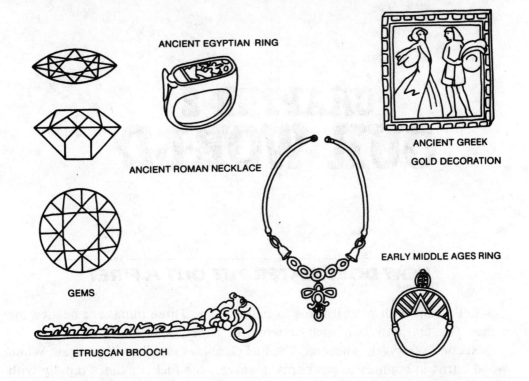

ANCIENT EGYPTIAN RING

ANCIENT GREEK GOLD DECORATION

ANCIENT ROMAN NECKLACE

GEMS

EARLY MIDDLE AGES RING

ETRUSCAN BROOCH

tians were making beautiful jewelry out of gold, silver, enamel, turquoise and other gemstones. They wore rings, earrings, and brooches, just as we do now. They also wore heavy jeweled collars, breastplates, and headdresses.

To the ancient Greeks the beauty of a piece of jewelry was as important as the value of the materials used to make it. Fine threads of gold were shaped to look like butterflies or grasshoppers. The Greeks also liked cameos. Jasper, amber, and coral were among their favorite gemstones.

The most beautifully made jewelry in history was made by the Etruscans, who lived in northern Italy. They designed jewelry in intricate patterns and made it with great skill. Instead of a shiny surface, their gold jewelry had a grainy surface, as if fine gold powder has been evenly sprinkled on it.

The Romans wore very elaborate jewelry, designed to show off their wealth. Both men and women wore large gemstones. They especially liked pearls and emeralds. The Romans loaded their fingers, sometimes all their fingers, with rings.

During the Middle Ages most of the jewelry craftsmen were monks. The monks devoted their energy to making religious decorations for the churches. Guilds of jewelry makers began after the 9th century. By 1327, goldsmiths had formed their own association in London.

CHAPTER 2
OUR WORLD

HOW DOES WATER PUT OUT A FIRE?

Let's start with what it takes to make a fire. Three things are needed for a fire. The first is a fuel, such as wood or paper or alcohol or gas.

Secondly, oxygen is needed. The fuel combines rapidly with oxygen. When wood burns in bonfires or gas burns in stoves, the fuel combines rapidly with oxygen in the air.

The third thing needed is heat. Paper or wood that is simply exposed to air does not catch fire. Usually a burning match is applied to paper to make it catch fire. When the paper becomes hot enough, oxygen can begin to combine freely with it. The paper then bursts into flames.

There are three main ways in which a fire can be put out. In each, one of the three things needed for burning is removed. The first way is to remove some of the fuel. A second way of putting out a fire is to keep oxygen from getting to it. If there is no oxygen supply, the fire goes out. For example, a fire cannot burn in carbon dioxide. Some fire extinguishers blanket a fire with carbon dioxide. The oxygen is thus blocked from the fire.

A third way to put fires out is to remove heat from the fire. That is why water is sprayed on fires. The water absorbs heat from the burning materials and lowers their temperature. Once the temperature drops below the kindling temperature, the fuels stop burning.

Some fires cannot be put out with water. For example: oil and grease float on water. If you try to put out an oil fire—such as a burning pan of cooking oil—with water, the flaming oil will come to the top of the water and continue to burn.

HOW ARE AMENDMENTS ADDED TO THE CONSTITUTION?

The Constitution of the United States has grown with the needs of the American people. One of the ways this has happened is through amendments. An amendment means that the words that make up the Constitution can be changed.

When two-thirds of the members of Congress agree on an amendment, the amendment may then be given to the states for their approval. The states may consider the matter either through their legislatures or through special conventions. Congress decides which. And when three-quarters of the states have ratified an amendment, the amendment is in force and the Secretary of State announces the fact.

The first ten amendments, the Bill of Rights, were really unfinished business of the Constitutional Convention. In other words, they were part of the creation of the Constitution. Amendments Eleven and Twelve were also added in that way.

After a long period with no amendments, Thirteen abolished slavery. Fourteen further protected the rights of citizens, and Fifteen granted equal voting rights regardless of race or color. Sixteen permitted Congress to levy an income tax. Seventeen called for the election of senators by the people instead of by state legislatures.

Eighteen outlawed alcoholic drinks—and was repealed by amendment Twenty-one in 1933. The Nineteenth amendment gave women the right to vote. Twenty changed the terms of office of the president, vice-president, and Congress. Twenty-two limits presidents to two terms. Twenty-three gives the presidential vote to the District of Columbia. Twenty-four bars the poll tax as a requirement for voters in federal elections. And Twenty-five covers presidential disability.

HOW DOES THE SOIL HELP PLANTS GROW?

Soil is a mixture of organic and inorganic materials. The organic part consists of living things and the remains of once-living things. The inorganic part is made up of particles of rocks and minerals.

The decaying organic matter in soil is called humus. Humus separates otherwise tightly packed rock particles, thus allowing more air and water to enter the soil. Humus also provides food for bacteria and other micro-organisms in soil. These micro-organisms decay, or break down, dead organic matter, forming substances that plants can use. So humus is very important to the fertility of the soil, or helping plants grow.

Many kinds of animals live in the soil. The body wastes of these animals enrich the soil. Earthworms are important, too. They turn over the soil, and improve it in many ways. Micro-organisms present in the soil feed on particles of organic matter. This breaks the organic material into minerals, gases, and liquids. These decay products are broken down still further and result in new combinations of the basic elements. Plants can then use the substances for growth.

There are ten elements that all plants need to grow. Three of these, oxygen, hydrogen, and carbon, are present in either air or water or in both. The others are obtained from the soil by the plants. They are: nitrogen, phosphorus, potassium, calcium, magnesium, iron, and sulfur.

HOW DO SEEDS GROW?

Each seed is like a tiny package of plant life. It contains a tiny new plant and food to nourish it. You can see the plant and its food if you split a large seed, like a bean, in half.

You will see that it is made of two pale, thick leaves, called cotyledons. These are filled with starch for the developing plant. If you look carefully, you will see a tiny white sprout at one end between the cotyledons. This is the future bean plant. Some plants have only one cotyledon.

Some seeds germinate, or sprout, as soon as they fall from the plant, but most need a resting period of several months. The root appears first. Then a leafy shoot pushes upward.

Seeds enclosed in fleshy fruits, such as apples and tomatoes, do not sprout until they have been removed from the fruit. This is because the fruit contains substances that prevent sprouting.

The tiny new plant in the seed, called the embryo, has an upper part called the plumule. This grows into stems and leaves. The rest of the embryo is the hypocotyl, a very short stem that produces a root at its lower end.

Seeds sprout into new plants when conditions are favorable. The conditions that make seeds sprout are warmth, abundant moisture, and an adequate oxygen supply. Given these conditions, the food stored in the cotyledons passes to the growing regions of the embryo. The embryo bursts through the seed coat and emerges as a young plant that gradually comes to look like the parent plant.

WHAT ARE DIATOMS?

Diatoms are tiny one-celled plants. They are found by the billions and billions in all the waters all over the earth.

The largest diatoms are barely visible to the naked eye and the smallest are less than a thousandth of an inch long. Yet even though they are so tiny, each of them builds for itself a stone shelter hard as granite. There are more than 10,000 species of diatoms, and they have many shapes.

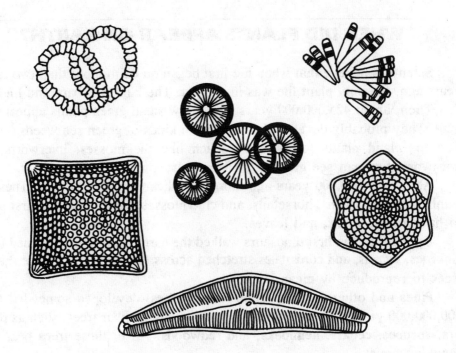

A diatom shelter consists of two shells or valves, one fitting over the other like the top and bottom of a box, and held together along the edges by a girdle. Inside lies the living plant.

Most diatoms float about in the water or fasten themselves with a sort of jelly to stones or larger water plants. A few are able to swim slowly from place to place, but how they propel themselves is not clearly understood.

Diatoms usually reproduce by splitting in two. The interior living cell divides, the valves separate, and each half grows a new valve on its exposed surface.

Diatoms are very important to us. Together with certain other tiny forms, they are the main plant life of the oceans. While alive, they change nutrient materials that are dissolved in the water into organic substance, and so they are a source of food for all kinds of creatures in the sea, even including fish and whales. The oil which they produce is rich in vitamins and is accumulated in fish livers, from which commercial vitamins are produced.

WHEN DID PLANTS APPEAR ON EARTH?

Scientists believe that when life first began on earth more than two billion years ago, the only plant life was in the sea. The land was bare and lifeless.

Then, about 425,000,000 years ago, a few small green plants appeared on land. They probably developed from certain kinds of green sea weeds (algae). The first land plants looked very much like the mosses, liverworts, and hornworts you can see growing in damp, shady places.

About 400,000,000 years ago more complicated plants existed. These resembled modern ferns, horsetails, and club mosses. Ferns were the first plants to have roots, stems, and leaves.

By the time the first dinosaurs walked the earth, vast forests of seed ferns, ginkgoes, cycads, and cordaitales stretched across the land. These were the first trees to reproduce by means of seeds.

Pines and other conifers (cone-bearing trees) developed somewhat later, 300,000,000 years ago. This group includes many familiar trees, such as pines, firs, spruces, cedars, hemlocks, and redwoods. All of these trees bear their seeds on cones.

The first flowering plants developed about 150,000,000 years ago. Their well-protected seeds gave them a great advantage over plants with more exposed seeds, and they increased in numbers and kinds. Today flowering plants are found almost everywhere.

WHO CARVED THE FACES ON MOUNT RUSHMORE?

In the Black Hills of South Dakota, about 25 miles southwest of Rapid City, is one of the most impressive sights to be seen anywhere. It is Mount Rushmore National Memorial.

It honors four American presidents: George Washington, Thomas Jefferson, Abraham Lincoln, and Theodore Roosevelt. Giant likenesses of the four are sculptured into the granite of Mount Rushmore, which is 5,725 feet high. Each face is about 60 feet from chin to forehead, which, by the way, is twice as high as the great Sphinx.

The work was designed by the American sculptor Gutzon Borglum. Borglum was a man who was interested in producing American art, art that related to this country and its history. Well-known works done by him include the colossal head of Lincoln in Washington, D.C., the statue of General Sheridan, and the figures of the twelve apostles for the Cathedral of St. John the Divine, New York City.

Borglum began his work on Mount Rushmore in August, 1927. The first figure, that of Washington, was dedicated on July 4, 1930. After Borglum died on March 6, 1941, work on the memorial continued until October under the direction of his son, Lincoln. But the last sculpture, of Roosevelt, was never quite completed.

Fourteen years passed between the beginning of the project and its termination. But only about six and one-half of these were spent in actual work. The lapses of time without any work being done were due to bad weather and a lack of funds.

The total cost was just under $1 million. The federal government gave 84 percent of this; the rest came from private donations.

WHEN WAS THE GREAT SPHINX BUILT?

One of the greatest "wonders" that still survives from an ancient civilization is the Great Sphinx at Giza, in Egypt. A sphinx is a mythical animal that has the head of a human and the body of a lion.

The sphinx became part of Egyptian religion and many sphinxes were made, but the most famous and the oldest is the Great Sphinx. This sphinx was built in the 26th century B.C. The face had the features of the king at that time, King Khafre, so that his people could worship him in this special form.

It is carved from a natural bluff of rock that lies in the center of a large quarry. The body and the head are carved right from the rock, while the outstretched paws are added in masonry. The figure was originally covered with painted plaster, and there are still some traces of this.

While we can still see and admire the Great Sphinx, it is quite different now than it was originally because of all the damage it has suffered. Drifting sand has caused a great deal of erosion and created a kind of ripple effect on the body.

It has also been injured by humans. In 1380 a ruler of Egypt did great damage to the face. At one time the monument was used as a target for guns.

The Great Sphinx is 66 feet high, its length is 240 feet. The nose is 5 feet 7 inches and the mouth 7 feet 7 inches in length. The face is 13 feet 8 inches wide.

ARE THE CONTINENTS MOVING?

The theory that the continents have moved or drifted about ("continental drift") was first advanced by a German scientist, Alfred Wegener, in 1912.

He pointed out that coal was present all over the northern hemisphere, yet coal forms from plants growing in tropical forests. And among other things, he said the west coast of Africa and the east coast of South America matched so well that they looked as if they had been torn apart.

Wegener thought all the continents had at first been together in one great land mass. Then they had drifted apart to their present location. Most geologists didn't agree with him because no one could think of any way by which continents would move about.

Then scientists began to suggest ways in which this could happen. One was that heat from the interior of the earth creates convection currents that make the continents move. Other scientists now think that the ocean floor is being pulled apart by currents in the mantle of the earth's crust.

So there is no agreement on the subject. Earth scientists tend to accept the idea; those who study under-ocean geology are more ready to accept it. If all geologists were to accept the theory that the continents have drifted, and may still be moving, a great revolution in our ideas on earth science will have to take place.

Science would have to come up with new answers about our climate, about how plants and animals evolved, about how mountains were built, and many more areas.

WHAT IS MAGMA?

Inside the earth it is very hot. This great heat melts some rock material that is there and makes it liquid rock. Liquid rock lies in huge underground pockets. This liquid underground rock is called magma.

Magma is lighter in weight than the colder, hard rocks around it. So it is slowly pushed upward by the pressure of the rock around it. In many places

43

the magma never does reach the surface but slowly cools and hardens underground.

It takes many thousands of years for magma to harden into rock. In other places the cold, hard rocks near the surface cannot withstand the pressure of the magma beneath them. They crack a little bit and the magma rises up along the cracks.

Magma often remains hot enough to stay in liquid form until it reaches the surface of the earth. It then flows through the cracks and spreads out on the ground. Magma that reaches the surface of the earth is called lava.

Magma usually starts cooling while it is still being pushed upward. As the magma slowly rises, certain minerals in it grow into big crystals sooner than the other minerals do. The crystals float in the magma. When this magma reaches the surface of the earth, the liquid rock turns to a solid in a short time. The big crystals carried in the liquid are "frozen" into the fine-grained lava rock. The whole rock is then made of many large crystals embedded in a very fine-grained rock, such as basalt. Such a rock is called porphyry. It is very attractive when polished and is often used as a building stone.

WHY IS LAVA HOT?

The center of the earth is a very hot place. If we could dig down thirty miles into the earth, the temperature would be about 2,200 degrees Fahrenheit. At the core or center of the earth the temperature may be about 10,000 degrees Fahrenheit. At such temperatures, rock exists in a molten form.

Lava is the molten rock, mixed with steam and gas, that is forced out of the interior of the earth. It comes from the center of the earth through cracks in the solid surface.

Sometimes the crack may be a rounded hole. When the lava comes out, it spreads out into a kind of round puddle and cools into rock. If more lava is forced out later, it flows over the first deposit and makes it a little higher. As this continues to happen, layer after layer is built up and there is finally a mountain of rock which we call a volcano.

When a flow of lava occurs and spreads over the land, it destroys everything in its path. This is because it is a heavy stream of molten rock with a temperature of 2,000 to 3,000 degrees Fahrenheit.

Cities that are close to volcanoes are always in danger of being destroyed by such a flow of lava. Sometimes a very long period goes by without this happening, and people assume they are now safe forever. Then suddenly the flow of lava begins again.

This happened two thousand years ago to a Roman city in Italy, called Pompeii. It was buried completely under the flow of lava from the famous volcano, Mount Vesuvius.

WHY DOES THE MOON HAVE DIFFERENT SHAPES?

The moon circles the earth in an orbit that takes about one month to complete. It also spins, or rotates, on its axis, and it takes 27 days, 7 hours, and 43 minutes to make one rotation. Because the orbit and the rotation take about the same amount of time, the moon always keeps the same side facing the earth.

The moon does not shine with its own light the way the sun does. It only seems to shine, because it reflects the sun's light. As the moon travels around the earth different parts of it are lighted up by the sun.

Sometimes you see the whole visible face of the moon lighted up, and at other times you see only a part of the moon's face lighted up. This is what makes the moon look as though it were changing shape in the sky. These changes are called phases of the moon—and it only means we are seeing different parts of the moon.

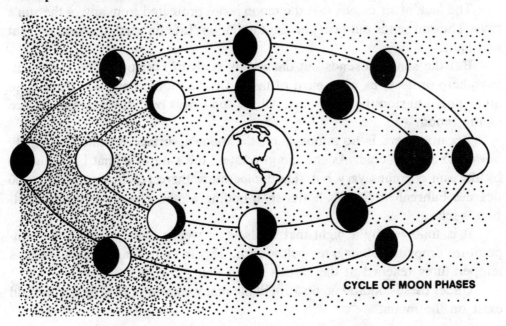

CYCLE OF MOON PHASES

45

The cycle of phases begins with a new moon. This is when the moon is between the earth and the sun. A new moon is not visible. Then the side of the moon facing the earth begins to be lighted up by the sun. The lighted part looks like a thin curved slice of a circle. This is called a crescent moon.

The sunlit part of the moon grows larger until it becomes a half-circle. This is called the first quarter. When the whole face of the moon is lighted by the sun we call it a full moon. Then the moon's face becomes less and less lit, and we reach the last quarter. The cycle ends with a crescent moon that changes to the next new moon. The whole cycle, from one new moon to the next new moon, lasts just over 29½ days.

WHY IS THERE NO LIFE ON THE MOON?

Now that man has actually explored the surface of the moon, he has learned many new things about it. But one thing man knew before he ever reached the moon was that there was no life on it.

There is no atmosphere on the moon. Astronomers knew this because there is no twilight on the moon. On earth darkness comes gradually because the air reflects the sun's light even after the sun sets. On the moon, one moment there is sunlight, the next moment night has arrived.

The lack of air means that the moon is not protected from any of the sun's rays. The sun sends out heat and light radiation. Life on earth depends on heat and light.

But the sun also sends out dangerous kinds of radiation. The earth's atmosphere protects us from most of them. On the moon, however, there is no atmosphere to stop the radiations. All the sun's rays beat down on the surface of the moon.

Because there is no atmosphere, the moon's surface is either extremely hot or extremely cold. As the moon rotates, the side of it that is lighted up by the sun becomes very hot. The temperature there reaches more than 300 degrees Fahrenheit. This is hotter than boiling water. The hot lunar day lasts two weeks.

It is followed by a night that is also two weeks long. At night the temperature drops to 260 degrees below zero. This is more than twice as cold as temperatures reached at the earth's South Pole.

Under these conditions, no form of life that we know of here on earth could exist on the moon.

DO OTHER PLANETS MOVE LIKE THE EARTH?

The earth moves in two ways. It travels around the sun in a fixed path called an orbit. The time it takes to do this is called a year. The earth also rotates on its axis. The time it takes to do this is called a day. The other planets also orbit the sun and also rotate, but at speeds different from the earth's.

The earth travels around the sun at an average distance of about 93,000,000 miles and takes slightly more than 365 days to make one orbit. It takes a little less than 24 hours to rotate once on its axis. Now let's consider the other planets. Mercury's average distance from the sun is about 36,000,000 miles and it takes 88 earth days to complete one trip around the sun. It is believed that Mercury rotates once every 58 or 59 days.

Venus, about 67,200,000 miles from the sun, takes about 225 days to make one trip around the sun. It is believed that Venus takes 243 days to rotate just once—and this planet rotates backward! In other words, on Venus you would find the planet turning from east to west.

Mars, an average distance of 141,600,000 miles from the sun, takes about 687 days for one orbit, but rotates nearly as fast as the earth. Jupiter, 483,300,000 miles from the sun, takes about 11.9 earth years to complete one orbit, but takes less than ten hours to rotate once. Saturn, 886,200,000 miles from the sun, takes nearly 29½ earth years for one orbit, but only about ten hours to turn once on its axis.

Uranus, 1,783,000,000 miles from the sun, completes an orbit in 84 years. And Neptune, 2,794,000,000 miles from the sun, takes almost 165 earth years to complete one orbit.

WHAT MAKES A BEAUTIFUL SUNSET?

The sun itself has nothing to do with creating a beautiful sunset. And strangely enough, one of the things that helps create that effect is the dust in the air. In fact, dust particles help make the sky blue and give us those red sunsets.

The sun's white light is actually made up of all the colors of the rainbow. Each color has its own wavelength. Violet has the shortest wavelength, red has the longest.

At sunset the sun is near the horizon. We see it then through a much thicker layer of dust and air. All these particles change the direction of more and more short-wave light from the sun. Only the longer wavelengths—red and orange—come through directly.

Violets, blues, and greens are scattered out of the direct beam; they mix and make a gray twilight glow all around the sky. The disk of the sun itself looks red. Sometimes there are clouds in the part of the sky where we see the sun. They reflect this red light and we see a blazing sunset.

Violet and blue light waves are scattered more than the longer red ones. The scattered violet and blue light bounces from particle to particle in the atmosphere, thus spreading light through the whole sky. Since our eyes see blue light more easily than violet, the sky looks blue to us. This, of course, is what happens during the day.

By the way, the redness of a sunset depends on the kind of particles in the air that will be scattering the sun's light. Tiny water droplets are especially effective at this, which is why certain cloud formations appear so red at sunset.

WHAT IS THE DIFFERENCE BETWEEN TOADSTOOLS AND MUSHROOMS?

The answer is, there is no difference! In fact, scientifically speaking, there is no such thing as a "toadstool." Many people call poisonous mushrooms "toadstools." But a botanist never uses that term at all, and there is no difference between a mushroom and what is called a toadstool.

There are a great many other ideas about mushrooms that people have which are completely wrong. The kinds of mushrooms which are poisonous are quite few. But these few are deadly. So no one should ever eat or even taste a mushroom unless he is certain that it is wholesome.

But the "tests" that some people believe in for detecting poisonous mushrooms are worthless. For example, it is not correct that all mushrooms with umbrella-shaped caps are poisonous. It is not true that poisonous mushrooms when cooling will blacken a silver spoon if they are stirred with it.

The poisonous mushrooms contain a poison so powerful that to eat them is almost certain death. There is a story that the Emperor Nero once killed off a whole party of guests by feeding them poisonous mushrooms. The best thing to do is to eat only the mushrooms you buy in stores—and not pick your own.

Mushrooms are fungi. Like other fungi, they lack the green coloring matter called chlorophyll without which a plant cannot manufacture food for itself. They must grow near, and depend for food on, plants that have this green coloring matter. Mushrooms are very delicate plants. They consist chiefly of water, which is why most of them cannot bear hot dry winds or the summer sun.

HOW WAS PETROLEUM FORMED IN THE EARTH?

Petroleum is believed to have been formed from the remains of ancient living things. Millions of years ago many land areas of today were underwater. The sun shone on these waters and the living things in them.

Marine plants and animals stored the sun's energy in their bodies. As they died, their remains sank to the bottom and were covered by sediments (tiny particles of rock and soil).

While organic remains of these animals and plants settled under layers of sand and mud, chemicals and bacteria were at work. How these agents actually formed gas and oil from the fats and oils of sea life is uncertain. But over long periods of time tiny oil droplets were formed. . .or what we call petroleum.

Later on, the layers of muds and clays became rocks of sandstone and limestone. These rocks are called sedimentary because they were formed from sediments. In time, tiny droplets of oil seeped into layers of these porous rocks and were held there the way a sponge holds water.

Over millions of years the earth's crust was shifting. Old sea floors, and the oil they held, were in some cases changed to land areas. Others were pushed deeper into the sea. The earth shifted and continents changed in appearance.

This is why oil-bearing rock layers are today sometimes found far inland, and also why some of the most productive oil fields are located in desert regions. Millions of years ago they may have been areas under water.

WHY DOES A CACTUS HAVE SPINES?

The cactus is a remarkable example of how, if plants and animals are to survive, they must be fitted for the climates and places in which they live.

Cacti are plants that live in hot, dry regions, so going without water for long periods is a problem. As the climate became drier, the roots of cacti gradu-

ally spread out, closer to the surface of the ground. That's why cacti can absorb water quickly from the earth when there is a rainfall.

The water has to be stored. This is done in the spongy or hollow stem of a cactus plant. What's more, the outer layer of the plant is thick and waxy, to prevent the escape of water.

Other plants have leaves which give off water in sunlight. Cactus plants have spines—and these prevent the loss of water. But the spines help save the life of the cactus in another way, too. Suppose there are thirsty animals roaming about in search of water. There is water in the cactus plant—but can you imagine any animal taking a bite at a cactus?

Except for their special structures that enable them to store water, cacti are regular flowering plants with blossoms that develop into seed-bearing fruits. In fact, the flowers of most cacti are very beautiful. When a desert is in full bloom, you can see bright yellow, red, and purple blooms springing from the polished stems of the cacti.

True cacti are native only to the Western Hemisphere. They grow mainly in the dry lands of South America, Central America, and the southwestern United States.

50

WHAT IS AN EARTHQUAKE BELT?

Earthquakes are tremblings or vibrations of the earth's surface. The real cause of earthquakes is usually a "fault" in the rocks of the earth's crust—a break along which one rock mass has rubbed on another with very great force and friction.

Because of this, earthquakes do not occur in all parts of the world. They are confined to certain definite areas, which are called "belts." The most important belt is the rim of the Pacific Ocean, where most of the world's earthquakes have occurred.

This belt begins at the southern tip of Chile, reaches up the Pacific coast of South America to Central America (branching into the Caribbean), runs along the Mexican coast to California, and on to Alaska.

But that isn't the end of it. The belt continues from Alaska to Kamchatka. Passing through the Kurile Islands and the Aleutian Islands, it stretches on to Japan, the Philippines, Indonesia, New Guinea, and through various South Pacific islands.

Most of the big earthquakes in history have taken place within the Pacific belt. However, another earthquake belt branches off from Japan. It runs through China, India, Iran, Turkey, Greece, and the Mediterranean.

In some regions, such as Japan, earthquakes occur almost every day. Fortunately, most of these earthquakes are not severe and cause no damage. On the other hand, in the New England states there have been no destructive earthquakes since the last Ice Age, many thousands of years ago.

WHERE DOES MONEY FOR TAXES GO?

Taxation is the process by which governments get the money to pay for the things that the people want governments to do. In the United States, city and state governments and the national government collect taxes to pay for the many services which the people have decided the government should provide. It is much cheaper and more efficient to have schools and streets, fire and police departments, and the armed forces run by the government than to have each family try to provide its own education, highways, and protection.

The expenses of all kinds of governments have increased greatly over the years. The main reason for the increase in the cost of running the national government is national defense. In the states, cities, and towns the need for government spending has also increased.

It is necessary to have better streets and highways to take care of the large number of automobiles. More and better schools are needed, and larger universities are necessary. People want to have better hospitals, parks, and other facilities that may be provided by cities and towns.

The federal income tax is the most important source of funds for operation of the United States Government. Cities and towns get most of their money from property taxes. States get their money more and more from income taxes and sales taxes. Without these taxes, none of the services, help, and protection that people want would be possible.

WHAT IS INFLATION?

Basically, inflation is a rise in prices. Families, businesses, and government groups are all buyers. The things they buy are called goods and services. During an inflation people spend money faster than goods are being made. It is a period when too many dollars are chasing too few goods. During an inflation a dollar buys less.

Even if we knew all the causes of inflations, we might not be able to keep them from happening. Sometimes government spending is blamed for starting an inflation. Sometimes businesses and labor unions are blamed. Even family spending is blamed. Often inflations are caused by wars.

In an inflation, a steady rise in prices cuts back the amount that a dollar will buy. Then people hurry to buy before costs get any higher. Then businessmen think that there is a growing demand for their products. So they put money into new products, machinery, and factories.

This creates a greater demand for workers. People get bigger incomes and they spend their extra money. Businessmen see that their goods are selling well and borrow money to expand their businesses.

The people who suffer during an inflation are the savers, creditors (the people who have loaned money), people on pensions, and those who earn a fixed salary.

Before a government tries to control an inflation, it tries to understand what is causing it. If the wrong controls are used, they may not solve the problem.

WHY DON'T ALL COUNTRIES HAVE A COMMON FORM OF MONEY?

Money is not a metal coin or a piece of printed paper. It is not a nickel or dollar bill, a French franc, an Italian lira, a Spanish peseta, or a Russian ruble. Why? Because, while these things are used as money, so is a pile of stones on a certain Pacific island.

In other words, all of these things are only symbols. They represent something real. The simplest way to define money is to say that it is a convenient means of exchange and a measure of the value of goods and labor. When a person wants something, he can exchange his form of money for the desired object. He can also exchange his services for money.

Down through history, money has gone through many changes. Cattle was an early form of money. Grain and salt later came into use as money. In early societies around the world, different objects and products were used as money. Later on, coins came to be used, and then—about three hundred years ago—paper money came into general use.

As these more modern forms of money developed, local governments began to control the form of money and its value. Each country had its own form of money—and this is still true today. We simply haven't reached the stage of civilization in the world where all the people, wherever they live, use the same money.

WHAT IS A STOCK?

Stocks and bonds are certificates that business companies sell to the public to raise money. To start a new company, or to buy new equipment for an existing company, usually requires a very large amount of money. To raise the money, the company sells thousands, sometimes millions, of shares of stock.

When a person buys stock in a company, he becomes one of the company's owners. As an owner, a shareholder hopes to receive a dividend, or a share in the company's profits. The amount of the dividend may change from year to year, depending on the kind of business the company has done during the year.

There are two types of stock: common stock and preferred stock. The owner of the common stock has the right to attend the yearly stockholders' meeting and vote for the directors of the company.

Preferred stock is so named because its owners have certain rights that owners of common stock do not have. When dividends are paid, first preference goes to the holders of preferred stocks. The dividends paid on preferred stocks have a set rate, while dividends on common stocks depend on how well the company is doing. If the company goes out of business, holders of preferred stock are paid off before the holders of common stock.

When a person buys stocks or bonds, he buys from another investor. When he sells, he sells to another investor. The marketplace for this selling and buying of stocks is the Stock Exchange.

Stocks are bought and sold through a broker. His business is to buy and sell stocks for investors. The price of stocks may go up or down for a variety of reasons relating to the company concerned, business conditions in general, and so on.

WHAT IS ECOLOGY?

Every living thing has its own way of life. The way of life depends partly on its own form and activities and partly on its environment (surroundings). Every organism (living thing) is affected by all that surrounds it—whether living or nonliving. And in turn each organism has some effect on its surroundings. Each organism is part of a complex web of life.

At the same time, every organism lives as part of a community, or group, of other organisms. These organisms, too, make up part of the surroundings.

Therefore, when we study an animal or plant in its natural surroundings, we are really studying a web of life. A scientist who studies these webs of life is called an ecologist. His subject is ecology, which comes from two Greek words meaning "study of the home, or surroundings."

Ecology studies the relations of living things to the world in which they live and tells us, among other things, how we can most effectively use and conserve our resources. It deals with such things as: How can we make the best use of our land? How can we save our soil, our forests, our wild life? How can we reduce the great losses caused by harmful insects? These are examples of the practical questions the ecologist asks and tries to answer.

HOW WERE THE GREAT LAKES FORMED?

The five Great Lakes together form the greatest connected area of fresh water on earth. In fact, one of them, Lake Superior, is bigger than any other fresh-water lake in the world. The only saltwater lake that is bigger is the Caspian Sea.

The basins of the Great Lakes were probably scooped out by glaciers during the Ice Age. As the glaciers pushed down from the north, the great moving weight of the ice made these valleys deeper and wider.

Then, when the ice melted, it left huge beds of sand, gravel, and rock where the rim of the glaciers had been. These beds blocked what used to be the outlets of the valleys.

THE GREAT LAKES

LAKE SUPERIOR

LAKE MICHIGAN

LAKE HURON

LAKE ONTARIO

LAKE ERIE

At the same time, as the weight of the ice was removed, the land began to rise, beginning in the southwest. This caused the surface of the region to be tilted, so that water flowed from the southwest to northeast. By the time the ice had retreated, all the lakes were draining down this tilt into the St. Lawrence River and the Atlantic Ocean.

What keeps the Great Lakes filled with fresh water? Some streams do drain into them, but most of the rivers in the area flow away from the Great Lakes basin. The main source of supply for the lakes is the ground water that lies close to the surface of this whole region.

The lake beds are like basins that dip below the level of this ground water, and so they are kept filled by seepage and by the flow of many small springs. So the Great Lakes are really like huge drainage ponds or rain pools—and in this way have a constant supply of fresh water.

The combined area of the Great Lakes and their channels is 94.710 square miles.

WHAT IS OLIVE OIL?

The ancient Greeks had a legend that the olive tree was a gift to them from the goddess Athena, which was why they named the city of Athens after her. The boundaries of estates in Greece were marked by olive trees. The tree was to ancient Greeks a symbol of freedom, hope, mercy, prayer, purity, and order. A crown of olive leaves was the reward given to winners at the Olympic games in ancient Greece.

Olive oil has been obtained from the olive and used for many purposes since very ancient times. Before soap was discovered, wealthy Greeks and Romans had the custom of anointing the body with olive oil. In the Mediterranean countries it has been used as we use butter and other fats for cooking.

In ancient times the oil was extracted from olives by crushing the fruit with large stone rollers. After crushing, the mashed olives were put between cloth mats and squeezed.

Today the process has been refined and mechanized. Modern grinders crush the olives. Hydraulic presses squeeze out the oil. The oil is then carefully filtered to clarify it, that is, make it clear and pure. The oil is about 15 to 30 per cent of the total weight of a fresh, ripe olive.

WHAT IS THE HIGHEST MOUNTAIN IN THE WORLD?

First, what is a mountain? A mountain is a part of the earth's surface that stands high above its surroundings. Mountains differ greatly in size and ruggedness. Some are huge, steep masses several miles high. Others are low and gentle. A mountain rises at least 1,000 feet above the surrounding land.

Some mountains are isolated peaks. But more often they are grouped together in a mountain range. Some mountain ranges have hundreds or even thousands of peaks.

Mountains rise not only from land areas but also from the bottom of the sea. In fact, the deep ocean basins hold some of the mightiest mountains on earth. If we would consider the total height of a mountain to include what is below the sea and what is above the sea, the tallest mountain of all would be Mauna Kea on the island of Hawaii. It is 13,796 feet above sea level and 16,000 feet or so below the sea. So its total height of about 30,000 to 32,000 feet would make it the tallest in the world.

The highest mountain above ground is Mount Everest, on the Nepal-China border. It is 29,028 feet high. The second highest is K2 or Mount Godwin Austen in Kashmir. It is 28,250 feet high.

The highest mountain in North America is McKinley, 20,320 feet. The highest in Europe is Mount Elbrus, in the Soviet Union. It is 18,481 feet high. The highest in Africa is Kilimanjaro, 19,565 feet. The highest mountain in South America is Aconcagua, on the Argentine-Chile border, 22,835 feet high. The highest in Australia is Kosciusko, which is only 7,305 feet high.

WHY IS IT COOLER ON TOP OF A MOUNTAIN?

Our atmosphere is divided into layers, each different from the others. The main layers are called the troposphere, the stratosphere, and the ionosphere. Together, they form a blanket several hundred miles thick.

The troposphere is the bottom layer of the atmosphere. This is where we live. Above the United States and southern Canada, the troposphere is about 40,000 feet (nearly eight miles) thick.

Instruments carried aloft in balloons have proved that the temperature drops steadily in the troposphere. The higher one goes into the troposphere the lower the temperature becomes. For each one thousand feet, the temperature drops about 3.5 degrees Fahrenheit.

So when we go up a mountain to the top, we are going up into the troposphere. A mountain that is about a mile high can thus be about 15 degrees cooler in temperature at the top. And there are mountain peaks that are more than five miles (more than 26,000 feet) high! No wonder it's always cold up there. At the top of the troposphere, the temperature is nearly 70 degrees below zero.

The air is always warmest near the earth's surface. The reason is that the sun heats the earth and the earth gives off heat that warms the air. The sun does not warm the atmosphere directly.

WHY DID INDIANS TAKE SCALPS?

Most of us think that only the Indians took scalps, and that the white man would have nothing to do with this practice. But there are some interesting facts concerning scalping.

Scalping means partly cutting and partly tearing off the skin of the head, with the hair attached. The victim could be living or dead. Scalping goes back to very ancient times. It was done by savage and barbarous peoples of Asia and Europe long before it was done by the American Indians.

And among the Indians it was not done by many tribes. For example, the Indians in the Canadian Northwest and along the whole Pacific Coast never practiced scalping.

A scalp was regarded, by those who did this, as a trophy of victory. It was a sign that the scalper had courage and skill in fighting. Among some tribes the scalps were used in religious ceremonies.

When the American colonies were fighting the Indians, many of the colonies offered rewards of money for Indian scalps. In 1724, Massachusetts offered about $500 for each Indian scalp. In 1755, the same colony offered about $200 for the scalps of male Indians over 12 years of age, and about $100 for the scalps of women and children. So this is something in our history not to be proud of.

HAS THE ICE AGE REALLY ENDED?

Ice ages are times when thick sheets of ice have spread over large parts of the continents. The ice sheets form when glaciers of high mountains and polar regions grow to great size.

There have been several ice ages. The last one, often called the Ice Age, began about 2,500,000 years ago. Four times during the Ice Age great sheets of ice advanced over the land and four times they melted and drew back. The last advance ended about 18,000 years ago. About 6,000 years ago the continents of the Northern Hemisphere were once more almost free of ice.

But Antarctica and Greenland did not lose their ice. They are still covered by ice sheets between one and two miles thick. This raises the question: Has the Ice Age really ended, or will glaciers advance again?

Scientists don't have the answer, because it really depends on what causes ice ages. And this is one of the great mysteries of science. There are many theories about what makes the earth's climate become colder and warmer. One is that there are actual changes in the amount of energy given off by the sun from time to time. Another is that dust from volcanic eruptions could cut off large amounts of sunlight from the earth.

Another theory is that changes in the amount of carbon dioxide in the air would cause great climate changes. Or climate changes could be related to changes in the distance between the earth and the sun and in the tilt of the earth's axis. And there are still other theories. So until we know exactly what causes sheets of ice to advance over the land and then melt and draw back, we won't know whether the last Ice Age has really ended.

WHAT IS A FOLK SONG?

Since the beginning of the human race, people have been singing folk songs. There are so many different kinds of folk songs that it is hard to define a folk song. Basically, folk songs tell us how people feel about life.

One type is work songs, sung by workers on plantations and the railroads, songs for building roads, and so on. There are songs about occupations, which are sung at any time. They may be about shepherds, shoemakers, blacksmiths, tailors. They can be about mills and mines—and about cowboys.

Another type of folk song has to do with love and marriage. Songs such as "I know where I'm going," and "Frankie and Johnny," and "Matilda," are examples of this type. Children's songs and games can also be folk songs.

Some folk songs combine fact and fancy and are sung just for fun. They might be nonsense songs or tall tales. A type of folk song—the play-party song

—developed from children's games, such as "London Bridge" and "All Around the Mulberry Bush." There are also folk songs that have to do with animals.

Still another type is the religious folk song. The "spiritual" is one of the most beautiful of this kind. There are also folk songs that have to do with the seasons.

And there are still more: wedding songs, lullabies, songs of mourning, songs of war and military life.

DO ANY CANNIBALS EXIST TODAY?

It is possible that the earliest humans fed on human flesh, as on any other. There is some evidence that cannibalism existed in central Europe in the late ice age, and possibly among the most ancient Egyptians.

At one time cannibalism was customary in most of Polynesia, in New Zealand, and in Fiji. It also occurred in Australia and New Guinea. Most of equatorial Africa had cannibalism at one time. It was also widespread in northern South America and the West Indies.

But cannibalism was seldom practiced only to obtain food. It had to do with warfare, or with the idea that one could acquire the enemy's strength by eating him, or that certain magical things happened when this was done.

As civilization spread throughout the world, cannibalism ended or was prohibited by police and government. During the last few hundred years it has existed only in certain tropical and subtropical areas.

It is probable that cannibalism today occurs only in the most remote districts of New Guinea, perhaps in the northeast Congo, and in certain inaccessible parts of South America.

DID THE VIKINGS VISIT NORTH AMERICA?

The homeland of the Vikings was Denmark, Norway, and Sweden. Starting in A.D. 787, for about 250 years, they explored, discovered, and plundered countries all over Europe. They built cities in Ireland, penetrated all of England, gained a province in France, raided Spain, Italy, and North Africa, established a kingdom in Russia, settled Iceland, and founded a colony in Greenland.

Did they also discover America? There is now evidence that they did. About the year 1000 Leif Ericson sailed west from Greenland with 35 men. They made two landfalls, and finally reached a pleasant place where game, grass, and salmon abounded. They called this Vinland (Wineland).

The site of Vinland was long sought and never found by modern explorers. Many scholars refused to take seriously the old Scandinavian sagas that told of Viking expeditions to the New World—because there was nothing to confirm them. There were no ruins, no buried arms, no stones with inscriptions.

Then, in 1963, a Norwegian explorer, Dr. Helge Ingstad, unearthed on the tip of Newfoundland the remains of nine buildings and a smithy, which were unquestionably Viking in origin.

By modern methods these relics can be dated at about the year 1000, almost five hundred years before the voyage of Columbus. They may have been Leif Ericson's Vinland or they may have been built by other Viking voyagers to the New World. But they are proof that the Vikings did visit America.

WHAT ARE ABORIGINES?

The earliest known inhabitants of a region are the aborigines. They are the people who were there before any new settlers arrived from another part of the world.

The word comes from the Latin *aborigine*, meaning "from the beginning." It was first used by Roman writers to describe the tribes who originally lived in the territory on which Rome developed.

Bushmen are described as the aborigines of South Africa because they occupied the land before Bantu-speaking Negro tribes. The primitive tribal people who occupied Australia before the coming of the Europeans are called the Australian aborigines.

They are probably the best-known aborigines in the world today. The Australian aborigines live mainly inland and in the remote northern coastal areas. They total about 50,000 people. Their ancestors led a nomadic life and wandered about in tribes. Today, fewer than a third of these aborigines live that way.

The Australian aborigines belong to a separate family of man, and are known as Australoids. It is not known how long they have been in Australia. Before they were influenced by the Europeans, they wore no clothes, built no permanent dwellings, cultivated no crops, and lived as nomadic hunters.

Now many of them have organized together to fight for their rights in Australia. They have the right to vote at federal elections and are entitled to all the social benefits available to other Australians.

WHAT IS WITCHCRAFT?

At one time a great many people believed in witches and in witchcraft. A witch was a person of great power and authority, whose goal was to do harm, and who worked with the help of the devil. The mischief that such a person was able to commit was witchcraft.

Witchcraft could be directed against a personal enemy, or even against a community. Even hurricanes and epidemics were thought to be the result of witchcraft. Because people then lived in fear, ignorance, and superstition, witchcraft was an easy way of explaining unforeseen disasters.

Early societies and religions forbade witchcraft on pain of death. The Old Testament says: "Thou shalt not suffer a witch to live." In later times, the Christian churches fought against witchcraft. In 1484, the Pope issued a papal bull formally condemning witchcraft.

Witch hunts took place in the American colonies. Between 1647 and 1663 hundreds of people in Massachusetts and Connecticut were accused of witchcraft, and 14 were hanged. But with the beginning of the 18th century, belief in witches faded. For the first time people began to understand the real causes of the things they had feared—drought, thunder and lightning, mental and physical illness.

WHERE DO METALS COME FROM?

Pure metals are chemical elements. This means that they cannot be broken down into other substances. There are over a hundred chemical elements known, and about 80 of these are metals.

A few metals, such as gold, platinum, silver, and sometimes copper, are found in the earth in their pure state. Most metals, however, are not found free in nature. They are found only in chemical combinations with other elements.

Chemical compounds that are found in nature are called minerals. Minerals that are valuable for the metals they contain are called ores.

The value of an ore depends on how much metal is in the ore and how costly it is to remove the metal from the ore. It also depends on the demand for the metal.

Many processes are used to obtain pure metal from ore. Some ores need to go through only a few steps, while other ores must go through many steps.

When ore comes from the mine, it usually contains large amounts of unwanted material, such as clay and stone. This worthless material is usually removed before the valuable part of the ore is processed further.

Copper and gold were probably the first metals man learned to use. They occur in nature in a free state as well as in ores. Copper was used as long ago as 5000 B.C. Gold was first used some time before 4000 B.C.

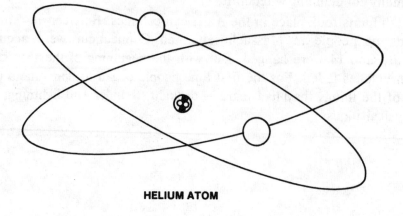

HELIUM ATOM

WHO DISCOVERED ATOMS?

The idea of the atom as the smallest possible particle of any substance goes back to the ancient Greeks. Today we know the atom is not the smallest particle—there are other particles within the atom itself. And we also know that we still don't know a great deal about the atom.

The first man to develop a scientific atomic theory was John Dalton, an English chemist who lived at the beginning of the 19th century. He found that gases, as well as solids and liquids, were made up of unbelievably tiny particles which he (like the ancient Greeks) called atoms. He figured out relative weights for the atoms of those elements with which he was familiar.

At the end of the 19th century, Ernest Rutherford developed the idea of a "solar-system" atom. In an atom there was supposed to be a center, a heavy nucleus carrying a positive charge of electricity, which was surrounded by negatively charged electrons. The electrons traveled around the nucleus like planets around the sun.

Later on, Niels Bohr developed a new theory about the atom. He showed that the electrons could revolve only in certain orbits or energy levels. When electrons moved from one level to another they gave off energy.

But what man knows about the structure of the atom is constantly changing as new experiments give us new information.

WHAT IS THE OZONE LAYER?

Man is becoming more and more aware that things he does in his daily life can have an effect on the climate, the water and food he takes in, the air he breathes, and so on. There is now some concern that things we release into the air can have a harmful effect on "the ozone layer."

What is the ozone layer and why is it important? The earth is surrounded by a thick blanket of air, the "atmosphere." Earth's atmosphere is one of the things that make it a planet of life. It is the air we breathe. It shields us from certain dangerous rays sent out by the sun. It protects the earth from extremes of heat and cold. And it serves us in many other ways.

Our atmosphere is divided into layers, each different from the others. The bottom layer, about ten miles high, is the troposphere. Most of our weather takes shape in the troposphere. The second layer of air, going from a height of ten miles to a height of 30 miles, is the stratosphere.

Somewhere between 12 and 22 miles up, in the middle of the stratosphere, is the "ozone layer." It is a layer of ozone, which is a form of oxygen. Here the winds have died away and the air is warm. It is the ozone that makes the air warm.

This gas absorbs most of the ultraviolet rays sent out by the sun. One result is the band of warm air. But more importantly, the ozone stops most of the ultraviolet rays from reaching the earth. A few of them are good for us, but a large dose would actually broil us alive. So you can see why it is important not to let anything we send into the air have an effect on the ozone layer.

CHAPTER 3
THE HUMAN BODY

WHAT CAUSES AN EARACHE?

There are many different conditions that cause an earache, and even the form of the earache varies a great deal. Aside from mechanical injuries, most earaches arise from some type of bacterial infection.

In many cases an earache is caused by a foreign body that has become trapped in the ear. Children sometimes deliberately put something into their ear or another child's ear.

Sometimes earache is caused by hardened wax in the ear. This, and the removal of any object in the ear, should be done by a physician, because he knows how to avoid injury to the delicate parts of the ear.

Infection of the outer ear may be the result of using unclean hairpins, matches, or other objects to relieve itching of the ear caused by wax. These objects may break the skin and introduce infection. This causes a boil to form, the ear swells up, and there will be painful earaches.

A fungus infection of the outer ear and canal can produce a swelling of the canal which causes pain. Sometimes shooting pains are felt in the ear after a cold or other respiratory infection. The eardrum, which divides the outer ear from the middle ear, may become inflamed.

The middle ear may become infected simply because the person has blown the nose incorrectly. Both nostrils should be blown at the same time, because blowing only one side at a time may force infectious material into the sinuses. And there are many other causes of earaches, too. So it is advisable to see a doctor when one has frequent earaches.

WHAT IS YELLOW FEVER?

Did you know that when the French tried to build a Panama canal, they had to give up chiefly because the construction crews were struck down by yellow fever?

In 1900, Walter Reed discovered the cause of yellow fever and how it was transmitted. As a result, work on the canal was able to be done and the canal was completed in 1914.

Yellow fever is an acute disease in which the patient has fever, jaundice, and vomiting. If it is an isolated case, the attack may be mild and the patient is fairly certain to recover. But if there is an epidemic of yellow fever, as many as 50 per cent of the patients may die.

Yellow fever is caused by a virus which attacks the liver chiefly. The liver cells are extensively damaged, which results in jaundice. In fact, it is the yellow-to-brown color of the skin which gives the disease its name.

The virus is transmitted by mosquitoes. The female mosquito of a certain species sucks the blood of a person with yellow fever during the first three days after that person became infected. After about twelve days, the virus in the mosquito becomes infective. Then, when it bites a person who is not immune to yellow fever, that person will develop the disease.

There is no drug that can cure yellow fever, so prevention is what is important. There is a vaccine that makes people immune to yellow fever. Also, once a person has it, he is immune. And, of course, mosquito control in those areas where yellow fever is found is also a way to prevent it.

WHY IS THERE STILL NO CURE FOR CANCER?

First, what is cancer? Basically, it is when the process of cell division in the body gets out of hand. As the new "wild" cells continue to divide, they form a larger and larger mass of tissue. So cancer is an uncontrolled growth (and spread) of body cells.

Cancer can occur in any kind of cell. Since there are many different kinds of cells, there are many different kinds of cancer. In man alone there are hundreds of different kinds of cancer—so cancer is not one disease but a large family of diseases. This is one of the problems in finding a cure for cancer.

One approach in dealing with the problem of cancer is to learn what agents cause cancer. Scientists also need to know exactly how such agents cause normal cells to produce cancerous cells. In this way they hope to be able to prevent the disease. Other lines of research involve the search for agents to destroy the cancer cells in the body, just as modern antibiotics destroy bacterial cells.

Scientists have found many cancer-causing agents that are chemicals. Steps have been taken by governments to keep such chemicals out of food and to prevent other forms of contact with them. Such actions do help prevent cancer.

Because of the close links between cancer and viruses in certain animals, more and more scientists are coming to believe that many types of cancer are caused by viruses. But exactly how a virus can produce cancer in the human body is still not known.

So the search for the causes of cancer is a difficult one, but much progress is being made. Eventually, it may be discovered that the different kinds of cancer have little in common. Or it may be that all the different agents work in the same way. But at present we still don't know.

WHAT IS CEREBRAL PALSY?

Cerebral palsy is a condition in which the patient has little or no control over the movements of his muscles. It happens when one of the three main areas of the brain that control muscular activity is damaged.

One such area of the brain is called the motor cortex. This is where all movements that are planned and controllable start. When it is damaged, there is stiffness of the muscles.

A group of nerve cells in the brain, called basal ganglia, hold back or restrain certain types of muscle activity. When there is damage in this area, unplanned movements of the muscles occur. It might be slow, squirming, and twisting movements of the arms. Or it may be slight shaking or violent jerking.

The third area of the brain, called the cerebellar area, controls muscle coordination and balance. If this area is injured, there is a lack of balance and clumsiness.

There are many causes of cerebral palsy. The brain may not develop as it should before birth. The mother may be sick or injured during pregnancy. The brain may be injured during birth. Difficulty in breathing at the time of birth may prevent oxygen from getting into the blood and injure nerve cells.

Treatment is a long, slow, and continuous process. The aim of it, which must be realized, is not to restore the child to a normal condition. It is to make the child useful to himself and the world, so that he will be happier. Muscle training is the most valuable way of treating children with cerebral palsy.

HOW DOES THE BRAIN SEND MESSAGES TO THE BODY?

The brain can get signals, add them up, and signal back for action in a split second. Different parts of the brain do different things.

The medulla, at the top of the spinal cord, controls nerves that are in charge of certain muscles and glands. The medulla keeps your heart beating, your lungs taking in air, and your stomach digesting food.

The cerebellum controls body movement and balance. The cerebrum is where thinking, learning, remembering, deciding, and awareness take place. The sensations of seeing, hearing, smelling, tasting, and touching are centered here. So are body feelings.

Scientists still do not understand how the brain does its work. But they have learned that the messages that travel through the nervous system—to and from the brain—are weak electrical charges.

Nerves are made up of nerve cells. A nerve cell consists of a central cell body with a number of threadlike parts reaching out from it. Messages are passed from cell to cell through these threads.

The billions of nerve cells in the body form a huge network that leads toward the spine. Along the way nerves from different parts of the body come together in thick bundles. A thick cable of nerves runs up the hollow of the spine to the brain. One set of nerves in the cable carries messages from the senses to the brain. Another set carries messages from the brain to the muscles and glands. The brain sorts out the signals and makes the right connections.

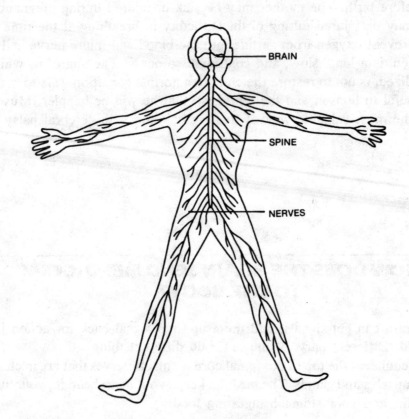

WHY DO WE NEED OXYGEN?

Animals can go for weeks without food, and for days without water. But without oxygen they die in a few minutes.

Oxygen is a chemical element. It is the most abundant element on earth and it is all around you. It makes up about one-fifth of the air (most of the rest of the air is nitrogen).

Oxygen combines with almost all other elements. In living creatures, oxygen is combined with hydrogen, carbon, and other substances. In a human being it accounts for two-thirds of body weight.

At normal temperatures oxygen combines with other elements very slowly. When oxygen combines with other elements, new substances, called oxides, are formed. The combining process is called oxidation.

Oxidation goes on all the time in living creatures. Food is the fuel of living cells. As food is oxidized, energy is released. This energy is used for moving the body and for building new body substances. The slow oxidation in living creatures is often called internal respiration.

In man, oxygen is breathed in through the lungs. From the lungs, oxygen passes into the bloodstream and is carried to all parts of the body. The breathing process supplies the cells with oxygen for respiration. So we need oxygen for the energy to keep the body functioning.

People who have trouble breathing are often placed in oxygen tents. Here the patient breathes in air that is from 40 to 60 percent oxygen. The patient thus uses little energy to get the oxygen he needs.

While oxygen is continually being removed from the air, the supply of oxygen never seems to get used up. Plants give off oxygen as they make food, and this helps keep up the supply of oxygen.

WHAT IS ENDOCRINOLOGY?

Certain organs in the body produce chemical substances that keep the body in proper working order. These chemical substances are called hormones. The group of organs that produce hormones is called the endocrine system. And the study of these organs and hormones is called endocrinology.

The organs of the endocrine system are called "glands of internal secretion" because they send their substances directly into the bloodstream to be distributed throughout the body.

The endocrine glands are: the pituitary, the thyroid, the parathyroids, the adrenals, the testes, the ovaries, part of the pancreas, and the thymus. Some of these produce many hormones and others produce only one.

The endocrine system is responsible for regulating many functions of the body. For example, the rate of growth and final size of the body, the body contour, the distribution of hair, total weight, and the masculine or feminine aspect of the body are all influenced by hormones.

They also regulate the amount of urine produced, the body temperature, the rate of metabolism, the calcium and sugar levels in the blood, the transformation of proteins into energy-giving substances. How they are able to do all this is still not fully understood by experts on the subject.

The reproductive system is especially affected by hormones. And they are also a great factor in the personality of the individual. A person's mental and physical alertness, and masculinity or femininity, are influenced by hormones.

WHAT IS HEMOGLOBIN?

Most of the cells in the blood are red corpuscles. Millions and millions of red cells circulate in the bloodstream.

The red corpuscles contain a protein called hemoglobin. Hemoglobin is a pigment (coloring matter) containing iron. Our blood is red in color because of the combination of hemoglobin and oxygen.

But hemoglobin has a more important function than just giving the blood its color. It has the ability to combine loosely with oxygen. It is this ability that makes it possible for the red corpuscles to deliver oxygen to the cells of the body.

Oxygen is part of the air breathed into the lungs. The red corpuscles in the bloodstream pass through the lungs, where the hemoglobin picks up oxygen. The red corpuscles, traveling through the bloodstream, release oxygen to the body's cells.

When the oxygen is released, hemoglobin takes up carbon dioxide from the cells. This gas is waste that is formed when the cells burn food. The red blood corpuscles, loaded with carbon dioxide, return to the lungs.

Here an exchange takes place. Carbon dioxide is dropped (to be breathed out) and fresh oxygen is picked up. Then the red corpuscles continue on their way, carrying oxygen to cells throughout the body.

This is why foods containing iron are important to our health. Iron stimulates the production of red blood cells and increases the amount of hemoglobin in those cells.

HOW DO WE SWALLOW?

The act of swallowing food is quite a complicated process. It is done by nerves, muscles, ligaments and glands. Included in the process are the larynx, the uvula, the epiglottis, the soft palate, the tongue, lips, nose, lungs, diaphragm, the abdominal muscles, and the brain!

First our teeth cut and grind the food, which is moistened by saliva. The tongue kneads the food into a bolus (a large pill). In the act of swallowing, the soft palate in the back of the mouth is raised so that food won't enter the nose.

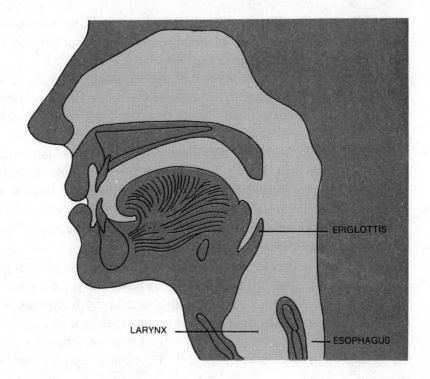

Then the food enters the pharynx. Here the windpipe is open on top. To prevent food from entering the windpipe, the epiglottis, which is at the root of the tongue, comes down to cover the entrance to the windpipe. The bolus then passes into the gullet, or esophagus, which is about ten inches long.

The walls of the gullet consist of muscle fibers, and the food is pushed through the gullet by the contractions of its walls. Liquids pass quickly down the esophagus; a bolus of food takes about eight seconds to go through. So swallowing of food is not a matter of having it fall down into the stomach. It requires muscular action. That's why it's actually possible to eat and drink while hanging with one's head downward.

What makes the muscles contract during swallowing? In the wall of the alimentary canal are nerves which react to the presence of food. The food touches the wall of the canal, stimulates the nerves, and the nerves cause the muscles to contract—pushing the food through.

WHY DO WE SMOKE?

Millions and millions of people know that smoking is believed to be harmful and even dangerous to the health, yet millions and millions continue smoking—or even start smoking. Why?

Experts in various fields say that the beginning of smoking, and the process by which it becomes a habit, are complex and not fully understood. Of course, certain things can be pointed out, as those that get people started on smoking, and others that keep them at it—but the point is that it isn't just a simple matter.

For example, we know that most people start smoking because other people around them do it. Do you know that in the 12th grade, from 40 to 55 percent of children are smokers? By the age of 25, about 60 percent of men and 36 percent of women are smokers. Children feel it makes them seem "adult" to smoke, and other children urge them to smoke, and they see their parents smoking—so they start smoking, too.

The effect that smoking has on a person then acts to strengthen the habit. For example, nicotine has an effect on the heart and the nervous system. Smoking one or two cigarettes causes an increase in the heart rate and a slight rise in blood pressure. The effect on the nervous system is chiefly tranquilizing and relaxing. People want these effects, or feel they need them, or come to depend on having them at certain times and in certain situations—and so they go on smoking.

WHAT ARE PHAGOCYTES?

In the body there are millions of lymph nodes, which are balls of cells surrounded by connective tissue and muscle fibers. The cells that come from the lymph organs are called lymph cells.

But they also have several other names. They are called white blood cells. They are called leukocytes, because they float in the blood as colorless bodies alongside the red blood cells. They are called wander cells, because they wander about through the body.

And they are called phagocytes, which means "scavenger" cells, because they have the ability to ingest foreign bodies. There are about a thousand times as many red blood cells as white cells.

The number of white cells in the blood increases during digestion, after strenuous exercise, during fever, and in the course of various infectious diseases. This is why every complete medical examination includes making a white blood cell count.

The white blood cells, or phagocytes, can be compared to policemen, soldiers, street cleaners, firemen, and first-aid men of the blood. Whenever there is a foreign substance in the body, a dying cell, or some vital activity is disturbed, they go into action.

For example, if a splinter penetrates the skin, it is attacked by a whole army of these cells. They gnaw at it. They secrete digestive substances around it and try to dissolve it. They eat into the tissue around the splinter so it will become liquefied.

This liquefied tissue is called pus. If we have a wound that gives off pus, it is a sign that there is something there which the body wants to remove. A large collection of pus is called an abscess.

WHY DO WE NEED SO MUCH SLEEP?

If we think of the human body as a "machine," it has one big weakness compared to other machines. They can work around the clock. The human machine must have a chance, at regular intervals, to restore tired organs and tissues of the body, to do repair work, and to get rid of wastes that have accumulated during the day. This is done during sleep.

When the body is asleep, everything slows down. The rate of metabolism is at its lowest. The blood pressure drops. The pulse rate is slower. Breathing is slowed down. Even the temperature drops a little.

So the body needs sleep just to "keep going." But how much sleep does a person need? The surprising thing is that it varies with the individual. Of course, babies need more sleep than grownups. But as one grows older, less sleep is required. The one thing that matters is that we should have enough sleep so that when we wake up we are rested and refreshed.

There are some people who say that four hours of sleep a night is all they need, but this is not enough for most people. There are some who are "long sleepers" and seem to need ten or more hours. The great German philospher Kant needed so much sleep that he had his servant wake him up after seven hours and force him to get out of bed—or he would sleep on and on!

By the way, a short sleep—which may last only 15 minutes or a half hour—may be more restful than a long sleep. This is because it is a deep sleep, when our body really relaxes and goes to sleep.

WHAT CHANGES THE RATE OF A HEARTBEAT?

Each beat of the human heart lasts about 0.8 seconds. The heart beats about 100,000 times a day. It also rests an equal number of times between beats. In one year, the heart beats about 40,000,000 times.

The beating of the heart is really a wave of contraction that takes place in the heart to send blood circulating through the body. So the rate of the heartbeat (or pulse rate) depends on the body's need of blood.

Change in the heartbeat is most often caused by work. Here is how this happens. When a muscle begins to function somewhere in the body, it produces carbonic acid. The molecules of carbonic acid are carried by the blood to a certain part of the heart, the right atrium, within ten seconds.

There are cells there that react to the presence of the carbonic acid molecules. And the reaction adjusts the rate of the heartbeat to the carbonic acid content of the blood. If the muscle stops working, and the carbonic acid content of the blood becomes lower, the action of the heart becomes slower.

But the action of the heart is related to the needs of the body as a whole. Mental excitement stimulates a nerve which makes the heart beat faster. When we are depressed or frightened, a different nerve is stimulated, which makes the heart beat slower.

The ordinary person cannot change the rate of his heartbeat by just wanting to do it. But there have been certain people who had this ability. There is the case of one man who was able to make his heart "stand still" so that people thought he was dead—and then was able to make it beat again.

WHY DO ALCOHOLIC BEVERAGES MAKE YOU DRUNK?

Alcohol is a narcotic, which is how we describe a substance which enters the nerve cells quickly and tends to paralyze them. But before any narcotic paralyzes, it stimulates nerve cells, putting them in a state of excitement. So alcohol first acts as a stimulant.

How does alcohol affect the brain? The first effect is a feeling of stimulation. Action and speech seem to be speeded up. The skin gets redder, blood pressure rises, the heart beats faster, and breathing is quickened.

But alcohol soon exerts a depressing effect on the brain. Our ability to observe, think, and pay attention is affected. As the higher functions of the brain are paralyzed, the power to control moods is lost.

Another serious effect is that inhibitions are relaxed. In our body nerve fibers called inhibitory fibers act as brakes in the nervous system. They are developed as the result of education and training, and make us disciplined, restrained people.

Under the influence of alcohol, these inhibitory fibers are paralyzed. Our controls become relaxed, our judgment is unclear, and we are ready to say and do things that we would never do if our minds were normal. Alcohol has produced a state of drunkenness!

Since alcohol does first act as a stimulant, if it is taken into the body in weak solutions, it will continue to act as a stimulant rather than as a narcotic.

WHAT CAUSES GOUT?

Gout is a disease that has been known since ancient times. At one time it was thought of as a "rich man's disease." This was because it was believed that gout was caused by eating too much and drinking too much wine—and, of course, this couldn't be done by poor people.

Gout is a condition of having too much uric acid in the blood. A person who has gout is unable to metabolize, or break down, certain proteins taken into the body. These proteins are called "purines" and are obtained from the diet of the person.

Among the foods with a high purine content are: sweetbreads, liver, kidney, sardines, anchovies, turkey, pork, beef, and many others. So a person with gout is usually advised by his doctor to avoid such foods.

Gout is a very painful disease, and the pain seems to come very suddenly. In 70 per cent of the cases, the first attack is in the large toe, and in 90 per cent of the cases the large toe is involved eventually.

Within hours, the joint swells, becomes hot, red, and tender. It hurts so much that a person with gout is very much afraid of being touched on the painful part. This feeling is typical of a patient with gout.

The acute condition lasts a few days or weeks, and then disappears completely—until the next attack. A person who is subject to attacks of gout may have them brought on not only by his diet, but by such things as physical strain, overwork, emotional strain, and allergy.

WHAT GIVES FOOD ITS TASTE?

The whole process of tasting is actually quite a complicated thing. First, we start with the taste buds, tiny wart-like bumps on the tongue called "papillae." An individual has about three thousand taste buds.

We taste when the molecules in a fluid strike the hairs in the taste buds and produce a reaction. Only substances in solution, where the atoms move about freely, can be tasted. A glass ball, for example, has no taste.

Anything that makes atoms move faster intensifies taste. Heat does this, and that's why hot coffee has a more bitter taste than cold coffee, why salt pork is saltier when it is warm, and why meat tastes better when it is hot.

Our taste buds register three or four different sensations: sweet, salt, bitter, and perhaps also sour. Different parts of the tongue are more sensitive to different tastes. The back of it is more sensitive to bitter, the sides to sour and salt, the tip to sweet.

Since almost all our foods are composed of various substances, they produce mixed sensations of taste. An apple is sour and sweet. And the taste sensation itself is a mixed sensation. There is no pure taste. We experience pressure, cold, heat, odor impressions as we taste. The combination of many sensations results in what we call the taste of food. And at least half of what we think of as "taste" is really odor! Coffee, tea, tobacco, apples, oranges, lemons, and other things really stimulate the sense of smell, as we enjoy them more than the sense of taste.

HOW FAST DOES OUR BLOOD FLOW?

Blood doesn't flow through the human body the way water flows through a regular series of pipes. The vessels through which blood is pumped out of the heart to all parts of the body are the arteries. But the arteries that are some distance from the heart keep on dividing and dividing until they become tiny vessels called capillaries. And the blood flows much more slowly through these vessels than it does through arteries.

Capillaries are fifty times thinner than a human hair, so that the blood corpuscles pass through them in single file. It takes a quantity of blood about one second to flow through a capillary.

Blood is constantly flowing through the heart. It takes about 1.5 seconds for a given quantity of blood to pass through the heart. Blood flows from the heart to the lung and back to the heart. This takes about 5 to 7 seconds.

Blood flows from the heart to the brain and back to the heart. This takes about eight seconds. The longest trip the blood has to make is from the heart through the trunk and the legs to the toes and then back to the heart. This takes about 18 seconds.

The time required for the blood to circulate through the entire body—that is, from the heart to the lung to the heart to the body to the heart—is about 23 seconds.

But the condition of the body has an effect on how fast the blood flows. For example, fever or work can increase the number of heartbeats and make the blood flow twice as fast. A single blood cell makes about three thousand round trips through the body's circulation in one day.

WHAT VITAMINS DO WE NEED?

The answer is simple: we need them all. When we don't get a particular vitamin, the conditions that result are known as deficiency diseases.

Vitamins are very different from each other in structure. But each vitamin is a substance that the body cannot manufacture, but must have. So a vitamin is essential for some vital function of the body and must be supplied by food.

Here is a brief description of what vitamins do for us. Vitamin A is essential for growth, for vision, and for healthy skin and mucous membranes. It is supplied by milk and milk products, eggs, liver, fruits and vegetables.

Vitamin B1 (thiamin) makes possible the proper use of carbohydrates and is required by the nerves. It is found in whole-grain bread, milk, vegetables, beans, nuts, and pork. Vitamin C prevents scurvy and is essential for healthy teeth, gums, and blood vessels. It is obtained from fresh fruits and vegetables.

A vitamin called niacin is needed to prevent pellagra, a disease that causes great suffering in undernourished people. It is supplied by meat, vegetables, and whole-grain cereals. Vitamin D prevents rickets. It is manufacutred in the body through the action of sun on skin. Vitamin D is now made synthetically in chemical factories and is often added to the milk you buy.

Other vitamins such as E and K and riboflavin have been isolated. Each one has a special duty to perform. That's why one should have a well-balanced diet to ensure an adequate intake of all vitamins.

WHY IS HAIR DIFFERENT COLORS?

Our hair has a very interesting structure. It develops from the horn layer of the skin, actually growing downward. It strikes root and then shoots upward through the layers of the skin.

Hair, like the epidermis from which it is derived, has a tissue of cells which form the "soil" in which it grows, and a horny shaft which is nourished and pushed upward by this "soil."

Among the cells at the root of the hair are cells that contain a pigment called melanin. These cells (like the others) multiply and move upward with the hair shaft as it grows. They die and leave the granules of pigment in the hair.

The pigment granules are all shades of brown, from a reddish color to a deep black-brown. The horn substance of the hair, in which the pigment is embedded, is yellow. The color of the horny material and that of the pigment granules mix together. And that's how all the different colors of human hair develop, from blond to black. Our genes, which we inherit, help decide what shades the pigment granules will be, and so what the color of our hair will be.

The average person has from 300,000 to 500,000 hairs in his skin. Blond persons have finer hair and more hairs than others. Dark persons have coarser hair and about a quarter less hair. Red-haired persons have the coarsest hair and the fewest hairs.

Your hair grows at the rate of about half an inch a month. And it grows at a different rate at various times of the day.

WHAT MAKES HAIR CURLY?

Hair is the slender, threadlike strands that grow out of the skin. There are many kinds of hair. Hair may be thick or fine, long or short. It may be white or colored. It may be straight, wavy, or curly.

Scalp hair is not the same among the many peoples of the world. Oriental people generally have hair that is quite straight. The Negro has tightly curled hair. The hair of Caucasians, or members of the white race, can be straight, slightly curly, or very curly.

So the color, curliness, and thickness of a person's hair are inherited. A person is born with a certain structure and type of hair. But there is something about the structure of hair that determines whether it will be curly or not.

Imagine that you cut across a shaft of straight hair and a shaft of curly hair, as you might cut across two tree trunks. If you were to look at the cut section of straight hair under the microscope, you would see that it is round. The cut section of curly hair is oval or flat. The flatter the hair is, the more easily it bends and the curlier it is.

The color of a person's hair depends largely upon a substance called melanin. Melanin is a pigment, or coloring matter. It is contained in the hair cells at the time they are formed in the root. It is the amount of this coloring in the cells that makes hair dark or light.

As people grow older, there is less and less melanin in the newly formed cells. That's why the hair gradually turns gray or white.

WHY DO WE GET SUNBURNED?

Most of us have no idea of the many ways in which light from the sun affects us. For example, sunlight destroys fungi and bacteria that may have settled on the skin. The action of sunlight on the skin produces a substance which contracts the blood vessels of the skin and thus raises the blood pressure. Ultraviolet light from the sun produces vitamin D in our bodies.

And one of the other things sunlight does to our skin is create the condition we call sunburn. There is a substance in the skin called histidin. Ultraviolet light from the sun transforms histidin into a substance that dilates the blood vessels, causing the skin to become red.

How do we get a "suntan"? The skin also contains a substance called tyrosin. Ultraviolet light acts on tyrosin and transforms it in the brown pigment called melanin. This melanin is deposited in the outside layers of the skin and makes it look "tanned." The melanin acts to protect the skin against further action of the light rays.

Because sunlight affects our skin and our body in so many ways, a person should be very careful in taking "sun baths." Did you know that if you expose only your feet to the sun's rays, you can raise the blood pressure, produce vitamin D that will go to the bones of the body, and so on?

Most people can't be bothered to do it right, but the healthiest way to take sun baths is very gradually. This would be exposing only one-fifth of the body for five minutes the first day, another fifth of the body for ten minutes the second day, and so on.

WHERE DO WARTS COME FROM?

Many people have superstitions about warts. They believe that if you handle toads, you get warts. Or that certain animals can pass them on to you.

None of this is true. You can't get warts by handling toads, and while dogs and cattle do have warts, there is no animal that passes warts on to human beings.

Warts are caused by a virus, which is a very small germ. This virus may be picked up by contact with others who have the virus.

A wart is usually a small raised area of the skin which is quite rough or pitted on the surface. It is flesh-colored or slightly darker than the normal skin. Since the wart is caused by a virus, it can be spread by scratching it and spreading the virus on the skin. That's why there are sometimes many warts on the skin.

Most warts disappear after a year or two. But there is really no guarantee that they won't spread or continue on and on. That's why it's a good idea to see a doctor about the warts.

In treating the patient for warts, the doctor usually uses some form of local medication, or he may inject special preparations into each wart. When there is constant pressure on a wart, such as those on the palms or soles, the problem becomes a bit more serious. The wart may become quite hardened and have to be removed.

HOW ARE BACTERIA USEFUL TO MAN?

When you say "bacteria," most people think of germs that are harmful and cause disease. But the fact is that there are over two thousand different kinds of bacteria, and most of them are either harmless or helpful to other forms of life—including man.

Bacteria cause the decay of dead plants and animals, both on land and in water. Without such bacteria the earth would be covered with dead matter. While eating, the bacteria break down the complicated substances in these organisms into simpler ones. The simpler substances are then restored to the soil, water, and air in forms that can be used by living plants and animals.

Bacteria play an important part in the digestive processes of man and other animals. There are a great many in the human intestine. As the bacteria eat, they break down foods. At the same time, they make certain vitamins, which the body then uses.

Bacteria are a vital link in the food chain that supports life. Some bacteria, called nitrogen-fixing bacteria, live in the soil and help change nitrogen into substances that plants can use. Man depends on such plants for food.

Bacteria are responsible for the fermentation process by which such products as cheese and vinegar are made. The same fermentation is also used in industry to make substances essential for paints, plastics, cosmetics, candy, and other products. It is also used to make certain drugs. In other industries bacteria are used in curing tobacco leaves, in tanning hides, in eating away the outer covering of coffee and cocoa seeds, and in separating certain fibers for the textile industry. So you see in how many ways bacteria are useful to man. And there are still many more ways they are used and will be used in the future!

CHAPTER 4
HOW THINGS ARE MADE

WHAT CAUSES CEMENT TO HARDEN?

Cement is one of the most useful materials in modern building. By itself, it is a soft powder. But when it is mixed with water and allowed to harden, cement can bind sand or gravel into a hard, solid mass.

Cement is used chiefly as an ingredient of mortar and concrete. Mortar is a mixture of cement, sand, and water. Concrete is the same mixture with gravel or broken stone added to it.

Modern cement is made by heating a mixture of limestone and clay or slag to a very high temperature. This mixture is heated until large, glassy cinders—called "clinkers"—are formed. The clinkers are then ground to powder.

When water is added to the cement powder, a very complicated chemical reaction takes place. The result is a durable artificial stone that will not dissolve in water.

What is this chemical reaction? What takes place that enables the cement to harden?

Chemists are still not sure of the exact answer. There are four major compounds in the cement, and it is believed that each of these compounds, when water is added, becomes crystals. These crystals interlock—and the result is the hardened cement.

The kind of cement that will harden under water is called hydraulic cement. An amazing thing is that the Romans discovered how to make a type of hydraulic cement in the 2nd or 3rd century B.C. by mixing volcanic ash with lime. This discovery was one of Rome's outstanding achievements.

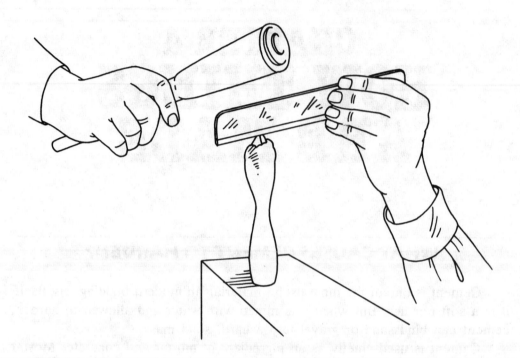

HOW CAN A DIAMOND BE CUT?

If a diamond is the hardest substance known, how can a diamond be cut? It is possible to do it because of two things: the structure of a diamond, and the way the cutting is done.

A diamond is highly crystallized carbon. The carbon atoms that make up a diamond have a geometrical arrangement. This means it is possible to cleave a diamond parallel to the planes in which the atoms are arranged and get smooth flat faces.

To cleave a diamond, a small diamond fragment is used as the cutting tool. A small groove is cut into one of the edges of the crystal. Then a thin, blunt-edged knife, or "cleaving iron," is positioned in the groove. A sharp blow is struck on this and the diamond crystal breaks apart. This is often done with large diamonds in order to remove flaws, or get a shape that provides more brilliancy, or to get more usable weight from the original stone.

In sawing or cutting a diamond, it is also necessary to go only in certain directions. A diamond is sawed by a thin phosphor bronze disk with its edge impregnated with diamond dust mixed in oil. In other words, it takes diamond to cut diamond. The saw revolves very fast, but it cuts the stone slowly.

The "facets," or little faces of a diamond, are ground on a high-speed cast-iron wheel impregnated with the same combination of diamond dust and oil.

Diamond cutting is a very skillful art which requires years of training.

WHAT IS A DETERGENT?

A detergent is a substance that makes things clean. So soap is really one kind of detergent. But when we say "soap," we usually mean a cleaning agent made from natural materials. And when we say "detergent," we usually mean a detergent made of synthetic materials.

Synthetic detergents are put together from many different chemicals by complicated processes. Petroleum, fats, coal tar, and other materials go into the complex formulas of these detergents. They are manufactured in chemical plants with special equipment. The ingredient in the detergent that does the actual cleaning is called the surface-active agent—surfactant, for short.

Surfactants can be made from a wide variety or raw materials, including petroleum, animal fats, and vegetable oils. The chemical processes involved are quite complicated. For example, animal fat may be treated with a series of different chemicals—an alcohol, hydrogen gas, sulfuric acid, and an alkali—to make one surfactant that is being used.

The surfactant must be mixed in a crutcher with other chemicals that help it remove dirt more thoroughly and keep the dirt from settling back on the cleaned material. Special bleaches, coloring, and suds stabilizers may also be added.

What has made synthetic detergents popular is that they produce suds in any kind of water, hard or soft, hot or cold; and they don't produce the curds that cause "bathtub ring." Today, about 90 percent of the packaged dishwashing and laundry products used in homes in the United States are synthetic detergents. Soap is still the most popular type of detergent for personal uses.

HOW ARE COLORS FORMED?

Light from the sun or from any very hot source is called white light. But that white light is really a mixture of light of all colors. This can be seen when light passes through a glass prism and is dispersed. We then see all the colors—red, orange, yellow, green, blue, and violet.

What creates the different colors? Color is determined by the wavelength of light. The wavelength of light corresponds to the distance between one crest and the next in a wave traveling on water. But the wavelengths of light are so small, they are measured in millionths of an inch.

The shortest visible waves are violet, with a wavelength of about 15 millionths of an inch. The longest are red, with a wavelength of about 28 millionths of an inch. In between are all the colors of the spectrum, and each shade has its own wavelength.

Most of the colors we see are not of a single wavelength, but are mixtures of many wavelengths. Purple is a mixture of red and violet; brown is a mixture of red, orange, and yellow. Different shades of any color can be made by adding some white light; for instance, a mixture of red and white is pink.

Why does a piece of cloth have a certain color when we look at it? When white light falls on an object, some wavelengths are reflected and the rest are absorbed by the material. A piece of red cloth absorbs almost all the wavelengths except a certain range of red colors. These are the only ones that are reflected to our eye—and so the cloth looks red.

WHAT IS A PHOTOELECTRIC CELL?

There are many types of photoelectric cells, and they are used for many things. One of the most familiar ones is when a door seems to open by itself when we approach it, as we often see at airports. This happens because our body blocks a beam of light and a photoelectric cell makes the door open.

Light is a form of energy. When light strikes certain chemical substances, such as selenium and silicon, its energy causes a push on the electrons in the substances.

If two different substances happen to be touching one another, some of the electrons may leave one substance and enter the other. Suppose an outside wire is attached to these substances so as to make a path for the electrons. Then, as long as light shines on the chemical substances, a continuous flow of electrons will take place through the substances and the wire.

Such a flow of electrons is an electric current. The entire path that the electrons travel along is called an electric circuit. A device that produces or increases the strength of an electric current when light shines on it is called a photoelectric cell.

Photoelectric cells are used in many ways. For example, solar batteries, placed in satellites and spacecraft, are a number of photoelectric cells connected together. In an exposure meter used on cameras, a dial is connected to a circuit that has a tiny photoelectric cell. The dial registers the amount of current flowing through the circuit. This tells how much light is shining on the cell.

CAMERA EXPOSURE METER

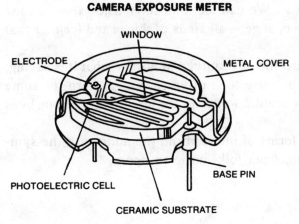

WINDOW

ELECTRODE

METAL COVER

BASE PIN

PHOTOELECTRIC CELL

CERAMIC SUBSTRATE

DOOR ENTRY

BEAM OF LIGHT

WHAT IS MUSIC?

Suppose you hit a wooden table with your hand. It makes a sound. Now suppose you hit a bell. It makes a sound. The second sound is called a tone. A tone is a single musical sound.

Music is the art of organizing tones into meaningful patterns of sound. We might call it the language of tones. Sometimes the language of music speaks to us in tones sounding after one another in melody. Or the tones could be sounding together in harmony.

When tones clash with one another, it is called dissonance. But this clashing is often full of meaning. What we call melody is given meaning by its rising or falling or moving straight ahead. It is also given meaning by its rhythm of beats and phrasing, its speed or tempo, and how loud or soft it is at any moment.

All of this sounds very technical, or mechanical. But it doesn't have to be understood or thought about for us to enjoy music. What music means to us can often not be put into words. We can feel that the music expresses joy or sorrow, gaiety, tenderness, love, anger—all kinds of things and feelings that words alone could never do.

Music can also be enjoyed just for its beauty, and not for what it is saying. We can get pleasure from even a single tone of voice, violin, horn, or some other instrument. We may love a beautiful melody for many years of our lives and always enjoy hearing it.

There are, of course, many forms of music, from the anthem to the symphony; and many types of music, from folk music to opera.

WHAT IS IRRIGATION?

Irrigation is the artificial application of water to land in order to increase the growth and production of plants.

In ancient times, irrigation was a natural process. For example, the annual flooding of the Nile River spread a thin layer of silt (mud) across the land. At the same time, the land received enough water so that crops could be grown.

Where irrigation was a natural process, people sometimes built canals, reservoirs, and drainage ditches. Floodwaters could then be directed where needed or stored for future use. This was the earliest form of man-made irrigation.

Today, in order to supply enough water for irrigation, costly dams and reservoirs are needed. Irrigation water may be so expensive that only good land can be irrigated profitably. Only such crops as vegetables and fruits can produce enough income to cover the costs.

The kind of irrigation used depends on the type of crops grown. Occasional flooding may be enough for hay, pasture, and the small grains. Furrow distribution (spreading water in ditches between rows) may be required for such crops as sugar beets and vegetables. In some cases, underground pipes with overflow standpipes are used.

Irrigation is not done only in dry lands. In Asia, irrigation is needed to raise rice, because rice fields must be covered with water at all times, until the rice crop is ready to harvest. In some parts of the world, supplemental irrigation is used. Pipes and sprinklers carry water to where it is needed most. This may save a valuable crop from serious damage by drought.

HOW IS CARBON-14 USED TO DATE OBJECTS?

All living things contain carbon. They also contain small amounts of carbon-14, a radioactive variety of carbon. Using carbon-14, scientists can determine the age of wood and clothing—in fact, anything that was once alive. Dating an object by means of carbon-14 is called radiocarbon dating. Radiocarbon dating is used to date objects up to 50,000 years old.

The rate at which a radioactive element breaks down is described by its half-life. An element's half-life is the time in which half the element's atoms break down.

Carbon-14 has a half-life of about 5,500 years. This means that about 5,500 years after a plant or animal dies, half the carbon-14 atoms present at the time of death are left. After 11,000 years, one quarter of the original carbon-14 atoms are left, and after 16,500 years, about an eighth of the original amount, and so on.

Suppose an old piece of wood is found in an ancient tomb. In the laboratory it can be heated and turned to carbon, or burned to release various gases, including carbon dioxide. The carbon or the carbon dioxide contains a few carbon-14 atoms. These atoms of carbon-14 are breaking down. With each breakdown a tiny particle is sent speeding out of the atom.

The carbon or the carbon dioxide is placed in a sensitive instrument—called a Geiger counter—which detects the particles given off by the atoms of carbon-14. From the number of particles given off, scientists can determine the amount of carbon-14 in the sample.

Scientists know how much carbon-14 is contained in an equal amount of wood from a living tree. From the amount of carbon-14 left in the ancient sample, scientists can tell its age. For example, if the ancient sample contained half the original amount, it would be about 5,500 years old.

WHAT IS AN AUTOPSY?

Quite often we read in the papers that an autopsy has been performed on a person who died from a disease, or from unknown causes, or who was murdered.

An autopsy is the examination of the body after death. Its purpose is to try to determine the cause of death. It is done by inspecting the organs of the body, and by making microscopic and chemical studies of pieces of tissue removed from the body.

Permission for an autopsy must be granted by the nearest of kin. It is similar to a surgical operation and is performed by medical personnel. An autopsy is performed in such a way that there will be minimal disturbance of the body. There is no visible evidence of an autopsy when memorial services are held for the person.

Why are autopsies done? Sometimes a doctor doesn't know the exact cause of a person's death. An autopsy can clarify this problem and might save someone's life in a future situation of the same kind.

An autopsy might reveal something about a disease that could be important to save the lives of surviving relatives. Sometimes an autopsy is done to identify a dead person who cannot be identified in any other way. An autopsy can help establish the time of death, which can be important when the person died from unknown causes or because of an act of violence.

Autopsies performed hundreds of years ago enabled man to begin to know about the human body and started the science of anatomy.

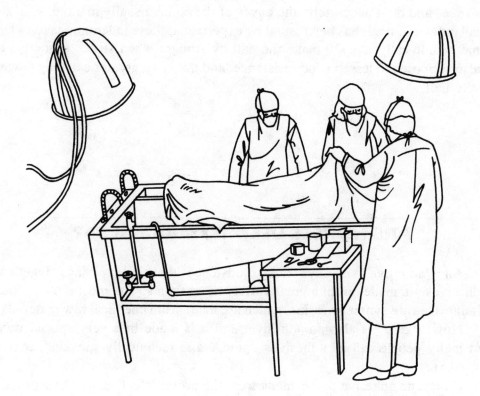

WHY DO GOLF BALLS HAVE HOLES?

To begin with, those are not "holes" in golf balls. They are small indentations, called dimples.

Like any sport, golf has certain rules and regulations. These also apply to the balls used. A golf ball is about half the size of a baseball or tennis ball.

But it just can't be any size. United States rules provide that a golf ball shall not weigh more than 1.62 ounces nor be less than 1.68 inches in diameter.

In Great Britain and most other Commonwealth nations, the rules allow for a slightly smaller ball.

Early in the history of golf, the balls were made of heavy leather, stuffed with feathers. Today the ball is made by winding strip rubber tightly around a core and covering it with a hard, rubberlike composition material.

Since one of the objectives of the game is to be able to hit the ball a long distance, and do it accurately, the cover of the ball is usually marked with the small indentations. It has been found by experts that these indentations (or what some people call "holes") make the ball fly straight when struck properly. It is also supposed to lessen wind resistance, and thus give greater carrying power to the ball.

ARE HORSES USED TO MAKE GLUE?

An "adhesive" is any sticky substance that holds things together. Adhesives are made out of a great variety of materials. The most modern kind of adhesives are synthetic resins, which are made from chemical raw materials.

Now, "glue" is also an adhesive, and it is made in a very special way. But many people call all adhesives "glue," and technically speaking, that is not correct.

Glue is an adhesive that is made from the protein "collagen." This protein is the chief thing found in the connective tissues of animals and fish. The chief way of obtaining the raw material for glue is by boiling animal hides and bones. And so that would include the bones and hides of horses (as well as other animals) when the animals have died. Actually, the bones of the animals make one kind of glue, and the hides make another.

The need for adhesives by man goes back to very ancient times. Primitive man used resins and plant gums to stick things together. But glue—the animal kind—has also been known for thousands of years. As far back as 1500 B.C., the Egyptians used glue to join pieces of wood.

The biggest change in the history of adhesives came with the development of the synthetic resins in the 1930's. They proved to be stronger and more durable than the natural adhesives, and they stood up against water, mold, and fungi as well. (Animal glue dissolves easily in hot water.) Today's synthetic adhesives are so strong that they are used in bonding the metal skins of some airplanes and missiles.

HOW CAN THE DISTANCE TO A STAR BE MEASURED?

Most stars are very large, yet to us they look like points of light. This is because they are so far away from the earth. In fact, while we can measure the distance to stars, we cannot really imagine how great that distance is.

The stars are so far away that the distance to them is measured in light-years, not in miles. One light-year is the distance that light travels in one year—nearly 6,000,000,000,000 (trillion) miles.

The closest star that can be seen with the unaided eye is just over four light-years away. Its name is Alpha Centauri. If the sun (which is a star) were as far away from the earth as Alpha Centauri, the sun would also look like a point of light.

Here is one way astronomers can estimate the distance to a star. They observe the star from two positions that are a known—and very large—distance apart. For example, they may observe the star from opposite sides of the earth. Or they may make observations a half year apart, when the earth is at opposite sides of its path around the sun.

When they do this, the star appears to have changed its position. This apparent change in position is called parallax. By measuring a star's parallax, an astronomer can calculate how far away the star is.

Because the stars are far away, they must be studied with telescopes. Through telescopes astronomers have observed and photographed hundreds of millions of stars. The most distant objects that can be seen through telescopes are thousands of millions of light-years away.

HOW ARE RAISINS MADE FROM GRAPES?

Raisins are small, very sweet grapes that have been carefully dried in the sun. There aren't too many regions in the world where grapes can be produced. The reason is that when the grapes are ripe, there must be many weeks of hot, rainless weather in which the grapes can dry.

There are regions near the Mediterranean, parts of Spain and Greece, and areas in Asia Minor that have the required climate; so do parts of southern Australia.

The San Joaquin and Sacramento valleys of California are ideal for making raisins, and lead the world in production. The drying season, from August to November, is hot and rainless, while the nearby mountains provide water for irrigation during the growing season.

In California, the grapes ripen in August. They are cut from the vines and allowed to lie in trays between the rows for from two to three weeks. Then they are put in boxes and allowed to dry some more. Then they are taken to the packing plant.

Here they are carried on conveyors to go through the process which prepares them for market. Special machinery removes stems and dirt from the grapes. Then the grapes are washed, steamed, or soaked in special solutions. Then they are dried and packed. About three-fourths of the original weight of the grapes is lost in drying them to make raisins.

Seedless raisins are made from the Sultana grape and from the Sultanina, both of which types grow in California.

WHAT IS LEATHER?

Leather is an animal hide or skin that has been tanned, or treated. The word "hides" is usually used to denote skins of large animals, as in cowhide or horsehide. The word "skins" is usually used for the smaller animals, as in goatskin or pigskin.

Cattle hides are the single most important source of leather raw materials. Calfskin leather is finer grained and lighter in weight that cattle hide. It is used for the most expensive shoes and handbags. The skin of any goat, old or young, is known as kidskin. Most suede leathers are kidskins buffed on the side that originally was next to the flesh.

The hide of the horse is used for shoes, jackets, and sports equipment. Pigskin leather is produced from hogs. The kangaroo provides the strongest of all leathers. It is used for track and baseball shoes. Alligator leather is used for shoes, handbags, wallets, and luggage. Even the skins of snakes and lizards are used as leathers for shoes, bags, and luggage.

Tanning turns animal hides and skins into soft, flexible leather. Tannin, the bark extract used in tanning, causes a chemical reaction. Different types of leathers are produced by slight changes in the chemical processes.

Before the hides are tanned, they must be preserved, or "cured." This is done in the packing house by salting the skins to prevent rotting. After the leather has been tanned, waxes, resins, shellac, or other chemicals are applied to make it shinier. Dyes are used to add color. The application of enamel paint called japan, or of plastics, gives patent leather its shiny surface. Suede leather is made when the underside of the leather is buffed or sandpapered to produce a nap.

HOW DO ESKIMOS BUILD IGLOOS?

To most of us the word "igloo" means a house built from snow. But "igloo," or "iglu," is the Eskimo word for shelter. An igloo need not be made of snow. It can be a tent, a schoolhouse, a church, or even a railroad station. Only the Eskimo of Canada and northern Greenland ever build snow houses, and these are used only in winter.

A snow igloo is called an "apudyak." It is made of frozen snow—not ice—which is carved into neat blocks. Snow has hundreds of air spaces, and this is what provides excellent insulation against cold weather.

An Eskimo can build a snow house quite quickly. Blocks of snow are cut about two feet long, eighteen inches high, and five inches thick. These are set on edge slanting inward to form a circle ten or twelve feet across. The blocks spiral upward and inward to form a dome. A small "breathing hole" is left open at the top of the igloo. Snow and ice platforms inside the igloo are covered with animal skins. Sometimes several snow houses are built together with connecting tunnels. Eskimo families can visit each other without stepping out into the cold.

Eskimos of Alaska never built snow houses. Their winter houses were partly underground. A white settler in Alaska once showed his young daughter how to build a snow igloo. His Eskimo neighbors were all amazed—they had never seen a snow igloo before!

HOW CAN A HELICOPTER HOVER IN SPACE?

A helicopter can fly in any direction: forward, backward, to the side, or straight up. It can even hover over a single spot. To understand how this is done, we must understand how a helicopter flies.

As the rotor blades of a helicopter slice through the air, the air beneath the blades has greater pressure than the air above them. This pushes the blades up and creates lift.

The wings of an airplane create lift in the same way. In fact, the rotor blades of the helicopter are really moving wings. The difference is that the whole airplane has to move forward in order to get lift, while the helicopter needs only to move its rotor blades through the air. This is what enables a helicopter to go straight up or down or hover over one spot.

In front of the pilot in a helicopter there is the "cyclic stick" or go-stick. He moves it in the direction he wants to go and the helicopter flies that way. The cyclic stick works by changing the pitch of one blade at a time as it passes one side of the helicopter. This means that one side of the disc—the circle made by the whirling blades—has more lift than the other, and the disc tilts.

When the disc is flat, the helicopter hovers because all the lift force is straight up, keeping the helicopter in the air. If the disc is tilted, most of the force is still up, keeping the helicopter in the air, but some of the force pushes slightly forward, backward, or to the side, and the helicopter moves in that direction as a result.

WHY DOES SILVER TARNISH?

Silver is a precious metal with remarkable qualities. It has been known and used by mankind before the dawn of history.

Silver conducts electricity and heat better than any other metal. Silver is the whitest of all metals. It reflects light better than other metals, which is why it is used as the backing material for mirrors.

Silver is also very easy to shape. Only gold can be worked with greater ease. Pure silver is very soft. Therefore, to increase its usefulness, small amounts of other metals are added to it. Sterling silver is 92½ percent silver and 7½ percent copper.

People who own objects made of silver often get annoyed because the silver begins to tarnish. The reason for this is that silver reacts very strongly to sulphur and many sulphur compounds.

With sulphur and hydrogen sulphide it forms black silver sulphide—and we notice this as the tarnishing or blackening of our silverware. The sulphur may be contained in certain foods, such as eggs, or by the tiny amounts of sulfurated hydrogen in the air. When buildings are heated by coal or oil, this can produce that effect in the air.

Silver is sometimes found in nature as native, or solid, metal. But more often it is combined with other metals and non-metals in mineral ores.

HOW IS BUTTER MADE?

Most butter sold in the markets today is made in creameries that buy milk and cream from many farmers.

After the cream is unloaded, it is pasteurized. Most butter is made from sweet cream. Sometimes a starter—lactic-acid-producing bacteria mixed with other organisms—is added to the cream. The starter causes the cream to ripen. Some coloring is usually added, too.

Then the churning begins. It is done by a revolving drum that shakes the cream back and forth until it is a grainy mass. Churning takes about an hour. The buttermilk is then rinsed off by spraying the butterfat with water. What is left is butter.

The churn is filled with water and rotated for a few seconds to wash the butter. Salt is sometimes added. The butter is then kneaded mechanically until it has the right texture and the proper amount of moisture. The butter is then smooth and firm and ready for packaging.

Butter is usually packed in bulk containers weighing about sixty pounds and shipped to central markets. There it is repackaged into smaller pound or quarter-pound boxes or bars.

Butter has been made by man since the earliest times. It is mentioned in the Bible many times. In Proverbs 30:33: "Surely the churning of milk bringeth forth butter.'' The Hindus used butter as long ago as 900 B.C., and it was often a part of their religious ceremonies.

WHY DOES SWISS CHEESE HAVE HOLES?

We enjoy different kinds of cheeses because they have different flavors. The flavor of most cheese develops while it is curing. Curing takes place when the cheese is held in storage under carefully controlled conditions of temperature and moisture.

During curing, harmless bacteria, yeasts, and molds are allowed to grow in or on the cheese to develop its flavor and odor. For example, many different microorganisms grow in cheddar cheese to give it a distinctive cheddar taste. Other kinds of bacteria and yeasts produce the special flavors of brick, Limburger, and Liederkranz cheese.

In the making of Swiss cheese, a special kind of bacteria is also used. It is called propioni-bacteria, and it gives Swiss cheese its sweet, nutty flavor.

It is the action of these bacteria that also gives Swiss cheese its odd appearance. While the cheese is curing, the bacteria give off gas. The gas bubbles form the round holes, or ''eyes,'' of the cheese.

Other cheeses get their special appearance and flavor from certain molds. The blue veins in Roquefort and blue cheeses come from the mold *Penicillium roquefortii*, which produces the flavor and smooth body. A grayish-white mold, *Penicillium camemberti*, grows on the surface of Camembert and causes the creamy texture and that special flavor.

HOW DO SCIENTISTS DETERMINE OCEAN DEPTHS?

Finding the depth of water is called ''sounding the depth'' or ''taking a sounding.'' In the old days, a weight was attached to one end of a rope. The rope was marked by a knot at every fathom (six feet). By counting the number of knots that went over the side before the weight hit bottom, one could determine the depth.

Today an echo sounder uses echoes of sound to explore the ocean floor. A device on board the ship sends out a sound signal which travels through the

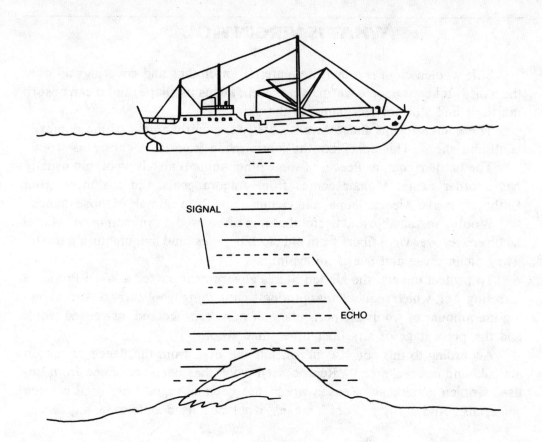

SIGNAL

ECHO

water at nearly one mile a second and is reflected—or echoed—back to an instrument. The deeper the water, the longer it takes for the echo to reach the ship.

In a modern echo sounder, high-frequency sound waves are beamed down from the ship. The instrument then records the echo as a dark mark on special paper. The paper is usually printed so that the depth can be read off in fathoms right away.

The echo sounder does more than just find the depth of the sea. It produces a continuous profile, or line, showing exactly what the ocean floor is like beneath the ship.

The soundings are so close together that the depth changes very little between one sounding and the next. If the ship passes over an undersea mountain, the echo sounder records the exact shape of the mountain. And if the bottom is flat, the record shows it as flat. The sounder does not miss a bump even a few feet high.

WHAT IS VIRGIN WOOL?

Soft woolen cloth is a favorite material for clothes and coverings all over the world. It keeps people warm, wears well, keeps its shape, and it can absorb moisture and still not feel damp to the skin.

The source of this fine fabric is chiefly the hairlike coat of the domestic lamb and sheep. This coat, like the fabric made from it, is known as wool.

The hairlike coat, or fleece, of some other animals also is wool, but usually has another name. Mohair comes from Angora goats and cashmere from Cashmere goats. Alpaca, llama, and vicuna come from animals of those names.

Wool is so valuable and useful that it is often used more than once. Manufacturers recover wool fibers from old clothing, rags, and manufacturing waste. They clean these and use them again.

To protect buyers, the United States government passed a Wool Products Labeling Act, which requires that products containing wool carry a label showing the amount of wool; the percentage of new, reprocessed, or reused wool; and the percentage of any fiber other than wool.

According to this act, "wool" means the fiber from the fleece of certain animals and not reclaimed. "Reprocessed wool" has been reclaimed from unused woolen materials. "Reused wool" has been salvaged from used woolen materials. And "virgin wool" means wool not used before in any way.

WHAT MAKES GASOLINE BURN?

Gasoline is very important in our lives because it is used as a fuel to make our automobiles go. Gasoline is a liquid fuel. It burns so rapidly and with such heat that it explodes.

Gasoline is a mixture of hydrocarbons or compounds made of hydrogen and carbon. These compounds are light liquids which boil at low temperatures. Carbon and oxygen are attracted to each other almost the way a magnet and iron are. When carbon combines with oxygen, burning takes place. This burning produces heat energy. When gasoline burns, the hydrogen joins with oxygen to form water vapor. The carbon and oxygen form carbon dioxide.

How does the burning of gasoline make a car go? The liquid gasoline is changed into a vapor and mixed with air by the carburetor of the engine. This mixture then flows into a cylinder where it is compressed by the piston moving up in the cylinder.

When the mixture of the gasoline vapor and air is compressed, a spark from a spark plug ignites the fuel. A great deal of gas is produced by the explosion (rapid burning). The pressure of the gas pushes hard on the piston and drives it down in the cylinder. The piston is connected to a crank which is free to turn. Thus, the push produced by the burning gasoline makes the crank go around. The crank is connected to the wheels and makes them turn.

WHY IS THERE LEAD IN GASOLINE?

Gasoline is a mixture of hydrocarbons. These are substances composed of hydrogen and carbon atoms.

The gasoline sold as motor fuel is usually a blend of several different hydrocarbon liquids. Special substances, called additives, are mixed with the gasoline to make it burn better.

At temperatures about 70 degrees Fahrenheit, gasoline turns from a liquid into a vapor. In an automobile engine, the gasoline is mixed with air and sprayed into the engine. The heat in the engine turns it into a vapor. A spark plug then sets off a spark that burns the mixture.

Sometimes the gasoline mixture may be ignited too soon. When this happens, the engine makes a sound, usually called a knock. There are two ways to reduce engine knock. One is to use a slow-burning gasoline.

The other is to put a chemical into the fuel to slow down the burning. The best-known chemical used for this is called tetraethyl lead, or simply ethyl. And that's why there is "lead" in gasoline.

Different kinds of gasoline are classed according to how much they are likely to knock in an engine. They are rated by an octane number. A gasoline with a high octane number will produce less knock than a gasoline with a low number.

Gasolines with an octane rating of 85 or more are considered good enough for most modern engines. Airplane fuel has an octane rating of 115 or more.

WHAT IS A SATELLITE?

In astronomy a satellite is a body that revolves around a larger body and is held captive by the larger body's attraction. Our moon is a satellite of the earth. The earth is a satellite of the sun.

Today when we say "satellite" we usually mean a man-made spacecraft circling the earth. Artificial satellites are sent into space for many purposes. Some are used for scientific research. Some send back information concerning the weather.

Some satellites relay television and radio broadcasts over long distances. Satellites may be used in navigation and map-making. Manned satellites give scientists information about how the human body reacts in a spacecraft.

Satellites can be of any size, from a tiny package of instruments to a huge balloon more than a hundred feet in diameter. They can weigh a few pounds or many tons. They can be shaped like balls, hatboxes, tin cans, bell buoys, and cigar boxes.

A satellite is launched at a velocity of 18,000 or more miles an hour. If no outside force acted on the satellite, it would travel off into space in a straight line. But the satellite cannot continue in a straight line because the earth's gravity attracts it, so the satellite is pulled into a curved path around the earth. The satellite is then in orbit.

Some satellites have orbits as near as 110 miles from the earth. Some have orbits as far as 22,300 miles from the earth. A satellite's orbit is chosen by scientists in advance, according to the task the satellite must perform.

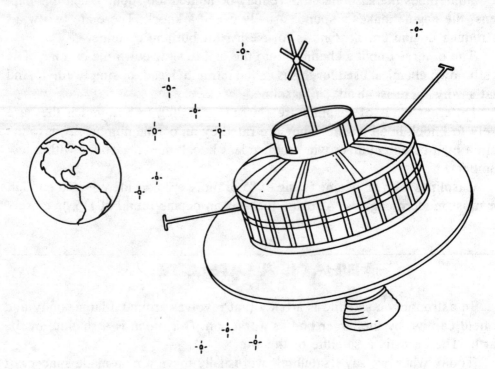

WHAT IS A LASER BEAM?

The word "laser" is formed from the first letters of some long scientific words. The first two letters stand for "light amplification." The *s, e,* and *r* stand for "stimulated emission of radiation."

So a laser amplifies light. The laser can take a weak beam of light and make it into a strong beam. Some lasers produce beams so strong that they can burn tiny holes in strips of steel in less than a second.

Laser beams can travel long distances through space without spreading out and growing weaker. Because of this, they may become an important means of communication in the space age. Many uses have already been found for lasers in medicine, science, and industry.

Scientists think of light as traveling in waves. The distance from the crest of one wave of light to the next crest is called a wavelength. Light from the sun or from a lamp is a mixture of many wavelengths. Each different wavelength produces a different color.

A laser beam is made up of rays that are all exactly the same wavelength. Light rays in ordinary light are all traveling in different directions. The rays in a laser beam move in exactly the same direction. A laser beam does not spread out and grow weak.

All the rays in a laser beam are in step. That is, the crests of one light ray are lined up with the crests of all the other rays. When light rays are in step like this, they strengthen one another. That's why a laser beam is very powerful. A laser beam is started in the laser by a weak flash of light that has the same wavelength as the beam.

WHAT KEEPS YOU UP ON A MOVING BICYCLE?

Of course, when you go spinning down the street on a bicycle, you don't think of what forces are at work to keep you balanced upright. But there are at least two things that enable you to stay up on a moving bicycle.

One is the gyroscopic force. A gyroscope is a heavy-rimmed wheel-and-axle mounted so that its center stays in one place no matter how the gyroscope is turned. When the wheel is set spinning, it holds its position in space until an outside force changes it.

Your bicycle wheels, when they start spinning, react in the same way. They will stay in the same plane unless considerable force is used to change the direction. So gyroscopic forces tend to keep the bicycle upright.

The second thing is centrifugal force. Centrifugal effect pushes things away from the center of a rotating body. It is the force that pushes you against the side of the car when it turns sharply.

As you start to fall just a little bit on the bicycle, you turn the front wheel in the direction of the fall. The centrifugal force pushes you upright again. The path of the bicycle curves first to the right and then to the left as you compensate for each tendency to fall. In other words, you move the wheel, without thinking, in such a way that the centrifugal force will keep you upright.

WHAT IS INCENSE MADE OF?

Incense is a compound of gums and spices which produces a fragrant smoke when burned.

A resin is a substance that exudes from plants. A gum resin called frankincense, which comes from a certain tree, is the base of most incense, but other gum resins are used, too.

Incense has also been made from many other substances, including the bark, wood, and roots of trees, aromatic herbs, and plants, seeds, flowers, and fruits that give off an odor.

The custom of burning incense is ancient and found all over the world. One of its earliest uses was in religious ceremonies, to fumigate and purify animal sacrifices and fruit offerings at the altar. Among the Jews, following the Exodus, the burning of incense was a rite that was ordered to be done. It was part of the memorial worship.

Incense has been used by many peoples, including the ancient Egyptians, Romans, Hindus, Chinese, Persians, Aztecs, and Incas. The Catholic Church began to use incense extensively about the 5th century.

Today, both the Latin and Greek churches use it in worship. Among Roman Catholics, it is used chiefly at High Mass, and in processions, funerals, and the consecration of churches. The Anglican Church at one time stopped the use of incense, but then began doing it again in the middle of the 19th century. So the burning of incense has played a significant part in the religious ceremonies of man.

WHAT IS A DAM?

A dam is a barrier that holds back or controls the flow of water. Dams create lakes (called reservoirs) for storing water and supplying it as needed.

Dams help man to preserve and use water and land resources. A dam built in the right place can help prevent floods. The reservoirs behind dams store up drinking water for people and livestock. Dams provide water for irrigating dry fields. Electric power is produced at many dams by harnessing the power of falling water to turn machines called turbines, which drive generators.

There are several types of modern dams. Solid concrete gravity dams are designed so that the sheer weight of the solid concrete is enough to keep the dam from sliding or being overturned by the pressure of the water behind it. They are called gravity dams because they depend on the force of gravity to hold them in place.

Hollow concrete dams are made of concrete reinforced with steel. They require less concrete than solid dams, so they may cost less. Embankment dams are made of piles of earth and rock. They are also called earth-fill or rock-fill dams. Dikes and levees, which control floods along coasts and rivers, are embankment dams.

For almost every dam a spillway is important. A spillway is a sloping ramp or tunnel that is used to let water out of the reservoir gradually. Spillways are used to control the water level in the reservoir and to prevent water from suddenly overflowing the top of a dam.

Dams have been built on rivers and streams all over the world for thousands of years. The earliest known dam in Egypt is over 4,500 years old.

WHERE DO THEY GET IRON TO MAKE STEEL?

Basically, steel is an alloy of iron and carbon. Other ingredients may be included to give the steel different characteristics, such as hardness, toughness, and resiliency. But the most important material for steelmaking is iron. Iron does not usually occur in nature as a pure metal. Most of it is found combined with other elements in the form of iron ore.

In the United States, the area around Lake Superior—which includes Michigan, Minnesota, and Wisconsin—is the chief source of iron ore. This region at one time supplied about 80 percent of the iron ore used in the United States and Canada. Today, imports of iron ore from abroad have increased.

Lake Superior ores average about 51 percent iron. These high-grade ores are mostly near the surface of the earth. They can be mined simply by stripping away the covering layer of earth and scooping up the ore. The high-grade deposits have been running low, however.

The richest sources of iron are iron ores, such as magnetite, hematite, limonite, and siderite. Magnetite contains a higher percentage of iron than any of the other iron ores, sometimes as much as 72 percent. It is a black mineral in which three parts of iron are combined with four parts of oxygen. Sizable deposits of magnetite are found in the Adirondacks region of New York, in New Jersey, and in Pennsylvania. Magnetite is also found in Sweden, Norway, Russia, and Germany.

Hematite is the most common iron material now used as a commercial source of iron. It is a soft, sandy or earthy, red-colored ore. The best grades of hematite contain 70 percent iron.

HOW ARE BRICKS MADE?

Did you know that bricks are one of man's oldest permanent building materials? They were first used over 5,000 years ago.

All bricks are made from clay. Clay is a common mineral substance composed of very small rock particles. Some types of clay are formed by the disintegration of rocks by weathering. Clay is found over most of the earth's surface, often in lake and river beds.

Clay becomes slippery and plastic (easily molded) when it is wet. When it is dry, it becomes hard and stony. When clay is heated to a high temperature (about 850 degrees Fahrenheit), it changes chemically so that it no longer becomes plastic when it is wet.

This means that bricks of baked clay will not soften and lose their shape when they become wet. Bricks are baked, or burned, at 1600 to 2200 degrees Fahrenheit. At about 1000 degrees Fahrenheit the brick turns red and its color becomes darker as the temperature increases.

Basically, the manufacture of bricks has changed little since ancient times, except that machines now do most of the work. The clay is dug by power shovels. After drying, it is ground in mills and screened to get particles of uniform size. The clay is mixed with water into a stiff paste, then forced out under pressure through shaped nozzles, like a giant square-cornered strip of toothpaste. The strip is automatically cut into pieces of the proper size by knives or wires. The soft brick is then dried in heated tunnels and finally carried in small railroad cars to the kilns for firing.

The average brick can take a load of about 5,000 pounds a square inch before it is crushed.

HOW ARE SYNTHETIC FIBERS MADE?

Some fibers, such as cotton, wool, silk, linen, and hair, are natural. They are produced by plants and animals. Others, such as rayon, nylon, Dacron, Saran, are man-made. To understand how man-made, or synthetic, fibers are made, we have to know something about fibers.

Most fibers are made up of organic (carbon-containing) chemicals, such as are found in all living things. Some organic chemicals have a special quality. Their molecules (groups of atoms) attach themselves to one another somewhat like the links of a chain. This is called polymerization. Each fiber consists of millions of such molecular chains held together by natural forces called chemical bonds. Different fibers contain different numbers of each kind of atom in their molecules, and the atoms are arranged differently.

In making synthetic fibers, chemists take atoms of carbon, hydrogen, oxygen, and other elements, and combine them in such a way that new substances are created. The raw materials for synthetic fibers are coal, oil, air, and water.

Atoms from these raw materials are combined and arranged into long molecular chains called polymers. In other words, the polymerization is created by the chemists, instead of by nature.

These polymers are liquid when they are hot. They can be cast into solid plastics and films like Saran wrap, or they can be extruded through spinnerets (nozzles with tiny openings) to form filaments. From these filaments fabrics are made.

Of all the fibers produced every year, about one-fifth are synthetic fibers.

WHAT IS SONAR?

Let's start with an echo. When a sound bounces back from a large object, we call the returning sound an echo. When a radio signal is bounced back from an object, the returning signal is called a radio echo. Producing and receiving radio echoes is called radar.

A radar set produces radio signals. It radiates (sends out) the signals into space by means of an antenna. When a radio signal strikes an object, part of the signal is reflected back to the radar antenna. The signal is picked up there as a radar echo. A radar set changes the radar echo into an image that can be seen.

The word "sonar" comes from the first letters of "sound navigation ranging." Sonar is very much like radar. Sonar can detect and locate objects under the sea by echoes. Since radio signals cannot travel far underwater, sonar sets use sound signals instead.

Compared with ordinary sounds, sonar signals are very powerful. Most sonar sets send out sounds that are millions of times more powerful than a shout. These outgoing sound signals are sent out in pulses. Each pulse lasts a short fraction of a second.

Some sonar sets give off sounds that you can hear. Other sonar signals are like sounds from a dog whistle. Their pitch is so high that your ear cannot hear them. But the sonar set has a special receiver that can pick up the returning echoes. The echoes are then used to tell the location of underwater objects.

Sonar is used in searching for oil on land. A sonar pulse is sent into the ground. Echoes come back from different layers of soil and rock underneath. This helps geologists predict what may lie deep in the earth.

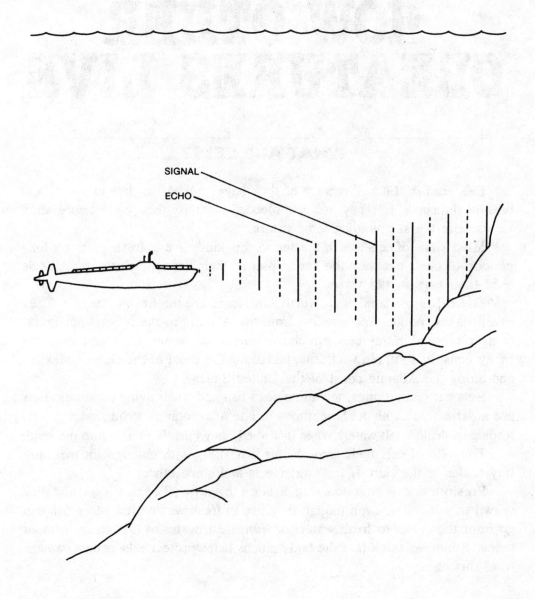

SIGNAL

ECHO

CHAPTER 5
HOW OTHER CREATURES LIVE

WHAT ARE EELS?

Eels are fish. Like all other fish, they have backbones, live in water, and breathe through gills. They are cold-blooded—that is, their body temperature varies with the surrounding temperature.

Most kinds of eels live in the sea. A few kinds live in fresh water for long periods of time, but they too spend part of their lives in salt water. All eels shed their eggs in salt water.

The eels most familiar to North Americans are the freshwater eels. They live in lakes, ponds, and streams from the Atlantic to the Mississippi River. Conger eels and moray eels, which live only in salt water, are found along the rocky coast of southern California and along the coast of the Gulf of Mexico, and along the Atlantic coast of the United States.

Eels eat many things, including dead fish and small living creatures. Eels are most active at night. Sometimes in late afternoon you can find tiny eels feeding in shallow salt water. When disturbed, they burrow rapidly into the sand.

The skin of eels feels smooth, for it is slimy with mucus. But there are tiny scales in the skin of freshwater eels and some others.

Freshwater eels migrate a long distance to spawn (shed their eggs) and they spawn in salt water, even though they live in fresh water. Few other fish can go from the ocean to fresh water, or from fresh water to the ocean, without dying. Biologists think that the body mucus helps protect eels against damage from this change.

Freshwater eels, moray eels, and some others, have a remarkable ability to recover from wounds that would kill other fish. A substance in their blood prevents possible infection.

DO HYENAS REALLY LAUGH?

There is actually a kind of hyena that is called the laughing hyena. It is the spotted hyena and is the largest member of the hyena family.

When this creature is on the prowl, or becomes excited by something, it utters a kind of eerie howl and chuckling gurgle that sounds like a laugh. But, of course, it is not "laughing" in the sense that human beings laugh. It is just making a shrieking noise that—to us—sounds like it is laughing.

The laughing hyena is a fierce-looking animal that stands about three feet high at the shoulder and is about six feet long. A big one may weigh as much as 175 pounds.

By day this hyena sleeps in a burrow or cave. When darkness falls, it comes out to seek food. Hyenas often hunt alone, but they may gather in packs around the remains of a kill left by lions or other beasts of prey. Their keen senses lead them to the kill, and they clean up all the remains.

The hyena is usually cowardly and sneaky, and it prefers to eat what others have killed and left. But it also lingers around camps and villages and sometimes attacks people sleeping in the open. It often follows herds of cattle or antelope. Closing in for the kill, it attacks a sick or crippled animal or else a very young or very old one.

The spotted, or laughing hyena, is an African species and it ranges from Ethiopia to the Cape of Good Hope. An unusual thing about the spotted hyena is that, unlike most animals, the female is larger than the male.

CAN SNAKES HEAR?

Snakes have no ears on the outside of their heads. This means that they do not hear airborne sounds as you do.

But snakes are sensitive to vibrations through the ground. So when a snake seems to "hear you coming," it is really feeling the ground shaking under your footsteps. Although a snake seems to have no sense of hearing, it more than makes up for it with other senses.

Most snakes can see very well. The eyes of snakes are always open, for snakes do not have movable eyelids. Snakes notice their prey more by movement than by shape or color. Snakes have a very keen sense of smell. They can recognize prey animals, enemies, and each other by odors.

Snakes also have another sense, related to both smell and taste, that human beings don't have. A snake can pick up chemical particles from the air, from the ground, or from some other animal or object, with the tips of its long forked tongue. The snake then thrusts these tips into a pair of openings in the roof of its mouth. These openings contain some highly sensitive nerve cells. And with these the snake can identify the chemical particles as food, enemy, friend, or whatever.

In fact, snakes have such a highly developed chemical sense that they can follow the trail of another animal like a well-trained hound. In addition, certain snakes—pit vipers and some boas and vipers—have a sense that no other animal has developed. They can sense a prey animal that is a little warmer or a little cooler than its surroundings.

This is a heat sense, and it enables these snakes to locate and strike a prey animal in the dark without ever seeing it!

HOW OFTEN DO SNAKES SHED THEIR SKINS?

There are over two thousand different kinds of snakes. They live on land, in the earth, in water, and in trees. So snakes vary quite a bit. But all snakes, young and old, shed their skins.

When they do this, even the film covering the eyes is cast off. During the process of shedding, the skin is turned inside out. The snake removes the skin by rubbing against rough surfaces. And snakes shed their skins several times a year.

The skin of a snake is scaly, and this is very important to them. In general, snakes have no legs, though a few types, such as the boas and pythons, have the remains of hind legs. These legs are imbedded in the muscles, and only spurs or claws show on the outside of the body.

It is the scales on the skin that enable snakes to move gracefully and even quickly. The broad scales on the underside can be moved forward in such a way that the rear edge of each scale pushes against some irregularity in the ground. When they are pushed back against these irregularities, the whole snake moves forward.

When the snake wants to move with great speed, it combines this with another method. This consists of swinging the body sideways into loops and, by pushing against any stone or plant it touches, gliding along the twisted path formed by the loops.

WHAT MAKES A RATTLESNAKE POISONOUS?

Scientists think that there are between 3,000 and 3,500 kind of snakes now living. Of these, 10 to 15 percent are poisonous kinds. They stun or kill their prey with venom. The rattlesnake happens to be one of the poisonous kind.

Rattlesnakes belong to a group of snakes called vipers, all of which are venomous. Rattlesnakes are pit vipers, and they get this name because of the two large pits on their heads. These pits are sensitive to the slightest change in temperature. They enable a viper to detect the presence of a warm-blooded animal even in the dark.

Vipers have a complicated type of venom system. Their fangs are very long. Each fang is set on a very short upper jawbone that can rotate. When a viper closes its mouth, the jawbone is rotated so that the fang lies lengthwise in the mouth and the mouth can close. When the mouth is opened for a strike, the jawbone is turned forward, bringing the fang at right angles to the throat.

The venom that vipers put into their victims with their fangs affects mainly blood cells and blood vessels. It may cause great swelling and bleeding. The venom of a few species, such as the South American rattlesnake, affects the nerves also.

There are 15 kinds of rattlesnakes, of various sizes and colors, in the United States and Canada. All of them have rattles at the tips of their tails. The "rattle" is made up of dry, horny rings of skin that lock loosely onto one another. When the snake shakes its tail, as it does when excited, these horny pieces of skin rub against one another. This results in a rasping or buzzing sound. This rattle helps the snake warn other animals away.

WHAT IS THE RATTLE OF A RATTLESNAKE MADE OF?

Rattlesnakes belong to a poisonous group of snakes called pit vipers. The pit vipers get their name from the two large pits on their heads, one on each side of the head, between the nostril and the eye. These pits are sensitive to the slightest change in temperature, so a viper can detect the presence of a warm-blooded animal even in the dark!

There are 15 kinds of rattlesnakes, and all of them have rattles at the tips of their tails. Even a young rattler has at least one round, shiny "button" at the tip of its tail.

The rattle is made up of dry, horny rings of skin that lock loosely onto one another. When the snake shakes its tail, as it does when excited, these horny pieces of skin rub against one another. This results in a rasping or buzzing sound. It serves to warn some other animal that it is too close for comfort.

Does a rattlesnake always give warning that it is going to strike by rattling? They usually do rattle when they become angry or frightened. But experts who have studied the habits of rattlesnakes report that this isn't always so. Many give no warning at all. So it isn't safe to depend on that warning rattle.

On the other hand, one can avoid being bitten by a rattlesnake by staying out of its range. A rattlesnake can only strike as far as it can raise its head. Even if it is coiled, it can strike only one-third to one-half its body length. And since rattlesnakes are rarely longer than six feet, one can be alert and stay out of its range.

WHY CAN'T THE OSTRICH FLY?

In the air the force of gravity is felt even more than when standing on the ground. This is because air gives little support to a creature's weight. Only small birds are able to fly by flapping their wings, because very large breast muscles are needed for this purpose.

A large bird does not have room for such muscles. And so the real giants among birds cannot fly at all. These include the ostrich, the rhea of South America, the emu of Australia, and a few others. All are much too heavy to fly. No bird can be truly a giant and still fly.

Is the ostrich really a giant? It certainly is! It is the largest of living birds. A full-grown ostrich is seven, and sometimes eight, feet tall. It weighs from 150 to more than 300 pounds!

But birds that cannot fly in some cases make up for this by having tremendous running speed. The ostrich is believed by some experts to be the fastest running bird. It has long, strong, thick legs and it can speed across the desert faster than the swift Arabian horse.

Some people claim they have seen ostriches run as fast as 50 miles an hour. But biologists believe that the fastest an ostrich can run is from 28 to 37 miles per hour—which is very fast, indeed.

The stride of the ostrich as it runs, moving one foot and then the other, can cover as much as 28 feet in a single leap.

WHAT DO HORNETS USE TO MAKE THEIR NESTS?

Several large members of the wasp family of insects are called hornets. They have thick bodies, usually black or dark brown, marked with brilliant white or yellow. This is why some of them are called "yellow jackets."

Hornets are social insects. They live together and build nests. If their nests are attacked, they become so angry that they sting the enemy very painfully. No wonder we have the expression "as mad as a hornet."

Hornets build large nests, sometimes a foot long, with a hole at or near the bottom. These nests are attached to branches of trees, or on bushes, or sometimes under the projecting roofs of buildings.

What are the nests made of? Paper. Yes—paper! We might say the hornets were the first paper-makers on earth. The paper is produced from wood pulp. The hornet collects it from boards or trees that have had the bark removed by accident or other means.

In collecting the pulp, the hornet goes backward, scraping off the pulp with its jaws and moistening it as it goes. This forms a round ball of paper pulp. The pulp is then spread into a sheet in building the nest.

Most people don't like hornets because they are afraid of their sting. And hornets do some damage to fruit. But, actually, hornets are a friend to man in destroying flies and other harmful insects.

HOW DO BEES STING?

First of all, not all bees sting. There are hundreds of different species, or kinds of bees, and many of them don't sting at all. When it comes to stinging by bees, what most of us are familiar with is the sting of the honeybee.

At the rear of the abdomen of the bee is the sting and other organs that surround it. The sting is quite a complicated thing. For one thing, it is an egg-laying apparatus, and actually part of its job is to deposit eggs.

The spearlike sting is made up of three pieces which surround a central canal. Connected to the base of the sting are two poison sacs. There are also two very sensitive, fingerlike projections. These tell the bee when the tip of her abdomen is in contact with the object she wishes to sting.

In the act of stinging, the spearlike sting is pushed outward and the poison sacs force the poison into the wound. It is this poison, in addition to the pain of the sting itself, that people want to avoid, for that poison can be very harmful to some persons.

Once the bee has inserted the barbed sting into the skin, it cannot be taken out easily. So when the bee flies away, her sting and its attached organs are pulled from her body, and she eventually dies.

If a bee does leave its stinger in a person's skin, it should be removed by scraping the stinger out with a fingernail or knife. Trying to pull the stinger out by its end may produce a squeezing of the poison glands if they are still attached and thus force more poison into the wound.

HOW DO WORMS CRAWL?

There are many different kinds of worms, but we will discuss the earthworm, the kind most familiar to us.

The body of the earthworm is divided into little rings, or segments, separated by grooves. So an earthworm belongs to the group known as "annelids." The name annelid means "little rings."

An earthworm stays underground most of the time, tunneling through soft, damp topsoil and feeding as it goes. It produces a slime that makes travel easy. An earthworm burrows along, using two sets of muscles.

One set of muscles runs around the body, with one muscle in each segment. When the segment muscles tighten, the body becomes longer and thinner. The front end is pushed forward. The second set of muscles runs lengthwise along the body. When these muscles tighten, the segments are pulled up close together. The body shortens.

An earthworm is like a tube within a tube. The long, segmented body is one tube. Within this is the long digestive tube through which the food passes. The digestive tube is open at both ends. Food passes in at one end, and the undigested remains pass out at the other.

In heavy or deep soil a worm tunnels by swallowing the soil. This method of moving is also a way of eating, for there are decaying bits of plants and animals in the soil. These are digested as the soil passes through the digestive tube.

This activity of swallowing soil and bringing it up to the surface plays an important part in turning over and enriching the soil. Scientists say that in each acre of land earthworms turn over ten to eighteen tons of soil each year.

HOW ARE FISH ABLE TO SMELL THINGS?

It probably surprises many people to learn that fishes can smell things just as other creatures can. Fishes smell with their noses.

There are two pairs of nostrils in a fish. That is, each nostril has two openings, which are called pits. One opening is in the front. The other is directly behind it. The two are separated by a small flap. The nostril can be in a number of different locations on the face. As is true with everything about fishes, there are many variations.

A current of water enters and leaves each pit. It flows in the front one and out the rear one. As the water flows, it stimulates the sense cells that tell the fish about odors. Many fishes have a keen sense of smell. They can detect the very smallest traces of substances.

In fact, the sense of smell may be important to fish in helping them find their way home. As we know, salmon return to their original home to spawn. How do they do it? Scientists believe that perhaps salmon can tell their childhood stream by its odor.

Researchers have trained salmon to distinguish 14 different kinds of colors. Some fish could tell the difference between water from two creeks. But if their noses were plugged up, they couldn't tell.

In other experiments a large number of salmon were taken out of their home stream. One half had their noses plugged; the other half didn't. Those with plugged noses got lost. The others found their way home again.

DO ALL FISH LAY EGGS?

Most fishes lay eggs and these eggs are fertilized outside the body. Fishes that emit eggs are described as oviparous. But some fishes give birth to living young. These are described as viviparous.

Among the viviparous fishes are guppies, platies, swordtails, and mollies.

The eggs are fertilized inside the body of the female and grow into baby fish there. At the appropriate time, they are born. In platies it is 21 days after fertilization.

The number of eggs that are laid and fertilized vary a great deal from one kind of fish to another. Some fishes expel their eggs and then abandon them, showing no more interest in them. These kind of fishes lay great numbers of eggs. Those fishes that watch over their developing young lay far fewer eggs.

Fishes also lay two types of eggs. One type floats and the other sinks. Eggs that float are called pelagic eggs. They are usually tiny and transparent and do not have much yolk. Eggs that sink are called demersal eggs. They are usually heavier and yolky.

As an example, herring lay demersal eggs and show no care for these eggs. They may deposit 20,000 to 40,000 eggs. Cod, on the other hand, lay pelagic eggs. An average-sized cod can lay one hundred million eggs!

Mackerel lay 400,000 to 500,000 eggs in a season, but they never lay more than 50,000 at a time. Large halibut can lay over two million eggs!

Eggs vary in size, too. Herring eggs are 1/25-inch in diameter. Cod eggs are about 1/15-inch. Halibut eggs are ⅛-inch. Eggs that are guarded until the young are larger have greater chance for survival. But billions and billions of fish eggs are eaten by other creatures.

HOW DO JELLYFISH REPRODUCE?

One of the most common jellyfishes in the world is the moon jellyfish. It has long, milky-looking threads streaming down from its round, cuplike body.

On the upper side of a fully grown moon jellyfish there is a pink or orange pattern like a four-leaf clover. The four "leaves" are the reproductive organs. In male jellyfish they produce sperm cells, which are released through the animal's mouth into the water. In female jellyfish the reproductive organs produce eggs. The eggs remain inside the body until they are fertilized, or joined, by sperm cells from the water.

The eggs develop in four long, trailing folds that hang down from the mouth. When the eggs hatch, the young settle on the bottom of the ocean. They develop into a shape very different from the parent animal. They become polyps (which means "many feet").

The young polyp catches food with its tentacles and grows for several months. Then something strange starts to happen. The polyp begins to develop grooves. Gradually, the polyp begins to look like a stack of fringed saucers.

One by one the saucers pinch off from the polyp and swim away. Each becomes a separate little jellyfish.

Apparently the jellyfish way of life and of reproducing works out quite well. Jellyfish have been doing this for more than 600,000,000 years! They are among the oldest forms of life on earth and have changed very little.

HOW DO FISH REPRODUCE?

Most fishes lay eggs. They either sink or float in the water. The outside shell of the egg is a transparent membrane. Inside, the egg itself is made of yolk and of protoplasm. Protoplasm is the living matter that becomes the future fish. The yolk, like the yolk of a chicken egg, nourishes the developing fish.

The egg cell is fertilized by a sperm from the male. The sperm swims into the egg cell through the shell, or membrane. The membrane has a small opening in it, just above the cell. Sperm swimming to the egg can get into the egg only through this opening. If sperm pass through, the egg is fertilized by one of the sperm.

Then life within the egg begins. The cells begin to divide until they form a thin sheet that encloses the entire yolk. The sheet then gradually begins to take the shape of the future fish. There is a bulge where the head will be, muscles appear as small blocks, the tail bud appears, and so on.

This embryo fish continues to grow inside the egg. After a certain number of days, the shell softens. The embryo hatches out of it. It is free to drift and to grow into an adult fish.

We have been discussing eggs that are laid and fertilized outside the body. Fishes that shed eggs are known as oviparous. But other fishes are viviparous, which means that they give birth to living young. Among such fishes are guppies, swordtails, and mollies.

The eggs are fertilized inside the body of the female and grow into baby fish there. At the appropriate time they are born.

DO FISH EVER SLEEP?

Can you sleep with your eyes open? No, you have to close your eyelids to go to sleep. And that's why most fishes do not sleep as we do. They do not have eyelids that they can close. But they do rest when the light dims. Some fish, such as the triggerfish, even lie down on their sides to rest.

The eye of a fish is similar to ours in many ways. But there are differences because a fish sees in water, while we see in air. As in people, there is an iris that surrounds the lens in fishes. The opening in the iris is called the pupil. The pupil of the eye always stays the same size in most fishes.

This means it does not close in bright light or open in dim light, as ours does. So if we turn on a bright light, the fish may be dazzled. It can't close out some of the light, as we can. However, a few fishes do have pupils that can narrow. By the way, fishes can't shed a tear, for they have no tear glands. Their eyes are kept moist by the surrounding water.

In most fishes the eyes are placed on each side of the head. Fishes see different images out of each eye. They have a large field of vision on both sides. Their field is much larger than ours. They can see in front, behind, above, and below themselves. Just in front of its nose a fish can focus both eyes on the same object.

Experiments have shown that some fishes can see colors. They can also distinguish between red and green, and probably between blue and yellow. However, not many species have been tested. So we cannot say that all fishes can see color. Also, there are many differences among the species.

WHAT IS A VULTURE?

The vulture is a large bird of prey. The word "vulture" has become a kind of symbol for creatures that feed on other animals.

Vultures belong to the same order of birds as the falcons, hawks, and eagles. There are five vultures to be found in North and South America. They are the turkey vulture, the black vulture, the king vulture, the California condor, and the South American condor.

All vultures feed on carrion (dead animals), which is why most people don't like them. Actually, these large birds are very graceful in flight, and one can admire the way they glide about in the air. But when a vulture discovers a dead animal, it swoops down, is joined by other vultures, and the birds tear the animal apart with their hooked beaks.

The South American condor is the only member of the vulture family that sometimes kills animals for food. It eats eggs, young sea birds, and young mammals. It also eats any dead animals that it can find.

How do vultures discover dead animals they eat? Many experiments have been made to get the answer. It is known that vultures have much better eye-

sight than human beings have. They can see small things from great distances. But they have hardly any sense of smell. So we still don't know exactly how they do it.

By the way, the North American vultures are quite welcome during stock-killing time on western ranches. They gather in numbers and save the rancher the labor and expense of getting rid of the unused parts of the animals killed.

WHEN DID HORSES COME TO NORTH AMERICA?

This question should really be: when did horses come *back* to North America? The horse developed into its present form in North America millions of years ago.

From time to time during their long history, horses traveled over land bridges from their North American homeland. They spread into South America, Asia, Europe, and Africa. On all these continents they evolved into numbers of different species. But during the Ice Age all the horses living in the Americas became extinct. At the dawn of recorded history there were no horses in North America. Horses then lived only in Europe, Asia, and Africa.

It was the Spanish conquistadores who brought horses back to America. In 1519 Hernando Cortes carried 16 horses with him when he sailed from Havana for the conquest of Mexico. De Soto brought more than two hundred horses with him when he landed in Florida in 1539. He still had most of them when he pushed on across the Mississippi River in 1541. And Coronado, exploring the Southwest at the same time, had one thousand or more horses in his expedition.

Spanish missionaries and settlers followed the explorers, bringing still other horses with them. At first the Indians were frightened by the horses, for they had never seen such beasts. But they quickly discovered how useful horses could be. Soon they began to steal horses from the Spaniards and to capture runaways. Tribe after tribe acquired horses.

Possession of the horse changed the whole way of life for many western Indian tribes. Horses made it possible for them to move from one campground to another quickly and easily. Horses also allowed them to follow the bison herds and kill all they needed. Plains Indians also used horses in warfare against one another and against the invading white man.

HOW DO SCIENTISTS KNOW ANIMALS ARE COLOR BLIND?

To find out whether animals can see colors, scientists have conducted certain experiments. All they can say is that, according to the results of these experiments, certain animals cannot see colors.

Let's consider dogs, for example. Dogs were able to be trained so that their mouths watered (salivated) when definite musical notes were sounded. This was because when those notes were sounded, the dogs would be given food. Then the same kind of experiment was tried with different colors. It was impossible to make dogs tell one color from another as signals for food. Conclusion: dogs are color blind.

A similar type of experiment was made with cats. An attempt was made to train different cats to come for their food in response to signals of six different colors. But the cats always confused their color with shades of gray that were shown. So it is believed that cats are color blind.

We know that monkeys and apes can see colors because certain experiments prove it. They have been trained to go for their meal to a cupboard, the door of which was painted a certain color, and they wouldn't go to doors painted with other colors—and which had no food.

But even scientists say that the evidence that most animals are color blind is not complete. Maybe more tests will reveal things we don't know about animals. For example, tests were made that showed that horses are able to tell green and yellow from any shade of gray and from one another. But they don't seem to be very good at recognizing red or blue as colors.

HOW DO WE KNOW BATS USE RADAR?

Most bats are active only at night. They come out at night to find food. For centuries men who studied bats wondered how they found their way in the dark. How could a bat with no light to see by find a flying insect and catch it in flight?

Many people used to think that bats had unusually keen eyesight and could see by light too faint for human eyes to detect. Scientists now know that a bat's ability to navigate depends not on its eyes, but on its ears and vocal organs.

Way back in the 1780's an Italian zoologist named Spallanzani did an experiment. He blinded some bats and released them into a room crisscrossed with silk threads. The bats flew through the maze without touching the threads. When he plugged their ears, they became entangled in the threads. Spallanzani felt that bats used their ears rather than their eyes to find their way in the dark.

In 1920 a scientist suggested that bats sent out signals that were beyond the range of human hearing. Such sounds are called ultrasonic. In 1941, two other scientists decided to use a new electronic instrument that detected ultrasonic sounds in an experiment with bats.

The machine showed that the bats were uttering high-pitched cries, and that they were constantly squeaking as they flew through a maze of wires that had been set up in the dark. When they taped the bats' mouths shut, the animals blundered badly.

A bat sends out signals—high-pitched squeaks that bounce off anything in its path. A sound is bounced back, or reflected. It is an echo. The bat uses echoes to locate things in the dark.

DO POLAR BEARS HIBERNATE?

The word "hibernate" comes from the Latin and means "winter sleep." Many people think that certain animals hibernate because the weather gets cold where they live. And since polar bears live where it's very cold, they must hibernate.

But animals who hibernate do it because their food supply becomes scarce in winter. They do not store up a food supply for the winter. Instead, they lay up a reserve supply of fat on their body. Then the hibernating animal sleeps through the cold winter, living on the fat it has stored up in its body.

During this sleep, all life activities nearly stop. The body temperature goes down, the breathing is slow, the heart beats faintly. Do polar bears do this?

The answer is no. They do sleep more in the winter than in summer, but their sleep is not the deep sleep of hibernation. Their temperatures and breathing remain normal. They sleep in hollows or caves in the ice or snow. During warm spells they may even venture forth for a day or so.

Female polar bears do more sleeping in winter than the males. They go into dens and are often snowed under for weeks. The cubs are born during this winter sleep. The cubs are often very small, weighing no more than six or eight ounces at birth. So the mother bear nurses them and cares for them for several months during the winter.

Hibernating animals are awakened in the spring by the change in temperature, moisture, and by hunger. They crawl out of their dens and start eating again.

WHY DO OPOSSUMS CARRY THEIR YOUNG?

Opossums belong to a group of animals called marsupial. The females of this troup have pouches on the underside of the body in which the young develop.

An interesting thing about opossums is the fact that the young are so small. You could put all of the 5 to 18 babies in a tablespoon when they are born! At birth they are blind, hairless, and practically shapeless.

Because they are so small, and still quite helpless, the mother opossum carries her young. They ride on her back. She brings her tail up and they wrap their tails around it. When they are about three months old, they leave their mother; and at one year they are ready to raise families.

The babies climb into their mother's pouch, and attach themselves to the milk glands. When they are a month old they begin to poke their heads out of the pouch. A few weeks later they crawl out for short periods of time.

Opossums spend a lot of time in trees, hunting and eating. They like to eat upside down. To do this, they wrap their tails around a branch, hang down, and grasp their food by all four feet.

Opossums eat small mammals, insects, small birds, eggs, poultry, lizards, crayfish, snails, fruit of all kinds, corn on the cob, mushrooms, and worms. At night opossums invade orchards for fruit and henhouses for poultry and eggs. So man doesn't exactly like all their eating habits. But opossums do help farmers by killing mice and insects.

CAN A BUTTERFLY SMELL?

It may surprise us, but butterflies and moths have keen senses of sight, smell, and taste. The organs of taste in most butterflies are in the mouth, which is what you would expect. But most organs of smell in butterflies are on the antennae. And there are some butterflies that smell things through "noses" on their feet!

Many butterflies have odors, or scents, which they use for two purposes. One kind of scent is used to attract the opposite sex; the other is used to drive away enemies.

The scents of male butterflies come from scales in pockets on their hind wings. During courtship a male monarch butterfly may scatter these scent scales over the female. The scents of many male butterflies resemble those of flowers or spices and are often pleasant to humans.

Female butterflies produce their scents in special glands in their bodies. Most of these female odors are disagreeable to the human nose.

Did you know that the taste organs of a butterfly are far more sensitive in some ways than that of humans? They are far more sensitive to sweet things than our tongues are. Their chief food is flower nectar, which is a sugar solution, and they are easily able to find it. When a butterfly finds nectar in a flower, it uncoils its long, hollow "tongue" and sucks in the liquid.

Butterflies are able to see colors very well. They can even see certain ultraviolet colors that the human eye cannot see.

WHY DO A CAT'S EYES GLOW IN THE DARK?

People who own and love cats consider them to be sweet little creatures and wonderful pets. Which they are. But cats are members of a family of animals of a very special kind. These include tigers, lions, leopards—and, of course, the domesticated cat.

No matter where they live, no matter what their size and appearance, all cats are alike in many ways. All have bodies adapted for hunting and killing. All are highly specialized beasts of prey.

One of the things that helps a cat to be a good hunter is its eyes. The cat's eyes are adapted for seeing in the dark, since it does most of its hunting at night. During the day the pupils contract to slits, or very small openings. But at night they open wide, letting in every bit of light possible.

The backs of the eyes are coated with a substance like polished silver. It reflects every bit of light that comes into the eye. That is why a cat's eyes shine like glowing lanterns if you point a flashlight toward them at night.

What are other things about the cat that make it a great hunter? In the front of its mouth the cat has four long, pointed canine teeth—deadly weapons for biting and tearing flesh. On its feet the cat has an arsenal of needle-sharp, curved claws. To follow its prey silently, there are soft pads cushioning the bottom of its feet. And the cat has unusually keen sight, hearing, and smell.

WHY DO CATS HAVE WHISKERS?

The cat family includes everything from the small domestic cats we keep as pets to Siberian tigers weighing 600 pounds or more. But no matter where they live, no matter what their size and appearance, all cats have bodies adapted for hunting. All are highly specialized beasts of prey.

A cat has whiskers to help it perform in this way. When a cat is on the prowl, and its eyes and ears are not receiving any information to help it, or are busy, whiskers help the cat learn more about its surroundings.

For example, when a cat puts its head into a dark hole, the whiskers touch the sides of the hole and tell the cat where the boundaries of the hole are. Or the whiskers may brush against the body of a mouse and tell the cat at once that its prey is there.

So the long hairs of the cat's whiskers are what it depends on to know where it is, what's there, when the other sense organs, such as sound and smell and sight, can't provide that information.

But cats do have very keen senses. Their hearing and sense of smell are highly developed. They have keen eyes and they are directed forward (as ours are). This allows the cat to focus both eyes on the same subject at the same time and to judge its distance.

The cat's eyes are also adapted for seeing in the dark. During the day the pupils contract to slits, but at night they open wide to let in every bit of light possible. The backs of the eyes are coated with a substance that reflects every bit of light that comes into the eye.

HOW DID THE HIPPOPOTAMUS GET ITS NAME?

There are many amazing things about this beast, including its strange name. The word "hippopotamus" means "river horse." The animal got this name partly because it spends much of its time in the water. And it may have been called a horse because of its great size or its wide nostrils or its little horselike ears.

Actually, the closest living relative of the hippopotamus is the pig! The hippo is far larger than any horse. A big hippo can be twelve feet long and weigh up to four tons.

The hippo has the biggest mouth of any mammal except the whale. It has two tusks in the upper jaw and four in the lower. When it attacks, it can kill a smaller animal with a single bite. Usually, however, the hippopotamus would rather hide than attack. Most of the time it will run to the water to hide.

A hippo can run as fast as a man. In the water it can drop out of sight like a stone or it can float. When the hippo floats, only its bulging nostrils and eyes and its little ears show above the surface. It is almost hidden, but it can still breathe, smell, see, and hear.

When it sinks, the hippo closes its nostrils to keep the water out. It can walk around on the bottom and gather the juicy water plants it likes to eat. It can easily stay under for eight or nine minutes!

The hippo has an appetite to match its size. A big hippo that lives in a zoo may eat about one hundred pounds of food every day. A herd in the wild will eat many kinds of river plants and grasses. Hippos usually feed at night and rest during the day.

WHAT IS A MAMMAL?

Mammals are the most advanced of all the different classes of animal life. They are also the animals that we know best, and include dogs, cats, rabbits, horses, cows, pigs, elephants, bears, mice—and human beings. And there are hundreds and hundreds of other kinds of mammals.

Mammals have certain characteristics, some of which are shared by other creatures, some of which are not. Mammals are vertebrates—animals with backbones. (So are fishes, reptiles, and birds.) All mammals have lungs and breathe air. (So do birds, reptiles, and many amphibians.) All mammals are warm-blooded. (So are birds.)

All mammals, except two primitive types that lay eggs, give birth to living young. So do many fish, reptiles, insects, and other animals.

There are two important characteristics that set mammals apart from all other animals. They are the only animals that possess true hair, or fur. They are the only animals that produce milk. The word "mammal" comes from the Latin word *mamma,* which means "breast." All female mammals nurse their young with milk that comes from glands, usually called breasts, on their bodies.

Mammals have certain other characteristics. The mammal's lungs and heart are separated from its stomach and intestinal tract by a wall of muscle called the diaphragm. The mammal's lower jaw consists of a single bone on each side. And—most important of all—mammal brains are much more highly developed than the brains of any other animals.

WHAT IS A SLOTH?

When we say a person is a "sloth," we mean he is sluggish and lazy. What we are saying is that he takes after the sloth, an animal that is very sluggish and sleeps 18 hours a day.

Sloths are strange-looking animals found in Central and South America from Nicaragua to Brazil. They live in trees and are never seen away from forest areas. Sloths are mammals and are related to anteaters, armadillos, and aardvarks.

There are two types: three-toed and two-toed sloths. The three-toed sloths have three toes on each foot. The two-toed have two toes on their front feet and three on the back.

They use their toes and claws to hang from branches in an upside-down position. At night they inch slowly along the branches in search of tree leaves and twigs, which they eat.

Sloths sleep in the trees, on the upper side of a strong limb. Sometimes they crawl over the ground, and where there is a stream or a lake they jump in without fear and swim easily.

Sloths are very low in intelligence, because their brain is very small. Their body temperature is also the lowest of any mammal, and in fact they sometimes behave more like cold-blooded animals than warm-blooded animals.

The fur of a sloth is gray and shaggy. Sometimes algae grow in the fur, and this gives it a greenish tinge. But this actually helps sloths — because the green color helps them stay unnoticed by eagles, jaguars, and other animals that feed on them.

WHEN DID REPTILES FIRST APPEAR?

The first reptiles walked on the earth about 300,000,000 years ago. In those days the largest animals on land were amphibians. Their eggs were laid in water.

The first reptiles looked like amphibians, but the big difference was that their eggs could hatch on land. The young had lungs and legs, and could breathe air. They walked on damp ground in forests, and probably fed on insects.

Later on, reptiles became larger and stronger. Some looked like lizards and some like turtles. There were also reptiles with short tails, thick legs, and large heads.

One group of early reptiles were very important because of their descendants. They looked like lizards that were about three feet long, but they walked on their hind legs.

From these creatures many new types of reptiles developed. Some were true reptiles with wings. One group developed feathers and warm blood—they became the first birds. Other types that developed were crocodiles and the first dinosaurs.

At one time, all the types of reptiles that existed dominated life on earth. But after millions of years, many of the ancient types of reptiles became extinct. There are many theories that try to explain why this happened. The chief explanation seems to be that changes in the earth and its climate made it impossible for them to live on. Swamps dried up and they couldn't live on dry land. Their food disappeared. Climates became seasonal, shifting from summer heat to frost in winter. Most reptiles could not adjust to these changes, and those that couldn't died out.

HOW DO TURTLES BREATHE UNDERWATER?

Many turtles spend all or most of their lives in fresh water. They may live in swamps, ponds, running streams. They come up on dry land to sun themselves or lay eggs. How do they breathe when they are in the water?

Turtles have lungs and breathe air. They do not get oxygen from the water as fish do. So turtles have to fill their lungs with air to enable them to stay underwater.

They cannot do this by moving their ribs, as we do. Their ribs are firmly fixed to their hard shells. Turtles fill their lungs in another way. A turtle has two special sets of belly muscles. One set pulls the other body organs away from the lungs. Then a second set of muscles pulls the organs against the lungs, forcing the air out. One deep breath may last a land or sea turtle several hours.

Some freshwater turtles may remain underwater for several days without surfacing. They can do this because they use up very little oxygen while lying still on the bottom.

A few kinds of turtles have a special lining in their throats or in the cloaca. This is the opening through which wastes and other substances leave the body. This lining can take oxygen from the water, as the gills of fish do. Such turtles still need to come up for air, however.

A soft-shell turtle can breathe without moving from its shallow river bottom. Its neck is long enough to reach up to the surface of the water.

WHERE ARE BLUE WHALES FOUND?

First, what are blue whales? Well, to most of us, whales are whales. We are not aware that there are many different kinds of whales.

Scientists divide whales into two groups: Odontoceti and Mysticeti. Odontoceti means "whales with teeth." Mysticeti means "moustached whales." These whales have "moustaches" of baleen, or whalebone, hanging from the roof of the mouth. Baleen is a fibrous, horny substance, fringed along the inner edges. Using their baleen, these whales strain huge quantities of small food out of the water.

The baleen whales are the largest animals ever to live on earth. Bigger than the dinosaurs? Yes! The blue whale, which is the largest of this type, may be 100 feet long and weigh more than 120 tons—and even the biggest dinosaur didn't reach this size.

There are three families of baleen whales: the right whales, the fin whales, and the gray whales. Blue whales are the largest species of fin whales. The chances are that you will never see one swimming about—but, actually, these whales are found in seas the world over. There is no particular area or ocean which they prefer.

These huge whales feed mainly on small fishes and on shrimplike creatures known as krill. The whale takes a huge mouthful of water and closes its mouth. Slowly it presses its tongue against the blades of baleen, which hang down from the upper jaw. In this way the seawater is strained off, and the food remains in the whale's mouth.

CAN BIRDS SMELL?

Living creatures tend to have, or develop, those senses which are necessary for them to survive. How important would the sense of smell be to a bird? Apparently, not very important, since the sense of smell seems to be almost or entirely missing in most birds.

What senses are important to birds? Well, a large part of the brain and nervous system of birds is connected with the senses of sight and balance—because they are important in flight. Fine eyesight is vital for a flying animal, and birds have remarkable eyesight.

They usually have a wide angle of vision. Many birds are also "out-eyed." Each eye looks out at right angles to the bird and sees a completely separate area.

The ability of birds to see color is more-or-less like that of a human. Night birds also have large lenses. This type of eye (in birds like owls) is able to gather and concentrate dim light.

The sense of hearing is excellent in birds. So are the senses of balance and of place in and movement through space. All these senses are centered in the ears. Many birds also have a good sense of taste. They can select their proper food instantly.

Most of the habits of birds are the inherited abilities we call instincts. Birds are born knowing almost everything needed to know to carry out their normal lives. They have no need to learn very much.

WHY DO WOODPECKERS PECK ON TREES?

Most of us, when we hear a woodpecker at work on a tree, imagine that it is harming the tree. The fact is, the opposite is true! The woodpecker is actually helping keep the tree alive.

First of all, the woodpecker is an arboreal bird; that is, it lives in trees. And it eats in trees. Hidden down deep in the crevices of the bark of trees are many grubs and insects. The woodpecker finds them with a kind of instinct—even when they cannot be seen on the outside. Then he drills a hole straight down to them and eats them. Quite often these insects and grubs are the kind that are harmful to the tree.

How can the woodpecker reach down into the wood? For one thing, the woodpecker's beak is sharp and strong and has a chisel-shaped point. Then the woodpecker also has an amazing tongue. In some species it is twice as long as the head itself.

The tongue is round and at the outer end has a hard tip with tiny barbs on the sides. Inside the beak the tongue is curled up like a spring. When the woodpecker goes after insects in the tree, it is able to thrust that tongue quite some distance from the beak and go far down into the crevices of the bark.

Woodpeckers don't always peck away at live trees. They use their chisel-like beak also for cutting holes in decayed wood. This is to make a place for their nests. They like trees which are hollow part of the way up.

Sometimes woodpeckers make two openings, like a front and back door. This is to enable them to get away if an unwelcome visitor should show up.

HOW DO SNAILS GET THEIR SHELLS?

Soft-bodied animals that have shells are known as mollusks. There are many different kinds of shell-bearing mollusks.

Some have two shells, or valves, which are hinged together. These mollusks are called bivalves. This group includes clams, oysters, scallops, and mussels. Other mollusks have only one shell, which may be cap-shaped but is usually twisted into a spiral. These mollusks are called snails.

The snail builds its shell like all mollusks. The shell is a mollusk's skeleton. The shell is part of the animal, and the mollusk is attached to it by muscles.

The soft animal inside can never leave its shell and return to it. As the mollusk grows bigger, its shell increases in size and strength. The shell is made of a form of limestone and is built by the mollusk itself. Of course, the mollusk does not know that it is building a home for itself.

In the case of the mollusk, certain glands are able to take limestone from the water and deposit it in tiny particles at the edge of, and along the inside of, the shell.

As a mollusk grows, its home becomes larger and stronger. Some of its shell glands contain coloring matter. As a result, a mollusk's shell may be spotted, all one color, or marked with lines.

Most mollusks live in the sea. None of the bivalves live out of water. Many snails, however, are air-breathing. These land snails are generally found in moist wooded places.

WHAT IS THE DIFFERENCE BETWEEN BACTERIA AND VIRUSES?

People usually link bacteria and viruses in terms of disease. But they are quite different from each other. Some bacteria cause disease, but most do not. There are at least two thousand species of bacteria, and most of them are either harmless or helpful.

A bacterium consists of only one cell. A single drop of sour milk may contain 100,000,000 bacteria. Bacteria are everywhere. Some live in the mouths, noses, and intestines of animals, including man. Others live on fallen leaves, dead trees, animal wastes, in fresh and salt water, in milk, and in most foods.

Since bacteria have some features of both plants and animals, scientists have not agreed on how to classify them. Most bacteria reproduce by fission—the cell divides in two.

Viruses are very small organisms, so small that they can only be seen in detail with an electron microscope. Viruses grow and multiply only when they are inside living cells. Outside living cells, viruses do not change in any way and seem lifeless. They cannot grow unless they are inside the cells of animals, plants, or bacteria.

Viruses that attack man and animals are called animal viruses. Those that attack plants are called plant viruses, and those that attack bacteria are called bacterial viruses.

The viruses that infect man and animals may be breathed in or swallowed, or enter through an opening in the skin. Some of them destroy cells simply by growing in them. Others cause the membranes separating two cells to dissolve, and still others cause cells to become malignant.

WHAT ARE LICE?

Sometimes when a person wants to describe something terrible he says, "It's lousy." "Lousy" is not a dirty word. It refers to the louse—which is a very obnoxious insect.

Actually, there are more than one thousand different insects that are called "louse" (plural: "lice"), but the one that people usually have in mind is the one that attacks human beings.

These are bloodsucking creatures. They are true parasites—their food is human blood. And these lice are more closely associated with man than any other members of the animal kingdom. This is because they exist upon his body during all stages of their development.

The "pediculus humanus" is typical of this kind of louse. It develops from eggs that are glued to the hair or clothing. In the hair, the eggs, or "nits" are sometimes easily seen. The body louse is passed from one person to another by wearing clothing from an infested person or by contact with bedding that is infested. The body louse is known to carry the disease typhus fever.

There is another kind of louse that attacks human beings and stays in hair in all parts of the body, including even the eyebrows. The control of these lice is done by dusting DDT powder or other insecticides under the clothing or in the hair.

An interesting thing about lice is that certain kinds attack other creatures as well. There are lice that live on birds, other mammals, and even lice that live on honey bees. There are also plant lice that suck the juices of plants.

WHY DO PEOPLE HUNT WALRUSES?

The walrus is a huge mammal that lives in Arctic waters off both coasts of northern North America and also off northeastern Siberia. It measures from eight to twelve feet in length when full-grown, and weighs up to three thousand pounds.

Walruses have a thick hide which is tough and wrinkled and which has almost no fur. Both the male and female walruses grow tusks which are used in digging for mollusks and for fighting.

Walruses live together in herds. They stay in far northern waters during the summer. In the fall they drift southward with the ice, and in the spring they swim northward again.

Walruses are hunted by man for many reasons. Eskimos and other Arctic peoples have depended on the walrus to supply them with food, fuel, clothing, and equipment. Practically every part of the body is used.

The blubber supplies oil for fuel. The leathery hides are used for clothing. The flesh is used for food. And the ivory tusks are used to make many different kinds of objects. Eskimos have used these tusks to carve small decorative objects that can be traded or sold.

WHAT IS THE 17-YEAR LOCUST?

There is no such thing! What is called the 17-year locust is really the 17-year cicada, an entirely different kind of insect. True locusts are grasshoppers, and calling the cicada a locust is a mistake that is commonly made.

The 17-year cicada is quite an unusual insect. It probably lives longer than any other insect (except perhaps the termite queen). Its life cycle goes like this:

the nymphs, the cicada's young, hatch from eggs on the twigs of trees. Then they drop to the ground.

Then they burrow into the ground and attach themselves to rootlets. And they remain there, without moving, as they suck the sap, for 17 years! Then instinct calls them out into the light.

Now they climb the trunk of a tree, and their skins split open. Out comes the mature cicada. For about five weeks they seem to live a happy life in the light of the sun. The males, and only the males, are able to make a piercing, metallic noise, the "voice" of the cicada. This sound is probably a mating call to the females.

The sound is made by one of the most complicated musical organs in nature. There are little drumlike plates at the base of the abdomen, and they are kept vibrating rapidly by muscles that seem never to get tired.

After the five weeks are over, the cicada dies. So it took 17 years to develop—for just five happy weeks of life. This 17-year cicada (in the South it matures in 13 years) is peculiar to the United States. Altogether, there are about one thousand species of cicada, and most of them live in the tropics.

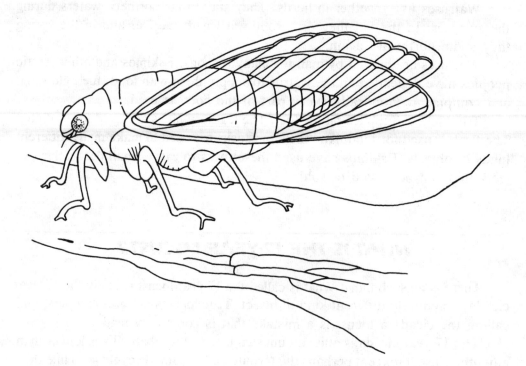

WHERE DO PENGUINS LAY THEIR EGGS?

During the Antarctic winter, February to October, the penguins live at sea. In October, which is early spring there, they come out of the sea and start a long trek to their rookeries, or breeding grounds.

The penguins may have to walk and slide, scramble and toboggan 60 miles across the sea ice to reach the rocky Antarctic coast. Usually the males arrive first and go directly to their nests of the previous year. The nests are made of stones. So you see, the penguins find a rocky area along the coast, where deep snow is not a problem, to lay their eggs.

The male and female penguin make a nest together before the eggs are laid. They go back and forth, collecting stones, carrying the stones in their beaks. They collect and guard the stones in turn. The stones are dropped by one partner; the other arranges them into a neat pile.

In mid-November the female penguin lays two bluish-white eggs. Now a very interesting process begins. The female and the male take turns guarding and hatching the eggs. After a certain period the female returns from the sea where she has been feeding and the male goes out to the sea to feed. Then he returns and she goes out to feed. But the timing is such that it is always the female who returns just as the chicks are coming out of their eggs. This taking turns in guarding and feeding goes on after the young are born for about four weeks.

WHY ARE DOLPHINS CONSIDERED INTELLIGENT?

Dolphins and porpoises are small whales, ranging in length from four to about twelve feet. Whether they are called "dolphins" or "porpoises" seems to be a matter of preference. Either name is correct.

There are several reasons why scientists consider the dolphin to be an unusually intelligent animal. Many of them have been known to imitate human speech quite distinctly—and without even being urged to do so. They can also learn to understand human words and respond to them.

Students of animal behavior have two other reasons for considering the dolphin intelligent. Dolphins are able to invent and play games. For example, suppose there is a feather floating about in a tank of water. A dolphin will get the feather and bring it near the jet of water entering the tank. The feather drifts into the jet and goes shooting off. The dolphin pursues it, catches it, brings it back, and again releases it into the jet.

Dolphins have invented games with small rubber inner tubes. They will toss the tube to someone standing by the tank and wait for the person to toss it back to them so they can catch it. This kind of play is considered a sign of intelligence.

Dolphins can also solve problems. If a piece of food is stuck under a rock, they can find a way to "blow" the food out from under the rock.

WHEN DID MAN FIRST FIND OUT ABOUT DINOSAURS?

No human being ever saw a living dinosaur. Dinosaurs were animals that lived in most regions of the world, but they died out everywhere about 65,000,000 years ago. It is believed that the first kind of man appeared less than 2,500,000 years ago. So dinosaurs were extinct by the time man appeared.

We know about dinosaurs from their remains. These are bones, found either in skeletons or separately; footprints in rock; impressions of skin, also in rock; and eggs.

There is some doubt as to when the first recognizable dinosaur bones were discovered. Footprints have been known for many years. A dinosaur skeleton may have been seen at Haddonfield, New Jersey, toward the end of the 1700's.

The first bones that are still available for examination and identification are some that were discovered in England. One set was found in 1822 and is now in the British Museum of Natural History in London.

Another set of dinosaur bones, found about the same time, was the basis for the first scientific description of any dinosaur. This was done in 1824 by a professor at Oxford University.

So you can see that man has found out about dinosaurs quite recently. Dinosaur specimens have been found in great numbers in the United States, Canada, Argentina, Brazil, India, Africa, Australia, Mongolia, China, France, Germany, Portugal, and the Soviet Union. This indicates that dinosaurs really lived all over the world.

WHAT IS AN AMOEBA?

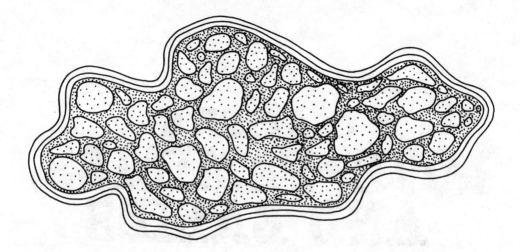

When we use the word "animal" we tend to think of pretty large creatures that move about on earth. But did you know that the amoeba is considered an "animal"?

It is a jellylike one-celled creature, so small that it can be seen only under a microscope. The common species of amoeba lives in freshwater streams and ponds, while other amoebas live on the bottom of fresh- and salt-water bodies, and in damp soils and foods.

The amoeba constantly changes its shape. It moves by pushing out one side and then another. As some of the jellylike substance is pushed out, it forms what are called false feet, or "pseudopodia." When the pseudopodia reach food, they wrap themselves around it and take it into the main body. This is the way the amoeba eats—it has no mouth.

The amoeba belongs to the Protozoa, which is the lowest division of the animal kingdom. It has no lungs or gills. But it absorbs oxygen from the water, gives off carbon dioxide, and digests its food, as more complex animals do.

The amoeba even seems to have feeling. If it is touched or disturbed, it immediately rolls itself into a tiny ball. The amoeba also tries to avoid bright light and water that is too hot or too cold.

In a full-sized amoeba, the nucleus, a tiny dot in the center of the protoplasm, divides into two parts. After this the amoeba itself divides, forming into new individual animals. When these become full-grown, each of them may divide again.

CHAPTER 6
LOVE, FAMILIES, AND BABIES

AT WHAT AGE DO PEOPLE FALL IN LOVE?

There is no specific age when this happens, but a person must be mature in certain ways to experience love. Young people do feel strong attachments for each other, and imagine at times they are "in love." But the full, deep meaning of loving another person can only be understood when one is mature. There is a responsibility that comes with love, and a dedication of oneself to the person one loves, that very young people cannot feel as yet.

IS A MOTHER'S LOVE FOR HER CHILDREN THE SAME AS HER LOVE FOR HER HUSBAND?

No. And it shouldn't be. It is not a question of "less love" or "more love," it is simply a different kind of love. A mother can love a child "with all her heart," and this will mean being devoted to the child, caring for it, helping it in every way, being close and warm and under-

standing, and even sacrificing for the child. But it is still different than the love for her husband.

That love — for her husband — involves her in a different way. It shows itself, among other things, in wanting to be physically close to him, in making love (having sexual intercourse). It reaches a beautiful closeness that is just as precious to her as closeness to her children — and it need not conflict with the love for her children.

IS IT POSSIBLE TO LOVE A FRIEND AS MUCH AS A SWEETHEART?

Of course. But it will be a different feeling with a dear friend. Having good times together, enjoying each other's company, admiring a friend, even feeling completely devoted to a friend, all this is a kind of "love." At the same time, one can feel strong emotional attachment to a sweetheart. Each has its place in our lives.

CAN PEOPLE OF DIFFERENT RACES FALL IN LOVE?

Yes, and often do. They have been doing it for thousands of years all over the world.

But society hasn't made it easy for such people. Laws have even been passed in certain places forbidding relationships or marriages between people of different races, in some cases because of prejudice, or ignorance about the other race, or a feeling that it is harmful to "mix" races.

Many people today feel it is perfectly natural and acceptable for men and women of different races to love each other and marry.

WHY DO PEOPLE SOMETIMES FALL OUT OF LOVE?

There is no single or simple explanation. It is sad when it happens, and seems to be something beyond "control." A person may simply begin to feel that he or she is no longer happy in the relationship. New interests or tastes by one of the partners can often bring it about. Sometimes people realize they didn't really love each other much in the first place, or were unsuited to each other.

AS MARRIED PEOPLE GET OLDER DO THEY LOVE EACH OTHER LESS?

If they loved each other all their lives together, then they still will when they are older. But the expression and quality of that love may change with age. Instead of passion, there may be tenderness. Instead of a desire to kiss, hug, and make love, there may be only the need and desire to be together, keep each other company, take care of each other. This stage of love can be just as meaningful and beautiful to older people as their young love was.

DO THE CHILDREN IN A FAMILY ALWAYS LOVE EACH OTHER?

Unfortunately, no. It often happens that there is jealousy, or basic differences in character, temperament or interests that set children in a family against each other. It has happened in many families for thousands of years.

But usually, even if they don't all "love" each other, the children in a family still feel the close ties and are concerned with each other.

CAN A CHILD HATE HIS FATHER OR MOTHER?

At any early age, many children say, "I hate you, Daddy!" or, "I hate you, Mommy!" And they feel they really do. This may be because of enforced discipline, or because of attitudes or opinions the parents have, or because certain things the children feel they want are being denied to them.

As these children grow older, they realize that they didn't really "hate" the father or mother, and may even forget they ever felt that way.

But there are cases where a child really does hate his parent or parents. There may be many reasons for this, but it is a sign that "something went wrong" in the relationship. Sometimes the parents are to blame. Their lack of understanding of the child, or the way they treated the child, may be responsible. In other cases, the child may be wrong in his own attitudes and feelings, bringing about "hate."

Whatever the reason, such things do happen and cause much unhappiness to children and parents.

WHY DO WE SOMETIMES FEEL THAT NOBODY LOVES US?

Because sometimes nobody does — at least, in the way we want to be loved. We all want other people, friends and parents, to think of us, remember us, do things for us. Sometimes these "other people" don't do it exactly when — and in the way — we'd like. They may have their own problems and disappointments, or be busy, or simply forget.

But very often those same people — our parents and friends — later *do* come through and show they love us. It's a mighty good feeling when that happens!

DOES A PARENT HAVE TO LIKE THE PERSON WE FALL IN LOVE WITH?

We *hope* they do. We *wish* they did. Because that would give us a feeling of all being together, and of approval, and of the person we fell in love with being accepted.

But in some cases it doesn't happen. Some young people today are not even asking their parents' approval of the person they're going to marry.

So there is no "must" about it. It varies from family to family, depending upon the relationship. But it *is* nice when it happens.

IF WE "LOVE" A PET, LIKE A DOG OR A HORSE, IS THAT REALLY LOVE?

It is a natural, wonderful, even exciting kind of love one can have for a pet — but it's not the same kind of love one can feel for another person. The great thing about it is that one can feel both kinds of love at the same time, enjoy them both, and still know which is really the more important and more meaningful.

ARE THERE SOME PEOPLE WHO NEVER FALL IN LOVE?

Yes. It doesn't mean they can't, or don't want to. It may be because they've never met the right person for them. Or it sometimes happens that certain people are "afraid" to fall in love, because it would mean changing their way of life, assuming responsibilities, sharing their home and possessions with someone else. Such people may love their parents, or brothers and sisters, but never be "in love."

WHAT DOES IT MEAN TO "LOVE YOUR FELLOW MAN"?

It means one should be concerned with other people, with their happiness, security, and progress. It means one should care what happens to other people, even if they are strangers, or quite different from ourselves. It means one should be willing to help them, even at some sacrifice to ourselves. Love for our fellow man is one of the basic principles of all great religions of the world.

DO ANIMALS FALL IN LOVE?

"Falling in love" among human beings involves not just sexual attraction, but also a mental and emotional involvement. Our whole person feels something for another individual's whole person.

But animals have a more limited attraction for each other. It is a sexual attraction that involves courtship and mating, but it takes place because of an instinct, the instinct to reproduce the species.

Sounds that are created, such as songs, colors that are displayed, such as in feathers of birds, certain "dances" that are done by animals and insects — all of these attract animals to each other. And this is quite different from what happens when humans fall in love.

WHAT DOES THE HEART HAVE TO DO WITH LOVE?

Nothing, really. The heart is like a pump in our body whose job it is to circulate our blood. And even though people will say, "I love you with all my heart," it is not in the heart that we feel all the things we do when we are in love. Still, the heart has become a kind of symbol of love.

Why did this happen? Probably because when we do feel a very strong emotion, the action of our heart is affected. When we're excited, the heart beats more rapidly. When we're frightened, our heart seems to "stand still." When we're upset or sad, our heartbeat slows up. So, since the heart reacts to what we are feeling, we have come to think of the heart as being the seat of love.

CAN PEOPLE WHO LOVE EACH OTHER LIVE TOGETHER WITHOUT GETTING MARRIED?

Of course they can, and many people have done it. Some young people today even feel that it's not "necessary" ever to get married formally.

There is no law that forces a man and woman who live together to be married — though members of certain religions are condemned by that religion if they don't.

But the society in which we live, including many of its laws and customs, is built around the idea of marriage. Wives have certain rights and protection that marriage gives them. Children of a legal marriage are entitled to certain things under law. And most people we meet believe in marriage and have strong attitudes about it.

So a couple that decides not to get married must be prepared to give up certain benefits, and face certain problems for themselves and their children. But they do have the right to make that choice.

WHY DO PEOPLE GO ON HONEYMOONS?

In very ancient times, a bridegroom had to "capture" his bride. He then would have to hide someplace with her until her relatives or tribespeople grew tired of searching for her. It is believed that the honeymoon developed as a symbol of what took place in those days.

So, to some extent, people still go on honeymoons because it is the traditional thing to do, just as they do many other "symbolic" things connected with marriage.

But newly married people enjoy going on a honeymoon because it gives them a chance to get to know each other intimately, and relate to each other. It is ideally spent in a place and atmosphere far from the bothers or problems of workaday life.

WHAT IS PUBERTY?

We say a young person has reached puberty when certain changes begin to take place in the body.

In a boy, hair (called "pubic hair") begins to grow in the genital area above the penis. Hair also starts to grow under the arms. The penis becomes larger. The voice becomes deeper. He begins to grow taller. All of these changes take place over a period of about two years.

In a girl, her breasts begin to develop. She also grows pubic hair. Her figure becomes larger and she may gain weight. Puberty can begin in a girl at the age of 11, but the average age is about 13 years.

WHAT IS ADOLESCENCE?

Adolescence is the period in a young person's life from puberty to adulthood. It begins in girls at ages from 11 to 15, and in boys about a year later. It lasts till they are about 19.

During the first period of adolescence, there is physical growth and change, and the sexual organs develop and begin to function.

During the last period of adolescence, many emotional changes take place, and problems may arise. The young person may feel adult in some ways, but still not want to act as an adult. New relationships with people will develop, and relationships with parents may be difficult. Adolescents begin to identify with groups of young people, or with some older person, or even form romantic attachments.

It is a period of so much change and development that the adolescent is constantly adjusting to new feelings in himself and in those he lives with.

WHY DOES IT USUALLY TAKE NINE MONTHS FOR A BABY TO BE BORN?

In mammals, the period between the fertilizing of an egg and the birth of the young that develops from that egg is called gestation. In human beings, the gestation period is about 280 days. It takes that long for all the changes and growth and development to take place so that the baby will be able to survive when it is born.

Among animals, the gestation period varies and is both longer and shorter than for human beings. For example: mice, 19 days; squirrels, 44 days; dogs, 63 days; horses, 336 days; elephants, 624 days.

IN WHAT PART OF A WOMAN'S BODY DOES THE BABY DEVELOP?

Almost immediately after the egg is fertilized, the cell begins to grow. It does this by cell division — one cell becomes two cells, and so on. It is now called an "embryo," and it still remains in the tube where fertilization took place, but it is moving toward the uterus, or womb.

Then it enters the uterus, and by the time the embryo is ten days old it begins to burrow its way into the walls of the uterus. Here is where it will grow and develop until it is ready to be born as a baby.

The uterus, a pear-shaped organ about the size of a fist, provides nourishment and protection for the developing child. As the baby grows, it stretches or expands. It can do this because the walls of the uterus are elastic, capable of being stretched to almost 500 times original size!

The baby is protected inside the uterus by two coverings. The outside covering keeps it attached to the wall of the uterus. The inside covering is filled with a liquid in which the baby floats. The liquid is like a cushion that protects the baby from being bumped while the mother moves about.

The baby grows and develops here until it is ready to be born.

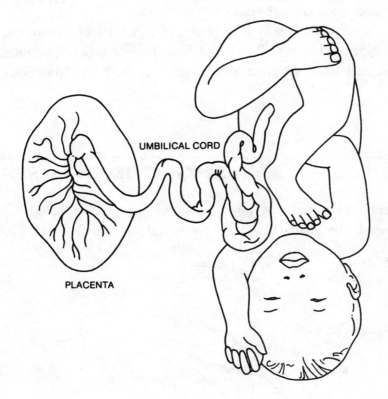

UMBILICAL CORD

PLACENTA

HOW DOES A BABY BREATHE INSIDE THE MOTHER'S BODY?

The baby receives oxygen — and nourishment — directly from the mother by means of a collection of blood vessels, called the "placenta," shaped like a flat cake. The placenta is connected to the embryo by a cord called the "umbilical cord."

Food, water, and oxygen from the mother's blood go into the blood vessels in this cord, and so into the baby. But the baby is already manufacturing its own blood, so the mother's blood doesn't go to the embryo.

WHAT EXACTLY HAPPENS IN THE PROCESS OF GIVING BIRTH TO A BABY?

The process is called "labor." It is the muscular contractions of the uterus which push the baby out into the world.

When the baby is ready to be born, the muscles of the uterus, or womb, start to contract. This is the first stage of labor. The muscles contract and relax, contract and relax. This may last from 9 to 14 hours.

WHEN DOES A BABY'S HEART BEGIN TO BEAT?

The heart of a baby is formed by joining of two blood vessels underneath the head. This tube grows quickly, bends around itself,

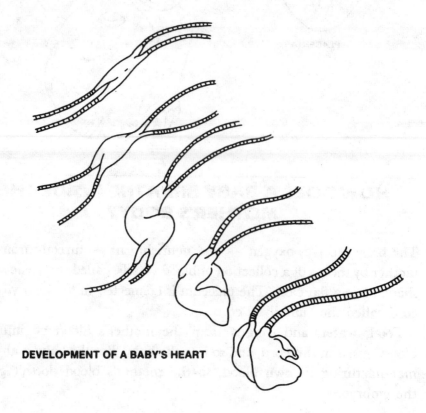

DEVELOPMENT OF A BABY'S HEART

and forms the structure that becomes the heart.

The heart begins to beat during the third week of the baby's life.

WHY ARE THERE SOMETIMES TWINS OR TRIPLETS INSTEAD OF ONE BABY?

Twins occur once in every 88 births. Triplets occur once in about 7,700 births.

There are two types of twins, fraternal and identical. Here is what happens to produce fraternal twins. A female has two ovaries where eggs are produced. It sometimes happens that one ovary releases two eggs at once, or each ovary releases an egg at the same time.

So there could be two eggs in one Fallopian tube, or an egg in each tube. Since these tubes are where sperm cells fertilize eggs, both eggs could become fertilized when sperm cells appear there.

If two eggs have been fertilized, each will become an embryo in the uterus, and will be born at the same time.

Fraternal twins may be of the same or opposite sex, and will only resemble each other as brothers and sisters do.

Identical twins are produced when a fertilized egg, after it is in the uterus, divides itself into two parts. Each part becomes an embryo, and both embryos develop and then are born at the same time.

Identical twins are of the same sex and look alike, which is why they are called "identical."

WHAT IS AN EMBRYO?

An embryo is a fertilized egg cell. It becomes an embryo the moment it is fertilized, because it begins to grow at once — from one cell to many cells.

"Embryo" is the term used for an unborn baby from the time of conception to the ninth or tenth week. At this time, vital organs are already formed and the unborn baby is called a "fetus."

DEVELOPMENT OF AN EMBRYO

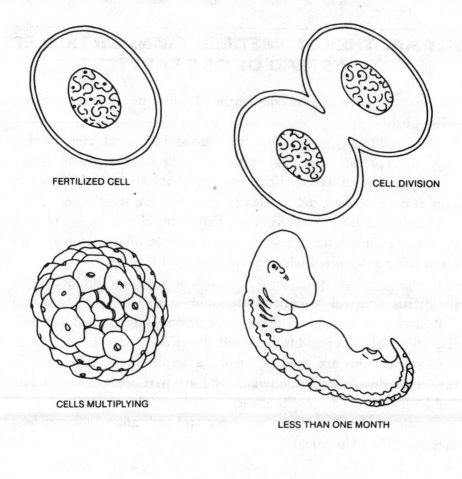

FERTILIZED CELL

CELL DIVISION

CELLS MULTIPLYING

LESS THAN ONE MONTH

WHAT IS A FETUS?

During the nine months the baby is in the mother's womb, it grows and develops.

At first it is called an embryo. An embryo is about an inch long at the end of six or seven weeks. In three months it is about four inches long.

At four months the embryo is six inches long, has arms and legs that can move, and is beginning to develop bones.

In general, however, the embryo is called a fetus after about the first two months of development.

IS IT TRUE THAT A HUMAN EMBRYO HAS A TAIL?

In the very first stages of life, embryos of all higher animals look so much alike that they cannot be told apart. Even in the third week of development, the embryo of a human being resembles that of a reptile, a bird, or another mammal.

So, during the first month, the human embryo does have a tail — which later disappears.

HOW BIG IS THE EMBRYO AT THE END OF ONE MONTH?

Here are the sizes of the embryo during its development. One month: about a quarter of an inch long. Two months: about one inch long.

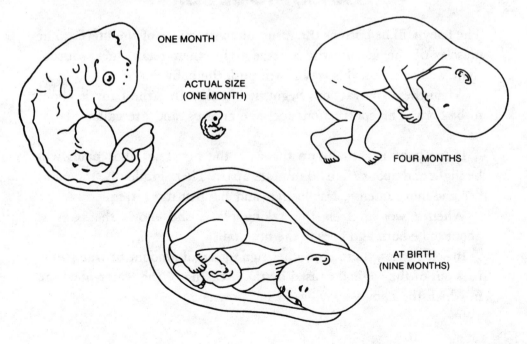

ONE MONTH

ACTUAL SIZE
(ONE MONTH)

FOUR MONTHS

AT BIRTH
(NINE MONTHS)

Three months: about four inches long. Four months: six inches long. It is usually termed a "fetus" after about the two-month period.

WHEN DOES THE FETUS BEGIN TO LOOK LIKE A HUMAN BABY?

It is hard to say exactly when this happens. But after eight weeks, when the embryo becomes a fetus, it definitely begins to look like an unborn human baby.

During the third month, the face changes a great deal. The eyes are in place, there is a bulging forehead, there are small, slit-like ears. There are nostrils, and a large, slit-like mouth. The upper limbs show the fingers, wrist, and forearms. By the end of the third month, the feet have toes, and the nails have begun to grow. There is no mistaking that it is a human baby now.

HOW DOES THE MOTHER KNOW WHEN THE BABY IS ABOUT TO BE BORN?

The baby will be born as the result of contractions of the uterus. The muscles of the uterus will squeeze tight, then relax, then squeeze tight, and so on. In this way it will push the baby out.

When these contractions begin, it is a sign that the baby is about to be born. The contractions feel like cramps, and are called "labor pains."

If the baby is actually on the way, the first few labor pains will be slight and about 15 to 30 minutes apart. Then, gradually, the pains become more intense, last longer, and happen more frequently.

When a woman feels this taking place, she knows the baby is about to be born and goes to the hospital.

In some cases, there is another sign: a small amount of water may pass out of the vagina, caused by the breaking of the water-filled sac in which the baby was lying during pregnancy.

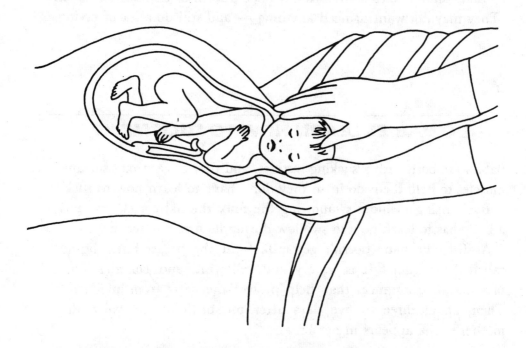

IS A BABY ALWAYS BORN HEAD FIRST?

·Almost always. But sometimes the buttocks comes out first, in which case it is called a "breech" delivery. Or the face, or the shoulders, or the legs may come out first.

A doctor can often tell weeks ahead if something like this is going to happen. He then may be able to change the baby's position before it is born. He moves the baby around from outside the womb.

A baby that doesn't come out head first usually takes longer to be born.

WHY DO NEW BABIES CRY SO MUCH?

A new baby cries because it may be uncomfortable, or it may be hungry. As it gets older, it can hold more food in its stomach at each feeding — so it doesn't cry as often out of hunger.

Sometimes babies cry because it's like a form of exercise for them. They may not want or need anything — and still do a lot of crying.

DO BABIES LEARN HOW TO SUCK MILK?

Babies are born with a sucking instinct, and they have strong sucking muscles to help them do it, so they don't have to learn how to suck.

But nursing includes swallowing the milk the baby sucks in, and a baby has to learn how to swallow during its first few feedings.

At first the baby doesn't get milk from the breast, but a liquid called "colostrum." It is watery and yellowish, and contains food plus certain substances that help protect the baby from infections. Then, about three to five days after the birth of the baby, the mother's milk appears in her breasts.

WHY DO CHILDREN RESEMBLE THEIR PARENTS?

In a child, certain things from both parents are mixed together. The male sperm cell and the female egg cell contain chromosomes. A chromosome is made up of genes — and the genes are the particles that transmit hereditary characteristics. This means that those things about a father and mother that can be passed on to a child are passed on through the genes.

This includes such characteristics as color of skin, type of hair, shape of face, body structure, and many other things about the person.

The way the genes mix — and the type of genes that come from the father and mother — decide what the new baby will be like. It may have hair like the mother's, a nose like the father's, and some features that don't resemble either one.

WHAT COLOR WOULD A BABY BE IF ONE PARENT WAS BLACK AND ONE WAS WHITE?

If the black parent has no white ancestors, and the white parent has no black ancestors, their children would usually be an "in-between" color, and called "mulattoes."

If the two people are mulattoes, their children may vary in skin color from black (going back to the black ancestor) to white (the color of the white grandparent or ancestor).

If one parent is light in skin color, but has black ancestry, and marries a white, the children will usually have skin color no darker than that of the near-white person.

WHY ARE BABIES "BURPED" AFTER FEEDING?

"Burping" a baby means holding it erect over the adult's shoulder and patting it gently on the back. It is done after each feeding and sometimes during the feeding.

Burping gives the contents of the baby's stomach a chance to settle toward the bottom. It also gives the air, which was swallowed with the milk, a chance to come up and be expelled.

HOW OFTEN IS A NEWBORN BABY FED?

Newborn infants require food about once every four hours. If the baby is smaller, it may have to be fed once every three hours. It depends on how long it takes for the baby's stomach to become empty — and this doesn't always happen on an exact schedule. During its first month, a baby usually has to be fed six or seven times a day.

HOW MANY HOURS DOES A NEWBORN BABY SLEEP?

A newborn baby sleeps 18 to 20 hours a day. Each period of sleep lasts from two to three hours, and then the baby is awakened by hunger.

As the baby grows older, and its stomach becomes larger, it can hold more food, so it can sleep longer each time.

When a baby is six months old, it sleeps less, about 16 to 18 hours a day, and it usually can sleep through the night without being fed.

INDEX

N

Nautical miles, 25
Nepal, 57
Neptune, 47
Nero, 48
Neumes, 32
New Fun, 16
New Guinea, 51, 60
New Year's Day, 18–19
New York City, 9, 11–12, 41
New York *Gazette and General
     Advertiser,* 29
New Zealand, 60
Newfoundland, 61
Niacin, 80
Nicaragua, 132
Nicotine, 74
Nile River, 90
Nitrogen, 38, 71, 84
North America, 57, 60–61, 123–25, 139
Norway, 27, 60, 108
Notation, 32

O

Ocean depths, 100–101
Octane, 103
Odontoceti, 134
Olive oil, 56
Olympic games, 33–34, 56
Opossums, 127–28
Orbits, 45, 47
Orchestras, 30
Ores, 63
Ostriches, 117–18
Otis, Elisha, 9
Ovaries, 72
Owls, 135
Oxford University, 142
Oxygen, 36, 38, 39, 65, 69, 71–73, 102,
     110, 143, 155

Oysters, 136
Ozone, 65

P

Pacific Standard Time, 21
Padlocks, 18
Panama Canal, 67
Pancreas, 72
Papillae, 78
Parallax, 95
Parathyroids, 72
Parents, 148, 149, 162, 163
Parma, Italy, 10
Pearls, 35
Peel, Sir Robert, 11
Pelagic eggs, 121
Pellagra, 80
Penguins, 141
Persia, 7, 23, 25, 106
Petroleum, 49
Pets, 149–50
    See also Cats; Dogs
Phagocytes, 75
Philadelphia, 9
Philippines, 51
Phoenicia, 13
Phonetics, 15
Phonograms, 15
Phosphorus, 22, 38
Photoelectric cell, 88–89
Pierced ears, 25–26
Pigs, 96, 97, 130, 131
Pines, 40
Pit vipers, 114–16
Pituitary, 72
Placenta, 155
Planets, 47
Plants, 37–41, 43, 49, 71, 138, 139
Platinum, 63
Plato, 29
Play-party songs, 59–60
Plumbing, 34

Uric acid, 78
Uterus, 154, 160

V

Venus, 47
Vertebrates, 131
Vesuvius, Mount, 45
Victoria, Queen, 27
Vicuna, 102
Vielle, 31
Vikings, 14, 60–61
Vinland, 61
Violins, 30–31
Vipers, 114–16
Virgin wool, 102
Virginia, 28
Viruses, 67, 68, 83, 137–38
Vision, *see* Eyes
Vitamins, 23, 40, 79–82, 84
Volcanoes, 44–45
Volunteer fire companies, 9
Voting rights, 37
Vultures, 123–24

W

Walruses, 139
Wander cells, 75
War of 1812, 29
Warts, 83
Washington, George, 28, 41
Washington, D.C., 20, 28, 41
Wasps, 118
Water, 34, 36, 38, 50, 65, 90, 91
Water buffalo, 22
Wegener, Alfred, 43
West Indies, 60
Whales, 40, 134–35
Whiskers, 130
White rice, 23
Wilson, "Uncle Sam," 28–29

Windpipe, 74
Windsor Castle, 27
Wine, 23
Witchcraft, 62–63
Wolves, 16
Woodpeckers, 136
Wool, 102
Words, 14
Worms, 119–20
Wrestling, 33, 34
Writing, 15

Y

Yaks, 22
Yale University, 24
Yeast, 12–13
Yellow fever, 67–68
Yellow jackets, 118

MP1U

TELL ME WHY #6

BY ARKADY LEOKUM

ILLUSTRATIONS BY CYNTHIA ILIFF KOEHLER, ALVIN KOEHLER, AND FRANK ALOISE

CONTENTS

Chapter 2
How Things Began

Chapter 3

The Human Body

Chapter 4

How Other Creatures Live

Chapter 5

How Things Are Made

TELL ME WHY #6

CHAPTER 1
OUR WORLD

HOW MANY GALAXIES ARE THERE?

Scattered throughout the universe are vast islands of stars, called galaxies. Our sun is a star in the Milky Way galaxy. This is our galaxy, too, and it has billions of stars in it. It takes light about one hundred thousand years to go from one end of our galaxy to the other (and light travels about six trillion miles in one year!).

Astronomers have discovered through the use of telescopes that there are millions of galaxies beyond our own and believe there are billions. There are basically three types of galaxies that we know about. Those that have a spiral shape (like our own Milky Way) are called spiral galaxies. The one nearest to us is about two million light-years away. It is the great spiral galaxy in the constellation Andromeda.

About 17 percent of the brightest galaxies that have been observed are called elliptical galaxies. (An ellipse is like a stretched-out circle.) These galaxies contain mostly stars and seem to have little or no dust and gas.

Some galaxies are called irregular galaxies because they appear to have no special shape. These galaxies contain stars, dust, and gas. The two galaxies nearest the Milky Way are irregular galaxies.

There are also some small galaxies that are called dwarf galaxies. The smallest are only a few hundred light-years across and contain only a few thousand stars. There may be more dwarf galaxies in the universe than larger ones.

Galaxies are separated from one another by hundreds of thousands of light-years. They usually occur in groups or clusters, each group containing ten or more large galaxies and some dwarfs.

The most distant clusters of galaxies so far observed lie billions of light-years from our Milky Way. And there are galaxies so far away from us that it is almost impossible for us to imagine the vastness of the distance. So the answer to the question of how many galaxies there are in the universe will probably always remain a mystery.

DO OTHER PLANETS ROTATE?

Let's consider them one by one and see what happens in each case.

Mercury goes around the sun in an orbit that takes 88 days to complete. Mercury rotates once every 58 or 59 days. This means that Mercury has a solar day (a period of day and night) that is about 180 Earth days long.

Venus rotates once about every 243 days. Mars rotates nearly as fast as the Earth. And because it is also tilted on its axis, it has seasons like the Earth's. Jupiter, which is the largest of the planets, spins very quickly. It takes less than 10 hours to rotate once. Saturn also rotates very quickly. It takes only 10 hours and 39 minutes to turn once on its axis. Uranus rotates in a very odd way because it is practically lying on its side.

Neptune and Pluto are the planets farthest away, and less is known about them than about the others. Neptune's orbit around the sun takes almost 165 Earth years to complete. It rotates every 18-20 hours in an elliptical orbit. And Pluto takes almost 248 earth years to go once around the sun, and rotates every 6 earth days in an elliptical orbit.

Scientists are learning more about the rest of the solar system than they ever knew before. We may soon have more knowledge about the motions of the other planets.

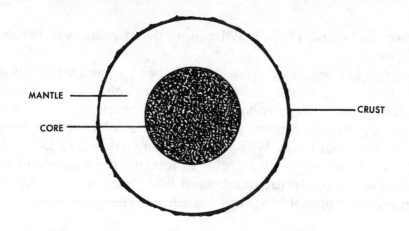

MANTLE

CORE

CRUST

HOW DO WE KNOW WHAT IS
AT THE CENTER OF THE EARTH?

Since scientists, and even instruments, are unable to go down very far into the earth, they have to use other means to find out about its interior.

One of these methods is the study of volcanic eruptions. These eruptions bring up hot gases and molten rock, indicating that the interior of the earth is hot. Another method is the study of earthquakes. Earthquake waves give us a kind of X-ray picture of the earth's interior.

When an earthquake occurs, different types of vibrations spread out in all directions through the rocks. These waves are called seismic waves. They travel at different speeds in different kinds of material. And their direction changes as they go from one kind of rock to another. By studying these waves with very delicate instruments, scientists can learn about the interior of the earth.

Scientists have noticed that at a depth of one thousand eight hundred miles, there is a sudden change in the way seismic waves travel. One kind of wave changes direction and another stops entirely. So there must be a great change in the material of the earth at that depth.

The shock waves from an earthquake reach different seismic stations at different times. This is caused partly by the material through which the waves travel. So here is another clue to what material is inside the earth.

Here is a brief idea of what is in the interior of the earth. The topmost layer, the crust, is made of solid rock. It is about twenty to thirty miles thick under the continents, and about three miles thick under the oceans.

Underneath the crust is the mantle, which is also made of solid rock. It goes down about one thousand eight hundred miles. The innermost part of the earth is the core. There is an outer liquid core, mostly made up of iron and nickel. Inside that, there is an inner core of solid metal about one thousand six hundred miles in diameter.

WHY IS THERE NO LIFE ON THE OTHER PLANETS?

We are not sure yet that there is no form of life on any of the other planets, and that is one of the things that space exploration is trying to find out. But we do know that for life to exist, certain conditions must be present.

There must be the right temperature. All living things must remain with certain limits of temperature. Living material must not be "cooked" by heat or frozen. Another condition is water. All living things require water. Light is essential for green plants, and so are certain minerals. Animals need a source of food. They cannot exist in places where they cannot obtain food.

Do all these conditions necessary for life exist on any other planet? It doesn't seem that way, judging by what we know so far about conditions on the other planets. Let's examine what they are on some of the planets.

Venus is more like the earth than any other planet. Some astronomers even think a form of plant life may exist there, because they have detected water vapor in the air above the clouds of Venus. The surface of Venus is approximately eight hundred degrees Fahrenheit. Life as we know it cannot exist there.

Planets like Jupiter and Saturn are covered by very thick layers of clouds made up of gases that are poisonous to us. Both of these planets may be very hot beneath the layers of clouds. So it goes for the other planets. Each seems to have some conditions that either make life impossible, or don't have the conditions necessary for life.

WHY DO COMETS DISAPPEAR?

A comet, like a planet or a moon, is a member of the sun's family, the solar system. A comet travels on a path or orbit around the sun on a regular schedule.

But most comets travel very elongated orbits. That is, the path they take resembles the shape of a long, fat cigar. Their orbits may carry them as far as halfway to the nearest stars. A comet following such an orbit takes thousands of years to complete one trip. So we may feel that it has "disappeared."

Comets are strongly influenced by the gravitational pull of the planets. A few comets have been pulled out of their regular orbits and forced into shorter ones. Jupiter, for example, has collected a number of comets, each of which takes about six years to orbit the sun. Comets which appear at fairly regular intervals are known as periodic comets.

But do any comets "disappear" forever? Some do. In 1826, the astronomer Wilhelm von Biela saw one of these "lost comets." It returned

several times and was observed each time by a number of astronomers. Then in 1846 it split in two, making a pair of comets. Finally, both parts of Biela's comet broke up into bits too small to be seen.

These pieces are thought to form the shower of meteors that appear in the heavens in the latter part of November. The history of Biela's comet shows that comets eventually die; that is, they break up and are scattered along their orbits in the form of meteoric dust. So comets *do* disappear eventually.

HOW FAR DOES OUTER SPACE GO?

Most astronomers think that the universe we can observe is only part of the whole universe. They picture the whole universe as extending much farther into space. But how far does it extend? Does it go on forever? Or is there perhaps an end to it somewhere? And if there is an end, what lies beyond it?

Astronomers think the answers may lie in the nature of space itself. According to the present theory, space curves around on itself. This means that you can never get "outside" space, for your path will always curve around and lead you back again.

Here is an example to help understand this: Imagine a plane flying from New York to San Francisco. If it flew in a straight line, by the time it was over San Francisco it would be a couple of thousand miles up in the air. The reason is that the earth is curved. A plane flying in a straight line is flying away from the earth into space.

To fly from New York to San Francisco, the plane actually follows a curved path. And if the plane continued in that same curved path, it eventually would come back to the earth.

Astronomers believe that space curves around in a special way. The curving is not as simple as the earth's. A picture of it cannot be drawn on paper, nor can a model of it be made. (The curvature of space, however, can be figured out by using complicated mathematics.)

So, just as it is possible to fly around the earth indefinitely without leaving it, so you could travel out in space for as long as you wished—but never outside it.

WHAT MAKES THE EARTH TRAVEL AROUND THE SUN?

Let's start with what made the earth, and all the planets, begin to move in the first place. According to one theory about the origin of the solar system, about 5 billion years ago a huge dust cloud was formed and began to spin. It flattened into a disk, and the hot central mass became the sun. The outer parts of the dust cloud broke away in swirling masses, and they condensed as planets.

So now we have the planets, of which the earth is one, in motion. Why didn't the earth and the planets just fly off into space? Gravitation, the pull of the sun, is the answer.

According to Newton's law of motion, an object in motion tends to remain in motion in a straight line unless acted upon by some outside force. Thus, a planet in motion would tend to fly away from the sun in a straight line. The outside force keeping it from doing so, and keeping it in orbit, is the sun's gravitation.

A planet moves in its orbit at a speed that depends on its distance from the sun. The planet moves faster when it is closer to the sun than when it is farther away. The earth moves at a speed of 18.8 miles per second when it is closest to the sun, and 18.2 miles per second when its orbit takes it farthest from the sun.

A planet in an orbit that is closer to the sun is attracted to the sun with more force than one that is farther away. The greater force also causes that planet to move faster than the one that is farther away. For example, Mercury moves at an average speed of 29.8 miles a second, Pluto at an average rate of 2.9 miles a second.

HOW CAN SCIENTISTS KNOW WHAT THE SUN IS MADE OF?

We know that the sun is a great ball of hot gases, made up of many layers of hot gases. But how do we know this, or any of the other things that make up the sun?

Astronomers have obtained many of their facts about the sun by using special instruments. Some of these instruments are the spectroscope, spectrograph, spectroheliograph, coronagraph, radio telescope, and space probe.

The spectroscope is used to study the glowing gases of the sun. It enables them to tell what chemicals produced the colors in the light from the sun. The spectrograph enables scientists to keep a permanent record of the colors.

The spectrohelioscope enables astronomers to see how different substances are distributed on the sun. And when this instrument has photographic equipment attached, it is called a spectroheliograph.

A coronagraph is a special kind of telescope. With a coronagraph astronomers can photograph the sun's corona without having to wait for an eclipse of the sun. A radio telescope enables scientists to study radio waves that are emitted by the sun.

Because the earth's atmosphere stops many of the sun's radiations from reaching the earth, scientists send instruments high up into the atmosphere. Such space probes help them learn more about the sun. While the technical ways in which all these instruments work have not been explained here, you can see that scientists do have instruments that enable them to learn a great deal about the sun.

HOW FAST DOES THE EARTH MOVE?

The earth, as most people know today, has two motions. It spins around on its axis, and it moves in an orbit around the sun.

The first motion of the earth that was discovered was its rotation about an axis. This rotation causes the apparent rising and setting of the sun, moon, and stars, and the changes of day and night. The period of rotation through 360 degrees (one complete turn of the earth) takes 23 hours, 56 minutes, and 4.091 seconds.

It was believed that the rate of the rotation of the earth never changed, or was constant within a thousandth of a second over centuries of time. But there are tiny variations. And because of the friction of ocean tides and changes in the earth's crust, our day may be getting longer at the rate of about one-thousandth of a second per century. (Scientists are interested in such tiny details and measure them.)

The earth also moves around the sun. At some points in its orbit it is closer to the sun than at other points. When it is nearest the sun it is at "perihelion": when it is farthest away, it is at "aphelion." The earth, and all planets, move in their orbit at a speed that depends on the distance from the sun. A planet moves faster when it is closer to the sun than when it is farther away. So it moves fastest at perihelion and slowest at aphelion. Since the earth's distance from the sun does not stay the same at all times, the orbital speed is constantly changing.

At perihelion the earth moves in its orbit at a speed of 18.8 miles per second. At aphelion it travels at the rate of 18.2 miles per second.

HOW WERE STARS FORMED?

First, what are stars? A star is a huge ball of bright, hot gases. Stars contain a great deal of hydrogen, which is their main source of energy. Stars also contain many different chemical elements, such as helium, nitrogen, oxygen, iron, nickel, and zinc. All the elements in a star are in a gaseous state.

Stars come into existence in the vast clouds of dust and gas that move through space. A star begins to form when a large number of gas particles whirl together within such a cloud. The whirling particles attract more particles, and as the group of particles slowly gets larger and larger, its gravitional pull gets stronger. The particles form a giant ball of gas.

As the ball grows larger, the particles press down on those below them and pressure builds up inside the ball. Finally the pressure becomes strong enough to raise the temperature of the gases, and the gases begin to glow. When the pressure and temperature inside the ball get very high, nuclear reactions begin to take place. The gases have become a star. How long does all this take? Probably a few million years.

If a large amount of matter comes together in forming a star, the star will be large, bright, and hot. Because it is hot, the star will burn up its nuclear fuel in about 100,000,000 years. If a much smaller amount of matter comes together in forming a star, the star will be small, dim, and cool. It will burn up its fuel slowly and may shine for thousands of millions of years.

Our sun is a star, and it is about an average-size star. It is about 109 times the diameter of the earth.

16

HOW FAR AWAY ARE THE STARS?

There are stars in the universe so far away from us that we have no way of knowing the distance, or how many of them there are. But how far away from the earth is the nearest star?

The distance from the sun to the earth is about 93,000,000 miles. Since light travels at the rate of 186,000 miles a second, it takes eight minutes for light from the sun to reach us.

The nearest stars to the earth are Proxima Centauri and Alpha Centauri. Their distance from the earth is 270,000 times greater than the distance from the sun to the earth. So their distance from us is 270,000 times 93,000,000 miles! It takes their light four and a half years to reach the earth.

Distances to the stars are so great that a unit for measuring this distance was worked out. It is called the light-year, and it is the distance that light travels in one year. This is about six million million miles (6,000,000,000,000). Four and a half times that amount is the distance to the nearest stars.

Of all the stars in the sky, only about 6,000 can be seen without a telescope. One-fourth of these stars are too far south to be visible in North America.

Actually, at any one time, looking up and counting the stars, the most one would be able to count would be a little over one thousand stars. Yet with a powerful telescope it would be possible to photograph more than one *billion*!

HOW MUCH DOES THE ATMOSPHERE WEIGH?

The earth is surrounded by a thick blanket of air. This is its atmosphere. The earth's atmosphere is made up of about 20 gases. The two main ones are oxygen and nitrogen. It also contains water vapor and dust particles.

Air is matter, and like all matter it has weight. Weight is the measure of the pull of gravity on matter. If a scale registers ten pounds when a stone is placed on it, this means that gravity is pulling the stone with a force of ten pounds.

Similarly, earth's gravity pulls on each particle of gas and dust in the atmosphere. Because our atmosphere is a vast ocean of air, it has considerable weight. If it could somehow be compressed and put on a set of scales, it would weigh about 5,700,000,000,000,000 (quadrillion) tons!

The air presses down on us and against us from all sides. Something like a ton of air is pressing against you at this moment. Yet you are not aware of this because your body is made to live with this pressure.

Air pressure is greatest at sea level, where it amounts to 14.7 pounds a square inch. It is greatest there because that is the bottom of the atmosphere. At higher altitudes the pressure is less. That is why space suits and the cabins of high-flying planes are pressurized—designed to maintain the air pressure our bodies must have.

Earth's atmosphere is one of the things that makes it a planet of life. It is the air we breathe, it shields us from certain rays of the sun, it protects the earth from extremes of heat and cold, and serves us in many other ways.

WHY IS GRAVITY IN SPACE NOT THE SAME AS ON EARTH?

Every object in the universe pulls on every other object. This is called gravitation, or gravity. But the strength of that pull—of gravity—depends on two things.

First, it depends on how much matter a body contains. A body (object) that has a lot of matter has a lot of gravitation. A body that has very little matter has very little gravitation. For example, the earth has more matter than the moon, so the earth's pull of gravitation is stronger than the moon's.

Secondly, the strength of gravitation depends on the distance between the bodies. It is strong between bodies close together. It is weak between bodies far apart.

Now let's take a human being on earth. The earth has more matter than the human being, so its gravitation pulls him to the earth. But the earth behaves as if all its matter were at its center. The strength of gravity at any place, therefore, depends on the distance from the earth's center.

The strength of gravity at the seashore is greater than at the top of a mountain. Now, suppose a human being goes some distance up into the air, away from the earth. The pull of the earth's gravity will be even weaker.

When people go out into space, they are away from the earth's gravitational field. There is no pull. They are in a condition of weightlessness. And this is why, in rockets and space capsules, weightless astronauts and objects float about in the air.

DOES WATER HAVE A TASTE?

Did you ever drink water from a well and say, "My, that tastes good"? Or perhaps you've heard people who live in certain cities say, "Our water tastes awful!" This might give you the idea that water itself does have a taste. But the fact is that water is actually tasteless. (It is also odorless and colorless.) We will see later why water seems to us to have a taste.

Water does not resemble either of the elements that compose it, hydrogen and oxygen. It has a set of properties all its own.

Water as it occurs in nature is never pure in the true sense. In the laboratory, the chemist can create chemically pure water. But in nature, water always contains dissolved mineral material, dissolved gases, and living organisms. These impurities give our drinking water its very slight but pleasant taste.

The reason water sometimes comes out "white" from a tap is the presence of these gases and other substances in water.

We might say then that the water we drink always does have a taste—simply because it is not chemically pure water.

WHAT CAUSES A WATER SHORTAGE?

Because of a water shortage in the 1960's, New York City was declared a disaster area. People were asked not to drink too much water, or to bathe too often, and they were urged to save water in every way. Considering that hundreds of millions of gallons of fresh water are fed

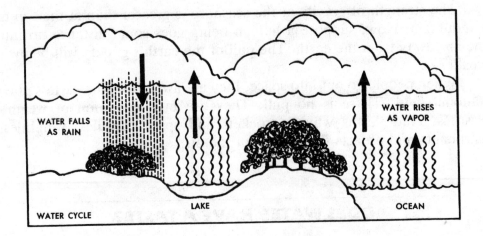

WATER FALLS AS RAIN

WATER RISES AS VAPOR

WATER CYCLE

LAKE

OCEAN

into New York City every day of the year, how could there be a water shortage?

Let's see what a water supply system is. All the fresh water in the world adds up to only about one-thirtieth of the water there is in the salty ocean. And one-third of that fresh water is locked up in snow and ice. Much of the rest is too far underground, or too loaded with minerals, to be usable. So all the fresh water needed by man and life on earth, must come from other sources.

Where does it come from? It is supplied by the "water cycle." Each year about thirty inches of water rises as vapor into the air. It falls again as snow or rain, runs to the sea, and then evaporates again into the air. It is a process that is a cycle, repeating itself over and over again. People use the water as it flows by in this never-ending process.

Since nature distributes water very unevenly, with some regions getting a lot of rain and others very little, a steady supply of water must be brought to all regions where people live. This is done through a water-supply system, and some cities bring water hundreds of miles through long and costly systems of canals, reservoirs, conduits, and pipes.

For very large cities, huge reservoirs are built and the water is stored in them. But suppose there is a dry spell with very little rain? The water in the reservoir is not replenished as it is used, and the reservoir gets lower and lower. From time to time in various parts of the country, there are long periods during which no continuous, heavy rain falls. Then a water shortage is declared, and people have to be careful about using water. By the way, the average person in the United States uses from one hundred to one hundred and fifty gallons of water every day!

WHY DOES IT RAIN ON CERTAIN DAYS
AND NOT ON OTHERS?

When you look up at the sky and see some big, heavy clouds, you might think it looks like rain. And we tend to think that this is all it takes to produce rain. But actually rain is the result of a long and complicated process.

It takes the combined influences of the sun, the earth, and the atmosphere to produce rain. The process starts when the earth is heated by the sun. This causes the water in the earth's oceans, lakes, and streams, and in damp soil, to turn into water vapor. The water vapor then mixes with the air. This process is called evaporation.

Now rising warm air carries the water vapor up into the atmosphere. Here it expands and cools. As this happens, the warm air gives up some of its load of invisible water vapor, and this forms clouds. This process is called condensation.

Inside the cloud, the tiny droplets gradually become larger and larger as they collect more moisture. Finally the drops become so large that they can no longer be held up by the air currents, and they fall to the ground as rain.

Now let's see why this process of forming rain only happens at certain times and not at others. The first step in the process, evaporation, is going on practically all the time during the day. Water vapor is rising into the atmosphere. But this invisible water vapor does not change into visible cloud droplets every day. And this is because the water vapor has to have a surface on which to condense. If there are very few or no dust particles in the air, condensation is not likely to take place. Also, small ice and snow crystals high up in the air help droplets to form.

What is usually needed for rain is the movement of a warm air mass against a cold air mass, or a cold air mass against a warm air mass. The warm air mass contains clouds and moisture, and when this warm air mass is cooled by the cold air mass, drops of water form and fall as rain. That's why weather predictions always mention movements of air masses. They give us an idea as to whether there will be rain or not.

WHAT ARE CAVERNS?

Although no two caves look alike, all of the really big caves in the world were formed in the same way. They were hollowed out of limestone (or related rocks like gypsum and marble) by acid water. They are called solution caves. Most people call them "caverns."

Some big caverns had their beginnings some 60,000,000 years ago. As rains poured down and rivers flowed, the solid rock of the cave-to-be was slowly eaten away.

The special kind of rock in such places is limestone. It is a fairly soft rock that can be dissolved by a weak acid. The acid that dissolves away limestone comes from rainwater. Falling drops of rain pick up carbon dioxide from the air and from the soil. This carbon dioxide changes the rainwater into carbonic acid.

So millions of years ago the acid rainwater fell on a bed of limestone. It nibbled away at the rock until thin cracks began to appear. More rain fell. The water trickled down, enlarging the cracks. It found new paths between the layers of stone. The paths widened into tunnels. The tunnels crisscrossed and grew into rooms. Over millions of years, the caverns took shape. As long as water filled its tunnels and flowed through its rock-walled rooms, the cavern grew bigger and bigger.

Caverns are not the only kind of cave. For example, there are sea caves, which are formed by the steady pounding of waves on the rocky cliffs along the shore. The waves don't dissolve the rock; they dig it out by grinding away at it year after year with pebbles and fine sand.

WHAT IS A STALACTITE?

Stalactites appear in many caves or caverns. To see how they are formed, let us examine one such cave, the Carlsbad Caverns in New Mexico.

The special kind of rock in Carlsbad is limestone. Limestone is a fairly soft rock that can be dissolved by a weak acid. The acid that dissolves limestone comes from rainwater. Falling drops of rain pick up carbon dioxide from the air and from the soil. This carbon dioxide changes the rainwater into carbonic acid.

About one million years ago a single drop of rainwater clung to the ceiling of the cave. As the water dripped, a tiny ring of lime crystallized on the ceiling. A second drop, and a third, fourth, and fifth left lime in the same place. As time passed, the rings of lime formed a little stone "icicle." It kept on growing.

Another drop of water dripped to the floor of the cave. Again the lime was left behind. As time passed, thousands of drops fell on the same spot. The specks of lime formed what looked like a stubby stone candle. The "candle" kept on growing.

The icicle of stone on the ceiling is called a stalactite. The stubby candle on the floor is a stalagmite. Each stalactite and stalagmite grows at a different rate, depending on the wetness of the cave, the temperature of the room, and the thickness of the limestone bed above it. Some stalactites grow an inch a year, others take one hundred years or so to grow that much.

Often the stalagmites growing upward meet the stalactites growing down and form columns. The largest column in Carlsbad is one hundred feet high. The ceilings of some caves are covered with short, hollow stalactites that look like soda straws. Others have glittering stone needles on their walls, or stone pincushions bristling from the floor. Some stalactites grow sideways and up as well as down.

When water stops reaching the underground caves, the stalactites stop growing, and the cave is considered "dead."

WHY DO PLANTS HAVE ROOTS?

A plant needs roots for two chief reasons: as a means of anchorage or support, and to absorb water and mineral salts from the soil.

The roots of most plants grow in the soil. They don't "just sit there," but seem to reach out in the soil to help the plant grow. By elongating near their tips, roots are always coming in contact with new portions of soil.

Thousands of tiny root hairs project from the surface of the young root and absorb materials from the soil. That's why when a young root is pulled from the soil, soil particles often cling to the root hairs.

Some plants have taproots. A taproot is a large, single root, much larger than any of the branch roots. It may be fleshy like a carrot, or woody like a hickory root. Other plants have not one large root, but several roots of approximately equal size. These form what is called a fibrous root system.

Grasses have fibrous root systems. Soil in which there are many fibrous roots is protected in this way from erosion. In still other plants, most of the roots grow from stems as, for example, the geranium.

As roots grow older, some of them store large quantities of sugar and starch. Beets and sweet potatoes are examples of this. A sweet potato is a root, but an Irish potato, with its eyes, is a stem.

Not all plants have roots that grow in the soil. Some tropical orchids that grow on trees have spongy roots that grow in the air and absorb moisture. Both the English ivy and poison ivy cling to walls or trees by means of tiny aerial roots.

Some plants have special roots that develop from the stem above the ground and grow down into the soil, forming props. A few roots, such as the sweet potato, form buds that grow into leafy branches and can be used to propagate the plant.

WHY DO PLANTS TURN TOWARD THE SUNLIGHT?

If plants didn't do this, they wouldn't be able to live. They would have no food.

Leaves produce food, in the form of sugar, for the entire plant. The leaves contain a special green substance that enables them to do this. This substance is chlorophyll. Chlorophyll can produce sugar only in the presence of light. This food-producing process is called photosynthesis, which means "putting together with light."

So we can see why plants have to turn their leaves toward the sunlight. But how can plants do this? Botanists say that the plant is "phototropic," that is, it turns toward the light, and it does it this way:

Plant cells contain growth substances known as auxins. These substances move away from the light. When the plant is not in the light, the auxins gather in the cells on the side of the stem away from the light. The auxins make the cells on that side grow faster than the cells on the lighted side. This makes the plant bend toward the light.

We do not usually think of plants as moving at all. This is because

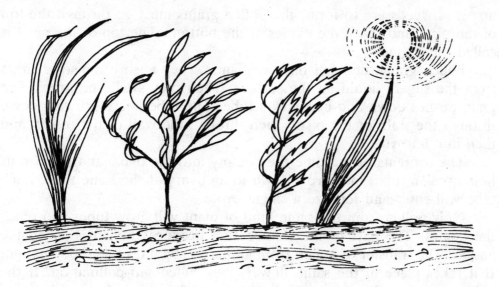

the movements of plants are usually too slow to be seen. But if you could see certain plants on a fast-motion film, you could see that the leaves, flowers, and stems are almost constantly moving—even when no wind is blowing.

Some plants move quickly. A pumpkin, squash, or cucumber vine may form a complete coil around a string support in ten minutes.

HOW DO NEW FLOWERS GROW?

Every living thing has some means of reproducing itself. In flowers, the process takes place as follows:

A typical flower has four main parts. There is usually a green outer cup made up of leaflike sepals. Within the sepals are the petals. Within the petals are the reproductive organs necessary for producing seeds.

In the very center of the flower are one or more pistils. Around the pistils is a ring of stamens. The pistil is the female part of the flower. The bottom of it is enlarged and is called the ovary. Inside the ovary are little round ovules, which later become seeds. But they become seeds only if they are fertilized by the contents of a pollen grain.

Pollen grains are produced by the stamens, the male organs of the flower. If seeds are to form, the pollen grains must go through the top of the pistil and reach the ovules at the bottom. The top of the pistil is called the stigma.

Pollen grains first fall on the stigma. They absorb moisture there from the sugary liquid on the surface. Then they swell and grow. The grain pushes down and becomes a tube. The tube keeps growing down through the stalk of the pistil, then through the wall of the ovary, and then into an ovule.

The contents of the tube then empty into the ovule and fertilize it. Many pollen tubes may grow down to an ovary at the same time. Each tube will enter and fertilize a single ovule.

Only pollen from the same kind of plant will grow tubes and reach the ovules. The part of the stamen that produces pollen is called the anther. The transfer of pollen from anther to stigma is called pollination. If it takes place in the same flower, it is called self-pollination. If the pollen goes to a flower on a different plant of the same kind, it is called cross-pollination.

Cross-pollination of flowers is done by the wind, by insects, by birds, and by certain animals. Later on, the seeds that develop also have to be carried to a place where they can take root and grow into flowers.

WHY DO TREES HAVE LEAVES?

Green plants and trees have to manufacture their food. The leaves are the food factories for the plants and trees.

Leaves of fruit trees manufacture the food that helps to make fruit. For example, peaches and maple sugar are sweet. So peach and maple tree leaves make sugar. They do this by taking materials from the air and the ground. One of these materials is carbon dioxide, a gas taken from the air. The other material is water, which comes from the soil. By a process called photosynthesis, the leaves manufacture sugar from the water and carbon dioxide.

Every factory must have machines and power to run the machines. The machines of the leaf are many little green bodies called chloroplasts. They are green because they have in them a green matter called chlorophyll. Sunshine is the power that runs the machines. Leaves change color in the fall when the chlorophyll disappears, and the red-and-yellow coloring matter can then be seen.

Chloroplasts work inside a leaf. The leaf is made up of cells. Some of these cells contain chloroplasts; others have few or none and do other jobs. "Guard" cells help regulate the size of the openings through which air passes. Many of these guard cells are on the underside of a leaf. A pair of guard cells and the opening between them is called a stoma (plural: stomata).

The roots of a plant or tree take water from the soil that eventually reaches the veins of the leaves. These veins carry back food the leaves have made. The air that goes into a leaf through the stomata has carbon dioxide in it. When the sun is shining, the leaves use the carbon dioxide to make sugar. The rest of the air, with additional oxygen, is given off through the stomata. But when it is dark and leaves are not making food, they do not need carbon dioxide. Then they give off air with carbon dioxide left in it.

Leaves give off water, too. Part of the water taken in through the roots is used to make sugar. The rest is given off from the leaves.

WHAT IS THE TALLEST TREE?

Trees are green plants. They have roots, stems, leaves, and seeds, just as other green plants do. Trees are also the oldest of all green plants. Some of the sequoia trees of the northwestern United States are more than four thousand years old. This means they were fully grown trees long before Columbus discovered America!

And trees are the biggest of all green plants. The tallest trees known to exist on earth are the giant redwoods of California. There is one tree there, growing in the Humboldt National Forest, that is believed to be the tallest tree in the world. It is called the Founder's Tree and is 364 feet high!

Some authorities believe that long ago the eucalyptus tree of Australia may have been as tall as these California redwoods, but those growing today average about fifty feet shorter. Two other kinds of trees that come close to the redwood are the Douglas fir and the sequoia, some of which have grown over three hundred feet tall.

The roots of a tree not only take water and mineral materials from the soil, but also hold the plant firmly in the ground. And with very large trees, it takes quite a bit of root system to hold the tree firmly.

Did you know that the roots of trees take up nearly as much room under the ground as their tops or crowns do above?

Scientists have learned to tell the age of trees by counting rings in the wood. There are rings in the cross-section of most kinds of tree trunks. New wood is formed each year in a layer outside the old wood and beneath the bark. It is this layer that becomes the ring. Each ring in the wood of the trunk of a tree represents one year of the tree's life. The trunk gets bigger and bigger around as new rings or layers are added.

A tree adds rings not only to its trunk but to its branches and twigs, too. Some new length is added to the tip ends of the twigs and branches each year. Because growth in height takes place only at the tips of branches, the limbs of trees never move farther from the ground than they were in the beginning!

WHAT IS GUM?

Gum has a whole variety of interesting uses—many of them more important than providing you with something to chew on! And, of course, there are a great many different kinds of gums.

One gum, called gum arabic, is used in making candies, medicines, and mucilage, and in the manufacture of silks. Like most of the true gums, it comes from the plant as a thick, sticky liquid, which hardens when exposed to air and dissolves in water.

Gum arabic is produced by several varieties of acacia trees, which grow in Africa, Australia, and Asia. It is sold in the form of clear yellow or reddish lumps. Some gums, instead of dissolving in water, absorb it and make a soft, gluey, gelatin-like mass. One such gum is called gum dragon, and is used in making cough medicines and as a sizing in cloth.

Another important gum is cherry gum, which is used in stiffening straw for the manufacture of straw hats and other articles. Other common gums are plum, peach, spruce, and chicle.

Chicle is produced by the naseberry and other trees and is used in making ordinary chewing gum. All these gums are used in the manufacture of ink, cloth, paper, and medicines. Some of the finest gums are used in medical and research laboratories for work with cultures.

Most gums are gathered in the dry seasons and brought to the markets in the form of nodules or "tears." Chemically, gums consist of an acid nucleus combined with sugar molecules.

In addition to the true gums we have described above, there are gum resins. They are also produced by plants, but they differ from true gums because they contain resin, and therefore will not dissolve completely in water.

Two famous gum resins are frankincense and myrrh. They are very fragrant and are used in making perfume and incense.

WHAT IS NEON?

When we walk down the main street of a city at night, we see all sorts of colored lights on stores and advertising signs. We think of them as neon lights.

But the fact is that not all of them are lights made by glowing neon gas. Other gases, such as helium, argon, krypton, and xenon, are also used in lights. Each gas gives out a different-colored light when electricity is sent through it.

The color of the light given out will vary, depending on such things as the temperature, pressure, and electric voltage. Neon gives out a red-orange light; argon gives out a reddish-blue light; the light from helium is white, yellow, or sometimes violet; from krypton it is yellow, green, or pale violet; and from xenon it is either blue or blue-green.

By passing electricity through neon gas, the atoms are made to give off light. What happens is that the energy of the electric current knocks electrons off some of the atoms of neon. When these electrons rejoin the neon atoms, energy in the form of light is given off.

All the gases we have mentioned here form a family of elements called the noble gases. Sometimes they are called rare gases because they are fairly scarce. All of these gases are relatively inactive chemically. This means they do not burn, and they form no chemical compounds under normal conditions.

The chief source of these gases is ordinary air (except for helium, which is obtained from natural gas). The gases are mixed together in the air with oxygen, nitrogen, carbon dioxide, and other substances.

To get the noble gases, the air is separated into its elements, and the gases are removed one at a time. This is done by chilling air to a very low temperature so that it turns into a liquid. The liquid air is piped into tall towers and heated.

As each gas reaches its boiling point, it boils off from the liquid air as a gas.

WHY DOES A DIAMOND SPARKLE?

Suppose diamonds were not as rare as they are. Suppose they didn't cost much and almost everyone could have them. Would diamonds still be valuable?

Two things would probably make people still want to have diamonds. One is that a diamond is the hardest substance known to man, so diamonds would still be very useful in industry. The second is that diamonds would still be beautiful, and so people would still enjoy looking at them.

Diamonds are the result of a process that took place in nature. Millions of years ago, the earth was gradually becoming cooler. At that time, there existed beneath the ground a mass of hot liquid rock. This mass was subjected to extreme heat and pressure. As a result of this, molecules of carbon became packed together in dense, clear crystals. A diamond is simply a crystal of pure carbon.

When a diamond is found in "rough" form, its outside appearance is rather dull. Now man takes over to make it into the sparkling gem we all know about. Most diamonds are sawed in two, and each half is shaped and cut into a round diamond called a brilliant.

Then little faces, or facets, are cut into the diamond. The average brilliant is cut into fifty-eight facets, or even more. These facets make a diamond sparkle.

The reason for this is that a diamond has a very high refractive power. This means that when light enters it, the diamond bends the light more than other substances do. The light, instead of passing through the diamond, is bent so that it is reflected back into the stone. So a greater amount of light is returned to our eyes when we look at a diamond and it looks more brilliant. The diamond also breaks up the light into its different colors, which gives a diamond its "fire."

Did you know that diamonds were not worn as personal ornaments until 1430, when a Frenchwoman called Agnes Sorel started the custom? From then on the custom spread.

HOW IS GOLD FOUND?

Probably the first metal known to man was gold. Because of the way it occurs in nature, man knew about it and valued it long before the days of recorded history! Just how is gold found?

Even though it's considered so precious and rare, gold is actually widely distributed in nature. The trouble is that in most cases there isn't enough gold present to make it profitable to extract it. For example, sea water contains a small amount of gold. But it's so tiny in quantity that no one knows how to separate gold from the sea. Yet there's so much water in the oceans that the total amount of gold in them might be as much as ten billion tons!

Gold occurs in two forms: native, which means it's not combined with other minerals, and in combination with the ores of other metals. Native gold occurs mostly in veins of quartz or in masses of iron pyrites.

Sometimes the quartz or pyrites have been exposed to water and wind. The particles of rock surrounding the lumps of gold have been washed away, leaving lumps or nuggets of nearly pure gold.

The nuggets are gradually washed down to the bottom of the valleys and become mixed with the sand and the gravel. In this form it is called "alluvial" or "placer" gold. When people first discovered gold, it was

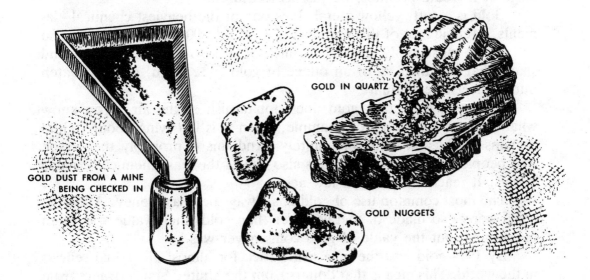

GOLD IN QUARTZ

GOLD DUST FROM A MINE
BEING CHECKED IN

GOLD NUGGETS

placer gold. These particles of gold vary in size from fine dust to the great nugget found in Australia, the "Welcome Stranger" nugget, weighing nearly 150 pounds!

Gold is often found in the ores of other metals. Silver nearly always contains quantities of gold. Copper ores quite frequently occur in combination with gold.

Today, most of the gold is obtained by mining methods similar to those used for other metals. A deep hole, called a shaft, is dug into the ground toward the gold deposit. This may be more than a mile deep! The ore is then blasted, loaded on carts, brought to the shaft, and hoisted to the surface. It is crushed and ground into a fine sand called pulp, and then by means of chemical action, the gold is extracted from the other material.

The five principal gold-producing countries of the world are South Africa, Russia, Canada, China, and the United States.

WHY IS GOLD EXPENSIVE?

There are three reasons why people have always placed a high value on gold: its beauty, its usefulness, and its scarcity. If iron were as scarce as gold, it would probably be just as treasured.

Gold is a soft, yellow metal. It is one of the heaviest chemical elements. A cubic foot of this metal weighs over 1,200 pounds. Gold is also one of the most easily worked metals. Gold is so easy to hammer and shape that less than $1/25$ of an ounce of gold (one gram) can be beaten into a sheet 6 feet square.

Unlike most metals, gold does not tarnish in the air. (You know what happens to silver, for example, when it is left lying about.) Gold remains bright and shiny indefinitely. And this is probably the reason why people first valued it. Gold is also one of the least chemically active metals. It reacts with only a few acids.

The most common use of gold has always been as money. Although coins were also made of metals other than gold, their value was often questioned, but the value of gold coins never was.

By 1914 gold was the measuring stick for almost all the currencies in the world. This means that dollars from the United States, francs from

France, marks from Germany, and so on—all had a set value in terms of gold. At any time the currencies could be changed into gold. This system is known as the gold standard and is no longer in use, but gold is still very important in international trade. Gold is used as a "reserve" that backs up a country's international trade.

There are a tremendous number of uses for gold. About 10 percent of the gold produced each year is used by jewelers. Gold is used in dental work. Since gold conducts electricity well, it is used in certain types of electrical contacts.

The scarcity of gold keeps its price high. Today, slightly more than half of all the gold mined comes from South Africa. The world's richest gold deposits were discovered there in 1886.

WHAT IS ALUMINUM FOIL MADE OF?

Aluminum is the most abundant metal in the earth's crust. Actually, it makes up between 7 and 8 percent of the crust. But aluminum is never found in a pure state in nature. Rather, it is combined with other chemical elements in compounds that are very hard to break down. The most important ore of aluminum is bauxite, a type of clay. This generally contains from 40 to 60 percent aluminum oxide.

Aluminum has a number of properties that make it useful for many products. Aluminum is light, weighing one-third as much as such metals as iron, copper, nickel, or zinc. Aluminum conducts electricity well and is also a good heat insulator, because its shiny surface reflects away heat rays. And aluminum resists corrosion; when it is exposed to air, aluminum immediately combines with some of the oxygen to form a thin, tough, colorless film that protects the metal against further chemical action, thus preventing rust.

For these and other reasons, aluminum is used in making foil. Foil is any metal sheet that measures 0.005 of an inch or less. To roll a metal this thin, machines of great precision are needed. Even the smallest change in measurement shows up in foil. Different kinds of mills have been developed to roll out aluminum and other metals to the exact thickness desired.

Aluminum is so malleable that it can be rolled into sheets of foil as thin as 0.0002 of an inch. In such cases pure aluminum is used. For most other things, and for greater strength in the foil, aluminum alloys are used. In these instances other metals are combined with aluminum.

The aluminum foil you use at home resists moisture and gas, is greaseproof, odorless, and tasteless, resists corrosion, reflects away heat, and shuts out light.

WHAT IS PEWTER?

Pewter is an alloy, which means it is a mixture of metals. The basis of pewter is tin. It is generally mixed with lead in the proportions of six or four parts tin to one part lead.

Pewter has been made for thousands of years, though it is hard to be exact about it. It is said to have been known to the ancient Chinese, the Egyptians, and the Greeks. The ancient Romans made it, too.

Pewter is usually associated with the English, and there is a reason for this. In Cornwall, England, there were mines with deposits of fine tin, and so the English made pewter in very early days, and tin from Cornwall was used for making pewter in other parts of Europe.

Pewter has been used for three basic purposes: for church vessels, for domestic needs, and in civic functions. Chalices of pewter have been used in church services in England since medieval times.

In England, pewter became very popular for use in plates and cups. But in time, the richer people began to prefer silver, and so the middle classes used pewter in place of silver.

In France, pewter was used for drinking vessels, plates, salt-cellars, and cooking pots as far back as the fourteenth century. Germany had a pewter industry established in the fourteenth century, and at about the same time pewter was also being made in Belgium, Holland, Switzerland, Russia, and the Scandinavian countries.

In the United States, pewter was much used in homes in the early Colonial period. There is some that goes back to the seventeenth century, but the great period of production was between 1750 and 1850. Pewter was used for every kind of utensil that was made.

Pewter was also made in China, Korea, and Japan more than one thousand years ago.

WHAT IS PLANKTON?

The word plankton comes from the Greek word for "wandering" or "drifting." And plankton is a drifting mass of life made up of billions of tiny living creatures.

Some of the organisms that make up plankton, such as tiny green plants, always remain plankton. Others, such as fishes and lobsters, are plankton only while they are very young. Sometimes plankton includes large jellyfishes, sometimes creatures so small they cannot even be seen with an ordinary microscope. But all plankton have means of staying afloat and share a drifting way of life.

The smallest plankton organisms are one-celled plants called microscopic algae. One of the most numerous of these is a kind of algae called diatoms. There can be two million diatoms in a single gallon of water.

The animal life included in plankton is quite interesting. One kind is the pear-shaped copepod. Copepod means "oar feet." A copepod swims by jerky, oarlike movements of its tiny legs. The largest copepod is less than one-half inch long.

Young crustaceans of many kinds are plankton. These crustaceans include shrimps, crabs, lobsters, and barnacles in salt water, and crayfish and water fleas in fresh water. The larvae, or developing young, of these crustaceans are tiny or even microscopic, and during this period they cannot move on their own, so they drift with other plankton.

This is also true of the young mollusks, such as snails, clams, and mussels. They are part of the plankton at the first stages of their life. Plankton may also include the eggs and larvae of many fishes.

In fresh water, animal plankton often includes developing insects. Mayflies, dragonflies, mosquitoes, water beetles, and many other insects lay their eggs in water. When the larvae hatch, they live and feed on the plant plankton.

And this is only part of what makes up plankton. So you can see how much this classification includes and how interesting it is to study.

HOW DO ARCHAEOLOGISTS KNOW WHAT THEY FIND?

An archaeologist digs up things buried by ancient peoples. The question is, how can he identify cities and people and objects and reconstruct the life of the past from what he has found?

The answer is that it can't always be done. An archaeologist doesn't always find the things he needs to build a complete picture of a people or a way of life. After all, what he finds is only what people left behind, usually objects that were used every day. These might be remains of houses, tools, jewelry, dishes, toys, and also bones of animals used for food.

But many of the things that were important to the lives of early people cannot be found. Objects made of leather, wood, cloth, wool, or straw usually decay and leave no trace. Another thing that must remain a mystery to the archaeologist is the clothing early people wore. He can probably tell whether they used cloth or animal skins, but unless they left drawings of themselves, he can't tell much more about their clothing.

The archaeologist also may have no clue as to whether the people were artistic, and he may know nothing at all about their thoughts and ideas. So his picture of the life of the early people may be quite incomplete.

But, despite this, the archaeologist can still tell us a great deal. He first finds out the order in which early towns were built, one upon the ruins of another. Then he must know the town in which each object was found. Each object is labeled, photographed, measured, and so on. If the site belongs to historic times, the archaeologist must know the ancient writing used in that place.

There are many experts who help archaeologists such as geologists, botanists, zoologists, and others, all of whom help identify and analyze what they have found. Sometimes it takes years of work and study before the archaeologists are ready to publish a work about what they have found. But when they do, it may give us an exciting view into the past—a picture of how ancient peoples lived.

WHAT WAS DARWIN'S THEORY?

For a long time people believed (and certain religious groups still believe) that each form of life appeared separately on earth and that none had ever changed. They also believed that the earth itself was about four thousand years old. And so there was hardly time for much change to have occurred.

CHARLES DARWIN

GALAPAGOS ANIMALS THAT LED
TO HIS THEORY OF EVOLUTION

IGUANA

SEA IGUANA

37

Scientists claim they have shown that these beliefs are wrong. Living forms have undergone many changes in their long history. These changes came about very slowly. All of these changes are summed up in the term, evolution. Evolution describes the many changes that have taken place, and is also a theory developed to explain those changes.

The man who laid the foundations for the modern theory of evolution was Charles Darwin. Darwin said that all life had evolved, and that descendants of a species could become different from the parent forms. These ideas were not new or unusual. But Darwin suggested how evolution might have occurred.

He called the process natural selection. He said that nature "selected" those organisms best suited to survive in the "struggle for existence." Each organism differed slightly from other organisms and had its own individual traits. Some had traits that made them better able to survive than others. Therefore they lived longer and had more offspring. In this way, "beneficial" traits were passed on to a larger number of descendants.

Little by little, living things became so different from their ancestors that biologists classified them as separate and distinct species. Darwin believed that this was how new species originated. His theory still forms the basis of modern thinking on evolution.

Biologists later discovered that certain small chemical units called genes determine the traits that are passed from one generation to another. The genes change, or mutate, from time to time. A changed gene causes a variation in a trait, and if the change is favorable to survival, it may be passed on to the next generation.

WHY IS SNOW WHITE?

Snow is actually frozen water, and as we know, ice has no color. Why then is snow white?

The reason is that each snowflake is made up of a large number of ice crystals. These crystals have many surfaces. And it is the reflection of light from all these surfaces that makes snow look white.

Snow forms when water vapor in the atmosphere freezes. As the vapor freezes, clear transparent crystals are formed. The currents that are in the air make these crystals go up and down in the atmosphere.

As the crystals do this, they begin to gather around tiny particles that are in the clouds. When a group of ice crystals is big enough, it floats down to earth as a snowflake.

The crystals that make up a snowflake always arrange themselves in a special way. They either form six-pointed stars or thin plates shaped like a hexagon. Each branch of the six-pointed star is exactly like the others.

While all the branches of a snowflake are identical, no two snowflakes have ever been found to be exactly alike.

We can only think of snow as being white. But there have actually been cases where colored snow has fallen. One famous case of this was reported by Charles Darwin. During one of his expeditions, he noticed that the hoofs of the mules were becoming stained red as they walked through the snow.

The red snow was caused by the presence of certain tiny plants, called algae, which had been in the atmosphere when the snow formed.

HOW IS HUMIDITY MEASURED?

Water in the atmosphere is the only reason we have clouds, fog, rain, snow—and warm, sticky days. The atmosphere carries water in three different forms: water vapor, liquid water, and solid water.

A hot humid day is different from a hot dry day only because of water vapor. The amount of water vapor in the atmosphere is called humidity. When we say "relative humidity" is 80 percent, we mean that the air is holding 80 percent of the water vapor it could hold. When air is at 100 percent relative humidity, it is holding all the water vapor it possibly can, and we call it saturated air. Warm air can hold more water vapor than cold air.

The instrument used to measure the amount of water vapor in the air is a hygrometer. The most accurate kind is called the wet and dry bulb hygrometer. Two thermometers are mounted side by side on a base. The bulb of one is covered with muslin or some other coarse material which is kept wet. The bulb of the other is left bare and dry.

Evaporation of water on an object cools it. If the air contains much water vapor, the moisture on the wet bulb evaporates slowly, and the wet bulb thermometer doesn't show much lowering in temperature. If the air is dry, the moisture on the wet bulb evaporates rapidly, and the wet-bulb thermometer shows a much lower temperature than the dry-bulb thermometer.

By consulting a prepared table, the relative humidity can be learned by comparing the two temperatures. There are other types of hygrometers that use currents of air, or chemicals, or a hair, to measure the increase or loss of moisture in the air.

WHAT IS CARBON DIOXIDE?

Carbon dioxide is a compound, usually in the form of a gas. It can become a solid if it is cooled enough.

There is a very small amount of carbon dioxide present in the air, about one gallon in 2,500 gallons of air. Most of this carbon dioxide gets into the air when plant and animal tissues, which are carbon, decay. Fuels that are made up of carbon, such as wood and coal, give off large amounts of carbon dioxide when they are burned.

The human body needs a small amount of carbon dioxide in order to live. It controls the rate at which the heart beats and also other functions in the body. But inhaling too much carbon dioxide can do harm and even cause a person to suffocate.

Human beings take oxygen from the air they breathe. This oxygen is taken into the bloodstream. There it combines with food and is changed to carbon dioxide. Then the carbon dioxide returns to the lungs and is breathed out.

Plants, on the other hand, take in carbon dioxide to live. Green plants draw carbon dioxide from the air through the pores in their leaves. This combines with water, and with the help of sunlight the carbon dioxide and water change to starch and other food for the plant. The plant then gives off oxygen as a waste product.

So plants give off oxygen and take in carbon dioxide. People and animals take in oxygen and give off carbon dioxide. This keeps the supply of oxygen and carbon dioxide in the air fairly stable.

Carbon dioxide also has many commercial uses, the best known of which is for "carbonating" soft drinks.

WHAT IS OZONE?

Ozone is a form of oxygen. Oxygen is a chemical element, the most abundant element on earth. Oxygen is all around you. It makes up about one-fifth of the air. (Most of the rest of the air is nitrogen.)

Ordinary oxygen exists in the form of molecules made up of two oxygen atoms. There is also a second form of oxygen, called ozone, made up of three oxygen atoms.

Most ozone is formed in the upper atmosphere by ultraviolet radiations. These radiations break apart oxygen molecules into separate oxygen atoms. When these atoms become attached to some other oxygen molecules, ozone is formed.

Ozone collects in a layer from 12 to 22 miles above the earth. This layer, called the ozone layer, tends to protect life on earth by filtering some of the sun's powerful radiations. Ozone is also formed close to earth during lightning storms and by X-ray and electrical equipment. You may have seen blue sparks shooting off when metal is cut with an oxygen torch. These sparks are an indication that ozone is being formed.

Ozone combines with other substances much more rapidly than oxygen does. Ozone destroys germs very quickly and for this reason is used to purify water and to clean public places. It is also used as a bleach for many common substances, such as flour, wax, and cloth.

Ozone has a strong "electric" smell and may harm lung tissues if too much is breathed in.

WHAT IS SAND MADE OF?

When a solid rock is exposed to the action of the wind, rain, and frost, and broken up into smaller particles, if the particles are small enough (between one four-hundredth of an inch in diameter and one-twelfth of an inch in diameter), these particles are called "sand."

Since sand is formed of small grains of the minerals making up the rocks, any of these minerals may be found in sand. The principal mineral found in sand is quartz, because it is very hard and is quite abundant. Some sands have as much as 99 percent pure quartz. Other minerals sometimes found in sand are feldspar, calcite, mica, iron ores, and small amounts of garnet, tourmaline, and topaz.

Sand is found wherever rocks have been exposed to the weather. One of the principal sand-forming regions is the beach of a sea. There the action of the tide upon the rocks, the action of windblown sand rubbing against the rocks, and the dissolving of some of the minerals in the rocks by the salt water, all combine to make sand.

What about the sand often found in deserts? Most of the loose sand there has been brought by wind. In some cases, the desert sands may have been formed by the decay of rocks. In still other cases, the desert was once really a sea bottom and the water retreated thousands of years ago, leaving the sand.

Sand is a very useful substance. It is used in making concrete, in making glass, in sandpaper, and as a filter in helping keep water pure.

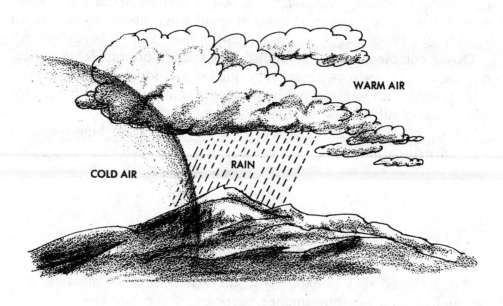

WHAT IS A CLOUD?

Here is how clouds are formed. Warm air, laden with moisture, rises into the sky. When it gets to a certain height, the warm air cools. At the cooler temperatures it can no longer hold all its moisture in the form of water vapor. So the extra moisture changes into small drops of water, or bits of ice, and this forms clouds.

No two clouds are exactly alike, and they are always changing their shape. The reason we have different types of clouds is that cloud formation takes place at different heights and temperatures. And clouds will be composed of different particles, depending on their height and temperature.

As the water vapor in the air changes back into a liquid (this is called condensation), it comes into contact with dust and other particles in the air. A droplet of liquid water forms around each tiny particle.

It takes about 100,000,000 droplets to form one large raindrop. And so it would take about a million million million droplets to make up a cloud a mile wide, a mile long, and a mile deep. Such a cloud may have about 1,400 tons of water in droplet (liquid) form and nearly 14,000 tons of water in water-vapor (gas) form.

The water vapor condenses into droplets to form clouds around many kinds of particles. There are dust particles blown from deserts, dry topsoil, and volcanoes. There are tiny crystals of salt from the oceans, solid particles from the burning of coal, and many other kinds.

WHAT IS THE EYE OF A HURRICANE?

In a hurricane, there are spiraling winds going around and around at great speed. When the winds are blowing at about 75 miles an hour, the pressure falls very rapidly in a small region of the center of the air column. The very low pressure region in the center is called the eye of the storm.

The eye may be from 10 to 20 miles across. The low pressure in the eye of the hurricane causes sea water to rise slightly within the eye. The water sometimes rises to about three feet.

Very heavy rains come down in the low-pressure area. The heaviest rains come from clouds surrounding the eye of the storm. The eye can be thought of as the hole in a doughnut. The winds rage around the eye, but within it all is calm. The sky overhead may be clear or have scattered clouds. The winds are light, usually less than 15 miles an hour.

If a hurricane passed directly over you so that you stood in the path of the eye, you would first be gripped by the winds and drenched by the rain of the front edge of the storm. Next, there would be a period of calm and of clear sky as the eye of the hurricane passed by. Then there would be another period of rain and strong winds, this time blowing from the opposite direction.

Why does the pressure fall very rapidly in a small region of the center of the air column that is a hurricane? Why does the eye of the hurricane form? Meteorologists, who have been studying this, are still not sure why it happens.

WHY DOES CORN HAVE SILK?

The silk on a corn plant is needed by the plant to produce seeds. Here is how it works:

The corn plant has a woody stalk that grows from 6 to 20 feet high. At the top there is a spiked tassel. This part grows the male flowers of the plant. Farther down, the stalk grows one or more spikes which develop into ears. The spikes have threadlike filaments (silk). These are the female flowers.

Each filament grows from a germ on the spike called an ovule. The ovules are arranged in rows along the spikes. Each one will produce a seed, called a kernel, if the filament of silk is fertilized by a grain of pollen. To catch pollen, the tender tips of silk stick out from the top of the leafy wrapping around the spike.

When the flower parts develop, the tassles produce yellowish dust-like grains of pollen. Each grain of pollen contains two sperms. Summer breezes shake the pollen-laden tassles and the pollen grains are jarred loose. The wind carries them to the silk of nearby plants.

Tiny receivers, called stigmas, at the ends of the silk, catch the pollen. The pollen grains quickly send tubes growing down through the silks to the ovules. Then the sperm cells pass down the tubes and fertilize the ovules.

The spike now grows into a large, pithy structure called a cob, while the ovules grow and ripen into seeds (kernels). The growing seeds are made up of a soft yellow hull filled with a milky liquid. When field corn is ripe, the kernel is hard, firm, and starchy.

CAN SOUND TRAVEL THROUGH WATER?

All sounds are produced by very fast, back-and-forth motions called vibrations. Vibrations are the source of all sounds.

Sound travels from a vibrating object to your ear by means of a medium, or sound carrier. The medium may be a solid, a liquid, or a gas.

Sound travels from a vibrating object to your ear by means of compression waves in the air. The vibrating object pushes against the tiny particles of air next to it and the particles are compressed, or squeezed, together. As it moves back, it leaves a space with fewer particles in it. The thinned-out air is called an expansion. Sound waves are made up of such compressions and expansions of air.

Not only does sound travel through water in this way, but it travels about four times as fast in water as it does in air. Sound travels through air at a speed of about 1,100 feet per second. Sound travels in sea water at about 4,800 feet per second.

The fact that sound travels through water is very useful to man. Ships and submarines are equipped with sonic devices for finding depth or for discovering the direction and distance of other vessels or of rocks.

By sending out a sudden pulse of sound from an underwater loudspeaker and finding the time it takes for the sound to return as an echo from the bottom of the sea, one can know the depth of the water beneath a vessel.

By sending out sound pulses horizontally and listening for echoes, one can detect other vessels or submerged rocks. The direction in which they lie and the distance can also be determined.

WHAT ARE GASES?

Matter can exist in a variety of forms. When the form resembles that of the air about us, it is a gas.

A gas is made up of tiny particles, which move about freely. They tend to spread out as widely as possible. So a sample of gas does not have any particular shape. If a gas is placed in a container, it spreads out and fills the entire container.

When a gas is inside a container, the moving particles strike the walls and bounce off. Trillions upon trillions of particles are constantly bouncing off all the walls. Each particle gives a little push as it does so. All these pushes make up the pressure of the gas.

If the container is made smaller—and has less volume—the gas particles are pushed closer together. The particles have less room to move about in. More of them hit the walls each second. So, as the volume goes down, the pressure goes up.

If a gas is heated, its particles move more quickly and the pressure increases. If the temperature is lowered, the particles move less rapidly. If the temperature is lowered enough, the attraction of the particles for each other causes them to come together and stay together. The gas is no longer a gas. It has liquefied and become a liquid.

There are many different gases. Air is the most common gas. It is actually a mixture of different gases, but mostly oxygen and nitrogen. Other common gases are ammonia, carbon dioxide (present in the air we breathe out), carbon monoxide (produced in automobile exhaust), helium, hydrogen, and methane.

WHERE DO GRASS SEEDS COME FROM?

The grasses make up the most widespread plant family in the world. There are about 7,000 different kinds. Great "seas" of grass cover natural fields, sometimes for thousands of square miles. These are called prairies, or plains, or ranges. The pampas of South America, the Russian steppes, the South African veld, are all "seas" of grass.

Most grasses reproduce by means of seeds. The seeds are scattered in many ways. Some grass seeds are covered with long hairs, and they are carried by the wind. Others are blown along the ground. Birds spread seeds by picking up the seeds in their beaks for food. As they fly away, they may drop some of them.

Some grass seeds have sharp spines. These seeds are spread by animals or by people who pass by the plant and carry away the seeds that stick to their fur or clothing.

Many kinds of grass seeds have been carried, sometimes by accident, along trade routes to distant parts of the world. For instance, ships brought seeds of molasses grass to the New World from Africa. The stalks of the plant were used as bedding for slaves. When the bedding was thrown away on the ground, the seeds took root. In this way the grass spread from Africa to North America.

Some of the grasses live for a season and then die. They must be planted again each year. Other grasses come up each year. The roots of pasture grasses, and the grasses you see growing on lawns, live through the winter. New blades come up in the spring. Such grasses are called perennial grasses.

HOW DO MUSHROOMS GROW?

Mushrooms are remarkable plants. They have no roots, no stems, and no leaves. They grow so fast that you almost feel you can see them grow. They are fungi, which means they have no chlorophyll to manufacture their own food. And some of them are delicious to eat while others are so poisonous that it is almost certain death to eat them.

The part of the mushroom plant that rises above the ground is only

the fruiting part of the fungus. The rest of the plant lies under the ground in the form of a mass of dense white tangled threads. These threads are called the mycelium or spawn.

The mycelium threads grow from little spores, which are tiny dust-like particles shed from the full-grown mushroom. On these threads small whitish knobs of tissue bud out, and they push upward, expand, and finally break out in an umbrella shape or in the form which is characteristic of each kind of mushroom.

On most mushrooms, underneath the umbrella, there are little radiating gills, set very close together. It is on these gills that the tiny spores are developed. The spores then drop out and are carried away by the wind. When the spores fall on surfaces favorable for growth, they develop into new plants.

Most mushrooms grow in moist shady woodlands, or in the bottoms of ravines where there is a lot of shade and plenty of warmth and dampness. The common field mushroom and a few other types are different. They grow best in open grassy meadows where they are fully exposed to the sun. But since mushrooms consist chiefly of water, most of them cannot live where there are dry hot winds or the hot summer sun.

48

HOW IS COPPER OBTAINED?

Copper is one of our most common and most useful metals. It is found in nature in two forms—as "native copper" (the metal itself) and in mineral ores (combined with other elements). There are more than 160 known mineral ores that contain copper.

About half of the world's copper supply is found in a bright-yellow mineral called chalcopyrite. This ore is a compound of copper, iron, and sulfur. It contains 34.5 percent copper. One of the richest copper ores is dark-gray chalcocite. It contains about 80 percent copper.

The first step in refining copper ore is to crush it into a fine powder. The finely crushed ore is then washed in flotation tanks. The tanks are filled with water with a layer of some oily substance on top. Compressed air is blown in through the bottom of the tank.

The air and the oil form a thick froth on top of the water, and the metallic ore particles cling to the froth. The next step is to roast the ore to burn out the sulfur.

After the sulfur is removed, the remaining ore is melted and treated chemically to help separate the iron that the ore contains. Finally the ore is transferred to a converter where the air blown through the molten metal burns away most of the remaining impurities.

The metal emerges as blister copper, which is about 98 percent pure. Blister copper must be refined still further before it can be used by industry. This is usually done electrically. The final product is about 99.9 percent pure.

Copper was probably one of the first metals people used because it could be found as a pure metal, not mixed with minerals.

WHY DO PINE TREES STAY GREEN ALL YEAR?

The leaves on a tree have several functions. One of them is to make food for the tree. Leaves take in carbon dioxide from the air and water and minerals from the soil. The chlorophyll in the leaves absorbs energy from the sun. Powered by the sunshine, the chlorophyll changes the carbon dioxide and water into sugar. The sugar made in the leaves is the tree's basic food.

But leaves also give off enormous quantities of water. Only a small fraction of the water that flows up through the sapwood pipes is used in making food. Most of the rest evaporates through millions of tiny holes on the surface of the leaves.

In much of North America a tree's water supply is cut off in winter. After the ground freezes, trees can't release gallons of water into the air. They would need more water than they could get from the frozen ground. So the trees "lock up" by shedding their leaves so that they won't lose water by evaporation through the leaves.

But certain trees have different kinds of leaves. Pines and firs and hemlocks have narrow, needlelike leaves with a thick, waxy outer covering. This prevents evaporation of water. And so the leaves on such trees remain for several years. When the leaves fall, new ones grow at the same time, and the branches never look bare. That's why these trees are called evergreens.

There are also trees with broad leaves that stay green all year round. The live oak and the California laurel have leathery leaves that help the trees keep their moisture during the cold months.

WHAT IS A WEED?

When we call something a "weed," we are not using a scientific plant classification. It is just a way people have of designating certain plants. Weeds are usually defined as plants that grow where they are not wanted.

A dandelion in the middle of a lawn is a weed; dandelions cultivated for fresh greens are not weeds. Clover sown in a pasture is not a weed; clover in a flower bed is a weed.

Sometimes one man's weed is another man's wildflower. City people gather daisies, buttercups, goldenrod, and black-eyed Susans. But the farmer who sees these flowers in his hayfield says, "Weeds!" and sets out to get rid of them.

Weeds, then, are plants that are out of place. And they are plants with a special ability for rapid and vigorous growth. In one way or another, weeds are better fitted to survive than most cultivated plants.

Some weeds are tall. Wild lettuce may be seven feet high, and great ragweed grows as high as 15 feet above the ground. Some weeds are small. Chickweed, carpetweed, and creeping spurge are weeds that trail along the ground. They are among the shortest of flowering plants.

Many weeds work underground. Wild carrot and dandelion, for example, have long, thick taproots. These help them get water even during dry spells. Some weeds have creeping roots that grow sideways just below the surface and send up whole colonies of new plants.

Chemical weed killers in the form of sprays have been developed to control the growth of weeds. Such sprays must be used carefully to prevent harm to people, animals, and the environment. Other methods of weed control include biological control (using natural enemies of weeds to kill them), efficient crop production and rotation, and the use of machines or manual labor to destroy weeds.

WHAT IS SPANISH MOSS?

Many people have seen Spanish moss without knowing what it really is. In the South, it can be seen on oak, pine, and cypress trees, in the form of long gray streamers.

The strange thing is that it is neither "Spanish" nor a moss! It is actually a flowering plant of the pineapple family. It grows in tropical and subtropical climates that have a moist atmosphere.

Nobody knows exactly how it came to be called "Spanish moss." In fact, it has other names as well, such as old man's beard, or southern moss, or Florida moss.

The seeds of this plant are carried by the wind to the rough bark of tree branches, where they stay and germinate. The plant gets its food from the air and dust and uses the tree on which it grows only for support.

Its long narrow leaves are covered with tiny hairs which absorb moisture. Its flowers are small. When Spanish moss is dried and cured, it is called vegetable hair. It is used for stuffing mattresses, pillows, cushions, harnesses, and dolls.

To obtain this stuffing material, the gray outer covering is soaked off or beaten off. Then the tough remaining fibers are dried in the sun until they are nearly black.

One problem in connection with Spanish moss is that in the South it provides a winter home for the cotton boll weevil.

WHY IS THE GREAT SALT LAKE SALTY?

Everybody knows the ocean is salty. But why should an inland lake like the Great Salt Lake be salty? To understand this, we have to know how lakes are formed and what happens to them.

Lakes result from the flow of water into low areas. Lake water comes largely from rainfall and melting snow. The water enters a lake basin through brooks, streams, rivers, underground springs, and groundwater. Dissolved mineral matter is in the fresh water entering the lake. This dissolved mineral matter is obtained from the ground and from rocks in the area.

In places where the climate is dry, lakes lose water rapidly by evaporation. When the amount of water that flows into a lake is matched by evaporation, salty minerals are left behind in the lake. Such lakes become salty, and the saltiness increases with time.

Great Salt Lake is such a lake. The mineral matter there has been accumulating over the ages and it now contains over 20 percent mineral matter, most of which is common salt. Because of the high salt content, only shrimp live in the lake. Great Salt Lake is more than 4,000 feet above sea level and is located in northwestern Utah.

The Dead Sea, which lies on the border between Israel and Jordan, is really another example of a salt lake. It is 1310 feet below sea level. The lake is fed by the Jordan River, but it has no outlet. This fact, plus little rainfall and high evaporation, cause the mineral matter to accumulate in the lake. It contains more than 24 percent mineral matter, one third of which is common salt.

WHY DOES WATER EVAPORATE?

Everybody knows that if you hang out wet clothes on a wash line, they will dry. Or that the wet pavement after a rain will gradually become dry.

Evaporation is the process by which a liquid exposed to the air gradually becomes a vapor or gas. Not all liquids evaporate at the same rate. Alcohol, ammonia, and gasoline, for example, evaporate more quickly than water.

There are two forces that act on the molecules that make up every substance. One is cohesion, which draws them together. The other is the heat motion of the molecules, which makes them fly apart. When the two forces are fairly evenly balanced, we have a liquid.

At the surface of a liquid, there are molecules of the liquid moving about. Those molecules which are moving outward more quickly than the neighboring molecules may fly off into space and thus escape the force of cohesion. Evaporation is this escape of molecules.

When a liquid is warmed, evaporation takes place quicker. This is because in a warmer liquid more molecules will have the speed to escape. In a closed container, evaporation stops quickly.

This is because when the number of molecules in the vapor reaches a certain point, the number of molecules that fall back into the liquid equal the number that are escaping from the liquid. When this happens, we say that the vapor has reached its saturation point.

When air is in motion above a liquid, it speeds up evaporation. Also, the greater the surface of the liquid exposed to the air, the faster the evaporation. Water in a shallow pan evaporates faster than in a tall pitcher.

WHAT ARE GEMSTONES?

In order to be considered a "gem," stones must have certain qualities. They must have beauty, they must be hard and tough enough to take considerable wear, and they must be rare enough for people to prize. Diamonds, rubies, and emeralds have all these qualities to a great degree and are the most prized gems.

Gemstones, with only four exceptions, are minerals. Minerals are inorganic (not formed from living things) combinations of chemical elements that are found naturally in the earth. There are four gemstones that are made of organic materials formed by plants or animals. These four exceptions are pearl, amber, coral, and jet.

The beauty of a gemstone depends on one or more of four things: its color, its brilliancy, its "fire," or its special optical features. Brilliancy means the stone's shininess, or ability to reflect light. Fire is the rainbow effect caused by the breaking up of white light. The glittering colors seen in a diamond when it is turned are an example of fire.

Gemstones can be found in almost any color. Rubies are intensely red, and emeralds are intensely green. Brilliancy is the amount of light that is reflected from a gemstone.

Each gemstone has a characteristic hardness and toughness. Hardness is the gem's resistance to scratching or wearing away. Toughness is its resistance to breakage.

Gemstones are formed by the same natural processes that form all minerals. But they are formed under unusually good conditions that yield transparent stones without faults.

WHAT IS THE QUANTUM THEORY?

Light is still one of the great mysteries. We know that light travels in waves, and that light waves are made up of electrical and magnetic forces traveling along together. They are one kind of electromagnetic wave.

In 1900, a German physicist named Max Planck found that waves do not tell the whole story about light. He was trying to explain how a hot object gives off radiation. His theory was that radiation is sent out in little bundles, or packets, instead of in a steady stream. Each little flash of energy is called a quantum (plural: quanta), and the idea suggested by Planck is now known as the quantum theory.

A single quantum of radiation energy is so small that the energy stream really seems to be steady. For example, even from such a weak source as starlight, about 60,000,000 quanta enter your eyes each second, and the light looks perfectly steady.

Today physicists think of light as waves for some purposes and as quanta for other purposes. Neither idea by itself is able to explain everything that is observed. Waves explain fully what happens when radiation passes through space or through a material. But the quantum idea must be used to describe how radiation originates and what happens to it when it is absorbed in matter.

Light and other kinds of electromagnetic radiation involve some of the most complicated events in nature. Neither waves nor quanta alone can describe everything that is observed.

WHAT WAS CRO-MAGNON MAN?

In the development of man over thousands of years, there was a time when he lived in caves. Probably the most interesting of the cave dwellers was Cro-Magnon man. He lived in Europe at the end of the Ice Age.

The first remains of these cave dwellers were found at a spot called Cro-Magnon in southern France. They are interesting to know about because experts who have examined the skeleton of the first Cro-Magnon that was found say he was very intelligent. If he had lived today he might have been a scientist, statesman, or business leader.

Cro-Magnons lived in very rough times, surrounded by wild beasts and other dangers. But despite this, they found time to draw excellent pictures on the walls of their caves. These pictures can still be seen and they are admired for their skill and beauty.

These people also had a well-developed social life. They lived in families, and since they hunted in groups, they must also have lived in tribes. They believed in a spirit world—that the dead would arise and live in another world again.

Gradually they developed better stone tools and new weapons. They learned to carve spearheads and harpoons from horn or bone.

They also invented throwing sticks for weapons. They learned to cure skins and sew them into garments with needles made of bone.

WHEN WAS THE GOLDEN AGE OF GREECE?

At certain times, in certain parts of the world, civilization seems to reach unusual heights and accomplish great things. The Greek poet Homer used the term "Golden Age" to describe a time in the past that he believed to be more enlightened than his own. Historians now use the term to describe the time when a nation is at its peak in development. The Golden Age of Greece dawned in the Age of Pericles, and lasted roughly from 461 to 431 B.C.

Early in the fifth century, the Persians invaded Greece, but the Greeks arose and pushed them out. The people of Athens led this fight. Because of this, Athens became the richest and most powerful state in Greece.

Athens built a fleet of ships that was larger than the combined fleets of all the rest of Greece. Wealth began to flow into Athens, some of it as tribute from other states, some from commerce, and some from silver mines. The population of Athens increased by four times. With all these new people, power, and prosperity, the arts in Athens flourished as never before in history.

During this period, construction was begun on the Parthenon, one of the most beautiful and famous buildings in the world. Among the men who lived in Athens at this time were Phidias, the great sculptor; Socrates, the teacher; and Sophocles and Euripides, the playwrights who wrote some of the greatest dramas in history.

Everybody was encouraged to help make Athens more beautiful, and many masterpieces were created. Also, because there was so much wealth and power, people had a great deal of leisure time. The citizens of Athens had more intellectual and cultural interests than any other society before or since.

The Golden Age of Greece created treasures and masterpieces and works of art that have had an influence on the whole world, even to this day. Later on in the fifth century B.C., fighting began between Athens and Sparta and their allies. Athenian culture began to decline and the Golden Age ended.

ARE THE MODERN OLYMPIC GAMES THE SAME AS THE ANCIENT ONES?

Even though the modern Olympic Games are patterned after those held in ancient Greece, there are many important differences.

The games are still held every four years, as in ancient times. In those days, wars were stopped so that the games could take place, but in 1916, 1940, and 1944, they were not held, because of World War I and World War II. Some countries and groups have used competing in the Olympics to express political protest. In 1980, the United States boycotted the Summer Games in Moscow to protest the Soviet Union's invasion of Afghanistan. In 1984, the Soviet Union, along with other Eastern European countries, boycotted the Summer Games in Los Angeles, citing poor security as the reason.

The original Olympics were always held in Olympia, Greece. Each modern Olympiad is held in or near a different city of the world.

The earlier games were open only to Greek citizens and athletes from Mediterranean countries. The modern games encourage all nations to compete in the spirit of friendship and world peace.

Another big difference is that events for women have become a major part of the modern games. And the female winners receive the same honors as the men who win.

In the ancient games, there were honors for cultural achievements. Modern competition is almost entirely athletic. Many of the contests held in the modern Olympics were unknown in early times. These include bicycle, canoe and yacht racing; soccer; basketball; judo; and water polo.

One of the most popular events of the modern Olympics is the marathon. This very tiring twenty-six-mile foot race over an open course is the supreme test of the runners' endurance. The marathon was not a part of the ancient Olympics although it originated in Greece.

And finally, a more recent development in the Olympics are the Winter Games, which were started in 1924. The Olympics have normally been held every four years with the Winter and Summer Games held in the same year. In 1994, the games are scheduled to occur in four-year cycles two years apart. The Winter Games are to be held in 1994 and 1998, and the Summer Games in 1996 and 2000. The winter Olympics provide competition in skiing, speed and figure skating, ice hockey, bobsledding, luge, and the biathlon. Such cold-weather sports could never have developed in the warm climate of Greece.

WHY DID ROME FALL?

For over four hundred years the Roman Empire governed all the lands around the Mediterranean Sea and most of the rest of Europe.

Much of what is now England and France, Belgium and the Netherlands, Spain and Portugal, Switzerland, Austria, Hungary, part of Germany, Romania, Bulgaria, Greece, Turkey, Israel, Syria, Arabia, the United Arab Republic, Tunisia, Algeria, and Morocco—all this was ruled by the Romans from their base in Italy.

The decline of this great Roman Empire in the west came very gradually. Contrary to the well-known expression, Rome did not "fall." Between A.D. 400 and 430 several large groups of people from the outside forced their way into the empire and settled down in France, Spain, and North Africa.

Little by little they asserted their independence from the Romans. By about 500 all the western parts of the empire—Italy, North Africa, France, and Spain—were ruled by Germanic kings who were independent of Rome.

The emperor Diocletian (A.D. 245-313) had divided the empire into two parts in 286. Long after the western part of the empire "fell," the eastern part remained strong. Its center was the old city of Byzantium, renamed Constantinople, and now called Istanbul.

For almost a thousand years this city was the chief city of the world and capital of the Roman Empire in the east. At last this empire fell when the Turks captured Constantinople in the year 1453.

The Roman Empire kept peace for two hundred years and did another valuable thing for civilization—it helped to preserve the literature and science of Greece and pass them on to the modern Western world.

WHAT DESTROYED THE EMPIRE OF THE INCAS?

In 1531 Francisco Pizarro first landed on the coast of what is now Ecuador. He entered an empire that extended nearly three thousand miles along the western coast of South America. This was the great Inca Empire.

With perhaps 16,000,000 people, it was larger than any kingdom in Europe at the time. It was well-governed. Every citizen was employed. The royal storehouses contained grain, so that no one went hungry even if the crops failed in some province. There were good roads to all parts of the kingdom. Messengers carried news and delivered orders to every village.

Life was so completely controlled in the Inca Empire, all the people were so obedient, that this may have helped lead to the downfall of the empire. When Pizarro entered the empire with 180 soldiers, a contest was going on between Huáscar and his half-brother Atahualpa over who would be the Inca (ruler). Atahualpa was winning the war.

Pizarro captured him by treachery. In the meantime Huáscar had been captured and killed by Atahualpa's army. Pizarro then killed Atahualpa. Now the Inca Empire had no leader, and it could not resist the brutal Spanish adventurers.

The average Inca was used to doing what he was told. Now the Spanish conquerors gave the orders. The Spaniards were interested in what the Inca mines produced, so they ordered the people to work in the mines. Farming was neglected. Many Inca died from overwork and lack of food. The Inca Empire was destroyed.

Many Inca survived this period, and their descendants still form the majority of the population in the Andes of Ecuador, Peru, and Bolivia.

WHAT WAS THE FAVORITE FOOD OF NATIVE AMERICAN INDIANS?

Most people refer to "the Indians" as if they were people who had one set of customs and way of life. But the Indians had many different tribes, who lived in different parts of North America, and had many different ways of life.

Some were hunters, some were gatherers, fishermen, and farmers. So naturally the food they ate varied quite a bit.

In what is called the Bison Area (from Saskatchewan to Texas and from the central Missouri River to the Rocky Mountains), Indians hunted bison. Bison meat and fat and berries were pounded into a pulp. The result was pemmican, the chief food of all the tribes in the Bison Area. It could be stored in rawhide bags for many months.

In the Caribou Area, Indians hunted caribou (their favorite food), as well as moose, elk, bear, beaver and porcupines. They also caught trout and whitefish in the lakes, as well as waterfowl.

There were many Algonkin tribes. In New England they were farmers; in other areas they were fishermen and hunters. In Algonkin country there were berries, fruits, roots, and nuts growing wild. In the summer they killed ducks, geese, herons, and cranes. Women and children gathered wild strawberries and blueberries, hazelnuts, wild apples, grapes, and roots.

Among some Indians the seeds of the mesquite tree were the chief food; among others it was wild rice they gathered. There was no single type of food that the Indians ate. It depended on where they lived, and whether they were chiefly fishermen, farmers, or hunters.

HOW DID THE CAVE MEN MAKE THEIR TOOLS?

According to scientists, Peking man, a type of prehistoric human being who lived between about 500,000-250,000 years ago, was the first cave dweller. Early man lived mainly by hunting.

Each man was his own toolmaker. With a hammerstone he broke large pebbles until they were a proper size for grasping. The resulting tool was a crude chopper, with one end slightly sharpened to make a rough cutting edge. Choppers could be used for digging, scraping, hacking, or cutting.

Other common early tools were crude hand axes. One end formed a heavy butt for grasping. The other end was chipped on both sides to a rounded or pointed tip. Hand axes were probably all-purpose tools, useful for digging up roots, cracking nuts, or cutting up dead animals.

Neanderthal man, who lived from about 100,000 to 35,000 years ago, was a real cave dweller. In addition to hand axes, Neanderthal man had flake tools. These were skillfully made of broad thin flakes of flint having a good sharp edge. Some of the flake tools were points in the shape of rough triangles. They probably served as knives for skinning and cutting up game animals. Other flake tools were side-scrapers having one curved edge.

During the next period, called the Upper Paleolithic (about 50,000 to 10,000 years ago), blade tools appeared. These were long, sharp flakes struck from specially prepared cores of flint. The blades were shaped into scrapers, chisel-like burins, and drills. Other tools were designed to do one particular job—for example bone needles with eyes were used in sewing animal skins together.

WHAT HAPPENED TO THE ANCIENT AZTECS?

One of the most remarkable peoples of ancient America were the Aztecs. They lived in the valley which now contains Mexico City.

These American Indians developed a way of life that was the equal in many ways of European civilization. They built temples and towers and homes of solid masonry. They were skilled in astronomy and in law and government. They were expert in many arts and crafts. They were fond of music, dancing, plays, and literature.

That isn't all. They had botanical gardens, or nurseries, which the Europeans didn't have. They had a system of canals for irrigation. They had a textile industry. They had hospitals, doctors, surgeons as good as those in Europe. They had quite a wonderful civilization!

In 1519, a Spanish captain, Hernando Cortés, with a small army, attacked the Aztecs. After much hard fighting he was able to destroy the Aztec power. The Spaniards then made Mexico into a part of the Spanish empire.

But even today there are many Indians living in Mexico who still speak the language of the Aztecs. Modern Mexico and Mexicans are proud of their Aztec ancestry. They have preserved much of the way of living, eating, and dressing that the Aztecs had before the Spanish conquest. Some of the Aztec words are still used not only in Mexico, but as part of the English language. They include chocolate, tomato, ocelot, coyote, avocado, among others.

So, while the power and the empire of the ancient Aztecs was destroyed more than four hundred years ago, their influence still lives on.

IS ALL MILK THE SAME?

People have used milk as a food since very ancient times. Yet in different parts of the world, different animals have been the source of its supply.

In the United States and among other English-speaking people, the cow furnishes most of the milk supply. In Spain, a great deal of the milk comes from sheep. The desert tribes of Arabia get milk from the camel. In Egypt, the water buffalo is a source of milk. In Lapland, reindeer furnish milk to the people. In Peru, the llama is a milk-producing animal. In Tibet, the people get milk from the yak. And in many countries, the goat is an important supplier of milk.

Is all this milk the same? The answer is no. Each animal produces milk especially suited for its own young. Cow's milk is intended for a calf and not for a human baby. It is much coarser than human milk.

But cow's milk is enough like human milk so that a baby can drink it and grow strong and healthy. Cow's milk has less sugar, more salts, and four times as much casein, an important protein substance, as human milk.

GOAT ON MILKING STAND

While milk differs a great deal, depending on the species of animal, it always contains fat, protein, carbohydrate, and minerals. No matter which milk people drink in different parts of the world, they obtain these vital substances for nourishment.

Just to see how different milks compare, let's look at cow's milk and reindeer milk. Cow's milk contains about 87 percent water; reindeer milk, only about 68 percent. Cow's milk has about 4 percent fat; reindeer milk, about 17 percent. Reindeer milk has half the amount of sugar of cow's milk, three times as much casein, and about five times as much other protein. So you see, it's quite different from cow's milk, and yet the people of Lapland get along on it very well indeed!

Even cow's milk may vary greatly, depending on the breed, the health of the individual cow, and the time between milkings. The last milk to be drawn at each milking is richer in fat than the rest, so a good job of milking can produce richer milk from the same cow than a poor job!

WHAT IS AN OBELISK?

An obelisk is a slender stone shaft with a pyramid-shaped top. The first and most famous of these monuments was made in Egypt.

These Egyptian obelisks are considered to be true obelisks, because each one was carved from a single stone. Some famous memorials in the United States, such as the Bunker Hill and Washington monuments, are shaped like obelisks, but they are made of many small pieces of stone.

The Egyptians believed that the obelisk was the home of the spirit of the sun. Obelisks were usually made in pairs and placed on each side of the gates to temples and tombs. The tops were often covered with bright metals, such as gold, to reflect the sun's rays. Inscriptions in hieroglyphics on the four sides praised the pharaohs who had ordered the obelisks.

All Egyptian obelisks came from a granite quarry near Aswan. Some of them were over eighty feet tall. How were the Egyptians able to move these tremendous shafts? No one knows exactly. It has been estimated that more than twenty thousand men would be needed to pull one. From the quarry the obelisks were dragged to the Nile River. They were loaded onto barges and shipped to different cities.

Throughout history, Egyptian obelisks have been sent all over the world. The ancient Romans were very impressed by them. After the Romans conquered Egypt in 30 B.C., they moved about fifteen obelisks to Italy. No one knows how they did this.

The obelisk that stands in front of St. Peter's Cathedral in Rome was brought to Rome at about that time. Sixteen centuries later, in 1585, it was moved to the square in front of the cathedral. The operation took nearly a year!

In the nineteenth century three obelisks were moved from Egypt. The first was set up in the Place de la Concorde in Paris in 1836. The second obelisk was set up on the banks of the Thames in London in 1880. The third was placed in Central Park in New York City in 1881. The London and New York obelisks are both called Cleopatra's Needle.

WHAT ARE BIRTHSTONES?

Many early civilizations believed that precious possessions, including gems, had strange and mysterious powers, and that certain gems could even prevent or cure diseases.

These ideas about gems are still preserved in the custom of wearing a birthstone for the month in which one was born. Even though the idea is a very ancient one, the actual wearing of birthstones started about the sixteenth century.

Here are the traditional birthstones used in America: January, garnet; February, amethyst; March, bloodstone or aquamarine; April, diamond; May, emerald; June, pearl; July, ruby; August, peridot; September, sapphire; October, opal; November, topaz; December, turquoise.

One of the most curious human beliefs is this faith in the power of precious stones. For example, some gems are supposed to have an influence on love and marriage. Turquoise is believed to prevent disagreement between a husband and wife. Aquamarine promotes the love of married couples. Topaz is a symbol of loyalty. Those who wear it are said to be devoted to their husbands or wives for life.

Among the stones believed to have the power to cure or prevent illness, the amethyst is considered especially effective against headache and toothache, and diamonds are believed to cure leprosy, insanity, and nightmares. Agate reduces fever.

Sapphire, it was thought, gave protection from spirits of darkness. The Chinese put jade bracelets or anklets on their children to protect them from harm. The Hindus believe pearls guard them against all evils. The garnet, because it is the color of blood, is worn to make its wearer immune to injury.

A turquoise is said to be a charm against falling from a horse. And there are people who believe an opal necklace guards the life and color of blond hair!

WHAT IS THE ZODIAC?

In ancient times, when people looked up at the sky at night, they noticed that many of the brightest stars were arranged in a certain pattern, or group. These groups are what we call constellations. The name comes from a Latin word meaning "group of stars."

In every ancient civilization people gave names to these constellations, calling them after gods and heroes, and after animals and familiar objects.

In studying the constellations, early peoples noticed that they seemed to march in a great procession across the sky. Certain constellations appeared in the spring, traveled across the sky, and then disappeared. They were followed by summer, fall, and winter constellations.

Within the process, twelve constellations were noticed in particular. The sun and the moon always rose and set within the part of the sky that held these twelve. And so the part of the sky through which the sun, moon, and the planets traveled was named the Zodiac, meaning "circle of living things." This was because most of the twelve constellations were named for living things.

The Zodiac was divided by the ancients into twelve sections, each named after one of the twelve constellations. We know these constellations as Taurus, the bull; Aries, the ram; Pisces, the fish; Aquarius, the water carrier; Capricorn, the goat; Sagittarius, the archer; Scorpio, the scorpion; Libra, the scales; Virgo, the virgin; Leo, the lion; Cancer, the crab; and Gemini, the twins.

The twelve constellations were called the signs of the Zodiac. Every month a different sign of the Zodiac appeared on the eastern horizon, and the sun and the moon seemed to rise in this particular sign.

In addition to the twelve constellations of the Zodiac, thirty-six other constellations were familiar to peoples of ancient times. These forty-eight are known as the "ancient" constellations. Later on, forty other constellations were discovered by astronomers, and these became known as the "modern" constellations.

WHAT IS JAZZ?

Jazz is a kind of music that originated in the United States. It was originally the music of the black people of the United States, but it developed into a coming-together of several different kinds of music from various parts of the world.

One of the basic features of jazz is its rhythm. Jazz melody combines elements from African and European music, but its harmony comes mainly from Europe. One important feature of jazz is improvisation. This means making something up on the spot on the spur of the moment. Much jazz is played that way. The music is made up as the players go along.

Over the years, jazz has changed and developed, but it has retained its basic quality. One of the forms of music that contributed to the development of jazz was the "blues." About a third of jazz music is in the blues form. So are over half of the popular rock-'n'-roll pieces. Even some of the country and western music of the United States is in the blues form.

A major step in the development of jazz was taken by musicians in New Orleans. New Orleans jazz, sometimes called Dixieland, had the deep emotion of the blues and the black spiritual as well as elements of Ragtime and European folk music.

Later on big-band jazz, or swing music developed. In the 1940's and 1950's came what was called "modern jazz." This modern jazz was more complex in harmony and melody than earlier styles of jazz. But its most outstanding feature was its new approach to rhythm. The players used new rhythms in making their melodies, and the drummers played in a more complex style.

Another major step in the development of jazz was the "new thing" of the 1960's. It is free-form jazz. A whole group of players may change the tempo or speed of a piece several times during a performance without planning to do so beforehand. This doesn't mean that the music is disorganized, but that it is simply freer in spirit and approach. So you see, jazz is a form of music that is always changing, yet one that keeps its basic approach and quality.

WHAT IS PSYCHIATRY?

Many people confuse psychiatry and psychology. There is a great deal of difference between them. Let us see what this difference is.

Psychology is the study of how people and animals behave. Psychologists study people to find out how and why people do such things as learn, think, remember, feel, see, hear, and talk.

Psychiatry on the other hand is actually a branch of medical science. It has to do with mental health. Originally, psychiatry was concerned only with insanity. But today this science offers help to people who have all kinds of emotional and mental problems.

Psychiatry moved forward in this way when two important discoveries were made. The first was that there are many kinds of mental disorders and that they have a wide range of seriousness. The other was that even serious mental disorders are more open to cure than was formerly thought possible.

A psychiatrist is always a physician. Psychiatrists look for the motives or causes underlying the illness of one who has a "nervous breakdown" or who is otherwise not in good mental health. He is sure that there are always motives or causes for the illness.

One thing a psychiatrist has learned is that these causes or motives are seldom the ones given by the patient. This is not because the patient deliberately lies about them. It is because the real reasons are often hidden in the unconscious part of his mind.

This means the patient is honestly not aware that there are any reasons other than those on the surface. Once the psychiatrist finds the hidden, unconscious causes that are making the patient sick, he tries to devise a treatment that will do away with these causes and promote the patient's health.

WHAT IS CAPITALISM?

Capitalism is an economic system in which most of the industries and businesses in a country are owned privately. By contrast, under communism, industries and businesses are owned by the state.

A capitalist is a person who uses his own wealth (or other people's money) to make more wealth. The extra money he makes is his profit. Some capitalists manufacture things to sell at a profit. Some are store owners who sell goods at a profit. Others are financiers or investors who lend their money in the hope of getting more back.

No matter what his business, the aim of the capitalist is to make a profit. But, of course, this does not mean that he can get away with any kind of business practice in order to make that profit. For example, he can't charge prices that are too high, or sell bad goods.

If he does, he will probably lose business to others who sell better goods or charge lower prices. So competition forces the capitalist to sell the best possible goods at the lowest possible prices. And that's why competition is an important feature of capitalism.

The profits made by the individual capitalist in free competition can benefit the economy of the whole country. As the capitalist makes profits, he can afford to expand his business and put more people to work.

Today in many capitalist countries, such as the United States, Canada, and Japan, governments own some businesses and regulate many more. For example, the United States Government has always supervised the post office. It regulates public utilities—necessary services like gas, electricity, and water. It also regulates railroads, airlines, television, and other businesses in which the public has a vital interest.

So in a capitalist system, government protects free enterprise and at the same time sees to it that no person is free to run a business in a way that harms other people.

HOW MANY DIFFERENT RELIGIONS ARE THERE?

What is a religion? The word "religion" can mean so many kinds of experiences that it is impossible to describe it in a few words. But there are six things that most religions have in common. Let us consider them briefly:

1. A belief in a greater power(s). 2. This power (or powers) is praised, feared, sacrificed to, and prayed to. 3. Ceremonies are developed for these sacrifices or prayers. 4. Certain places and objects connected with the worship and history of the religion are held sacred. 5. There is hope that through observing the religion, man can have a better

life, either on this earth or after death. 6. Proper conduct is one of the best ways to please God or the gods, and leads to a better life.

Almost all the religions of the world share these six basic concepts. The religions of primitive peoples, which include the worship of "spirits" in animals, rocks, rivers, and so on, are considered to be on a lower level.

But many of the religions of civilized people, who worshipped many gods, died as civilization progressed. For example, among the "dead" religions are the Egyptian, Babylonian, Assyrian, Greek, Roman, Celtic, and Norse.

Today there are many living religions. The chief ones are the Hindu, Buddhist, Confucian, Taoist, Shintoist, Zoroastrian, Islam, Jewish, and Christian. These religions together have a total of more than 3,000,000,000 followers, which includes most of the civilized world.

Here is the number of followers in each of the leading religions: Hinduism has about 647,895,000 followers, most of them in India. Buddhism has about 307,416,000 followers in China and Japan. Confucianism has about 163,000,000 followers, and Taoism about 21,000,000.

Shintoism has about 3,427,000 followers, and the Zoroastrian religion, about 161,000. Islam followers total about 840,221,000 in Asia and Africa. The Jewish religion has about 17,981,000 followers. The Christian religion today has more followers than any other, about 1,300,000,000 people.

WHO ARE THE QUAKERS?

In 1650, a man called George Fox was on trial in England because of his religious beliefs. He looked at his judges and commanded them to "tremble at the word of the Lord." One of the judges therefore called him a "quaker." And since Fox and his followers sometimes trembled during religious experiences, the nickname "quakers" became popular for these people. Their official name today is Society of Friends.

George Fox, the founder of the Quakers, taught that men should be guided in their conduct by an inner light, the Holy Spirit that dwells within each person. The Quakers refused to take an oath, even in the courts. They also agreed that they should never use physical force against anyone, or take part in military conflicts.

To set themselves apart from other Christians, they developed different customs, dress, and speech. They wore a plain gray costume, opposed amusements, and used the pronouns "thee" and "thou" in ordinary conversation.

Modern-day Friends have put aside most of the old Quaker customs. But their meetings are still conducted for the most part in the traditional manner. There is no prearranged program. The members gather and sit in silence until the Inner Spirit moves one of them to rise and offer a prayer, or perhaps read from the Scriptures or relate some spiritual experience.

They have no ministers in the usual sense and have no written creed. Men and women, young and old, have equal privileges in all the meetings.

The Quakers maintain many schools and have always been active in charitable and welfare work. They were among the first to establish free schools for the poor. As early as 1688 they took a definite stand against slavery.

WHAT LANGUAGE DO GYPSIES SPEAK?

Do you know why these people are called Gypsies? Years ago, people in Europe thought that they had originally come from Egypt, and "Gypsy" was derived from the word "Egypt."

But it is believed that about one thousand years ago several tribes from northwest India migrated into other lands, and these were the original Gypsies. Some of these tribes reached Persia; others wandered into what is now Turkey; and still others went into Syria, Egypt, and North Africa. Since they had originally come from India, they spoke an Indian language related to Sanskrit.

Later on, tribes of Gypsies wandered through the Balkans, Russia, Hungary, and then eventually to western Europe, including Germany, France, England, Spain, and even Sweden and Finland.

Through centuries of wandering, the Gypsy language became mixed with words borrowed from the countries in which they lived. An English Gypsy was said to speak *pogado tshib* (broken language), which is a mingling of Gypsy and English words. The English word for the Gypsy language is "Romany." The Romany word for a Gypsy's home on wheels is *vardo*.

Gypsies practiced trades that allowed them to roam the countryside. Some Gypsies were wood carvers, others mended pots and pans, some were minstrels or fortune-tellers.

It is interesting to learn how Gypsies in different countries developed in different ways. English Gypsies became horse traders. In Wales, the Gypsies are singers, violinists, and harpists. Spanish Gypsies are famous for flamenco dancing. In Hungary and Rumania many Gypsies are musicians. In Yugoslavia many Gypsies specialized in making gunpowder.

Did you know that the first groups of Gypsies in the United States came here as long ago as 1715?

דער טאָג
מאָרגען זשורנאַל

WHAT IS THE YIDDISH LANGUAGE?

One of the most interesting languages in the world, Yiddish, is the language spoken by the Jewish people practically all over the world. But isn't Hebrew, the ancient language of the Old Testament, the language of the Jewish people? The answer is yes. Hebrew is the language of scholars, of religion, of much of the great literature, and in Israel today, of the people, too. There are many Hebrew scholars who consider Yiddish only a dialect spoken by the noneducated classes.

The fact is, Yiddish originally developed in Germany. About a thousand years ago, many Jews from France and northern Italy began to settle in western Germany. As happens whenever languages mix (the German they found and the French and Italian they brought with them), a new dialect or language began to develop, and this became Yiddish. This word, by the way, comes from the German *Judisch*.

After the fourteenth century, many Jews migrated to Poland and nearby countries. In these new places they developed variations on Yiddish to include the local languages. And those who remained in Germany developed Yiddish to its highest form.

Yiddish is written with Hebrew characters, and many of its words are derived from Hebrew, but many are quite different. A curious thing about its development is that for a long time it was chiefly used by women. This was because among the Jews only the men used to be scholars, and they studied Hebrew. So Yiddish came to be called the "mother's tongue."

Probably no other language uses the words of the local country as much as Yiddish does. For example, most people who speak Yiddish in the United States will say the English words for "carpet, floor, dress, hat," and so on. Many learned Jews, however, try to speak a "pure" Yiddish without English words. And by the way, many Yiddish words are used by non-Jews in the United States. For example, you probably know what a *kibitzer* is!

WHAT MAKES STAMPS VALUABLE?

There are probably several million people in the United States who collect stamps. Some of them are experts, knowing exactly what each stamp in their collection is worth. Others have only the vaguest idea of what makes a stamp valuable. A stamp catalogue today lists about two hundred thousand different stamps. How is it decided what each one is worth?

A stamp that is damaged is next to valueless. A "damaged" stamp may be torn, stained, discolored, or soiled from bad handling. Unless it is a very rare stamp, such a stamp is practically worthless.

Unused stamps without gum are not in demand and can usually be bought cheaply. Stamps with perforations missing or heavily cancelled stamps are also less valuable.

Now, what makes a stamp valuable? The chief thing is obviously the rarity of the stamp. If only a very few of them were issued or are known to exist, or if some mistake was made and a few of these reached the public, the stamps are likely to be quite valuable.

One famous rarity is a one-penny orange Mauritius stamp of 1847. Instead of having the word "Postpaid," it was inscribed "Post Office." But most collectors can hardly hope to obtain such rare and valuable stamps. Many of them try to collect complete sets of stamps from certain countries. Others try to collect commemorative stamps, which are issued to honor some person, group, or event.

There is a great deal of pleasure in stamp collecting, even if you have no rarities and will never make money from your collection!

WHAT COUNTRY PRODUCES THE MOST CLOCKS?

In the early days of mechanical timepieces, there was no particular country that led in clock and watch production. Skilled workers migrated from country to country, and watchmaking and clockmaking became an international trade.

But soon different countries began to specialize in different types of clocks. For example, England has long been famous for its ship chronometers, which are large, accurate watches mounted in a special bracket to keep them level on a rolling sea. England also specializes in chime movements. Many chime-clock movements are shipped from England to case manufacturers all over the world.

The Black Forest of Germany supplies the world with hand-carved cuckoo clocks. The movements are not of the highest quality, but the wood carvings are very attractive. Some jeweled watches are also made there.

Watchmaking in Switzerland is a national industry and is very important to the economy of that country. The Swiss began to lead in the production of watches in the late nineteenth century, when the wrist watch made its appearance.

The Swiss are experts in the production of high-grade, small watch movements. Special-feature watches, such as alarms, calendars, automatics, and chronographs, are made almost exclusively in Switzerland.

What about the United States? Most of the American clock industry is devoted to the manufacture of electric clocks, automobile clocks, and inexpensive alarm clocks. The American watch industry also imports and assembles watches. Individual parts, complete movements, and complete watches are imported by some American companies from Switzerland, Germany, Japan, and France.

WHAT ARE PUBLIC-OPINION POLLS?

Occasionally you read in the paper or hear on a news program that a poll has been taken which indicates how most people feel about a certain question.

How did they find this out? It is done through a kind of survey that is called public-opinion research. This kind of research finds out what people think and how they feel about a variety of subjects.

For example, the survey, which is done by asking a representative number of people certain questions, may find out how they feel about labor unions, big companies, the government, the school system, or a certain law that has been passed.

Public-opinion surveys may find out what people's ambitions are, or who makes decisions in a family. They may ask whether people think prices are too high, or whether there should be a change in the draft law.

Probably the best-known kind of public-opinion research is the election poll. In elections for political office, such as for president, governor, or mayor, the polls can find out for whom people are going to vote, as well as the reasons. In some cases, the polls come very close to indicating the actual result of an election. In others, they may be somewhat incorrect, especially when the situation changes quickly or people are still undecided.

Such polls can also be helpful in showing leaders in government what people think about important questions that they may have to deal with when in office.

Another value of public-opinion surveys is that they often show what types of people are ignorant or uninformed about what subjects. With this information, educators can improve their methods of teaching.

WHO DISCOVERED AUSTRALIA?

Australia is the world's largest island and its smallest continent. Its total area of 3,000,000 square miles is about the same as that of the continental United States (excluding Alaska).

Even in medieval times there were stories about a large continent in the Southern Hemisphere. But no one had ever seen it. People wondered what it was like and whether it was inhabited. They called this land "Terra Australis Incognita," or "Unknown Southern Land."

The Dutch were the first Europeans to visit Australia. They discovered it while making their journeys between the Netherlands and the island of Java, a Dutch colony in Southeast Asia.

Ships sailing from the Netherlands to Java used to go around the southern tip of Africa (the Cape of Good Hope) and then sail across the Indian Ocean with the westerly winds. Many navigators sailed too far east before turning north toward Java and found themselves on the west coast of Australia. They later gave the name New Holland to this western part of the continent.

In 1642 Captain Abel Tasman was sent by the Dutch to discover what lay in the east of the continent. He discovered the island now named Tasmania, and also discovered New Zealand. Later he explored Australia's north coast.

In 1770 the English captain James Cook discovered the east coast of Australia and named it New South Wales. He visited Botany Bay, near what is now modern Sydney. In 1788, the first English colony was established in what later became the city of Sydney.

WHO DISCOVERED GREENLAND?

If there is any part of the world that you would not expect to be called a green land, it is Greenland!

Most of Greenland is covered by an icecap more than ten thousand feet thick in some places. Only the hardiest plants and animals can survive the climate at the edges of this icecap. Winters are bitter cold, and summers are short and cool.

There are thin patches of soil with grasses, heather, and low, flowering plants. But much of the ice-free surface is barren rock, thinly covered by mosses and lichens.

Why then is this place called Greenland?—for the same reason a real-estate development is called "Pleasant Hills," or some such name, when actually the place may be quite unattractive: the real-estate developer wants to attract customers.

In A.D. 982 an Icelander named Eric Thorvaldsson came to southwestern Greenland. This rugged man, better known as Eric the Red, had been exiled from Iceland for three years for killing a man. Eric spent his three-year exile exploring the western land described by Icelandic sailors.

Three years later he returned to Iceland and told the people about his explorations. He wanted settlers to be eager to go to this land, so he made it sound attractive by naming it Greenland!

Today there are almost fifty-seven thousand people living in Greenland, which is a small number for such a large place. Most of them live in the ice-free areas of the island's southwest coast.

WHAT ARE THE ROMANCE LANGUAGES?

There is a group of languages that is descended from the form of Latin spoken by the ordinary people of ancient Rome. They are known as the Romance languages, and they are: French, Provencal Catalan, Spanish, Portuguese, Italian, Romanian, and the Sardinian and Rhaeto-Romanic dialects.

These languages developed in the region of the Roman Empire in Europe. When the Roman soldiers, traders, and colonists came to these areas, they made the natives use their language.

In ancient Rome there was classical Latin, the speech of literature, oratory, and formal conversation. But at the same time there was the everyday speech of the common people, the vulgar Latin.

This grew in Rome and then was carried to the provinces by those who went to settle there. But there were local differences, and new nations began to grow, so this form of Latin then developed into separate languages.

As time went on, the various Romance languages began to change even more in pronunciation. Words from outside sources were used and changed to fit the language. For example, French picked up about four hundred Teutonic words. During the Crusades, French took over some Greek and Arabic words. Spanish has many words that were taken from the Arabic.

At the same time the Romance languages were developing dialects. People in one part of the country began to speak a language slightly different from that spoken in other parts. In Paris, for example, they still speak a slightly different French than in other parts of France.

WHY IS THE WHITE HOUSE WHITE?

The White House is the official residence of the president of the United States. But it wasn't always white, nor was it always called the White House.

It is the oldest federal structure standing, its cornerstone having been laid on October 13, 1792. It was designed by Irish-born architect James Hoban, who won an architectural competition to select a design for the president's house.

Originally it was called the President's House, and then the Executive Mansion. How did it come to be called the White House? The house was originally built of gray sandstone. During the War of 1812, British troops invaded Washington and burned the structure (August 24, 1814). Only a shell was left standing.

Under Hoban's direction the building was restored, and this was completed in 1817. To cover up the smoke stains, the gray sandstone walls were painted white. So the building came to be called the White House, but this didn't become its official name until 1902, when Theodore Roosevelt adopted it.

It is interesting how many rooms in the White House are known by their colors. The Blue Room, which is oval in shape, is the reception room for the president. The Red Room is furnished with objects of the American Empire period. The Green Room is furnished with objects going back to the days of John Adams and Thomas Jefferson. There is a Rose Guest Room upstairs where the president and his family live.

WHAT'S THE DIFFERENCE BETWEEN A COLLEGE AND A UNIVERSITY?

A university is an institution of higher learning that generally includes many kinds of schools and colleges.

In addition to an undergraduate college of liberal arts and sciences, the university has graduate schools. These are for students preparing for professions in law, medicine, engineering, or other special fields. A graduate student is one who has already earned a degree.

The typical college offers a four-year course that generally leads to a bachelor's degree in science or art. A college may be part of a university or, as in the United States and Canada, a separate institution. There are also schools called institutes, which stress scientific and technological studies.

The junior college is a 20th-century American development in education. It offers a two-year course of study in liberal arts or vocational training. With the credits earned in a junior college, a student may be able to transfer to the junior, or third, year of a four-year college or university.

Modern universities and colleges had their beginnings in the institutions started by the Christian Church in Europe during the Middle Ages. European universities were not the first in the world, however.

The University of Al-Azhar, founded in Cairo in the 10th century, is the oldest that is still in operation. One of the earliest in Europe was the University of Bologna, which was begun in Italy in the 11th century.

WHY IS MONEY BACKED BY GOLD?

Money is not a metal coin or a piece of printed paper. These are only symbols. But they do represent something real.

Money is backed by large stores of precious metal that is held by the government that issues the money. The standard of measurement for the value of money that is widely used throughout the civilized world is gold and silver. They are scarce enough to retain their value, yet plentiful enough to meet the demands of the marketplace.

In other words, the paper and coins that a government issued as "money" was accepted as having a certain value because there were supplies of gold and silver backing up that money.

In 1821, Great Britain made monometalism (one metal) the basis of its monetary system. Gold was adopted as its official currency. By 1914 gold was the measuring stick for almost all the currencies of the world. By having one standard of value, countries were able to trade more easily with each other. Dollars from the United States, francs from France, and marks from Germany all had a set value in gold. This is known as the gold standard.

By 1933 most countries had gone off the gold standard. But many currencies, including that of the United States, are still based on a set price of gold. And gold is still very important in international trade. Governments buy and sell gold bars known as bullion. Part of the gold is used to pay off international debts, and part of it is stored. The stored gold is called a "reserve."

HOW IS A BANANA TREE GROWN?

The banana "tree" is actually not a real tree. This is because there is no wood in the stem rising above the ground. The stem is made up of leaves growing very close together, one inside the other. The leaves spread out at the top of the stem and rise in the air, making the plant look like a palm tree.

To grow bananas, pieces of rootstock (bits cut from the base of growing plants) are planted in holes about 1 foot deep and 11 to 18 feet apart. Each piece of rootstock must have one or more sprouts, or "eyes," like the eyes of a potato. Green shoots appear above the ground three or four weeks later. Only the strongest shoot is allowed to become a plant. This plant forms its own rootstock, from which other plants later grow up beside the first one.

Banana plants need a lot of care and attention. They must be provided with water by irrigation if the normal rainfall doesn't supply enough. The area around the plants must be kept free of weeds and grass.

81

About nine or ten months after planting, a flower appears on the banana plant. This flower is at the end of a long stalk, which grows from the base up through the center of the stem and turns downward when it emerges from the top. Small bananas form on this flower stalk as it grows downward. Bananas really grow upside down. As the small bananas form on the stalk, they point downward, but as they grow they turn and point upward.

Bananas are harvested while they are still green. Even when they are to be eaten where they are grown, they are not allowed to ripen on the plant. A banana that turns yellow on the plant loses its flavor.

WHY DO WORDS HAVE CERTAIN MEANINGS?

Words are really "codes," or symbols that stand for something. They are produced by sounds that human beings make. When two or more human beings decide that a certain sound or set of sounds have the same meaning for them, they have a language.

So words have certain meanings only because certain groups of human beings have decided that they should have this meaning. When the sounds of D, O, and G are lined up, they produce the word "dog." English-speaking people agree that the word "dog" represents a particular animal. If one English-speaker says "dog," another English-speaker will automatically see the image of a "dog."

But what about a Russian? It will be meaningless to him. A Russian uses the word *sobaka* for the dog image. And an Italian uses the word *cane* when he means to indicate a dog.

Even the rules for using words are not the same in every language. It all depends on what has been agreed upon for that language. In English, if you want to speak about more than one dog, you add the letter "s" and get "dogs." In Italian you change the last letter of *cane* to "i" and get *cani*.

People learn the use and meanings of words of a certain language from childhood. As a baby, you begin to imitate the sounds produced by your parents and other people around you. You connected the sounds, with certain objects, actions, or ideas. You learned to string your words along in a certain way and to make changes in them when necessary for their meaning. You learned a language.

WHO OWNS THE STATUE OF LIBERTY?

The Statue of Liberty in New York harbor is the property of the United States Government. It became a national monument in 1924. It is maintained by the National Park Service of the U. S. Department of the Interior.

But the strange thing is that this statue, of which we are all so proud and which symbolizes the freedom we cherish, has a history of money problems associated with it.

The idea of the statue was suggested in 1865 by a French historian, Edouard de Laboulaye. It was to be a gift from the French people as a memorial to American independence and as a symbol of friendship between the two countries. A friend of Laboulaye's, sculptor Frédéric Auguste Bartholdi, designed the statue and selected its site.

To raise money for the statue, the French-American Union was formed in 1875. By 1882, Frenchmen had contributed about $400,000 for the statue. The statue was built in France in sections and in 1885 it was shipped in 214 cases to the United States.

An American fund-raising committee was formed so that the pedestal for the statue could be built. But work on the pedestal had to stop in 1884 because enough money hadn't been raised. Two months after the statue arrived in New York, the required amount of money, $250,000, was finally raised and the work was completed. The statue was dedicated by President Grover Cleveland on October 28, 1886.

In the early 1980's, millions of dollars were raised from private donations to pay for needed repairs to the Statue of Liberty, and also to restore Ellis Island's immigration station. July 4, 1986 marked the official opening of the restored monument. The Statue of Liberty remains one of the world's major tourist attractions. About 2 million people come to see it every year.

WHAT ARE ANTIQUES?

It is very hard to define an antique. Antiques are usually old objects made by skilled craftsmen. The nearest thing we have to the definition of an antique is based on certain government regulations.

Most governments allow antiques to be imported into the country without payment of import duties. But to qualify as an antique, the object must have been made a certain number of years ago. In Canada, it's before 1847. In Britain and the United States, the object must be 100 years old. In most countries, the object must be 60 years old to be considered an antique.

Of course, people can call any old object an antique. And there is no limit to the type of object. Furniture is one of the most common antique items, and certain pieces of furniture made in the 18th century bring very high prices.

Old glass objects, such as flasks, tumblers, goblets, vases, and pitchers, are also valuable antiques. Pottery of all kinds, from porcelain to stoneware, is a favorite of antique collectors.

Objects made of silver, such as spoons, cups, tankards, and mugs, are a familiar kind of antique. Early ironwork made by hand, such as latches and hinges for doors, andirons for fireplaces, pots and pans for cooking, are valued as antiques.

Many objects that were made of pewter, such as plates and tea and coffee pots, are collected by antique lovers. So are old objects made of brass, copper, and tinware.

People who collect antiques sometimes don't even care if they are rare or beautiful. They like them because they give a picture of the people and customs of other times.

WHAT IS ETYMOLOGY?

The word "etymology," comes from the Greek words *etymon* ("true") and *logos* ("word"). Etymology is concerned with the first, true meanings of words. Etymologists study words to uncover the changes that have occurred in them.

There is a wide variety of ways in which the words we use originated and developed. Greek and Latin supplied most of the words used in English today. For example, from the Latin word *manus* ("hand") we got the words manufacture, manicure, emancipate, and manipulate.

A Greek word, *graphein* ("to write"), gave us telegraph, "to write far away"; phonograph, "writing sound"; geography, "writing about the earth," and so on.

Latin and Greek prefixes gave us many words. Anti ("against") is used to make antiknock, antiseptic, etc. Astro ("star") gave us astronaut. There are over one hundred common prefixes that were used in creating words.

English includes words borrowed from many other languages of the world. From the Vikings we got: leg, gate, freckle, seat, dirt, bull, birth, ugly, and many other words. The Normans introduced such words as prayer, ministry, parliament, poverty.

Later, as explorers ranged throughout the world, English obtained words from everywhere. From India we got bungalow, punch, faker, and coolies. From the Dutch came freight, schooner, scour, and landscape. From Spain and Latin America came armada, potato, cargo, tobacco, and hurricane.

It is impossible in a short article to give even an idea of all the sources of words that today make up the English language. An etymologist, who makes this his study, has certainly a big and interesting field of work!

WHY DO PEOPLE KILL WHALES?

The killing of whales as an industry goes back quite a long time. The Basques were doing it in the Bay of Biscay as early as the 11th century. Whaling was being carried on in North America in the 17th century.

The chief reason for killing whales was to obtain whale oil. This was the oil from the large baleen whale, and the blue, fin, humpback, and sei whales. The oil obtained from sperm whales is called sperm oil.

Until the middle of the 19th century, whale and sperm oil was used for nearly every purpose where oil is required. It was used for lighting, for lubrication, steel tempering, leather finishing, and many other processes. Whale oil is used in some cosmetics, in the soapmaking industry and in the manufacture of margarine. Sperm oil is now used for a variety of purposes in the chemical industry.

The oil yield is highest from whales taken in Antarctic and Arctic waters in the spring and summer, when the whales are feeding heavily. A blue whale provides about 120 barrels of oil, and a sperm whale about 50 barrels.

As a result of this hunting of whales, certain ones—the blue whales, white whales, and gray whales—are almost extinct. The International Whaling Commission (IWC) was established in 1946 to regulate the number of whales taken. But it wasn't very effective. The blue and humpback whales became more rare, and the fin whale became scarce, too.

More efforts are being made now to protect whales from becoming extinct. The IWC voted on a temporary halt of commercial whaling in 1982, to begin at the start of the 1985 hunting season. In 1988, 111 nations ended commercial whaling. In the 1990's, the IWC plans to determine whether whale numbers have grown enough to warrant renewed hunting.

HOW ARE CALORIES MEASURED?

A calorie is a measurement of energy or heat. One calorie is the amount of heat it takes to raise the temperature of one gram of water one degree centigrade.

What does this have to do with food? Well, we eat food to supply us with energy, and so energy in foods is measured in calories. When foods are metabolized—that is, utilized—by being combined with oxygen in the body cells, they give off calories (energy). In measuring the energy value of food, we use the "large" or kilogram calorie, which equals one thousand regular calories.

Each type of food, as it "burns up," furnishes a certain number of calories. For instance, one gram of protein furnishes four calories, but one gram of fat furnishes nine calories.

The amount of calories the body needs depends on the work the body is doing. A man who weighs about 150 pounds needs only 1,680 calories per day—if he does nothing at all. If he does a little work, he may need about 3,360 calories per day. And if he does heavy work, he may need as much as 6,720 calories a day to keep the body functioning properly.

There are other factors that decide how many calories a person needs, such as age, sex, size, physical condition, and even climate. Suppose you take in more calories than you need? The body uses up what it needs and stores some of it away for future use. The body can store away about one-third of the amount it needs each day. The rest becomes fat! And that's why it's important to "watch your calories."

WHAT IS THE CASTE SYSTEM?

In India there is a system that divides people into different social classes, or castes. The particular caste a person belongs to is the one he is born into.

The major castes, starting from the top, are: the Brahmans, the priestly caste; the Kshatriyas, the warriors and earthly rulers; the Vaisyas, the merchants and artisans; the Sudras, the servants; and the Pariahs, or outcasts. The Pariahs really belong to no caste and are known

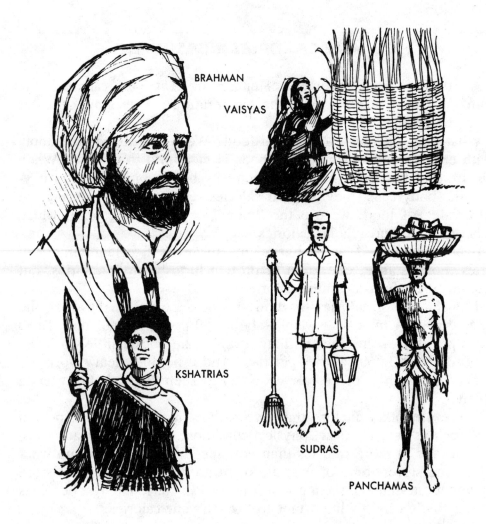

BRAHMAN

VAISYAS

KSHATRIAS

SUDRAS

PANCHAMAS

as "untouchables."

An Indian born in a low-caste family cannot change his caste to a higher group by education or wealth. There are many rules about the kind of contact people of one caste can have with members of another caste. The caste system controls Indian society very strictly.

How did the caste system start? One theory is that when the Aryans came to India about 1500 B.C., they established it. The Aryans were tall, fair of skin, with thin noses and straight black hair. Their life was well organized into social groups, and the caste system enabled them to guard their standing as a ruling minority.

The new Indian constitution prohibits discrimination on account of caste. But the caste system continues to flourish—and it is believed probable that it will continue there for a long time.

WHAT IS A RECESSION?

We might say that when business goes into a decline, a really bad decline, we have a depression. When the decline is not so great, we have a recession. A recession is a sort of minor depression.

What is a depression? It is a period of time in a country's history when most business is bad. It affects all kinds of people, from bankers to laborers to storekeepers. Workers lose their jobs in factories. Sales of things go down as a result. Stores order less goods, borrow less money. So banks are hurt, also. The entire economy suffers. And if all this happens—but on a smaller scale—it's a recession.

In the past 150 years, people have come to realize that business activity moves through a series of good times and bad times. These movements are known as business cycles. For a while there are good times. Business flourishes, people are fairly well off. Then, once in a while, something goes wrong, and business goes into a decline. After a while, business gets better, and the cycle starts all over again.

No one is sure exactly what causes recessions or depressions. There is no single explanation that is accepted by all economists. And while governments and businesses take various steps to end recessions and depressions, there is still no one sure way of doing it.

WHY DIDN'T SCHUBERT FINISH THE "UNFINISHED SYMPHONY"?

It is sometimes hard for people to understand that a creative genius, like a writer, composer, or artist, doesn't always lead a well-regulated life. He doesn't "produce" his work like someone in a factory.

Franz Schubert was one of the most productive composers. He lived to be only 31 years of age, yet he wrote over 600 songs, many beautiful symphonies and sonatas, and much choral and chamber music. And he had a hard time doing it.

Creating the music was not his problem. He couldn't get a permanent position to support himself. He was underpaid by the publishers of his music. He was usually short of money. So there could be all kinds of reasons why he could start a work and not finish it.

The exact date when he composed the Eighth Symphony in B Minor (Unfinished) is not known. It was dedicated to a music society in Austria, and Schubert delivered the first two movements to the society in 1824.

The manuscript gathered dust for more than 40 years until it was discovered in 1865 by a Viennese conductor and given its first performance.

Schubert's reasons for not finishing the Eighth Symphony remain a mystery. It is assumed that he intended to complete the work, for the first nine bars of a scherzo movement were fully written and the rest of the movement sketched out. Something must have happened to prevent him from finishing it. But it is still a masterpiece.

WHAT CAUSES NIAGARA FALLS?

Niagara Falls is located on the Niagara River, about 16 miles northwest of Buffalo, New York. The Niagara River flows out of Lake Erie, draining four of the Great Lakes into Lake Ontario. About midway on its 36-mile course, the swift water surges forward and plunges over the edge of a high cliff—Niagara Falls!

Actually, Niagara Falls consists of two cataracts—the Horseshoe, or Canadian, Falls and the American Falls. About 94 percent of Niagara's waters, or some 84,000,000 gallons, flows over the deeply curved Horseshoe Falls every minute.

Niagara Falls is considered by geologists to be quite young—perhaps no more than 10,000 to 15,000 years old. In the Ice Age, glaciers covered all of what became known as the Niagara region. As the glacial ice melted, Lake Erie was formed. The overflow from the lake found an outlet to the north and became a river.

As the river flowed northward, it spilled over an escarpment (cliff). The escarpment, topped by a hard layer of limestone rock, created the original Niagara Falls. Since then, the falls have been cut back by the powerful force of the water. They are now some seven miles upstream from their original location!

The first account of Niagara Falls appeared in 1683. It was written by a French missionary and explorer, Father Louis Hennepin. Father Hennepin had seen the falls in 1678 while on an expedition to the New World with Sieur de la Salle.

CHAPTER 2
HOW THINGS BEGAN

WHY DO MANY IRISH NAMES START WITH O'?

How do you feel about your name? Do you think it says anything about the kind of person you are? Would you have chosen it for yourself?

Nowadays, about the only people who have names made up for them to "fit" them are actors and actresses in Hollywood. The rest of us must get along with the names our parents gave us, even though they may say nothing about us.

First names have always been chosen by the parents for the child. At one time, the first name usually had a meaning for the parent. It might describe the appearance of the little baby, or express something the parents felt. For example, the name Samuel means in Hebrew "asked of God." And the name Blanche stands for "white" in French.

As towns grew and many people lived together in the same place, it became hard to tell people apart by their names. There were too many Johns and Williams and Davids. Suppose there were two men called John whom you knew and you had to tell someone which John you meant. You might say: "I'm talking about John who is William's son."

In this way the idea arose of telling people apart by mentioning the father's name. So this particular John came to be called "John Williamson." This might be expressed in many different ways. It might be "John Williams" or "John Wilson" or "John Wills"—all pointing out that John is the son of William!

In Ireland, the prefix O' means "of." So when the Irish wanted to say John, the son of Brian, they used this prefix and made the name "John O'Brian." All the Irish names that start with O' began with this way of identifying the son by the name of the father.

The Scotch did the same thing, only their prefix was Mac, which means "son." This could be shortened to Mc or M with c raised. So John, son of Donald, became known as John MacDonald.

There were many, many other ways in which last names originated. Sometimes the last names were given as the result of the place where a person lived. If Thomas lived near a wood, he might become Thomas Wood or Thomas Atwood. Sometimes the last name came from a nickname, such as Brown, or Longfellow, or Drinkwater.

If you could pick your last name today, what would you choose?

HOW DID FAIRS BEGIN?

In ancient times most people lived on farms or on large estates. There were no stores, for the small settlements of people were too far apart. Also, there were not enough goods or people for daily trade.

But people always came together for religious festivals. The merchants waited for the times when people gathered in large groups to sell their goods. This is how the fairs of ancient times began. In fact, the word "fair" comes from a Latin word *feria,* meaning "feast day" or "holiday."

The Egyptians set up markets for buying and selling when they gathered at their tombs and burying grounds for religious ceremonies. The Greeks held their fairs and festivals honoring their gods at Delphi, where there was a famous oracle.

Long before the time of Mohammed, thousands of people used to travel to Mecca, an Arab religious and trading center. After a week of religious ceremonies and feasting, they stayed on to trade precious jewels, oil, and hides. Trade fairs were also important in India, China, and Persia and among the Aztecs of Mexico.

In the Roman Empire, fairs were closely connected with religious harvest festivals. The country people brought their farm products to those festivals. There they exchanged them for cloth and other manufactured articles.

In olden days, only certain towns had the right to hold fairs. This right could be given by a king or an overlord to the lord of the town. The merchants who wanted to sell their goods at the fair had to pay money to the lord who held the license.

Special rules and laws were made for fairs. Honesty was of great importance so that people wouldn't be cheated. In the early civilizations people at war stopped their battles when they met at a fair. They considered the fairgrounds holy.

Fairs played an important part in the development of commerce. They made possible trade between the Orient and eastern and northern Europe.

HOW LONG HAVE PEOPLE BEEN GROWING VEGETABLES?

Vegetables are herbaceous plants, the kind of plant that has a soft stem and little or no woody tissues. The part of the plant that we eat may be a root (beets), a stem (asparagus), leaves (spinach), flower buds (broccoli), a fruit (tomatoes), or seeds (peas).

Early people probably gathered wild pod-bearing plants, such as beans and peas, and root plants, such as carrots. Vegetables such as these and leafy plants such as cabbage and lettuce are believed to have been in the first primitive gardens, though we don't know when such gardens were started.

The ancient Egyptians cultivated lettuce, cabbage, cress, melons, broad beans, radishes, onions, garlic, artichokes, and possibly peas. So thousands of years ago people were already eating quite a variety of vegetables.

The Greeks and Romans later were familiar with all the vegetables the Egyptians used. In addition, they raised cucumbers, asparagus, and celery.

When the explorers came to America, they found vegetables that were completely unknown in Europe. Even the familiar bean was not the same plant in the New World. Here they found string beans, lima beans, potatoes, sweet potatoes, corn, and tomatoes. These were all native to the New World and were not grown in Europe until the explorers brought back seeds and tubers. Many of these new vegetables didn't become popular until the nineteenth century.

In the nineteenth century a revolution took place in farming of all kinds. Farmers improved crops by using better farming methods and by selecting only seeds from the best plants for the next year's crop. In this way, vegetables became larger, better tasting, and more nutritious than they had ever been before.

WHEN WAS FERTILIZER FIRST USED?

Any material that is added to the soil to give it the elements that will help plants grow is a fertilizer. Why are fertilizers needed? Basically they keep up the fertility of good soils, and correct or cure the lack of fertility of poor soils.

When crops are harvested, all the food elements that have gone into them are taken away from the land. In this way, crops use up the supply of food elements in soil. The farmer uses fertilizers to put them back, or to build up the supply of elements that are naturally low in soil.

There are natural fertilizers that come from things that were once alive, such as humus, which is made from decaying plants; meal, made from animal bones or seeds; and animal manures. And there are chemical fertilizers that come from many sources.

People have used fertilizers for a long time. We do not know just how long, but we do know the Chinese used animal and plant wastes as fertilizers thousands of years ago.

The Romans as early as the second century B.C. rotated their crops, put lime in the soil, and added nitrogen by planting peas and beans. During the seventeenth century, in parts of Europe, manure was used as fertilizer, town wastes were taken to farms, and clover was used in crop rotation.

In 1748, Benjamin Franklin demonstrated in America the value of a lime fertilizer. He laid out lime plaster in the form of huge letters in a field along a highway near Philadelphia. The letters spelled out the message: THIS FIELD HAS BEEN PLASTERED. The white letters soon disappeared, but when the crop came up, the message reappeared, because the fertilized area was much greener than the rest of the field.

WHERE DID OLIVES COME FROM?

The original home of the olive is southwest Asia. For many centuries olives have provided food for people and have been carried by caravan to distant markets.

An unusual thing about the olive is that it cannot be eaten fresh from the tree. The bitter taste of the fruit must be removed by pickling, before the olive can be eaten.

Oil from olive trees was very important in trade between ancient peoples. Kings used to judge how wealthy they were by the number of jars filled with olive oil in their storerooms. On the tiny island of Crete the remains of storerooms for olive oil have been found that date back as far as 2000 B.C.

Olive trees were planted in all the countries that border the Mediterranean Sea. At one time even the bare desert regions of North Africa were covered with olive groves. It is said that once upon a time a person could travel from Mecca to Morocco in the shade of olive, date, and fig trees.

The Spaniards brought olive seeds and cuttings to the New World. They planted them around their missions in California, where the trees thrived in the warm, dry climate.

Today olives are a major crop in California, which produces almost all the olives grown in the United States. But Spain and Italy are still the leading olive-producing countries in the world.

Olive trees are raised either from seeds or from cuttings. A cutting is a stem or other part of the plant that will grow into a new tree if properly planted. An olive tree lives a long time. In the Garden of Gethsemane on the Mount of Olives, there are olive trees that have been alive for two thousand years, though they may not have the same trunks as originally. They were probably renewed by new shoots growing from their bases.

WHEN WERE PRETZELS FIRST MADE?

Pretzels may not taste or look like cookies, crackers, and biscuits—but all of these are actually alike in many ways.

They are all small and crisp, and keep well. They are even made on the same kinds of machines and packaged in the same way. Special baking plants turn out all four with only slight changes in equipment and recipes.

They are made with the same ingredients—flour, leavening, shortening, sweetening, and liquid. Usually the leavening in these products is baking powder instead of yeast. In the oven the baking powder creates carbon-dioxide gas, which makes the baked goods light without making them rise too high.

Pretzels have a long history. They date back to the early Christians in the Roman Empire. They were used at that time solely for religious purposes. Fat, milk, and eggs were forbidden during the Lenten season, and people ate dry pretzels instead of bread. They were especially popular on Ash Wednesday. It was only in modern times that they became popular as snacks to nibble on.

In northern Europe and the Scandinavian countries, the pretzel has become the sign of the baker. A large golden pretzel is usually seen hanging outside each bakery.

The original pretzel was a large twist with a soft inside and a crusty outside. By baking out almost all of the moisture, manufacturers produce the crisp, hard pretzel we eat today. Made from very stiff dough, the pretzels are actually salty baked biscuits. They are twisted or shaped into sticks.

By the way, the name "biscuit" comes from the early French word for "twice cooked." During the Middle Ages, French travelers, soldiers, and sailors carried a strange, hard bread. The bread had been cooked twice to keep it from spoiling. This hard bread was what we call the biscuit.

When we buy biscuits today, they come wrapped to keep the moisture out so that they will be as crisp as when they left the oven.

WHEN WERE STOVES FIRST USED?

Stoves were used as early as the fifteenth century, even though the fireplace was still the main source of heat in the house. Stoves were more efficient than fireplaces, because a stove sits inside a room and heats by convection as well as by radiation. Convection means air flowing around a room in a circular fashion, due to the fact that air rises as it warms and drops when it cools off.

The earliest stoves were made of clay or brick with wrought-iron or bronze doors. As wrought iron became less expensive, the stoves themselves were made of wrought iron. Metal conducts heat much better than clay or brick, so these iron stoves were a big improvement. They conducted more of the heat from the fire to the air in the room.

The first metal stoves were called five-plate stoves. They were just boxes made of five wrought-iron plates: one for the top, one for the bottom, and one for each of three sides. The fourth side was left open and was put into a fireplace so that the smoke could go up the chimney.

The first metal stoves that did not need to be set in a fireplace were made in Holland and Scandinavia. They were called six-plate stoves because they were made of six cast-iron plates, which formed the six sides of the box.

The stoves had a door for putting in fuel and removing ashes. They also had a hole that allowed air to enter for proper draft, and they had a hole at the top to which a chimney pipe could be attached. The Pilgrims lived in Holland for several years before they sailed to America, and were familiar with these stoves. When American colonists in Massachusetts began making iron and iron products, this was the type of stove they made before 1650.

Early stoves burned wood, coal, or the cheapest local fuel. In the 1820's a coal-burning stove, called the baseburner, came into use. The baseburner was designed to burn small pieces of coal, which were cheap. The coal burned on a grate near the bottom of the stove. Such a stove could stay lit for twenty-four hours a day.

HOW DID CLOTHES DEVELOP?

People have always wanted to improve their appearance. Early people put on animal skins and hung strings of beads and stones around their necks. Bark, leaves, straw, feathers, or whatever material was closest at hand were turned into clothing.

Clothing may also have had magical qualities. By wrapping themselves in a certain skin, people may have been trying to keep away evil spirits. During the ice ages, people had to wear animal furs to keep warm.

The hides were first scraped. Then holes were pierced in the skins. Strips of leather or animal tendons were drawn through the holes to tie the pieces of fur together and to help keep the garment on the body.

Gradually, people learned to make the skins softer and more supple. About forty thousand to fifty thousand years ago the needle was invented; it became a key tool for making clothes.

Later, people learned how to twist wool and animal hair into long strands. The Egyptians wove light fabrics out of the flax and cotton that grew in the Valley of the Nile. Wool was spun into yarn for robes and tunics by other ancient peoples.

In colder climates, clothes covered all of the body as a protection against the elements. Because of cold weather, the clothes that were developed here were closer-fitting. So trousers, tunics, and warm, protective cloaks came from these areas.

As communication improved between the sections of the globe, clothing styles from different regions began to influence each other. But different social groups wore different types of clothing. The clothes of the lower classes were looser and easier to work in. Wealthier people liked to wear clothing that showed everyone that they didn't have to do manual work.

WHEN DID WOMEN BEGIN TO STYLE THEIR HAIR?

Women have dressed and decorated their hair from as far back as we have any records in history.

Combs of some sort or other, for example, have been used by women since the very earliest times. Primitive peoples have made combs of bone, wood, or even bronze.

Savage races have always paid a great deal of attention to their hair. Some of them have dyed their hair black, white, or red. In the Belgian Congo in Africa, natives used the oil from the castor bean for dressing their hair, and many tribes would plaster their hair with mud.

In ancient Greek times, women used long hairpins that were quite elaborate and sometimes had sculpture on them. On special occasions they would adorn their hair with garlands and wreaths of flowers, and they also used ribbons for their hair.

As for what women did about arranging their hair in ancient times,

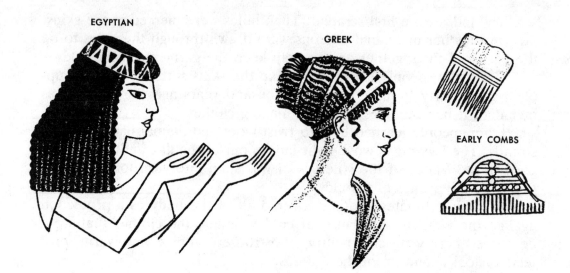

EGYPTIAN

GREEK

EARLY COMBS

it varied from place to place and customs were constantly changing. It seems that curled hair was considered more attractive than straight hair. There are pictures and statues that show women with rows of small curls arranged over the brows and temples, and these curls must have been made and kept in place by some artificial means. And not only did men also curl their hair, they even used to curl their beards!

WHEN DID MEN FIRST START TO SHAVE?

What decided whether men would let their beards grow or shave them off? All through history it was chiefly a matter of religious custom or just fashion.

We don't know exactly who the first men were who shaved their beards. But we do know that the ancient Egyptians did shave their faces for religious reasons. On the other hand, the ancient Jews were required to wear full beards, and there are many orthodox Jews who still do so for religious reasons.

The ancient Greeks wore beards, and many portraits of the great Greek philosophers show them with long flowing beards. Then Alexander the Great introduced the custom of shaving to the Greeks. He is said to have done this so that his soldiers wouldn't be grabbed by their beards in combat.

The early Romans didn't shave until about 300 B.C., when barbers were introduced. The first Roman known to have shaved every day was the great general Scipio Africanus (237–183 B.C.). Shaving soon became a regular practice among the Romans. In time of mourning the Romans let their beards grow—and the Greeks cut their beards.

The Roman custom of shaving influenced the Roman Catholic Church to have the clergy beardless and clean shaven. In the 16th and 17th centuries the wearing of beards was revived among popes, cardinals, and priests. Later Roman Catholic practice went back to the idea of shaving, except for members of monasteries.

The custom of shaving was introduced into England by the Saxons.

WHEN DID PEOPLE BEGIN TO USE KNIVES, FORKS, AND SPOONS?

Let's see if you can figure this out by using logic. Imagine the time when knives, forks, and spoons didn't even exist. Which one of them do you think people would "invent" first?

Not the knife—because man can tear his food apart with his hands. Not the fork—because he can pick it up with his fingers. But for picking up liquids, especially hot liquids, we need a spoon! Hence the spoon was invented first. In fact, spoonlike implements have been found going back to the Stone Age! The Egyptians had spoons made of wood, stone, and ivory. And the Greeks used spoons of bronze and silver.

When people began to use the knife and fork, however, they really made a great advance in dining. And this advance came about quite recently in history. Even only three hundred years ago, knives and forks were great curiosities. As a matter of fact, in France everyone ate with his fingers until the seventeenth century.

This doesn't mean that knives and forks didn't exist before that time. The primitive savage actually used a kind of fork, but it was nothing like ours. It may have been made of a small pronged twig.

As far as is known, the first real forks were long, two-pronged utensils made of iron, bone, and hard wood. They were used only in cooking and for holding the meat while it was being carved.

Forks were used for dining in the eleventh century, but only a very few people were so dainty that they had to have one. The knife, of course, was one of man's first inventions, in the sense that he made a cutting tool of flint or other stones. But there was no such thing as a table knife in early times. Even three hundred years ago, it was so rare, most people didn't know about it. After the seventeenth century, table knives were introduced in England, and soon they became popular. But the poor people couldn't afford them, and so most people still ate with their hands.

WHEN WERE EYEGLASSES INVENTED?

If you look around you, you'll notice that an amazing number of people wear eyeglasses. We are so used to seeing people wear glasses that it's hard for us to imagine a time when there was no such thing. People with poor eyesight simply had to get along as best they could.

Nobody is really sure when eyeglasses were invented. In the year 1266, Roger Bacon, an English monk who made many interesting experiments, found a way to make the letters in a book larger and easier to read. He simply put a piece from a ball of glass on the book! Of course, this wasn't the same as having eyeglasses to help him.

The first evidence we have of someone actually wearing spectacles is a portrait of a cardinal painted in 1352 in Italy. He wears two framed lenses with their handles riveted together and attached over the eyes.

When printed books began to appear, eyeglasses became a real necessity for many people and the use of them began to spread. During the sixteenth century, eyeglasses were being made in large quantities in northern Italy and southern Germany. In 1784, Benjamin Franklin invented bifocals, which are two different kinds of lenses in the same pair of eyeglasses.

To understand how eyeglasses can help a person see better, you must know something about the eye. The eye is shaped like a ball, with a slight bulge at the front. At the center of this bulge is the pupil, which lets the light into the dark inside of the eye. Light passes through the pupil to the lens. The lens focuses the light, forming a picture at the back of the eyeball. Here there is a screen of light-sensitive cells called the retina.

Some people have eyeballs that are a little longer than normal, front to back; with others the eyeball may be too short, and the lens may not be able to focus a sharp picture on the retina. Eyeglasses provide the eye with an extra lens. The extra lens corrects what your own lens does, so that there is a sharp picture focused on the retina and you can see better.

HOW OLD IS THE SPORT OF DIVING?

People probably learned to dive shortly after learning to swim. People started jumping into the water after they found that they were able to walk into the water from land.

After learning to jump, people probably began to enter the water by diving head first. But it wasn't until the late nineteenth century that acrobatic or fancy diving was developed. Gymnasts from such countries as Sweden, Germany, and Finland, who wanted to improve their acrobatic techniques, found during their practice sessions that water was softer to land on than the ground or tumbling pads. As a result of these practice sessions, the sport of fancy diving, now usually called competitive diving, was developed in Europe.

By 1904 there was great international interest in the sport. There were enough assorted dives to hold an Olympic diving championship during the Olympic Games of that year. The event was called high diving in the program of the Olympic Games.

Each dive that is permitted in competition has a value based on how difficult it is to perform. Since the first Olympic diving event, held in 1904, the list of competitive dives has been continually changing. Old-fashioned dives are discontinued, and new ones are added.

Platform diving is diving without a springboard. It is usually performed from a high platform. In springboard diving a long, flexible board that bends very easily is used. Springboard diving was developed after platform diving. It is performed closer to the water than platform diving.

Today competitive diving is one of the top sports in high schools and colleges. Many divers who enter competition during their high-school and college days continue to compete for many years.

WHO INVENTED THE BALL?

No one knows who first played with a ball. People have been playing ball since prehistoric times. Every civilization, from primitive times to the present, has played a game using some kind of a ball.

Some early people wove reeds into rounded shapes. Others used leather stuffed with feathers for playing ball. Later, generations of Greeks and Romans added a new idea—air. A blown-up leather ball called a *follis* was used in games of catch. They also inflated balls of larger sizes with which they played a kind of football and other kicking games.

Balls have been made from many materials, depending on what was available in the particular country. North American Indians, for example, were hunters, so they used balls made of deer hide. Japanese children, on the other hand, played with balls of tightly-wadded tissue wrapped with string.

It is said that Columbus found the Indians of Central America playing with solid, black balls of vegetable gum. He took some of these balls to Europe with him and thus introduced the idea of a bouncy rubber ball.

Many of our modern ball games started as religious and magical ceremonies. Ball games were once carried on seriously by older people. Often the games retold the old beliefs about war, gods and devils, life and death.

The Egyptians were among the first people to have ceremonial ball games. Each spring two large groups of people acted out a contest between two of their gods. A round, wooden ball and crooked sticks were used. The object was to drive the ball through the opposing goal. The side that was able to knock the ball past the defenders won a victory for the god their team represented.

U. S. FLAG OF 1777

UNION FLAG OF HOLLAND

WHY DOES THE AMERICAN FLAG HAVE STARS AND STRIPES?

It may surprise a great many people, but the exact reason why the American flag has stars and stripes is not really known. Scholars have studied the question and there are many explanations, but no one is really sure.

The Continental Congress, on June 14, 1777, resolved that "the Flag of the United States be 13 stripes alternate red and white, and the Union be 13 stars white in a blue field representing a new constellation." But nobody knows why Congress adopted that design. Perhaps the stars were chosen to represent a new country being born, the way a new constellation appears in the sky.

Some scholars believe that perhaps Congress had taken the idea of using stars and stripes from George Washington's coat of arms. But others believe that Washington would not have allowed his coat of arms to be used for the Republic's first flag.

There is also the story that relates how Betsy Ross made the first flag for George Washington. He is supposed to have come to her sewing shop with a rough drawing. Betsy Ross was a seamstress and official flagmaker for the Pennsylvania Navy. However, there is no actual proof that she made the first American flag that had stars and stripes.

WHY IS TEXAS CALLED THE "LONE STAR STATE"?

For a long time it has been very popular to make jokes about Texas. Usually these jokes refer to its tremendous size and the size of everything in it.

There's a good reason for this. It's as far across Texas as it is from New York City to Chicago. The area of Texas is 267,339 square miles, which makes it 25 percent larger than France and five times as large as England. It is as large as the whole of New England plus New York, New Jersey, Pennsylvania, Delaware, Maryland, Virginia, and West Virginia!

The first Europeans in the land now called Texas were survivors from a party of shipwrecked Spaniards. They were cast on the Gulf shore in 1528, and some of them later wandered across to the Gulf of California. As a result of their wandering, Spain claimed not only Texas, but all the region that is now southwestern United States.

But Spain made no effort to take possession of Texas for more than 150 years. In the meantime, France also established a claim to Texas. Then the Spaniards began to settle the country. By 1750 they had established several missions.

In 1821 Mexico, of which Texas was then a part, broke away from Spain and became an independent nation. That same year Stephen F. Austin came to Texas with a colony of immigrants from the United States. Quarrels arose between the colonists and the Mexican Government. The Texans revolted against Mexico in 1835.

The Mexicans tried to put down the revolt but were defeated by Sam Houston in 1836. This made Texas independent, and for ten years Texas was a republic, with a congress and government like that of the United States. The congress adopted a red, white, and blue flag bearing a single star. This gave Texas its popular name, the "Lone Star State." In 1845 Texas was admitted as a state into the United States.

WHEN WAS THE FIRST OIL WELL DRILLED IN THE UNITED STATES?

Long before people thought of drilling for oil, or petroleum, they were using it. Ancient peoples, including the Egyptians and Chinese, used it as a medicine. In India it was used for lighting. More recently, the Native Americans were using petroleum before the white man came. To hold it, they dug pits in the ground. The white men imitated the practice of the Indians and used to sell the mineral oil as a cure for many ailments!

Until the middle of the nineteenth century, people collected crude oil where it seeped naturally from the earth. At that time, people lighted their homes with lamps in which they burned whale oil. Then they began to distil oil from coal, which produced a product called kerosene. At the same time, work was being done on petroleum to make it a source of lamp oil. So the time was ripe for someone to find a way of obtaining more of this petroleum, which was becoming more and more useful.

Two New York lawyers named George Bissel and Jonathan Eveleth formed a company to prospect for oil in Pennsylvania. They secured the services of Colonel E. L. Drake, a retired railroad conductor, and set him to drilling near the little town of Titusville, Pennsylvania.

On August 27, 1859, after he had drilled down only 69½ feet, Drake struck oil. Soon he was pumping eight barrels a day, then twenty. The petroleum was a cheaper and surer source of lamp oil than the dangerous business of hunting whales. So it quickly found a market.

Excitement ran high. Thousands of people came to see the Drake well. Soon the first oil rush in history was on! Farms were leased. More wells were sunk. Many people became suddenly rich. Oil towns sprang up overnight. The flood of oil mounted, and now the refining and transportation of the oil became the big problems. But the age of petroleum had come!

Today the Middle East supplies about 64 percent of the world's oil.

WHO DISCOVERED THE X-RAY?

Did you know that the story of X-rays started more than a hundred years ago?

In the middle of the nineteenth century, a man named Heinrich Geissler discovered that when electricity was discharged under high voltage through tubes in a partial vacuum, beautiful light effects were produced. Later on, Sir William Crookes proved that the luminosity was caused by electrified particles.

Next, Heinrich Hertz showed that these rays would pass through thin sheets of gold or platinum. His pupil, Lenard, made "windows" of such substances, so that the rays could pass out of the tube to the outer air.

Now we come to the actual discovery of the X-ray. In 1895, Wilhelm Roentgen was experimenting with one of these tubes, but one without "windows." He noticed that certain nearby crystals were glowing brilliantly. Since he knew that the rays that had been discovered before (called cathode rays) could not pass through the glass to produce this effect, he suspected that there must be some other kind of rays present, too.

These invisible rays, which were so different from the other rays and from light, could not be explained so he called them X-rays. By this he meant "rays of unknown nature." Later on, scientists called them Roentgen Rays, and this name is still used by many scientists.

X-rays are produced in an X-ray tube. Most of the air is pumped out. There are two electrodes, and the electrons travel from one (the cathode) to the other (the anode). The target is made of tungsten, and it stops the electrons suddenly. Most of the energy of these electrons is changed to heat, but some of it becomes X-radiation. X-rays can penetrate objects, because they have a very short wavelength. The shorter the wavelength, the more penetrating the rays become.

HOW LONG HAVE SECRET CODES BEEN USED?

Codes are a way of writing something in secret; that is, no one will be able to read it who doesn't know the code. Ciphers are another way of doing this. In a code, each word is written as a secret code word or code number. In a cipher each letter is changed. Secret writing that uses codes and ciphers is called cryptography.

Codes and ciphers have played an important part in the history of the world. Julius Caesar, the Roman ruler who conquered almost all of

Europe about two thousand years ago, used a cipher when he sent secret messages to his generals. During the American Revolution, George Washington's spies used a code to send him information about the enemy. His spies had a code book that listed numbers for all the words they might need. The messages were written and decoded according to the numbers given in the book.

Do you know that today you see codes being used all around you? When you go into a store, you may find numbers or letters on certain goods. These are codes used by storekeepers. The codes show how much was paid for the goods, or when they were added to the stock.

Businesspeople use codes to hide plans from competitors. Sometimes personal letters or diaries are written in code. Many people enjoy working out codes and ciphers simply as a hobby.

In the sixteenth century, codes and ciphers were very popular among scientists. They wrote messages to each other in code so that no one would learn their secrets.

An Italian scientist of that time, Giambattista della Porta, wrote a book about codes. He is sometimes called "The Father of Modern Cryptography." When Galileo, the famous Italian astronomer and physicist, discovered the phases of Venus, he recorded his discovery in a kind of cipher.

WHO MADE THE FIRST PHONOGRAPH RECORD?

Thomas A. Edison invented recording in 1877, when he noticed two things about sound.

He noticed that a small disk inside a telephone receiver vibrated as the person at the other end of the line spoke. So he had the idea of attaching a tiny needle to the center of the disk; the force of the needle could tell him the amount of sound that was being sent out.

He also noticed that when he ran a paper tape covered with Morse code dots and dashes through an instrument at high speed, it produced little noises that were much like the sound of people talking. If the human voice could make a needle move, why couldn't the same needle prick the pattern of the sound waves on paper tape?

After a few experiments, he replaced the paper with a metal cylinder. He wrapped a piece of tin foil around the cylinder and attached two disk-and-needle units. One was to speak into; the other was for sound to come out of. When the "in" disk vibrated, the needle should make little indentations in the tin foil as the cylinder turned. When the "out" needle traveled over these same indentations, its disk should vibrate, too, recreating the sounds.

Edison put on the first cylinder, leaned close to the "in" disk, and shouted, "Mary had a little lamb." He then set the out needle in the same groove and turned the crank of the cylinder. Back came the voice! He had made the first recording of sound! This was in 1877.

In 1895, a man called Emile Berliner put the first phonograph record on the market. This was a record instead of a cylinder. It was made of zinc and coated with wax. When the "in" needle vibrated to the sound of a voice, it scratched a wiggly pattern in the wax. Then the record was put into acid, which ate into the zinc where the needle cut its path. This was a way of "etching" the human voice, and became the way to make records.

HOW DID MOVIES START?

"Movies" is short for "motion pictures," and the development of pictures that seem to move has taken place over many years, thanks to the work of many people.

Way back in the 1800's, experiments were being made using photographs which created the illusion of motion. For example, batteries of cameras were set up to take a series of pictures of a running horse.

In the late 1880's roll film was invented. Then cameras were invented which photographed a series of separate photographs of an action on a strip of film and then showed them back at the same rate of speed, thus reproducing the action. In fact, these were "movies."

They became quite popular. At first they were only scenes of something that moved: waves on the beach, horses running, children swinging, trains arriving at a station.

The first film which really told a story was produced in the laboratories of Thomas Edison in 1903. It was "The Great Train Robbery," and it caused a nationwide sensation. It was exhibited in black lightproof tents.

The first permanent motion-picture theater in the United States opened in November, 1905, in Pittsburgh, Pennsylvania. The owners called it a nickelodeon. Soon nickelodeons were opened all over the country and everybody began to go to the movies.

Most of the first films were made in New York and New Jersey and it wasn't until 1913 that films began to be made in Hollywood.

WHEN WERE JOKES AND RIDDLES FIRST TOLD?

Riddles have been asked since very ancient times. Today, we consider riddles as a form of amusement, but long ago people took riddles very seriously.

Ancient oracles often answered questions and gave advice in the form of riddles. Kings used riddles to send each other secret messages. These serious riddles were also called enigmas.

Greeks and Romans held riddle contests at their feasts and gave prizes to the winners. According to some legends, a man's life sometimes depended on his giving the correct answer to a riddle.

Riddles even appear in the Bible. At Samson's wedding feast, a riddle contest was held and the Queen of Sheba asked King Solomon a number of riddles.

Jokes are as old as the spoken word. In every country in the world and in every age in history, people have told funny stories to make one another laugh.

In the Middle Ages in Europe the court jesters, or fools, amused the king and his court with jokes and tricks. At first, court jesters sang of brave deeds, or gestes. But as time went by they became tellers of jokes and funny stories.

Jokes told by jesters began to appear in collections, or jestbooks. One of the best-known English jestbooks was "Tarlton's Jests," which appeared about 1611. So you see how long ago people were collecting jokes. The most famous joke-teller in history is Joe Miller, an English actor who lived from 1684 to 1738.

WHEN WERE HOUSES FIRST BUILT?

People began to build homes, shelters for themselves and their families, thousands and thousands of years ago. The kinds of homes people built long ago depended almost completely upon the climate in which they lived, the building materials that were close at hand, and the dangers they faced in their daily lives.

For example, when the stone ax was invented thousands of years ago, wood began to play an important part in home-building. So early people were already building houses of wood.

In ancient times, people living in warm climates found that grass houses were easy to make and comfortable to live in. So all over the wet, hot grasslands of Africa and on some of the islands of the South Pacific, houses were made of grasses, leaves, or vines that grew nearby.

Thousands of years ago people who lived in hot, dry climates found a way to make fine walls for their homes. They plastered a sticky mixture of clay or mud over house walls of loosely woven twigs. The mud plaster dried hard in the sun and stuck firmly to the house walls.

The ancient Egyptians are believed to have been among the first to discover how to make bricks. In Mesopotamia primitive people later developed a way of making the sun-dried bricks harder and stronger. They placed the molded bricks in a hot fire and "burned" them. Later on, the ancient Assyrians found out how to burn a glaze onto their bricks. Such bricks have lasted for thousands of years.

WHEN WAS THE FIRST U.S. CENSUS TAKEN?

Since early times, governments have been taking official counts of the population in their country.

The United States was the first nation in modern times to make the regular taking of a census part of its constitution. Article 1, Section 2 of the U. S. Constitution, adopted in 1789, provides that an "enumeration" should be taken every ten years.

There was a good practical reason for this. The number of delegates which a state was to have in the House of Representatives was based on the population of the state. So changes in the population had to be recorded in order to keep the proportion accurate. The first census was accordingly taken in 1790, and has been taken every ten years since.

In a census, much more information is gathered than just the number of people. There are questions about whether the people are married or single, about the kind of home they live in, the amount of schooling they had, their occupation, and so on.

This additional information is very valuable and important in making decisions in many areas. For example, it can help determine how many schools and teachers are necessary. It can help guide us about what social legislation is needed for older people. It can tell us what effects population changes will have on the labor market, and many other matters.

There are also other censuses taken at different times pertaining to agriculture, manufacturers, mineral industries, business, government units, and irrigation and drainage.

WHEN WERE WINDMILLS FIRST USED?

A windmill is a machine that converts the energy of the wind into work. The most common use for windmills is to grind grain or to pump water.

The wind-driven wheel, or windwheel, consists of a number of evenly balanced vanes or sails which radiate from a shaft. When the wind strikes the sails, the windwheel rotates, which turns the shaft. This turning force is transmitted by gears from the shaft to the parts of the machine that do the work.

The principle of the windmill has been known since ancient times, but little is known of its use before the 12th century. It was during that time that windmills began to be widely used in Europe.

The earliest kind of windmill, which is called the post or German mill, had a fixed vertical post around which the entire mill rotated so that the windwheel might face into the wind. The other principal kind of windmill, called the tower, turret, or Dutch mill, had its windwheel and shaft set in a rotating turret mounted on a stationary tower.

The horsepower developed by these windmills ranged from two to eight horsepower for the German type, and from six to fourteen horsepower for the Dutch type. About half the horsepower developed was lost in transmission, so they weren't very efficient machines. But they were used in great numbers until steam power was developed in the 18th century. There were as many as eight thousand windmills in the Netherlands alone in use in the 17th century!

A much smaller type of windmill, used for pumping water, was very popular in the United States at the end of the 19th century. They were used to pump water for livestock, household use, or for irrigation.

WHAT WAS THE FIRST ZOO?

About three thousand years ago, a Chinese emperor kept a collection of animals in what he called an "intelligence park." If the emperor kept the animals alive to study them and learn something of their habits, then this was perhaps the first zoo, because today this is what a zoo is—a large, enclosed area where wild animals, birds, and reptiles are kept for people to see and scientists to study.

Long ago it became a custom to keep animals at home. As time passed and villages and towns grew, some men kept wild animals in enclosures on their property.

In this way they had animals on hand when they wanted to go hunting. Also, the animals could be taught amusing tricks to entertain people. But people often collected wild animals to show how rich and powerful they were. To make themselves popular, they sometimes allowed people to enter their parks and look at their animals.

There were public zoos in Europe as early as the 19th century. Many more were created in the larger towns and cities during the next 700 or 800 years.

A zoo's size is rated by the number of kinds of animals it contains. Only four zoos have more than one thousand kinds of animals. Of these, the largest is the San Diego Zoo in California. Then come the West Berlin Zoo, the Bronx Zoo in New York City, and Belgium's Antwerp Zoo.

Years ago, zoos bought animals from dealers. But today, with wild animals rarer, zoos usually breed their own animals or exchange animals with other zoos.

WHY IS THE NUMBER 13 CONSIDERED UNLUCKY?

The idea that the number 13 is unlucky is a superstition. There are many different kinds of superstitions, based on things in nature, charms, spirits, objects, colors, accidents, and so on.

But there is probably no superstition that has as many people observing it, in one way or another, all over the world, as the one that 13 is unlucky. Hotels don't have a 13th floor—the count goes from 12 to 14. Hotel rooms don't have a 13. Many people would never have 13 persons at a dinner table.

Yet the strange thing is that there is no single, accepted explanation for the origin of the superstition about 13. There are many different ideas about the origin of it.

Some experts say 13 was unpopular from the time when man learned to count. By using his ten fingers and two feet as units, he came up with the number 12. But beyond that—13—was unknown and frightening to him.

Among religious circles, the 13 superstition is traced back to the Last Supper, at which were Christ and the twelve Disciples—thirteen in all. Other people go back to the story of the Valhalla banquet in Greek mythology, to which twelve gods were invited. Loki, the Spirit of Strife and Mischief, intruded, making thirteen. As a result, Balder, the favorite of the gods, was killed.

Another strange thing about 13 is that this number was regarded as lucky by the ancient Chinese and Egyptians.

HOW DID ANIMALS GET THEIR NAMES?

The names of animals, like the names of so many other things, didn't originate in one particular way. The names developed in many different ways, from many different sources.

For example, a strange name like "hippopotamus" is actually a descriptive name. In Greek, "hippos" means "horse" and "potamus" means "river." So the hippopotamus was a "river horse." "Rhinoceros" came from two Greek words, "rinos," the nose, and "keras," a horn. That's just what this creature has: a horn on the nose! "Leopard" is from the Latin "leopardus"—which meant a "spotted lion."

Some names of animals that we use are based on names used in other places. "Camel" comes from the Arabic "gamel," and "giraffe" from the Arabic "zirafoh," meaning "long neck." The name "ox" is an Icelandic term which became "oxa" in Anglo-Saxon. And "cow" also comes from Iceland, where the name was "ku." The name "bull" comes from the Anglo-Saxon verb "belan," which meant to roar, to bellow.

"Deer" comes from the Anglo-Saxon "deor," which meant "a wild animal." We get our name "cat" from the French "chat," which came from the Latin "gata." "Mouse" comes from the Anglo-Saxon "mus." The name "poodle" has an interesting origin. It comes from the German "pudel," short for "pudelhund," which meant "a dog that splashes in water." The duck is so named because this bird "ducks" in the water, from an old English word "duce," a "diver."

These are only a few names with explanations of how they started. But you can see that animals got their names in many different ways.

WHEN WAS THE FIRST PLASTIC MADE?

In making a plastic, the chemist starts with the molecule. The chemist causes molecules to form a long chain, the links being the molecules.

The new "long-chain" molecule acts differently from the single molecule. The whole process is called polymerization, and it is by polymerization that new materials are made.

Chemists knew about and had worked with plastics as early as the mid-1800's. Vinyl chloride was polymerized in 1838, styrene in 1839, acrylics in 1843, and polyester in 1847. But at that time there was no particular need for these synthetic materials.

In 1869, looking for a substitute for ivory, John Hyatt, a printer, and his brother Isiah Hyatt discovered Celluloid. This was a new, tough, easily made and shaped material, and resisted many chemicals. It stimulated chemists to think about developing additional synthetic materials.

In 1909 the Belgian-American chemist Leo Baekeland discovered phenolformaldehyde. This was the first of a type of plastics called thermosetting plastics. Baekeland was actually trying to invent a substitute for shellac. Instead, he produced a dark syrup that would harden when heated. The new material was not dissolved by ordinary solvents; it could be molded into any shape, it did not conduct electricity, and it was inexpensive.

Baekeland named the new material Bakelite, after himself. This plastic was the first entirely synthetic material to be produced in large quantities. It opened the way to the development of a whole world of new plastics.

WHO WAS THE FIRST MAN TO EXPLORE
THE NORTH POLE?

The polar regions surround the earth's two geographic poles. The geographic poles lie roughly in the centers of these two regions. They are simply called the North Pole and the South Pole. The north polar region is called the Arctic.

The Arctic has excited curiosity from the time of ancient Greece and perhaps even earlier. The man who is given credit for discovering the Arctic is the famous Greek explorer Pytheas. In the 4th century B.C. he sailed from the Mediterranean northward to the edge of the Arctic region. It may be that men from northern lands, such as Norway and Britain, ventured into the northern seas even earlier, but there are no written records to prove it.

In the 16th century the great search started for northwest and northeast passages from Europe to the Orient, and many explorers went to the Arctic region and learned more about it. This search continued right up to the beginning of the 20th century, when such a passage was discovered by the Norwegian explorer, Roald Amundsen, in 1903.

Now explorers were ready to try for the North Pole itself. United States Admiral Robert E. Peary led an expedition over the polar sea ice from a base at the northern end of Ellesmere Island. On April 6, 1909, he became the first man to reach the North Pole.

The first flight over the North Pole, a round trip from Spitzbergen, was made by the American explorer Richard E. Byrd on May 9, 1926.

WHEN DID PEOPLE START COOKING MEAT?

Early people did not cook their food. Whatever they were able to find in nature, they gathered up and ate raw. And this was simply because they had no way of cooking their food. They didn't know how to make fire.

Even when they learned how to make fire, they used it at first only for warmth and to frighten away wild animals. Cooking may have been discovered by accident. Some of the animals they killed may have been thrown near the fire. Or meat may have fallen into the glowing embers. The surface of the meat turned brown. It smelled good and tasted good—and people discovered their food would be improved by cooking.

One of the earliest means of cooking was on the hot stones around an open fire. Pits lined with stones and glowing coals formed the first oven for primitive man. Soon it was built above the ground, with an outlet for smoke, a draft, and a stone across the front opening to hold in the heat.

People learned how to boil foods in pits lined with a large hide or skin. This was filled with water and heated to the boiling point by red-hot stones.

Primitive kettles were made by smearing clay over reed baskets and letting it harden. These kettles were placed over the fire for cooking foods, either with or without water.

So early people, many thousands of years ago, worked out the two main methods of cooking: by baking or roasting in dry heat, and by boiling or steaming in moist heat.

WHERE DID SUGAR ORIGINATE?

There are many different kinds of sugar, and they are found in many living things, both vegetable and animal. But when people speak of sugar, they usually mean sucrose, the sugar that comes from sugarcane or sugar beets.

Plants whose stalks were lusciously sweet were probably growing wild in New Guinea thousands of years ago. Early peoples had wars between tribes over these stalks. Later on, as people advanced in culture, the stalks of sugarcane were bartered for other goods and their use spread. In this way traders carried sugar throughout the islands of the South Pacific and eventually to Indonesia, Asia, and the Philippines.

Sugarcane was probably known in India in prehistoric times. We do know that as long ago as 400 B.C. cane sugar was in general use in India. The first Europeans to see the sugarcane were the invaders who went to India with Alexander the Great in 325 B.C. One of them described it as a grass that produced honey without the help of bees.

From India sugarcane culture and sugar manufacture spread to Persia between A.D. 500 and 700. When the Muslims from Persia conquered Arabia, Syria, Palestine, Egypt, and the Mediterranean areas, they introduced the use of sugar in those countries.

Sugarcane was first introduced into the United States in 1751. Jesuit missionaries brought the sugarcane from Haiti to New Orleans, Louisiana. By 1795 the commercial production of sugar had already begun.

WHEN WERE THE FIRST ELECTIONS HELD?

The word "election" comes from a Latin root meaning "to choose." And the feeling people have had that they should have the right to choose their leaders goes back thousands of years.

The ancient Hebrews and Greeks fought for that right. The early kings of Israel were chosen by the people, and so were the generals of the ancient Greek armies.

The habit of freely choosing their leaders was brought to Britain by the Anglo-Saxon conquerors some 1,500 years ago. Thus, the right to vote for local officials became a part of English thinking and was brought to America by the early colonists. Even before the American Revolution, Americans had been voting in their town meetings and colonial assemblies.

But the matter of elections has always presented one big problem: who shall have the right to vote? In the early days of the American republic only about 120,000 people in a total population of more than 4,000,000 could vote. This was because each state had the right to restrict the vote.

Voting was usually limited to free white men with certain property and religious qualifications. Today we wouldn't consider that as being fair or democratic. By 1860 practically all the states allowed all white men over 21 to vote. But Negroes and women could still feel they were not being treated as equals.

After the Civil War the Constitution was amended to give the vote to Negro men. In 1920, the Nineteenth Amendment gave the vote to women. And in 1971 the 26th Amendment lowered the minimum voting age to 18. So, even though elections have been held for thousands of years, the right to vote has only recently been won by many groups of people.

WHEN WERE TOMBSTONES FIRST USED?

The first tombstones were used by Bushmen and other primitive tribes in Africa. They believed that there were evil spirits living in the bodies of dead people. By placing heavy stones on the graves they hoped to prevent these spirits from rising.

But the marking of graves in some way goes back to very ancient times. Primitive man placed stones or other markings on graves not only to keep the evil spirits from rising, but to mark the spot so he could avoid it.

The ancient Greeks used gravestones, and they were usually ornamented with sculpture. The Hebrews marked the graves of the dead with stone pillars. And, of course, the Egyptians marked the places where dead were buried with tombs and pyramids.

Different peoples used different things for this purpose. Some built vaults, others erected tall pillars of ornamented stone. Some marked their graves with simple slabs of wood or stone; others built magnificent shrines and mausoleums.

As Christianity spread, the marking of graves became common. The cross over the grave was the most popular grave mark among Christians.

Decorating graves with flowers and wreaths is a custom that goes back to ancient times, too. The Greeks used wreaths made of gold. During the early days of Christianity a custom started of making wreaths of ribbon and paper and giving them to the church as a memento of the person who died. These wreaths would be hung around the walls of the church and stay there for years and years.

HOW DID ADVERTISING COME ABOUT?

Advertising is a way of informing people of something. This can range from telling them of a product for sale, or a service, or urging them to do something, or even to bring one's name before the public.

Advertising took many forms from the very beginning. For example, there is a papyrus discovered at Thebes offering a reward for a runaway slave. It is three thousand years old—and it's really an advertisement! Signboards that notified people of services available were

placed outside doors in Greece and Egypt around 1500 B.C.—a form of advertising.

With the invention of printing, advertising began to take on new forms. About 1477, in London, the first printed advertisement in English announced a prayer book sale. The first newspaper advertisement appeared on the back page of a London newspaper in 1625.

It was not until 1704 that paid advertisements were printed in the United States. By 1771 there were 31 newspapers in the colonies, and all of them carried advertising.

Today, of course, we know that advertising is done not only in newspapers, but also in magazines, on the radio, and on television. The first "commercials" appeared on radio about 1920.

Commercials on television developed mostly after World War II. The idea spread very quickly and today the advertising that is done on TV is so familiar to all of us that many people can remember the commercials even better than the shows they see!

WHY WERE SCHOOLS STARTED?

From the time of the cavemen, human beings have always taught what they knew to their young. If they had not, no child would have survived. He would not have known which animals were dangerous, which plants were good to eat, or how to make a fire to keep warm.

After many centuries people learned to write down what they knew. In this way they could save up more knowledge and pass it on to their children and grandchildren.

Once systems of writing had been invented, schools began. The earliest schools we know about were in Mesopotamia and Egypt three thousand to four thousand years ago.

Schools were started to pass on knowledge and to help prepare young people for living in the world. But society in ancient times felt that schools and a good education were not for all young people. In Egypt, for example, there were higher levels of education for young men who were going to be priests, government officials, architects, or doctors. Only a very few young men received this much education.

Another ancient people, the Hebrews, had a long tradition of education. When they were an independent nation, the father of each family taught his sons the history of their people, their laws, and their religion. Later, when the Hebrews were conquered by outsiders, they were afraid that their own customs and beliefs might be lost. They set up formal schools where everybody, rich or poor, was taught the language, the religion, and the history of the Jews. This was probably the first time in human history that formal education was given to rich and poor alike.

WHO FIRST WROTE NURSERY RHYMES?

Hardly a child grows up without learning by heart "Hey Diddle, Diddle," "Pat-a-cake, Pat-a-cake," or "Jack and Jill." We call them nursery rhymes, and sometimes Mother Goose rhymes.

The name Mother Goose first appeared in a collection of fairy tales by a Frenchman, Charles Perrault, which was published in 1697. But it is possible that the name had been known long before that as a way of describing women who were village storytellers.

A Boston printer, Thomas Fleet, is reported to have published in

1719 a book called "Songs for the Nursery; or Mother Goose's Melodies for Children." But no copy of this book has ever been found.

Most nursery rhymes were never intended for the nursery. During the 16th century in England adults sang ballads, madrigals, and rounds. Mothers sang the songs to their infants, and so the songs were brought into the nursery.

There were also rhymes that referred to political events and were recited and sung everywhere. Children hearing them would take a catch refrain or phrase and make the musical rhymes their own.

WHEN WAS COFFEE FIRST BREWED?

An interesting thing about the use of coffee is that it was first enjoyed without being brewed. East African tribes have used the fruit of the coffee tree for centuries as an article of food. They would roast the berries in an open pan or prepare them with animal fat, and then eat them. What they enjoyed was the stimulating effect the coffee berries had.

The first coffee plants probably grew in Kaffa, a province of Ethiopia. This province may have given coffee its name. In the 14th century Arabian merchants came to Kaffa and became acquainted with the coffee seeds. They then began cultivating coffee in Yemen.

There the people began to brew coffee. The followers of Mohammed were forbidden to drink wine, and coffee was a stimulating beverage that could take the place of wine for them.

About the middle of the 15th century, the use of coffee as a beverage spread from Yemen to Mecca, and from there to Baghdad, Cairo, Damascus, and other places. There were coffeehouses in Cairo as early as 1511.

Coffee was first introduced to Western Europe around 1615. It created quite a lot of excitement, and many people were against the idea of drinking coffee. They thought it was poisonous. But coffeehouses soon became a part of the social life of England.

In fact, so many people used to gather in coffeehouses that King Charles II was afraid plots against the government were being hatched there. He ordered them closed. But by this time coffee was so popular that he was forced to open them again.

WHO INVENTED ARITHMETIC?

Arithmetic is the science of numbers. It is concerned with the meanings of numbers, with their symbols, and with ways of working with them.

Nobody "invented" arithmetic. It developed to meet people's needs. At first it had to do with quantity, not with counting. Before people could count, they had a "number sense." For example, early man could tell when he had picked enough berries. A hunter could tell by looking that he had lost a spear.

But as time passed, people needed numbers and number names. Herders needed to keep track of their animals. Farmers needed to keep track of the seasons. So at some unknown time, long ago, the first numbers and number names were invented. These are counting numbers, which we also call whole numbers, or natural numbers.

Later, people needed to have numbers that were less than 1, and numbers between other numbers. So fractions were developed. Much later, still other kinds of numbers came into use. One kind was negative numbers, like -2 or -7.

The idea of negative numbers was very hard to discover. In ancient Greece it was known that if you took 5 from 7 you had 2 left. But was it possible to take 7 from 5? The Greeks decided it was not.

Not until the 1500's did people begin to see that there could be a number that was less than nothing. For example, take 7 from 5 and you have 2 less than 0, or -2.

With counting as the basic process, people learned to add, subtract, multiply, and divide—the four basic operations in arithmetic.

WHEN WAS THE CROSSWORD PUZZLE INVENTED?

The crossword puzzle is both a new thing and a not-so-new thing. Since ancient times there was a word square. In a word square the letters spelled the same words horizontally and vertically.

The crossword is built on a pattern of black and white squares, with different words interlocking across and down. There are numbered definitions given as clues to the words. So the crossword puzzle added some new things.

The first crossword puzzle was put together by a man called Arthur Winn. It first appeared in a Sunday supplement of the New York *World* on December 21, 1913. It remained as a feature of this newspaper for some time, and various improvements were made in its form.

In 1924 the first book of crossword puzzles appeared. Up until that time, the crossword puzzle had not been very popular. But after this, the crossword puzzle became a nationwide craze.

Other newspapers began to print crossword puzzles. In 1924, the *World* started printing one every day. Then the New York *Herald-Tribune* did the same. Pretty soon most papers began to publish crossword puzzles regularly.

The British took up crossword puzzles in 1925. At first they imported American books, but they soon developed a type of crossword puzzle that was a little different.

WHEN WAS COPPER FIRST USED?

Copper was used earlier than other metals, with the exception of gold. Long before the dawn of history, men of the Stone Age were already using it.

One of the reasons for this early use of copper was that it is found in a fairly pure state. It can be found in lumps and grains of free metal. So ancient man probably picked up lumps of copper because they were attractive. Later on, people discovered that these red stones of metal could be beaten into any shape. So they began to make knives and weapons out of copper, which was easier than making them by chipping flints.

And then, much later, people discovered that by melting the red stones they could shape the soft mass into cups and bowls. Copper became so useful that people began to mine for it and make all sorts of utensils out of it.

Copper was the only workable metal known for thousands of years. The problem with gold, for example, was that it was too scarce, and also too soft to be practical.

It is believed that when the Egyptians built their pyramids they used copper tools. And a piece of copper pipe used by the Egyptians more than five thousand years ago has been found. It is still in good condition!

The use of copper for many purposes dropped when iron was discovered. Today, bronze (copper and tin) and brass (copper and zinc) are two ways in which a great deal of copper is used. In fact, aside from iron and aluminum, copper is the metal most used in the world today.

HOW DID THE GRAPEFRUIT GET ITS NAME?

A grapefruit is about twice the size of an orange, and certainly much larger than a grape. Yet it is named after the grape.

If you were ever to walk through a grapefruit orchard, you would probably see the reason why. This heavy fruit hangs down in clusters just as grapes do, and the clusters may be of three to eighteen fruit. It got its name because of this resemblance.

The Spaniards, who brought the orange and the lemon, also brought the grapefruit to Florida and the West Indies. But the tree was grown only for its beauty in gardens. It has sweet-scented blossoms and dark glossy leaves.

Very few people ate the fruit in olden times. They didn't like the slightly bitter taste. So whoever owned grapefruit trees would let the ripe fruit fall to the ground and rot there.

It was actually visitors from the north who first created the demand for grapefruit. In the late 19th century they began coming down to Florida by railroad to spend the winter. They got to like the grapefruit and wanted to have it when they returned home.

The first shipments were sent to New York and Philadelphia between 1880 and 1885. For the first time, a market for grapefruit was developed. Then grapefruit orchards were set out in California, but on a smaller scale than in Florida. Today the fruit is cultivated in parts of Texas, Arizona, Israel, and China.

The grapefruit tree is small, reaching a height of only about 25 feet. There are several varieties, but the best known are the Duncan, the Marsh seedless, and the Walters.

129

WHO WAS THE FIRST DOCTOR?

Even before people became civilized, they "practiced medicine" in a way. That is, they did things to lessen discomfort or pain. And the earliest civilizations that we know about had physicians.

The Babylonians left such lucid medical writings describing various diseases that doctors today can recognize them. Among the ancient Egyptians it was believed that illness was caused by evil spirits. But their medical treatments also included pills and ointments containing drugs such as opium and castor oil. And surgical operations were done on the outer surfaces of the body.

So there were "doctors" in very ancient times. But about 460 B.C. a man called Hippocrates was born in Greece, and he brought a great change in medicine. In fact, he is called the Father of Medicine.

What Hippocrates did was rescue medicine from magic and superstition. While he didn't have the scientific knowledge on which medicine is based today, he had the kind of approach and attitude that might be called "scientific."

He taught that the physician should observe the patient closely and accurately. He should use gentle treatment and try to encourage the natural healing process. The physician should never risk harming the patient.

Hippocrates recognized and described many diseases. Some of the medical facts he observed are as true today as they were over two thousand years ago.

WHEN DID PEOPLE BEGIN TO MINE FOR MINERALS?

A mineral is a chemical element or compound that occurs naturally in the earth. An ore is a deposit in the earth that is rich enough in some mineral to make mining it worthwhile.

No one knows exactly when mining began. One of the earliest mining ventures recorded in history was the Egyptian expedition into the Sinai peninsula sometime around 2600 B.C. The Egyptians went there to mine turquoise. They also found and mined a more useful mineral—copper.

The ancient Greeks mined silver in mines south of Athens as early as 1400 B.C. The Greeks worked the mines from about 600 to 350 B.C. Several of the shafts went to a depth of 400 feet. Other metals, such as lead, zinc, and iron, were later mined from these old diggings.

To supply their huge empire the Romans mined on a large scale. They had mines everywhere from Africa to Britain. Among the most valuable Roman mines were the Rio Tinto mines in Spain, which yielded large quantities of gold, silver, copper, tin, lead, and iron.

Mining became a really large-scale operation in the 18th century, when the Industrial Revolution was underway. Large amounts of coal were needed for smelting iron and stoking factory furnaces, and coal mining expanded rapidly. The development of modern mining techniques started at this time.

In the United States, "gold fever" reached its height in the 19th century. The California gold rush started in 1848. More than $500,000,000 in gold was mined in California within ten years. In 1896 a gold rush occurred in Alaska, and in 1886, the richest gold field ever discovered was found in South Africa. The world's largest diamond deposits were also found there in 1870.

WHO NAMED THE CITY OF LOS ANGELES?

Los Angeles is the second most populous city in the United States and the largest in area—465 square miles. In its early days probably no one could have believed it would become the great city it is today.

The first European visitors to the city's site were Capt. Gaspar de Portola and a party of Spanish explorers and missionaries. On August 2, 1769 they camped along the banks of a river which he named El Rio de Nuestra Senora la Reina de Los Angeles de Porciuncula ("The River of Our Lady the Queen of the Angels of Porciuncula").

Two years later Franciscans founded San Gabriel Mission, nine miles to the northeast. Not until September 4, 1781, was Los Angeles formally founded by the Spanish governor of California, Felipe de Neve.

With the aid of priests from San Gabriel Mission, Governor de Neve established a settlement of 11 men, 11 women, and 22 children and named it El Pueblo de Nuestra Senora la Reina de Los Angeles ("The town of Our Lady the Queen of the Angels").

The town did not amount to much until California became a part of the United States in 1848 after the Mexican War. Its population then was about 1,500. Soon farms were all around the town, and oranges, grapefruit, lemons, walnuts, avocados, and grapes were being grown. The Southern Pacific Railroad reached Los Angeles in 1876, and nine years later the Sante Fe came in.

Oil was discovered shortly after 1890, and then the city really began to grow.

HOW DID UNITS OF MEASUREMENT DEVELOP?

Long before there were established units of measurement, people measured one thing in terms of another familiar thing. And one of the most familiar things was the human body.

For example, if a person wanted to measure the distance from his house to a neighbor's house, he would pace off the distance and count the number of times his right foot swung forward. The distance was so many "paces" long. To measure a room, he would put one foot before the other. The distance was so many "feet" long.

Arms, hands, and fingers were useful for measuring such things as cloth. The distance from the tip of the nose to the fingertips of one outstretched arm, the distance from fingertips to elbow, the distance from the end of the thumb to the end of the little finger when he spread his fingers, the width of his hand, the width of his thumb—all these distances were used as units of measurement.

But the problem with this was that the distances varied from person to person. One person's arm, or foot, and so on, was longer than another's. So it became necessary to establish standard units of measurement. During the Middle Ages associations of tradesmen kept watch on the measures used. Later on, governments set up standards for all sorts of measures.

Today there is international agreement about standard measures. The governments of various countries have agreed to use the same basic units. Many of them have special departments in charge of standards. In the United States the National Bureau of Standards was established in 1901 to take care of standard measures. In 1791 the metric system of measurement was invented in France and it is used by most countries.

HOW DID HOROSCOPES ORIGINATE?

What is a horoscope? A horoscope is a diagram of the heavenly bodies showing the relative positions of the sun, moon, stars, and planets at a given time.

To make up an individual's horoscope, the exact time and place of birth must be known so that the positions of those bodies will be related to that time. By establishing the relative positions of the heavenly bodies at the exact time of a person's birth, astrologers claim to be able to predict his future or advise him on decisions to make or actions to follow.

You will notice that we said "astrologers" claim this to be so, and this indicates the origin of the horoscope. It is part of astrology, which is the belief that heavenly bodies have an influence on human affairs, and that future events can be predicted by making astronomical observations.

Western astrology goes back to the Chaldeans and Babylonians of the 2000's B.C. In its beginnings, astrology was an attempt to make practical application to human affairs of what was being studied and observed in astronomy, the stars and the planets.

These and other ancient observers noticed that movements of the sun, the moon, the stars, and the planets happened with certain regularity, or in certain periods of time. The seasons, the rains, the growth cycles of plants—also had a regularity and periods of occurrence. So they linked the two together—and started the belief that the movements and positions of the heavenly bodies had an influence on the lives of human beings.

WHY DO WE SAY "GOD BLESS YOU" WHEN SOMEONE SNEEZES?

We say "God bless you" when a friend sneezes. The Germans say *"Gesundheit,"* which means "good health." The Italians say *"Felicita,"* which means "happiness." In the Near and Far East, people may clasp their hands and bow toward the person who has sneezed.

One explanation for this has to do with superstition. It is said that these customs began when early peoples believed that a person's spirit or soul was in the form of air or breath, and that it was contained in the head.

So a sneeze might accidentally expel this spirit for a short time, or even forever, unless God prevented it. "God bless you" was an appeal to God to not let it happen. The act of bowing toward the sneezer was meant to say "May your soul not escape."

But there are some experts who claim that the custom of saying "God bless you" is not based on a superstition. They believe it started during a great plague that took place in ancient Athens. A sneeze was often the first sign that a person had contracted plague.

The Romans practiced the custom of "blessing" and brought it to Britain. And when Britain had the plague, the people there said "God bless you" for the same reason that the Athenians had said it—to ask God's blessing for a person who might die.

Of course, there are many superstitions connected with sneezing, including one that says different things will happen to you, depending on the day you sneeze.

CHAPTER 3
THE HUMAN BODY

IS CANCER HEREDITARY?

Cancer is a disease in which there is an abnormal growth of tissue. A tumor is considered malignant, and therefore a cancer, if it can spread to remote areas of the body. Cells from the original tumor break off and set up a "colony" elsewhere. Cancers grow locally by extending into the normal surrounding tissue. A cancer can arise in any of the body's tissues, wherever those tissues begin to grow wildly and uncontrollably.

Cancer is chiefly a disease of middle and old age, but may occur at any time of life. Certain peoples of the world seem, for some reason, to get one type of cancer more commonly than another type. For example, cancer of the stomach is twice as frequent among the Japanese as it is among Caucasians.

The question of whether cancer is hereditary is not an easy one to answer. What may happen sometimes is that the child may inherit the type of skin, for example, in which cancer is more prone to occur, rather than inherit the disease itself. As a rule, two factors are necessary: the susceptibility, which may be inherited; and some factor that incites the cancer in this tissue. It has been found that sometimes marriage between certain people magnifies the hereditary factor. For example, in some families cancer of the stomach is a common ailment, while in others it may be a cancer of the breast.

But to any one human being, the inheritance of a tendency to cancer need not be a source of fear. It is a good policy for people with a history of cancer in parents or close relatives to be alert and have regular physical examinations to detect any signs or symptoms.

WHAT MAKES PEOPLE LAUGH?

If this question had a simple answer, such as a formula that could be learned, every comedian would know it! But laughter is a complicated thing, and the best explanations of it are still only theories.

We know, of course, that laughter is an expression of many feelings and that laughter is found only among human beings. But psychologists

are still studying two basic questions about laughter: What makes people laugh, and what is the function or purpose of laughter?

When you try to think of what makes people laugh, or what people consider funny, you find yourself thinking like a psychologist or philosopher. You become concerned with people's reactions to other people in all kinds of situations—for example, why people laugh when they see awkwardness or some kind of weakness or imperfection in another person.

From the physial point of view, laughter is good for us. It's good for our lungs, and it's an outlet for some extra energy. Laughter also has a great social value. We usually laugh as members of a group. According to this theory, laughter is used by social groups as a way of commenting on the behavior of people and making them conform to our standards.

HOW DOES A BABY LEARN TO TALK?

What is usually the first word a baby says? We all know the answer—"Mama!" Now, that seems like a very simple thing to do, doesn't it? But it's a very complicated process indeed. It requires many steps of development. No other creature on earth is capable of accomplishing this.

Let's go through the process step by step. When a baby is born, his brain is like an unwritten page. There is nothing there. The areas in the brain that receive sense impressions haven't yet received any. The baby's eyes are open, but the nerves between the eyes and the brain are not yet developed, so the brain doesn't register anything.

After one or two months, these nerves are developed and now the baby "sees" its mother. As a result of seeing the same object again and again, the visual memory center in the brain develops. The infant's impressions of the mother register in this center as memories. So now the child "recognizes" the mother.

As soon as the mother realizes this has happened, she keeps pointing to herself and saying "Mama" at the same time. At first the child can't hear, but gradually the nerves develop and the baby "hears" the sound "Mama." Through repetition, the child forms a memory image of the sound. The baby now remembers and "understands" the word "Mama."

Now the mother has to teach the child to speak. By repeating the word "Mama" over and over, she makes this happen: A connection is made in the brain between the image of the mother in the visual center and the sound of "Mama" in the hearing center. This is called an association. Now the child not only recognizes Mama's face, but also thinks of the sound "Mama" when he sees the mother. He "identifies" her. The child now begins to imitate the mother. He forms the word without saying it at first. After trying to say the word many times, the baby can make the vocal muscles move when it sees the mother. Finally he is able to say "Mama." And, of course, the proud mother says, "My baby is talking already!"

DO HUMAN BEINGS ALONE HAVE FINGERPRINTS?

If there's one thing in the world you have that nobody else has, it's your own particular set of fingerprints! What are fingerprints, and what makes them so different for each person?

To begin with, our skin consists of two layers of tissue. One is a thick, deep layer, the "corium," and over it is a delicate membrane called the "epidermis." In cold-blooded animals, the epidermis fits smoothly on the corium. There are no "ridges" to make "prints."

But in mammals, these two layers of the skin are joined very closely. The under layer, the corium, buckles where it meets the upper layer, the epidermis. Some of the tissue of the lower layer projects up into the upper layer molded over these projections, so that they are firmly and closely attached.

Now, among the lower animals, these "pegs" that stick up are scattered at random. There is no pattern of any kind. Among the apes, these pegs are arranged in rows. So the ridges in the upper layer of skin form parallel rows. But since all apes have these parallel rows of ridges, their "fingerprints" are pretty much alike.

But in human beings, the rows of ridges form definite patterns. In fact, the system of classifying human fingerprints was developed by studying these patterns. An Englishman named Sir Edward Henry developed the system of classifying fingerprints that is the basis for the system used today by authorities all over the world.

According to this system, all ridges on human fingers can be divided into the following patterns: loops, central pocket loops, double loops, arches, tented arches, whorls, and accidentals. (If you press your finger on an ink pad and then onto a piece of paper, you should be able to see some of these patterns.)

By counting the ridges between fixed points in the pattern, it is possible to classify each of the ten fingers into a definite fixed group. The ten fingers are then considered as a unit to classify a person's fingerprints. By the way, the chances that two people will have the same ridge pattern on just one finger are one in twenty-four million!

WHAT IS EQUILIBRIUM?

If you've read about space ships with human passengers, you've probably noticed that one of the problems that scientists will have to overcome is that of loss of equilibrium as a human being moves away from the pull of the earth's gravity.

Equilibrium is the ability to adjust ourselves in relation to the earth, which constantly pulls at everything that is near it. Without equilibrium it would be impossible for a bird to fly, a person to walk, or for any living thing to have a sense of direction.

We have two organs of equilibrium; they are located in the head near the ear. Each organ is like a sack and is filled with a liquid called lymph. Inside the organ, growing out from the bottom, is a kind of hair that springs out of a sensory, or recording cell. When the head is kept erect, the pressure on these hairs is distributed equally. If the head is inclined to one side or the other, the pressure on these hairs changes. The sensory cells are stimulated by this pressure and send nerve impulses to the brain. The brain sets certain muscles into action, and the body readjusts itself and returns from an inclined to an upright position.

Our organs of equilibrium also enable us to know in which direction we are moving. Let's imagine we go out for a drive in an automobile. As the car starts forward, our body sinks back against the seat. The liquid, or lymph, in the "canals" of the organs of equilibrium, bends the sensory hairs back. This causes certain nerves with which they are connected to send a message to the brain, and we feel that we are moving forward.

After a while, the lymph moves with our body, the sensory hairs are erect, and we no longer have that feeling of suddenly moving forward. Now suppose we step on the brake! Our body keeps going forward and so does the lymph in the organs. It therefore bends the hairs forward. The message goes to the brain and we feel ourselves slowing up.

There are three "canals" in each organ of equilibrium, to correspond with the three planes of space. In this way, the sensory hairs tell us whether we're going up or down, from side to side, or backward or forward.

HOW MANY ODORS CAN WE SMELL?

Compared to many animals, a person's ability to smell is not very good at all. In fact, it is probable that as we developed, our sense of smell became less and less keen, until today we are chiefly "visual animals."

The dog, to take an example at the other extreme, is almost completely an "olfactory animal," meaning he lives by his sense of smell. Here are some comparisons that will show how inferior man is in this respect. In our nose, the area devoted to smelling is actually about the size of a fingernail on each side. In a dog, this area, if the membrane were spread out, would cover more than half the animal's skin!

In the human brain, where the sensations of smell "register," about a twentieth of the brain is concerned with smell. One-third of a dog's brain is concerned with the sense of smell! We, of course, have devel-

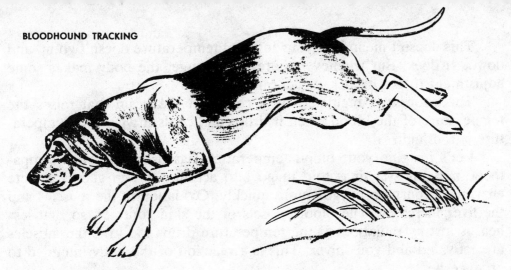

oped other senses, organs, and powers that more than make up for our weakness in smelling.

In our nose, smells are picked up by delicate hairs that are in the olfactory membrane. But the tips of these "antennae" don't stick out in the air; they are embedded in a special layer that covers the membrane. This membrane is always moist. If it becomes dry, we no longer can smell! In addition, in ordinary breathing, the stream of air does not pass over this membrane, so we really have to sniff—pull air in over this membrane—when we want to smell something.

Before we can smell anything, that substance has to dissolve in the fatty layer that covers the delicate hairs that pick up the smell. So these substances have to be volatile oils (as those from flowers), or be carried by such oils (as from coffee).

There are five important types of such substances that our sense of smell can detect. One is flowery (violet, rose, etc.). The second is spicy (lemon, apple, etc.). The third is burnt (coffee, tobacco). The fourth is putrescent (cheese, rotten eggs). And the fifth is ethereal (alcohol, camphor, etc.).

WHY DOES A FAN MAKE YOU FEEL COOLER?

When you feel hot or cold, you are actually feeling the temperature of your blood! The body maintains an average temperature of 98.6 degrees Fahrenheit, regardless of what the temperature is "outside."

This doesn't mean that your internal temperature doesn't go up and down. It does. But whenever there is a change, the body makes some adjustment to get it back to "normal."

This process is regulated by a center in the brain that raises the temperature of the blood when it drops and cools it when the temperature is too high.

Let's imagine your blood temperature has dropped. Your sympathetic nervous system is told to go into action. Certain glands secrete enzymes to burn up oxygen more quickly. Oxidation in the muscles and the liver increases. The blood vessels of the skin contract, so that less heat is lost by radiation. If the temperature drops too low, the muscles are activated and you shiver. This is a reaction of the body intended to produce heat.

Now suppose the temperature of your blood rises. The oxidation process is slowed up, and the vessels of the skin are dilated to eliminate excess heat by radiation and to help the evaporation of perspiration. When a liquid evaporates—changes into a gaseous state—it draws away heat.

This is what happens when you perspire. The sweat that comes out of the pores of your skin is like a shower that washes the body from within and from without. It comes out of your body in the form of microscopic drops through millions of tiny openings.

If the air near your skin is humid, the evaporation is cut down. You can't seem to cool off. But when you use a fan to move the air that comes near your skin, the rate of evaporation is increased. Your body is losing heat in this way and you feel cooler.

WHAT IS THE SPLEEN?

It is hard to believe that there is an organ in the body about which we still know little, and that what it does still cannot be fully explained. But such an organ is the spleen.

There is a well-known story about the spleen. A professor giving a medical exam asked a student to name the functions of the spleen. The student said: "I knew them all yesterday, but now I've forgotten everything." The professor said: "Too bad! We finally had someone who knew something about the spleen, and now this one person forgets it!" It's a joke, of course, but it indicates how much of a mystery the spleen is.

It is known, for example, that the spleen plays a part in making blood during childhood. It fights diseases of the blood and the bone marrow, such as malaria and anemia. Yet the amazing thing is that the spleen can be removed from the body and these vital processes will go on being performed! It seems that other parts of the body can then take over the work of the spleen.

The spleen is a large organ in the abdomen and lies next to the stomach, but it is not part of the digestive system. It is really attached to the bloodstream and could actually have been located in any other part of the body.

In a healthy human being, about ten million red blood cells are destroyed every second. They have to be replaced, and three different parts of the body help in doing this. One is the bone marrow, another is the liver, and the third is the spleen. Surplus red cells that might be needed in an emergency are stored in the spleen, among other organs. Old and worn-out red cells are broken down in the spleen.

Certain white cells, called lymphocytes, are manufactured in the spleen and in the marrow. When there is a sudden loss of much blood, the spleen releases large numbers of red cells to make up for the loss. So you see that the spleen does do important work for the body.

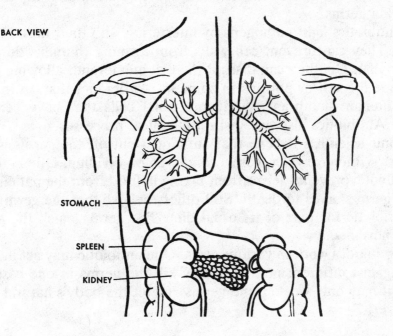

BACK VIEW

STOMACH

SPLEEN

KIDNEY

HOW DO ANTIBIOTICS WORK?

Antibiotics are chemicals. When these chemicals are put into the body, they kill or stop the growth of certain kinds of germs. They help your body fight disease.

The name "antibiotics" was first applied to these medicines in 1942. It comes from two Greek words meaning "against life." Antibiotics work against the forms of life that we call germs.

Many antibiotics are made from microbes. Microbes are tiny living things. For example, bacteria and molds are microbes. The microbes used in making antibiotics are chosen for their ability to produce chemicals that wage war on the microbes of disease. In other words, man takes advantage of the struggle that goes on in nature among microbes.

Microbes are engaged in a constant struggle for survival. In the course of this struggle, microbes produce complex chemicals in their bodies. By investigating the chemical products of microbes, scientists have discovered many chemicals that kill disease germs. If these chemicals can be made in laboratories—and made in large enough quantities—they may be used to make antibiotics.

How do antibiotics cure diseases? How do they get to the right part of the body to go to work there? How does an antibiotic stop the growth of certain germs?

Antibiotics fight pathogens by interfering with their normal cell processes. They can prevent cell walls from forming (humans do not have these walls). Or, they can disrupt the cell membrane, allowing nutrients to escape the cell or poisons to come in. Antibiotics that do this do not affect human membranes, only microbial cells that have certain elements. Antibiotics also can disrupt chemical processes.

Some scientists believe that antibiotics cut off the germs' supply of oxygen. Without oxygen, germs cannot go on dividing. Others think that an antibiotic prevents germs from taking in food from the patient's body, so the germ starves to death. Still others believe that the germ mistakes the antibiotic for part of its usual diet. The germ "eats" the antibiotic and is poisoned.

Antibiotics work in various ways. One antibiotic may act in different ways against different germs. It may kill the germs in one case. In another, it may only weaken the germs and let the body's natural defenses take over.

WHAT MAKES US DAYDREAM?

Is there anyone who doesn't daydream sometimes? It's rather nice in fact to daydream. We find ourselves doing some pleasant thing, or enjoying a great triumph, or accomplishing something we want very much, or getting something we strongly desire.

Daydreaming is actually a form of dreaming, only it is done while we are awake. Night dreaming is done while we are asleep. That is the only difference between them, since both are done when the dreamer is so relaxed that he pays no attention to what goes on around him. Then his thoughts can wander wherever they want.

For this reason, both sorts of dreams are often about strange persons, animals, or situations that could not possibly exist in real life. Night dreams are even more unusual and unrealistic than daydreams, because in sleep people have almost no control over what they think.

145

It is interesting to note that there are two kinds of daydreams that children have but adults do not: the daydream of the "imaginary playmate," and the daydream of the "adopted child." A child, if he has few friends to play with, may daydream that he has a playmate. Another child likes to imagine that he is "special"—that he is really a prince or princess and that his parents are a king and queen. Such a child then daydreams that he has been adopted, and that his real parents are royalty.

From this you can see that in daydreams we usually express something we need or want. In night dreams, we often express not only such things, but also things that frighten us. In either case, the dream is not something that comes from "outside," but is an expression from inside the person of needs, wants, fears, desires, and so on. The dream provides the opportunity for these to express themselves. Daydreams may give a person what he wants but cannot have in real life. In some cases they help the dreamer to plan ways of doing things in reality. Night dreams, in disguising the dreamer's feelings and granting his wishes, may help him to remain asleep and to get his rest.

A dream is something you tell yourself. A dream has special meaning for the person who creates it.

WHY DO WE AWAKEN FROM SLEEP?

Everybody has strange experiences with sleep. Sometimes we want very much to sleep and we just can't seem to. We stay awake or wake up early. And sometimes we feel we could sleep for hours and hours more when that darn alarm clock goes off!

What wakes us up is something that scientists still can't explain fully. There are various theories about it. One theory says that sleep and fatigue are pretty much the same. The nerve cells become tired because their reserve of energy is used up faster than it can be renewed.

Nerve cells can also become tired because waste materials accumulate faster than they can be eliminated. When we go about thinking and seeing and feeling and carrying on mental activities of all sorts, we use up energy. So the brain and other nerve centers need a rest. Sleep clears away our tiredness, and when we wake up we are rested and able to function again.

Some scientists believe that what really happens when we fall asleep is that one particular nervous center, called the vasoconstrictor center, becomes tired. This causes the blood vessels to cut off some supply of blood, and we go to sleep. When this center has its blood supply restored to normal, we wake up.

Another theory about sleep and waking up is quite different. According to this theory, we have a "wakefulness center" in the lower portion of the brain. Our mental activities and emotions during daily living stimulate this center. Now, if we can't shut off messages from the brain to this center, we remain awake. When we finally do it, by sending no more messages, we go to sleep.

Then suppose we get hungry while we're asleep, or feel cold or damp, or experience some emotion, such as fear. The wakefulness center is stimulated again and we wake up.

But don't forget that every adult person needs a different amount of sleep. It depends on your age, your body, your work, and even your sleep habits. An adult really needs only enough sleep so that when he wakes up he feels rested and well and can carry on his work during the day.

HOW IS BODY TEMPERATURE CONTROLLED?

A thermostat controls the temperature in a room or building by controlling the amount of heat the furnace produces. There is a part of the brain called the thalamus, which acts like a human thermostat. It controls the amount of heat in the body and keeps it at about 98.6 degrees Fahrenheit.

The body burns fuel and oxygen to make energy, which is mostly heat. Since the body makes heat all the time, it must have ways of letting some heat off, or it would keep getting hotter and hotter. The job of the thermostat is to control the amount of heat let off so that the body temperature stays at about 98.6 degrees.

Air from the lungs carries off some heat. Waste passing out of the body also carries off heat. The body lets off much more heat through the skin. It always lets off some heat this way, which is why the skin is warm to the touch.

But the thalamus can make the skin give off more—or less—heat as needed. If the body is getting too warm, more blood than usual flows to the surface of the skin; it gives off heat to the skin surface, which gives off heat to the air. If the body is getting cold, the capillaries under the surface of the skin become smaller; less blood passes near the skin and so less heat is given off.

When the body becomes very warm, we begin to sweat. Sweat is a salty liquid produced by the sweat glands. Little tubes lead from the sweat glands to the pores in the skin. From the pores sweat spreads over the skin. Sweating speeds up the escape of heat from the body because the liquid evaporates.

The liquid changes to a gas and is carried away by the air. At the same time, it carries away heat. That is why you feel colder when you are wet than when you are dry.

WHY DOES YOUR TEMPERATURE RISE WHEN YOU'RE SICK?

The first thing your doctor, or even your mother, will do when you don't feel well is take your temperature with a thermometer. They are trying to find out whether you have "fever."

Your body has an average temperature of 98.6 degrees Fahrenheit when it is healthy. Disease makes this temperature rise, and we call this higher temperature "fever." While every disease doesn't cause fever, so many of them do that fever is almost always a sign that your body is sick in some way.

Your doctor or nurse usually takes your temperature at least twice a day and puts it on a chart, showing how your fever goes up and down. This chart can often tell the doctor exactly which disease you have, because different diseases have different patterns or "temperature curves."

The strange thing is that we still don't know what fever really is. But we do know that fever actually helps us fight off sickness. Here's why: Fever makes the vital processes and organs in the body work faster. The body produces more hormones, enzymes, and blood cells. The hormones and enzymes, which are useful chemicals in our body, work harder. Our blood cells destroy harmful germs better. Our blood circulates faster, we breathe faster, and we thus get rid of wastes and poisons in our system better. So fever helps us fight off sickness.

But the body can't afford to have a fever too long or too often. When you have a fever for 24 hours, you destroy protein in your body. And since protein is necessary for life, fever is an "expensive" way to fight off disease.

WHY DO WE HAVE EYEBROWS?

All mammals have hair on various parts of the body. For most mammals it acts as an insulating layer, to keep the body warm and cool, and to protect the body.

Human beings have less hair on their bodies than animals. The development of the "hair coat" in adult human beings is regulated by the sex glands. The male sex hormone promotes the development of the beard and the body hair, and inhibits the growth of hair on the head. The action of the female hormone is just the opposite. It inhibits growth of hair on the body and promotes growth of hair on the head.

While scientists know this, they still cannot fully understand the purpose behind all the hair on the body. One thing seems clear: hair grows in certain places as a kind of protection against dust and insects. This is why there is hair in the ear and the nose. And the purpose of eyebrows and eyelashes is to help protect the eyes against dust.

Charles Darwin believed that the fine hairs of the body are intended to serve as "gutters" for perspiration and rainwater. And it is believed that the reason men have beards is that it helped render the difference between man and woman evident at a distance, to indicate the sex of the person, and to give the male an appearance of power and dignity.

Altogether, human beings have 300,000 to 500,000 hairs in their skin. Blond persons with finer hair have somewhat more than this, and dark persons with coarser hair have one-quarter less.

HOW DO WE GET OXYGEN?

Man cannot live without oxygen. We need it to keep our life processes going. Oxygen is all around us. It makes up about one-fifth of the air.

We have special groups of cells to enable us to take in oxygen. These cells are in the lungs. We breathe in oxygen through the lungs, and from the lungs the oxygen passes into the bloodstream and is carried to all parts of the body. The breathing process supplies the cells with oxygen for respiration.

The oxygen that the blood carries is part of the air we breathe. Air is usually taken in through the nose and is warmed and cleaned on its way to the throat. From the throat air goes through the voice box, into the windpipe, and then to the lungs.

In the chest the windpipe splits into two tubes called the bronchial tubes. Each tube leads to one of the body's two lungs. Here the tubes begin to branch into smaller and smaller tubes. Each of the tiniest tubes opens into a cluster of thin-walled air sacs, bunched like grapes and covered with a fine net of capillaries.

Waste-carrying blood is pumped from the heart into the capillaries of the air sacs. Here a quick exchange takes place. The waste gas—carbon dioxide—passes through the thin capillary walls into the air sacs. Oxygen from the air sacs passes into the capillaries and the red blood cells. Now the blood has oxygen and it moves to the left side of the heart. From there the heart pumps the blood with the oxygen to all the cells of the body.

WHY DO CHILDREN GET CHICKEN POX?

Chicken pox is usually considered to be a disease of childhood, but adults can get it, too. The reason we see it so rarely in grownups is that once a person has had an attack of chicken pox it ordinarily makes him immune to the disease. So if somebody has had chicken pox as a child, he's through with it.

Chicken pox is a very contagious disease. It is believed that a virus causes the disease. It is usually transmitted directly from person to person—and not by contact with clothing or other articles soiled by an infected person. A person who has chicken pox can be considered infectious for about 14 days.

This is why doctors say the patient should be kept isolated from members of the family who have not had the disease, especially young children. They are also kept from school and all other public places.

One of the problems in connection with this has to do with symptoms of the disease. Some of the symptoms are a slight rise in temperature, loss of appetite, headache and backache. But sometimes the first sign of chicken pox is a rash or eruption of the skin. Since a person with chicken pox can infect another person about two days before the rash appears—you can see how a whole group of children could become infected before anything was done to prevent it.

While chicken pox is usually a mild disease that requires little special treatment, it is important to have a doctor make a diagnosis and observe the patient to see if there are any complications.

WHY IS WATER GOOD FOR YOU?

If you asked a biologist to list the most essential things for life, water would be right at the top. Water is absolutely essential to every form of life that we know. Every living cell—of plant and animal alike—depends on this substance.

As you may know, of every ten pounds of your weight, about seven pounds is nothing but water. Much the same is true of other living things. Without water to drink, human beings die in a short time.

Why is this so? Why is water necessary to life? The reason every living thing needs a certain amount of water is because the cells—the basic units that make up living things—have water molecules in them. Without water these basic units would be very different and of no use to life as we know it.

In the course of a day, an adult human being takes in about two quarts of water as fluids, and one quart in what we call solid foods, such as fruit, vegetables, bread, and meat. These are really not dry, since they are thirty to ninety percent water.

Besides these three quarts that enter the body from outside in the course of a day, about ten quarts of water pass back and forth within the body between the various organ systems.

There are about five quarts of blood in the vessels of the body, and three quarts of this is water. And this remains unchanged. Even if a person feels "dried out" after a long hike in the summer heat, or has drunk two quarts of beer, his blood vessels still contain three quarts of water. No matter how much water you drink, you cannot dilute the blood.

DO WE KEEP THE SAME SKIN ALL OUR LIFE?

The skin consists of two tissue layers. One is a thick, deeper layer of fibers called the corium. On top of this is a delicate layer of cells called the epidermis.

The epidermis contains no blood vessels. In fact, it is made up of dead cells. Only the bottom layer of these cells receives nutrition and is alive. These cells are very busy. It is their job to produce cells. The growth of the epidermis takes place as a result of the cells that are being produced by the cells of the deeper layers.

The new cells are pushed upward by the other cells, and so are removed from sources of nutrition and die. As a result, a chemical change takes place in them and they become a horny material. So the lower half of the epidermis consists of cells that produce cells, the upper half of cells that have died and have been changed into horn.

The top layers of cells are detached at the same rate at which the lower layers produce new cells. So our skin manufactures many billions of new cells daily and sheds as many billions of dead horn cells.

This process goes on without interruption and is why our skin continues to look young year after year. So we do not actually keep the same skin all our life—we are always getting a new skin.

This is also why stains on our skin, such as ink, grease, iodine, tar, or rust, all disappear very soon. The top layer of cells is removed, a new one takes its place. And there are thirty layers of these horn cells, and when one is rubbed off, a new one pushes up from the lowest layer. We can never run out of layers of these cells.

WHY DO PEOPLE GET ALLERGIES?

What is an allergy? It is any condition in which a person reacts in a hypersensitive or unusual manner to any substance or agent. That seems to cover a lot of ground, and the range of allergies is very broad.

People may become allergic to various foods, drugs, dusts, pollens, fabrics, plants, bacteria, animals, heat, sunlight, or even many other things! The symptoms that result from an allergy may be of many different kinds, too. Generally, however, they affect the skin and mucous membranes. They are the result of changes that take place throughout the body.

Whenever foreign material invades the tissues, the body reacts to fight it. The body produces certain materials called antibodies. The antibodies combine with the foreign material and render it harmless. But when the foreign material enters the body a second time, the antibodies are torn away from the body tissues to attack the substance. This causes a chemical substance called histamine to be released, and when histamine reaches the skin and mucous membranes it produces the disorders which are symptoms of an allergy.

While many facts about allergy are still not fully understood, it is believed that allergies may be inherited in some cases. Certain weaknesses in the structure and function of parts of the body make the allergies possible.

It is also believed that the adrenal glands are involved, making certain people more likely to have allergies. And it is believed that even mental attitudes play a part in producing allergies in some people.

WHAT MAKES A BOY'S VOICE CHANGE?

To produce what we call a "voice," three things are used in the body. One is the vocal cords, which vibrate. The second is air, which normally serves for breathing, as a source of energy to set the vocal cords vibrating. And the third is the cavities of the throat (pharynx), mouth, and nose to reinforce, or resonate, the sounds.

The vocal cords are located in the larynx, or voice box. A voice has volume, pitch, and quality. Volume is related to the energy of the stream of air and to the type of resonance provided. The vibration of the cords produces vocal tone. The pitch is related to the tension, length, and thickness of the vocal cords.

Now that we see how a voice is produced, we can understand what makes a boy's voice change. A child has a small larynx (voice box) with short vocal cords. When the vocal cords vibrate, they produce short air waves, and this results in a high-pitched voice.

At puberty the larynx begins to grow and the vocal cords become longer. And this is what makes the voice change; it becomes deeper. In boys the growth is so rapid and the difference in size of the whole voice mechanism in the throat is so great, that boys cannot get used to it quickly and often lose control of the voice. This is what people sometimes call "the breaking of the voice." This happens with boys and not with girls because in an adult male the vocal cords are about 50 percent longer than in the adult female. Girls' vocal cords don't grow as fast nor as long.

While the general pitch of the adult voice depends on the length of the vocal cords, each voice has a certain range which decides to which class it belongs, such as bass, baritone, tenor, soprano, and so on.

154

WHAT IS AMNESIA?

Amnesia is a state of total loss of memory by a person. He cannot recall his identity or anything about his past. Amnesia may be permanent or temporary.

One type of amnesia may result from an injury to the head. The person cannot recall the accident or events following the accident. But he still may be able to carry on his activities and be aware of his surroundings. Unless there has been serious damage to the brain, memory usually returns within a few days.

There is another kind of amnesia called hysterical amnesia. It may happen when a person tries to remove himself from a situation he can't bear in his personal life. The anxiety has become so great that the person is forced to forget it. This amnesia often arises when the person feels he must suppress many of his natural impulses and feelings.

By forgetting his anxiety, he also forgets a great many other things, even including his identity. He may still act in a normal manner, but be unable to recall anything about the past.

He acts so normally that he may move about without attracting notice. Or he may wander restlessly from place to place. Or he may assume a new identity. Then he may suddenly recover his memory.

When this doesn't happen, psychiatric help may enable him to do it. When he does regain his memory, he doesn't recall events which took place during his period of amnesia.

CHAPTER 4
HOW OTHER CREATURES LIVE

WHAT WERE THE FIRST FISHES?

500,000,000 years ago there were no fishes. Fossils show that the first fishes occurred in the Ordovician Period, which began about 460,000,000 years ago. But it is not yet known whether the first fishes evolved in fresh or salt water.

In the next period, the Silurian, there were jawless fishes, the most primitive of fishes. Their mouths were a simple opening, suited to feeding on the tiny animals that lay hidden in the mud.

During the next period, the Devonian, fishes spread throughout the waters of our planet. They were the common animals of the period, which is why the Devonian is sometimes called the Age of Fishes.

During that age jawless fishes and fishes with jaws became abundant. But eventually the jawless fishes became extinct because of the evolving of fish with jaws. Jaws allowed fish to explore various food sources and to feed more efficiently.

Early fishes with jaws are called placoderms. The jaws evolved from a set of gill arches that were present in the jawless fishes. Gill arches are the bony supports of the gills.

There were quite a variety of placoderms in these ancient times. Some lived in midwater, some at the bottom. One group had tremendous teeth with sharp blades. Some were probably 30 feet long.

From these Devonian placoderms came our present-day fishes, the sharks and bony fishes. Sharks have a skeleton of cartilage. Bony fishes have a skeleton of bone.

HOW MANY KINDS OF FISH ARE THERE?

There were no people on earth in the days when the first fish swam about through the oceans. There were no dinosaurs or elephants or any other highly developed forms of life. Fish were the first backboned animals to appear.

Fish, like all creatures that existed ages and ages ago, have undergone many changes in their development. In the world today there are more living species of fish than of any other class of backboned animals. There are about forty thousand different kinds of fish, and they live in every imaginable kind of water, from mountain torrents and tiny ponds to the depths of the ocean.

Fish are divided, however, into three general types. One is the cartilaginous fish, which includes skates, sharks, and rays. Instead of a bony skeleton, they have a cartilaginous one; that is, it is made of a firm but flexible substance. They also often have a tough, horny skin in place of scales.

The second type is the bony fish, which includes by far the greatest number of fish now living. Fish of this group have a complete bony skeleton and are covered with bony scales.

The third group consists of lungfish, or fish having both gills and lungs. All the lungfish live in fresh water. Their fins bear a faint resemblance to legs, and sometimes they come out on land. The climbing perch is an example of this kind.

Most fish, however, breathe by means of gills through which water is constantly passing from the mouth. The blood of fish is cold, but they have a nervous system like other animals and suffer pain and discomfort.

Their sense of touch is very keen, and they taste, as well as feel, with their skin. Two small organs of smell are located in nostrils on the head, and they have ears that are internal, which means inside the body.

Some fish are great wanderers and have no particular home, but mostly they live in little communities, much as land animals do. Most fish are predacious, which means they eat other fish or aquatic animals, and insects.

WHAT IS THE LARGEST FISH?

Next to the blue whale, the largest living creatures are the whale shark and the basking shark. They are classified as fish, so they are the largest fish we know. They may reach a length of fifty to sixty feet!

Some people think of sharks as man-eaters, and since this is such a huge fish, you might imagine the whale shark capable of gobbling up a man. But it couldn't do it even if it wanted to. It has very small teeth, about an eighth of an inch long, and its throat is only about four inches in diameter. So this enormous fish actually feeds on some of the smallest creatures in the ocean, such as sardines and small squids.

When it comes to fresh-water fish, the largest is believed to be the arapaima or pirarucu, which is found in the waters of South America. This fish is said to reach a length of fifteen feet and a weight of five hundred pounds. If we consider the sturgeon a fresh-water fish, since some sturgeons spend much time in fresh water, then we have even larger fish. There have been sturgeons that measured twenty-six feet and weighed about 3,220 pounds.

What about the smallest known fish? They are found in lakes in the Philippine Islands. The smallest one is called *Pandaka pygmaea* and measures about one-quarter of an inch! In fact, they are the smallest living animals with a backbone.

HOW ARE GUPPIES BORN?

If you have an aquarium at home, you want fish that are beautiful, easily fed, have interesting life habits, and that are pretty sure to live. One fish that meets all these requirements is the guppy, sometimes called the "rainbow fish."

The guppy has very unusual and interesting breeding habits. You can actually see much of the process in your aquarium. Instead of the female dropping or scattering her eggs as most fish do, they hatch within her body. When fully developed, the eggs are delivered through her vent into their watery world as small but perfect fish.

They are ready to swim, eat, and to avoid the larger fish that would like to eat them. As a matter of fact, the mother herself is apt to gobble up a few of the babies, especially if she happens to be very hungry.

But there are easy ways to save the babies. The first instinct of the newly-born young is to swim toward the light. If the light side of the aquarium is thickly-planted with aquatic grasses, there will be few babies eaten. If the babies have a chance to hide, they'll outwit the adult fish.

The guppy comes from the northern part of South America, in and near Venezuela. Specimens were long ago collected by a gentleman from Trinidad named Lachmere Guppy, and were sent to the British Museum to be identified. The fish received different names at the hands of several scientists, but the one now used is *Lebistes reticulatus*. It was once named *Girardinus guppyi,* which was shortened to "guppy," and this is the name that has become famous in many parts of the world.

The male guppy has greater brilliance than the female, and every male is different. No matter how much you try, you can't seem to find two that are marked exactly alike!

WHAT ARE MUSSELS?

If you ever get a chance to walk along practically any shore of the Atlantic Ocean during low tide, you may see an interesting sight. Lying exposed on the shore could be thousands of black shellfish, which we call mussels.

Mussels are in many ways similar to clams and oysters. Mussels have one unusual feature: They can anchor themselves to such things as sand, rocks, or even other shellfish. This is done by a structure mussels have called a "byssus." The byssus is composed of threads produced by a gland in the foot, or narrow end of the mussel.

Mussels are bivalves; that is, they have two shells. But unlike the oyster, they have no muscular hinge holding the shells together. The surface of mussels is smooth, also unlike the oyster's, which is rough-surfaced.

Fresh-water mussels do not have a byssus, so they cannot cling to rocks. Mussels breathe and eat by means of a tube called the siphon. This is divided into upper and lower parts by a partition. As water is drawn through the siphon, the gills take oxygen from it so the mussel can breathe. A small mouth in the tube captures the food as it goes by.

In the breeding season, the female mussel discharges millions of eggs. These small black eggs are carried under its gills until the young are hatched. When the larvae hatch from the eggs, they swim about for a few days. But soon the growing shell becomes so heavy that the mussel sinks to the bottom.

There are many hundreds of species of mussels, but the two chief divisions are salt-water and fresh-water mussels. The salt-water kind are about two inches long, and the fresh-water kind, somewhat bigger.

In the United States mussels are eaten, but they are much more popular in Europe. The shell inside is a delicate pearly-blue color, and is used for making buttons. Sometimes pearls are found in fresh-water mussels, but they are usually imperfect.

WHY DO WE HAVE MOSQUITOES?

Mosquitoes exist on earth like other creatures. We may not want them around and wish to get rid of them, but that's our problem.

Mosquitoes are found all over the world. Some species are scattered in all districts, while others are found only in certain regions. About 70 species of mosquitoes are found in the United States.

It is because some types of mosquitoes carry disease that man has tried to get rid of mosquitoes. The mosquitoes that carry the virus of yellow fever, for example, are being wiped out of many tropical areas in which they were once found.

There are two other things about mosquitoes that are very annoying. One is the mosquito bite. When the female mosquito bites, it injects a poisonous liquid into the blood. This poison causes the pain and swelling of a mosquito bite.

The other annoying thing is the mosquito's hum. This hum is very important to the mosquito, for it is a sort of mating call. The males make a deep, low hum by vibrating their wings rapidly, while the females have a shriller note.

Can mosquitoes be of any benefit to us? Certain types of mosquitoes can help us get rid of other, worse types. What happens is that the wigglers (larvae) of some mosquitoes feed on the wigglers of other species. The first kind doesn't bite people, the second kind does. So they may be helpful in getting rid of the biting type.

WHERE DO MOSQUITOES GO IN WINTER?

We don't see mosquitoes in winter in parts of the world where winters are cold, but mosquitoes may still be there. They are alive in a

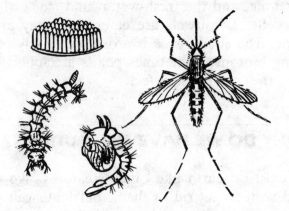

different form from that of the flying insect we know.

A mosquito spends the first part of its life in water and the rest of its life on land and in the air. The life of a mosquito begins when a female lays eggs on stagnant water. Soon larvae, or "wigglers," hatch out and begin to swim around looking for food.

In time the larvae change into pupae or "tumblers." Then each pupa becomes a grown insect and flies away. This whole process—from new egg to adult mosquito—may only take nine to fourteen days!

But when cold winter comes, the eggs lie dormant. They don't hatch. And in some species of mosquitoes, the fertile females spend the winter in a kind of sleep, too. So mosquitoes spend the winter as adults, eggs, or pupae.

An interesting fact is that while we think of mosquitoes as being the greatest pests in warm climates, they are actually far worse pests in the far northern regions of Canada, Alaska, and Siberia. This is because mosquito eggs are able to live through the winter in the snow. When the snow melts, the insects hatch out in such great swarms that stories have been told of men having been driven insane by them!

Of course, the danger that mosquitoes present to man is not that they are annoying pests, but that they spread diseases when they bite healthy persons after having bitten sick ones. The mosquito draws in the germs of viruses that cause diseases when it takes in blood from a sick person. Then when the mosquito bites a healthy person, it injects the germs with its saliva. The germs serve no purpose for the mosquito; it is interested only in the blood. Malaria and yellow fever are transmitted by mosquitoes.

HOW MANY KINDS OF BATS ARE THERE?

There are nearly a thousand different kinds of bats! They live in almost every part of the world except the polar regions. Each kind of bat has different habits, depending on where it lives. Yet despite all their differences the various species have many things in common.

Bats generally live in groups, but they do not make their own dwellings. They usually inhabit caves. In some caves there may be a colony of thousands of bats. But there may be bat colonies of only ten or twelve bats living in a hollow tree.

Some bats roost in trees, hanging like leaves from twigs and branches. Two kinds of tropical bats make little tents from palm leaves. There are bats living in the pyramids of Egypt and in the fruit trees of Australia. In North America and Europe, bats often live in homes of human beings. A bat can squeeze through narrow cracks and roost between layers of wall and ceiling.

While most bats are active only at night, there are some bats that venture out in bright sunlight. Most bats live on insects alone. Some eat only fruit; some eat both insects and fruit. A few kinds of bats eat meat, fish, and even flower nectar.

In India, there is one kind of bat that eats mice, birds, and lizards. The large spear-nosed bat of tropical America will eat almost anything once it is living in captivity. Such bats will eat bananas, horsemeat, liver, and hamburger. They will even eat smaller bats.

The bats with the most unusual diets are found in the tropics. The Noctilio bats of South and Middle America eat fish. Another group of jungle bats, the tiny hummingbird bats, eat chiefly the pollen and nectar of flowers.

Of course, there is the famous vampire bat of South and Middle America. It bites other animals—horses, cows, goats, or even people—laps up a small amount of blood, and flies away.

WHERE DO RHINOCEROSES LIVE?

There are five different kinds of rhinoceroses living today, of which two—the black rhinoceros and the white rhinoceros—are found in Africa. Both have two horns.

The other three kinds of rhinoceroses live in Asia. The Indian and the Javan rhinoceroses each have one horn. The Sumatran rhinoceros has two horns.

Rhinoceroses have huge, heavy bodies and usually move about very slowly. They pay little attention to their surroundings and do not hunt other animals for food. Rhinoceroses eat only grass and other plants.

This huge creature is usually quiet and retiring. But if it is cornered, it can become very fierce and dangerous. A rhinoceros can charge at a speed of thirty miles an hour and use its strong, pointed horns to attack its enemy.

The smallest rhinoceros, the Sumatran, usually weighs less than a ton and is about three to four-and-one-half feet high at the shoulder. The largest rhinoceros, the African white, weighs three-and-one-half tons or more and stands almost six feet high.

The great body of the rhinoceros rests on four short legs. Each foot has three toes. Rhinoceroses are hoofed animals and are related to horses.

The horns of some kinds of rhinoceroses are often very long; the longest ever measured was sixty-two-and-one-half inches. There may be one or two horns, depending on the kind of rhinoceros. The first lies above or slightly behind the nostrils; the second is behind the first, about even with the eyes. The horns are closely-packed masses of tough hairs.

The rest of the body is usually hairless, except near the ears and at the tip of the tail. The skin of a rhinoceros is tough and thick.

Rhinoceroses usually travel alone, but they are sometimes found in small family groups.

A female bears only one young at a time. The calf is born about eighteen months after the mating season and remains with the mother for several years.

In captivity rhinoceroses may live to be about fifty years old.

HOW LONG CAN A CAMEL GO WITHOUT WATER?

At one time, before automobiles and airplanes were invented, there was only one possible way to travel across the deserts of Asia and Africa. That way was by camel. That's why the camel has been called "the ship of the desert."

While there are many things about the camel that make him especially suited for living and traveling in the desert, the most important of these is the hump on his back.

When that hump is empty, it loses its firm shape and flops to one side in flabby folds. There is no bone in the hump; it is made of fat and muscle.

The purpose of the hump is to serve as a storage place for food. For days before a camel starts out on a journey, its master forces it to eat and drink. It eats so much that a hump of fat, perhaps one hundred pounds in weight, rises on its back. This fat can nourish the camel for several days if it is unable to find food on the journey.

The camel also takes its own water supply along. The camel driver forces the camel to drink about fifteen gallons of water. He does this by giving the camel salt to make it more thirsty.

The camel has three stomachs. It uses the first one to store food while it is grazing and to form it into a cud. In the second stomach are the digestive juices, and in the third stomach the chewed cud is digested.

In the walls of the first two stomachs, there are pockets for storing water. Muscle holds these pockets closed when they are filled. Whenever the camel needs some water, these muscles open and close to let out as much as it needs.

How long can a camel go without water? As you can see, it is not really without water. In fact, people who have been dying of thirst have sometimes killed a camel to obtain its precious water. If a camel travels slowly and with a light load, that water in its stomach can last from six to ten days!

HOW FAST CAN BIRDS FLY?

We have horse races and we have athletic events in which people race. It's easy to decide the speed in these cases because there's a starting line and a finish line; and there are accurate measuring devices being used by several observers. But how do we measure the speed of birds in flight?

Many figures have been published about the speed in flight of various birds, but there seems to be quite a bit of disagreement on the subject because not all authorities accept the records as accurate.

For example, birds called swifts are supposed to have been timed at more than 170 miles an hour in India. In Mesopotamia, someone claimed they were timed at about 100 miles an hour. A European peregrine was timed with a stop watch while making a dive at 165 to 180 miles an hour.

But most authorities doubt these figures. One expert believes that the fastest recorded flight for a bird was that of a homing pigeon going at 94.2 miles per hour.

Here are the generally accepted figures on the speed of flight of birds. The peregrine falcon can fly at about 65 to 75 miles per hour. The next fastest birds are ducks and geese, who can go at about 65 to 70 miles per hour.

The European swift can reach 60 to 65 miles per hour, and so can the golden plover and the mourning dove. Hummingbirds, whom we all think of as very fast, do reach speeds of 55 to 60 miles an hour. Starlings can go at about 45 to 50 miles. Swallows usually fly at about 25 miles per hour, but can fly as fast as 45 to 50.

The crow usually moves along at 20 to 30 miles, but can reach 40 to 45. Herons can fly 35 to 40 miles an hour. The pheasant can fly at 35 to 40 miles. And surprisingly enough, the wild turkey can fly at 30 to 35 miles. The blue jay moves along at 25 to 30 miles.

WHY DOES A BABY KANGAROO STAY SO LONG IN THE POUCH?

Pouched mammals form one order of mammals, the marsupials. Marsupials differ from all other mammals in the way their young develop and are cared for.

At birth, baby marsupials are tiny and only partly developed. The reason is the short time spent within the mother's body. It may be as little as 8 to 12 days with some of the smallest species; with the largest it is usually no more than 30 to 40 days.

At birth, a baby kangaroo is hardly an inch long and not even fully formed. Its tail and hind legs are like tiny stumps. Its eyes are closed, and its ears are not fully formed. Its mouth is just a tiny hole. Only its front feet are well developed, with toes and nails.

As soon as the tiny baby kangaroo is born, it begins to climb through the mother's fur toward the opening of her pouch. It seems to be guided by instinct. The mother, however, licks a path for it through her fur. Climbing hand over hand, the baby reaches the opening of the pouch and pops in.

Once inside, the baby quickly searches out a nipple and hangs. The little kangaroo remains firmly attached there for a number of weeks, nursing and developing. It grows, becomes covered with fur, its eyes open, and its ears form. Finally, it can let go of the nipple and peer out of the pouch.

When it is several months old, it starts to venture outside. But if danger threatens, it pops right back. By the time the baby is six months old, it is too big to fit into the pouch.

Now it eats grass and vegetable matter, like its mother. It is well on the way to growing up and taking care of itself.

WHERE DO DOGS COME FROM?

All the living members of the dog family are descended from a wolf-like creature called *Tomarctus*. This ancient canine, called "the father of dogs," roamed the earth's forests perhaps 15,000,000 years ago.

The characteristics and habits of the wild dogs are all shared by the domestic dog. Domestic dogs are brothers under the skin to wolves, coyotes, and jackals—the typical wild dogs. All belong to the branch of the dog family called *Canis*.

All are so closely related that domestic dogs can mate with wolves, coyotes, or jackals, and produce fertile offspring. But none of these species will interbreed with foxes. The foxes belong to another branch of the canine family.

At some time long ago early man tamed a few wild dogs. These dogs may have been wolf cubs. Or they may have been jackals or some other member of the wild dog family. People found that these animals

could be useful. They used them to help catch other animals and birds for food and clothing.

As people became more civilized, they found that the dog was a good friend and a helpful guard for home and cattle. In time, different breeds of dogs were developed for special purposes. Dogs with long noses, like setters, pointers, and beagles, were bred to track the scent of game, birds, and rabbits. Others, like greyhounds, chased rabbits and deer. Strong, heavy dogs like the mastiff pulled carts. Other dogs were bred to use for guard work and to scent the enemy in war. In addition to hunting and working dogs, other breeds came to be used in sport and as pets.

WHAT IS AN ORGANISM?

Scientists speak of all living things as organisms. A human being is an organism. So is a mouse, a fish, an insect, a tree, a daisy. So are bacteria and other tiny creatures.

All these living beings share some important features. That is one reason why scientists use the word "organism," thus giving each living being a name in common with every other living being.

The word "organism" also suggests that each living thing is organized. That is, its parts are arranged in certain ways and do certain work within the organism as a whole.

To be alive, a substance must be active. The activity of an organism is chemical and it takes place inside the organism. This chemical activity is a continuous process. Without it the organism would not be alive.

Energy must continually enter an organism so that the living machinery keeps going. Matter must also be continually flowing through an organism. A living organism has shape and substance (material). New material is continually flowing in to take the place of older material which is being pushed out or used up. The flow of energy and matter through an organism is called metabolism.

An organism grows until it reaches its full size. And an organism may reproduce—make small, new organisms which replace larger, older organisms. So we can say an organism is alive if it can metabolize, grow, and reproduce.

HOW DOES A CATERPILLAR SPIN A COCOON?

The larvae or young of butterflies and moths are called caterpillars. A caterpillar is really an insect in the making.

When a caterpillar hatches from the egg laid by the mother butterfly or moth, it is usually very small. But it grows rapidly, and all kinds of changes begin to take place.

The change caterpillars undergo is called metamorphosis. The first step for many moth caterpillars is to build cocoons. They spin them with threads of sticky fluid that flow from an opening in the lower lip. This fluid hardens in the air and becomes the thread we call natural silk.

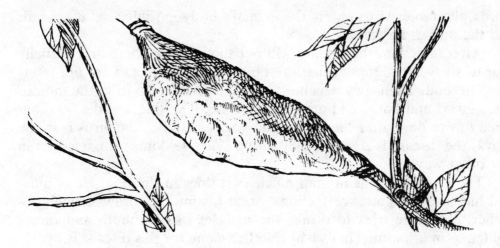

Some caterpillars form bags of silk that entirely enclose them. Others roll up a leaf, fastening the edges with the silk. Many of the hairy kinds of caterpillars pad the cocoons with their own hair. Some caterpillars, including most of those in the butterfly group, do not build cocoons.

But all caterpillars go through a resting stage, and in this stage it is called a pupa. The pupa does nothing except rest. This stage may last two weeks; it may last a whole winter. During this period the caterpillar changes into a full-grown butterfly or moth.

In its new and adult form, it emerges wet and shaky from the cocoon. As blood flows into the veins of the wings, the adult flutters its wings and dries them. In a few hours, when the wings are strong and dry, the butterfly or moth flies off to live as an adult.

HOW DO ANIMALS GET RABIES?

Viruses cause certain diseases in people and in animals. A virus is a germ which is too small to be seen with the ordinary microscope.

The virus which causes the disease known as rabies can infect all warm-blooded animals. People most often receive the disease from a dog infected with the virus. In the country, wild animals such as wolves, foxes, skunks, bears, and bats may also become sick with rabies virus. Even domestic animals, such as cows and cats, become infected. In other words, the rabies virus enters the animal's body, an infection is started, and the animal has rabies.

After infection, the disease will not show up for some time, usually four to six weeks. Dogs at first are quiet, have fever, and are not interested in food. Then they become excited. Saliva froths from the mouth. They growl and bark, and are likely to bite. The dog will die in about three to five days after these symptoms appear. Since the virus is in the saliva, the disease is passed on by biting. Very seldom is it passed on in any other way.

The disease begins in man much as it does in the dog. He is quiet and has fever and strange feelings. Soon his muscles draw strongly together. When he tries to drink, the muscles of his mouth and throat tighten as in a spasm. That's why another name for this disease is hydrophobia, which means fear of water. But the muscle spasms are due to changes in the nervous system. Death comes when the breathing muscles go into spasm.

Once the disease appears in people or animals, death is almost certain. That's why the disease must be prevented. The bite area is cleaned thoroughly. If the person or animal can be treated within three days of being bitten, a serum is used. The serum acts against the virus before it can increase and attack the brain. Injections are given each day for a period of two or three weeks.

HOW DO FROG EGGS HATCH?

Although frogs can live on land, many kinds go back to water when it is time to lay their eggs. This is usually done in the spring.

The frogs look for quiet places at the edges of ponds and small lakes, where the water is a foot or less in depth. In the night, or early morning, the female lays her yearly hatch of eggs. The eggs are enclosed in a mass of jelly that is attached to some kind of plant in the pond.

A small frog may lay two thousand to three thousand eggs; a large one, six thousand to eight thousand. Each egg is spherical, black above, light below, and about one-sixteenth of an inch in diameter. When first laid, the mass is as large as a teacup, but it swells up with water to several times this size by the time the eggs hatch.

After a few days or weeks, depending on the species of frog, the egg hatches. A tadpole swims out of the egg. It has a finned tail and gills, which look like small, furry branches.

At first the gills are outside the body. But in time, they are covered by a fold of skin. Inside the body lungs develop, and other changes take place. The legs develop. The hind legs are the first to show, and the front legs remain hidden until the last stages of metamorphosis. The tail is absorbed into the body. It has completely disappeared by the time the young animal—now a frog—is ready for life on land.

The whole change, from tadpole to frog, takes place within a week or less if the weather is warm. In cool weather it may take two weeks or more.

WHAT HAPPENS TO FROGS IN WINTER?

There are about 17 species of frogs that live in the United States. The most common are the bullfrog, leopard frog, and the wood frog.

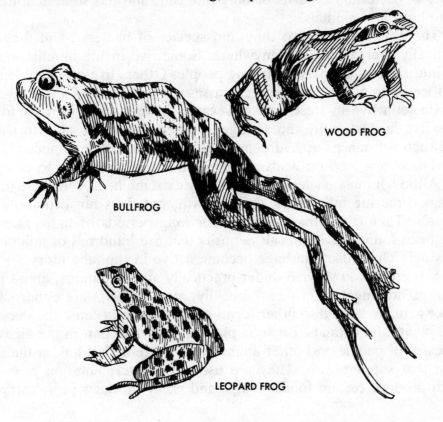

WOOD FROG

BULLFROG

LEOPARD FROG

Frogs vary considerably in shape, color, and size. Some little tree frogs are no more than one inch in length. Leopard frogs are about two to four inches long. Bullfrogs often reach eight inches and have legs that are ten inches long. A fully developed bullfrog is usually dark green or brown in color so that it can hardly be seen on a muddy bank or among the weeds.

What do these frogs do in the winter? In northern countries, when cold weather sets in, some frogs dive into a pond, bury themselves in the mud and stay there all winter. Ponds do not freeze solid, even when winters are very cold, so the frog does not freeze either.

WHERE DO BACTERIA LIVE?

Bacteria are probably the most common form of life on earth. They are microorganisms, which means they can be seen only under a microscope. A bacterium consists of only one cell, and has some features of both plants and animals.

There are at least two thousand species of bacteria, and they live practically everywhere and anywhere. Some live in the mouths, noses, and intestines of animals, including people. Others live on fallen leaves, dead trees, animal wastes, and carcasses.

Bacteria live in fresh and salt water, in milk, and in most foods. They live in dust, soil, and sewage. Some bacteria are able to use as food such substances as hydrogen gas, ammonia, iron compounds, and paraffin. A few feed on acids and gases that are poisonous to people.

Although most bacteria are killed by extreme heat, some live in hot springs. Freezing may check their growth, but does not ordinarily kill bacteria. They can remain inactive for long periods of time. Bacteria have been found frozen in salt deposits that are hundreds of millions of years old. These bacteria have become active in the laboratory.

If bacteria can survive under practically any conditions, aren't people in great danger from them? Luckily, most bacteria are either harmless or actually helpful to other forms of life. Bacteria cause the decay of dead plants and animals. Bacteria play an important part in the digestive processes of people and other animals. They are a vital link in the food chain that supports life. They are used in the fermentation processes which produce certain foods, drugs, and many products in industry.

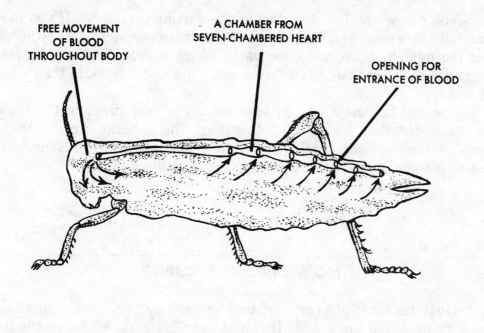

FREE MOVEMENT OF BLOOD THROUGHOUT BODY

A CHAMBER FROM SEVEN-CHAMBERED HEART

OPENING FOR ENTRANCE OF BLOOD

DO INSECTS HAVE HEARTS?

It is hard for us to believe that tiny creatures like insects have organs like hearts and brains. But insects do have them. An insect has nerves and a brain. A large nerve center in the head is the insect's brain. The brain receives sensations and sends messages to certain muscles to make them work. This is done automatically, because an insect's actions are automatic.

An insect's blood is not red like ours. It doesn't carry oxygen, so it has no hemoglobin, which is what makes blood red. The insect's heart is part of a long tube running along the top of the body, right under the skin. The tube opens just under the brain.

There are tiny openings with valves along this tubelike heart. Blood is sucked into the heart through these openings. The heart contracts and forces blood to flow toward the head.

In the head the blood pours out over the brain and then flows backward through the body. As it flows backward it bathes the body organs, muscles, and nervous system. It brings digested food and takes away waste material.

You can see an insect's heart in some living specimens. If you look carefully at a cutworm, a mosquito larva, or some caterpillars, you can see the tubelike heart along the back. Watch it beat. You may be able to notice that the heart beats faster when the insect is warm than when it is cold.

Another interesting thing about insects is their strength. Considering their size, they are remarkably strong. This is because of the thickness of their muscles, and because they have so many. People have about 600 major muscles. A grasshopper has about 900!

HOW DO OWLS HUNT?

Owls are birds of prey, and they are among the finest hunters for prey to be found anywhere. It's as if everything about the owl is designed to help it in its hunting.

The owl has powerful, needlelike talons (claws) that it closes over its prey like the jaws of a trap. The talons have one toe which the owl can change from a forward to a backward position.

In most species of owls the large eyes help it to see better during the evenings and moonlit nights than during the daytime. The owl has better ears than any other bird. Its two ears may be of different shapes and are hidden in the head feathers.

The owl has soft "furry" edges to the flight feathers of its wings. This makes the flight of the owl almost noiseless—and so helps it in its hunting. Not even the owl can see in complete darkness, but it can see on nights that people would call completely dark.

The owl hunts best at dawn or dusk, or on moonlit nights. It can hear a mouse scamper over the ground many yards away. When an owl is listening from its hunting perch, it spreads out the feathers and skin which cover its ears. This forms a large funnel which collects even the faintest sound. After it locates the prey by sound, the owl attacks swiftly and directly on noiseless wings and captures its prey with talons.

Owls eat mammals such as mice, squirrels, and rabbits. They also eat reptiles, frogs, birds and even fish. They are better at catching mice than most man-made mousetraps.

DOES THE MALE SEA HORSE HAVE BABIES?

Sometimes people who buy sea horses for their aquarium are told "the male is pregnant." There is a reason for this, even though it isn't true.

The sea horse is quite a strange creature. It has a head like a tiny pony and a body like a pigmy dragon. At times it swims upright through the water with the help of its single back fin.

But the sea horse is a fish. There are over 50 species of this fish found in temperate and tropic seas of the world. They range in size from two to twelve inches.

And the most peculiar thing about sea horses is the way they care for their eggs. The female lays about two hundred eggs. She places them in a pouch in the male's body just above his tail. After 40 to 50 days the male breaks the pouch open and the tiny baby sea horses come out. So you can see why people might get the mistaken idea that the male is giving birth to the babies!

Even after the young hatch out, they remain in the father's pouch for a time until they are old enough to take care of themselves. Sea horses eat small sea creatures and the eggs of other fishes. They refuse to eat dead things.

Sea horses were admired in ancient times. A sea horse was carved on a mummy case in Egypt. In ancient China they were ground up for medicine. In Italy a sea horse was considered good luck.

DOES A COW HAVE FOUR STOMACHS?

No. A cow does not have four stomachs. But its stomach is divided into four compartments, which seems to be almost the same thing.

Cows, sheep, goats, camels, llamas, deer, and antelopes all have the habit of swallowing their food and later bringing it back to the mouth. Then they chew it thoroughly at leisure. Such animals are called "cud-chewing" animals or ruminants.

The reason they developed this method of chewing their food is that their ancestors were easy prey to stronger, flesh-eating beasts. So, many thousands of years ago, to protect themselves, they began to swallow their food quickly and then go off to some more concealed places to chew at their leisure.

This is made possible by their complicated stomach with four compartments. They are the paunch, or "rumen"; the "reticulum," or honeycomb bag; the "omasum," or manyplies; and the true stomach, or "abomasum."

When the food is first swallowed, in the form of a coarse pellet, it goes into the paunch, the largest of the four compartments. It is softened there and goes into the reticulum. Here it is molded into "cuds" of convenient size. Later, these are passed up into the mouth by regurgitation, which is the opposite of swallowing. After chewing, they are swallowed again, passing into the third stomach or manyplies; then into the fourth compartment, or true stomach.

Cows, sheep, and goats have no front teeth in the upper jaw. Instead, the gums form a tough pad.

WHY DO BEES DO A DANCE?

Since all the bees who live in a hive together share their food, it is important for them to get all the food that can be found. So when foraging bees return to the hive, they get other bees from the hive to gather nectar and pollen from good flower sources.

They do this by performing dances on the combs of the hive. The bees around the dancing bees become excited and start to follow behind a dancer and imitate her movements. Then they leave the hive

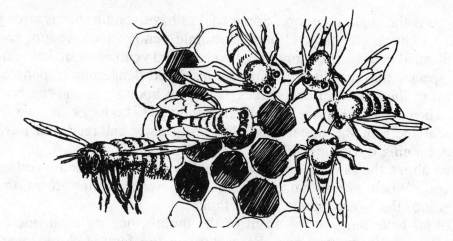

and—without the dancing bee to lead them—fly directly to the food source.

The dancing bees are able to tell the other bees, by these dances, the direction and the location of the food. If the bees do a round dance, then the bees fly out and look for food nearby. On the dancing bees is the odor of the nectar which tells the other bees which flowers to look for.

If the returning bees do a wagging dance, it means that the food is more than one hundred yards away. During this dance the bee goes in a straight direction for a short run, and this tells the other bees in which direction to look for the food.

If the straight run points directly upward, the feeding place is toward the sun; if it points downward, the feeding place is opposite the sun's position.

The speed of the dance tells the distance to the feeding place. If it is done quickly, the feeding place is near. The greater the distance, the slower the dance is. When the amount of food left at the source is very little, the returning bee does not do a dance, so other bees don't go there looking for food.

HOW DO SNAKES INJECT POISON?

In certain types of snakes, the venomous snakes, one of the saliva glands produces a substance that is poisonous to the snakes' prey. This substance is the snakes' venom. Some snakes have venom that is strong enough to kill an elephant. Others have mild venom; their venom can only kill small lizards. Probably only two hundred venomous snakes (out of 412 species that are known) can be considered dangerous to people.

Two of these are African snakes called the boomslang and the bird snake. Their fangs are in the rear of their mouths. The fangs are two or three rear teeth in the upper jaws that are greatly enlarged and have grooves running down one side.

Just above the fangs is an opening that leads to the venom-producing gland. When a rear-fanged snake bites, venom drips down the grooves into the wound made by the fangs.

Cobras have fangs at the front of the mouth, one on each side of the upper jaw. In most cobras the groove on the fang is closed over, forming a hollow tube. A muscle surrounds the venom gland. When the snake bites, the muscle presses on the gland. This forces the venom down into the fang and out through the fang tip directly into the prey.

The spitting cobra can spray venom from its fangs, the way water is sprayed from a squirt gun. These cobras aim at the eyes of a threatening animal. The spray goes about eight feet and causes almost instant blindness.

Vipers have a complicated type of venom system. Their fangs are very long and the fang lies lengthwise in the mouth so it can be closed. When the mouth is opened for a strike, the jawbone is turned forward, bringing the fang at right angles to the throat.

WHERE IS A SNAKE'S HEART?

When we look at a snake we see a long and slender animal that has no legs and that seems to be all tail with a head stuck on the front.

But between the head and the tail of a snake is a long and complicated body. A snake has a backbone and a digestive system, a liver, a heart, and all the other muscles, glands, and organs that are found in most backboned animals.

A snake's most striking feature is its lack of legs. Another characteristic is the absence of movable eyelids, which gives the snake that glassy, unblinking stare. A snake's eyelid is a clear cover that protects the eye.

Most snakes have only one lung. As a result, there is more room in the slender body for the other internal organs. But pythons and some other snakes have two lungs.

Snakes have no ears on the outside of their heads. But they are sensitive to vibrations through the ground. And they have other senses that make up for the sense of hearing.

Most snakes can't see very well. They notice their prey more by movement than by shape or color. Snakes have a good sense of smell and can recognize prey animals, enemies, and each other by odors.

Snakes can also pick up particles from the air or ground or some object and certain organs they have that possess a chemical sense will be able to identify the chemical particles as food, enemy, friend, or whatever!

HOW ARE INSECTS HARMFUL TO PEOPLE?

In nature there are many insects that are helpful and friendly to people. But there are also insects that may sting and bite and insects that carry diseases.

Some insects are harmful at all times and should be avoided. Black widow spiders are in this group. They may be found from southern California to Chile, usually in damp, sheltered spots. The poison of the black widow spider causes great pain and stiffening of the muscles of the abdomen. Many victims of the black widow spider die.

Most insect bites and stings hurt for a time but are not serious. But some people are allergic to the poison in a bee or wasp sting. If they are stung, they should see a doctor right away to get medicine to prevent an allergic reaction.

Some kinds of mosquitoes carry germs that cause disease, such as yellow fever, malaria, and sleeping sickness. The germs that cause the disease are picked up by the mosquito and then passed on to another person it bites.

Typhus is a disease carried by the body louse. It is a serious danger whenever people must live in crowded conditions. Flies play a part in the spread of such diseases as cholera, dysentery, hepatitis, and typhoid fever. These diseases, like all those that are spread or carried by insects, are less apt to occur if an area is kept free of dirt—and if the insects are prevented from breeding.

CAN ANIMALS COMMUNICATE?

The chief means of communication that humans have is words. No animals are able to communicate with words, of course, but many animals are able to communicate with one another.

Many animals communicate by making certain kinds of noises. When a horse neighs or paws the ground, this means something to other horses. A hen gives a warning noise to her chicks when danger is present.

Dogs communicate in a variety of ways: they bark, growl, snarl, whine, and howl. They bare their teeth or lift a paw. Other dogs understand these sounds and movements.

Bees have a fantastic ability to communicate. When they return to the hive, they do a dance that tells the other bees what kind of flowers they have found, how far away they are, the direction to go, and so on.

Birds, as we all know, have bird songs. And they are able to communicate in this way. In fact, there are "dialects" in bird songs. The song of the same kind of bird is slightly different in Switzerland than it is in England, and it even varies in different parts of the country.

Many people believe that their pet dog can understand human language. Actually, what dogs learn is what certain tones of voice mean, not the actual words. An interesting thing is that domestic animals, such as cats and dogs, have learned how to communicate with their masters. They beg for food, or mew until a door is opened. But wild animals do not seem able to express their desires, such as begging for food from each other.

But even when animals do communicate, the most they can express is feelings and intentions. They cannot have a "conversation."

WHY DO PEACOCKS HAVE SUCH BEAUTIFUL TAILS?

We often hear the expression "Proud as a peacock," or "Vain as a peacock." And that's because the peacock seems to take great pleasure in displaying its beautiful feathers.

There are some interesting things about this gorgeous display. First, it is done only by the male. The female, the peahen, doesn't have these beautiful feathers. The male, the peacock, does it for the sake of the peahen and for her alone.

What the peacock does, many birds do during the mating season. The male bird puts on a display to try to attract a female bird. He practically goes through a dance as he tries to convince the peahen that he's very handsome.

Most people think it is the "tail" of the peacock that contains those beautiful feathers. But it actually isn't the tail. Those feathers are from the lower part of the back, the "train." The tail lies behind it and acts as support.

The peacock has been known and admired since ancient times. The Greeks and the Romans considered it a sacred bird. But in the days of the Roman Empire the Romans enjoyed eating this bird, anyway.

Peacocks are natives of Asia and the East Indies. There are only two species and they are related to the pheasant.

WHAT DO SHARKS EAT?

There are about 250 different kinds of sharks, and they range in size from two feet long to the giant whale shark which is 50 or 60 feet long. Are there man-eating sharks? Yes, about 27 kinds are known to attack man. Among them is the white shark, the hammerhead, the tiger, the lemon, and the mako shark.

But no shark seeks people as food. Sharks feed mainly on bony fishes, squid, and crustaceans, such as shrimps and lobsters. Sharks also feed on turtles, dolphins, and birds. Some sharks eat other kinds of sharks.

The largest sharks, such as the whale shark, eat the smallest food. They eat tiny fish and other very tiny animals that feed on drifting sea-weeds. To find its food, a shark relies mainly on its nose. The hungrier a shark, the more sensitive its nose.

Sharks usually circle about their prey before closing in for the kill. Thresher sharks use their long, curving tails to herd their prey. They sweep their tails from side to side, sometimes stunning the prey with their mighty strokes.

Often a group of sharks become so excited while feeding that they bite anything and everything. The more they bite, the more excited they become. In this state they will eat rubber tires, tin cans, logs, boats, or anything else that happens to be in the way. Scientists call this state a feeding frenzy. Even the smallest and most sluggish of sharks is danger-ous during a feeding frenzy.

DO BIRDS HAVE EARS?

Since birds are flying animals, practically everything about them is adapted to this very difficult activity. This covers their whole body, the outside and the inside. And it also includes their nerves and senses.

For example, fine eyesight is vital for a flying animal. It is one of the most important features of birds. In proportion to the size of the animal, bird eyes are much larger than those of most other backboned animals. Many birds are able to see a separate area with each eye. Other birds are able to see very small objects and great detail at long distances.

It is important for birds to have a good sense of hearing, and they have an excellent one. Birds do have ears, and the sense of hearing, the senses of balance and of place in and movement through space are all centered in the ears.

In spite of the hard, horny character of the beak and mouth, many birds also have a good sense of taste. They can select their proper food instantly. But it seems that birds do not have to be able to smell. The sense of smell seems to be almost or entirely missing in most birds.

Flying, of course, is an activity that requires large amounts of energy. So their metabolism (the living processes that produce and use this energy) is rapid. Bird temperatures are high, usually between 104 and 112 degrees Fahrenheit. Their pulse and rate of breathing is very fast. For instance, a sparrow's heart beats more than 500 times a minute!

WHY DO FLEAS LIVE ON DOGS AND CATS?

Fleas are parasites. A parasite is a plant or animal that lives with, in, or on another living organism. The other organism is called the "host."

The flea (the parasite) lives on dogs and cats (the host) by sucking blood. It has a small round head and mouth parts that are adapted to sucking. It has a tiny body, no wings, and three pairs of legs.

By the way, those long hind legs of the flea make it a wonderful jumper. In fact, it is the champion jumper of all creatures. This tiny insect can jump seven to eight inches into the air, and can jump forward at least 12 inches. For a man, that would mean being able to jump 450 feet into the air and make a broad jump of about 700 feet!

There are hundreds of species of fleas. In the United States there are more than 50 different kinds. The dog-and-cat type of flea is found almost everywhere in the world.

Fleas don't just live in dogs and cats. They also infest rats, rabbits, squirrels, tame and wild birds, and nearly all other warm-blooded animals. In the United States, the flea that lives on dogs and cats also lives on human beings.

During the Middle Ages flea-infested rats spread bubonic plague throughout Europe. The flea lived on the diseased rat until the rat died. Then the flea jumped to a human being, carrying with it the disease germs. Cases of bubonic plague are rare now, but they still occur.

WHAT IS THE LARGEST ANIMAL IN THE WORLD?

When we think of ancient times, when dinosaurs lived on earth, we think of huge creatures that were bigger than anything else that ever existed. Yet the fact is that even the biggest dinosaur did not reach the size of an animal that is found in the world today.

This is the baleen whale, the largest animal ever to live on earth. One kind, the blue whale, may be 100 feet long and weigh more than 120 tons! The heaviest of the dinosaurs probably weighed no more than 50 tons and was about 90 feet long.

The largest animal living on land is the elephant. The largest elephant of which we have records weighed about 12 tons and measured 13 feet 2 inches at the shoulder.

The next largest land animal is considered by some to be the rhinoceros. But there have been cases where a hippopotamus, which is a shorter animal than the rhinoceros, weighed more. One such hippopotamus weighed 8,600 pounds.

The largest fish is the whale shark. Some of them have reached a length of 60 or 70 feet and have weighed as much as 13 tons.

The largest snake is believed to be the anaconda. The biggest ones may be 35 to 40 feet long. A 40-foot anaconda snake would weigh about 1,000 pounds.

The largest living bird is the African ostrich. It may reach a height of over 8 feet and weigh more than 300 pounds.

HOW DO PARROTS TALK?

When we say that parrots and some other birds can "talk," we mean they can imitate the sounds that human beings make when talking. But the birds do not use words in order to share thoughts and feelings or to get something they want. They probably talk simply because they enjoy making the sounds.

Many kinds of birds mimic various sounds that they hear about them. Some can copy the songs of other birds, some can mimic certain man-made sounds such as musical tunes. But birds of only three families—the parrots, crows, and starlings—can mimic the sounds of human speech.

The voice equipment of talking birds differs from man's in position and structure. Birds have no vocal cords. Most talking birds do not sing, although many can whistle. Talking birds, such as parrots, must be trained to talk while still very young.

Parrots and other talking birds do not learn human speech sounds easily. The words must be repeated slowly and clearly, many times over. Once the bird has mastered a word or phrase, it probably never forgets what it has learned.

But the words seldom seem to have meaning for the birds. Usually words are only sounds to them. A scientist tried to teach a parrot to associate words with feelings, but failed. The bird, an excellent talker,

could not learn to say "food" when it was hungry, or "water" when it was thirsty. Even the phrase "Polly wants a cracker" does not mean that "Polly" is hungry.

But a good many parrots have learned to say "Good morning" at the right time of day and at no other time. So in such cases the words may be more than just sounds to these parrots.

CHAPTER 5
HOW THINGS ARE MADE

WHY DOES THE NUMBER OF DAYS IN A MONTH VARY?

The first people to measure a year with any exactness were the ancient Egyptians. They started with a lunar (monthly) calendar based on the new moon's appearance every twenty-nine or thirty days. It was not very accurate.

The Romans also had a lunar calendar, and to make it agree with the solar year they added extra months whenever they needed to. Finally Julius Caesar adopted a new calendar based on a solar year of 365¼ days. Various changes had to be made in the months to make this calendar right. Here are the changes made by Caesar and others in the days of the month.

January was originally the eleventh month and had twenty-nine days. Caesar made it the first month and gave it thirty-one days. In Caesar's calendar February had twenty-nine days, with thirty in leap years. Emperor Augustus took one day from it and added it to August.

The number of days in March was always thirty-one. April, as a lunar month, had twenty-nine days. Caesar added a day to give it thirty. May always had thirty-one days and remained unchanged by Caesar. June had twenty-nine days and Caesar gave it thirty. July (named after Julius Caesar) was given thirty-one days by him.

When August was a lunar month, it had twenty-nine days. Caesar gave it thirty. Emperor Augustus, who named it after himself, added the day he took from February to make it equal to Caesar's month. September had twenty-nine days as a lunar month. Caesar gave it thirty-one, but Augustus reduced it to thirty.

October, in Caesar's calendar had thirty days, but Augustus gave it thirty-one. November also had thirty-one days under Caesar, and Augustus reduced it to thirty. December originally had twenty-nine days, Caesar gave it thirty, and then Augustus added another, giving it thirty-one.

The important thing for an accurate calendar was to have 365 days. The number of days in each month, as you can see, was decided first by Caesar and then by Augustus for whatever reasons they wished. We took our calendar from the Romans.

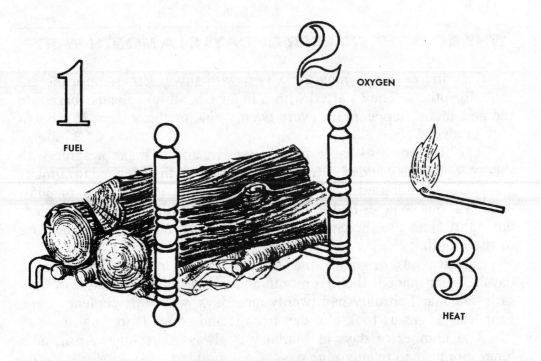

WHY IS FIRE HOT?

The answer to this question is really the definition of fire itself. Fire is a chemical action that occurs very quickly and gives off heat and light.

There are several kinds of chemical actions that can result in what we call fire. The most common is the chemical action between oxygen and a fuel. If heat and light are given off, you have a fire.

To make a fire, three things are necessary. The first is a fuel; the second, oxygen. The fuel combines rapidly with oxygen. When wood burns in bonfires or gas burns in stoves, the fuel combines rapidly with oxygen in the air.

The third thing we need to make a fire is heat. Paper or wood that is simply exposed to air does not catch fire. Usually a burning match is applied to make it catch fire. When the paper becomes hot enough, oxygen can begin to combine freely with it. The paper then bursts into flames.

Every fuel has its own particular temperature at which it begins to burn. This temperature is called the kindling temperature, or flash point, of the fuel.

Suppose a stick of wood is raised to its kindling temperature by a burning match. The wood as a whole does not catch on fire. The reason is that oxygen does not combine with the whole stick. Instead, the heat causes the surface layer of the wood to break up into a gas.

As the heating continues, the gas particles and the oxygen in the air move very fast. In this condition the gas and oxygen particles combine easily and quickly. Heat and light are given off—and we have a fire.

In some kinds of burning, no light is given off. If a fuel combines slowly with oxygen, heat alone is given off. That is what happens when iron rusts. Rusting is just a very slow kind of burning, so slow that you can't even feel the heat being given off. Fire is fast burning, or combustion. In combustion, both heat and light are given off.

HOW IS THE DEPTH OF THE OCEAN MEASURED?

Scientists who study the sea are called oceanographers. Since the deep ocean is cold and dark, they really know very little about it. Parts of the ocean floor have been seen through the windows of special submarines and through the eyes of deep-sea cameras, but it still adds up to very little information.

One of the things they're interested in is the depth of the ocean

water. Finding the depth of water is called "sounding the depth" or "taking a sounding." In the old days, this was done by lowering a rope with a weight attached. Later on, a very light line, usually made of piano wire, was used.

Today, scientists are able to get a much better idea of what the ocean floor is like because of the invention of a device called an echo sounder. An echo sounder uses the echoes of sound to explore the ocean floor.

A device on board the ship sends out a sound signal. The sound travels through the water at nearly one mile a second. It is reflected, or echoed, back to an instrument on the ship. The deeper the water, the longer it takes for the echo to reach the ship.

In a modern echo sounder, high-frequency sound waves are beamed down from the ship. The instrument then records the echo as a dark mark on special paper. The paper is usually printed so that the depth can be read off in fathoms right away (a fathom is six feet).

The echo sounder makes it easy to find the depth of the sea. But it does much more. It provides a continuous profile, or line, showing exactly what the ocean floor is like beneath the ship. This is like having a sounding every few yards along the path of the ship.

If the ship passes over an undersea mountain, the echo sounder records the exact shape of the mountain. And if the bottom is flat, the record shows it as flat. The echo sounder doesn't miss a bump even a few feet high!

HOW IS PAPER PROCESSED?

Paper is made of millions of tiny fibers. The fibers are cellulose, a substance from the cell walls of plants. The cellulose used in paper today comes mostly from trees.

When the bark of a tree log has been stripped off, the wood is ready to be turned into pulp. Pulping is done either by grinding up the wood or by cooking it with chemicals. Some pulping methods use both grinding and cooking.

The wood pulp is then screened and washed to clean out impurities and chemicals. It may then be bleached to make the paper whiter, so that printing or writing shows up better on it.

In the next step, the pulp is beaten in a large mixing machine and mixed with water. The beating frays the fibers, which helps them mat together. Starch, clay, or other materials may be added to improve the surface of the paper for printing and writing.

The pulp then goes into a machine called a Jordan refiner, where the fibers are trimmed evenly. At this stage the pulp consists of 99 percent water and 1 percent fiber. It is now ready to go into the paper-making machine.

In this machine, water drains out of the pulp through a screen, and suction pumps remove more water. The screen vibrates to make the fibers interlock and mat together. The wet mat then passes under a roller that presses it down into a smoother sheet.

The sheet goes through a series of pressing rolls, which squeeze out water and make the paper dense and smooth. Then it travels through a series of heated drums called dryers. At this time a coating can be applied to make the paper slick and shiny. Paper comes off the machines in large rolls. It is trimmed to take off the rough edges and cut to the desired width.

WHAT MAKES GLUE STICK?

Glue is an adhesive. An adhesive is any substance that is used to bond (join) two or more pieces of material without mechanical fasteners.

Adhesives are made out of a great variety of materials. Some are made from animal by-products, such as hides, bones, or blood; others are prepared from various vegetable starches. The latest developments are the synthetic resins, which are made from chemical raw materials.

Glue is one of the oldest adhesives known to man. It is an impure form of gelatin, and is obtained chiefly by boiling animal hides and bones. Some glue is also made from fish.

Glue makes a very strong joint, but it is not waterproof; it dissolves easily in hot water. Glue was by far the most important adhesive until the latter part of the nineteenth century. Even today many people call all adhesives glue, which they are not, of course.

Adhesives act in three different ways to join materials. They may penetrate the tiny surface pores of the materials and hold them together physically, the way a burr sticks to clothing. This is known as mechanical bonding.

Or, an adhesive may act by means of powerful but little-understood forces of attraction between its molecules and the surface molecules of the pieces being joined. This is called intermolecular bonding.

With certain materials, however, the adhesive actually unites chemically with the surface molecules of the pieces being joined. This is chemical bonding.

Whenever adhesives are used, the surfaces to be joined must be clean and must fit each other closely. The strength of the bond depends to a great degree on the surface areas that are actually in contact with the adhesive. If the surfaces do not fit closely, the adhesive may shrink away while drying and leave only small patches firmly bonded.

WHAT IS BEER?

Beer is a mild alcoholic beverage that man has made and used for thousands of years. The brewing of beer starts with grain. The chief grain for brewing is barley, though corn or rice is sometimes used as well.

The grain is mixed with water and kept in a warm room until it begins to germinate, or sprout. After a week of germination, the grain is roasted in a furnace and germination stops. The partly sprouted grain is known as malt.

The malt is mixed with water and boiled to form a sweet-tasting

liquid called wort. Then the dried seed cones of a plant called the hop vine are added to the wort, and the mixture is boiled again. The seed cones, called hops, give beer its tangy flavor.

All the solid matter is then filtered out, and yeast is added. As the yeast organisms feed on the sugars of the wort, they give off alcohol as a waste product. This change from sugar to alcohol is called fermentation. During fermentation, carbon dioxide is also given off. This gas gives beer its bubbles.

The beer is pumped into closed storage tanks where it ages for about 6 weeks. Then it is filtered again before it is put into barrels, bottles, or cans. From start to finish, the brewing process may take as long as 3 months. Bottled and canned beer is pasteurized to keep it from turning sour.

The most popular kind of beer in the United States is lager beer. This beer originated in Germany and gets its name from the German word for storage, "lager," because beer is stored for some time before it is used.

HOW IS WHISKEY MADE?

Whiskey is an alcoholic beverage that is distilled. Not all alcoholic beverages are distilled. For example, beer and wine are not. Distillation is the process of separating different kinds of liquids by boiling them.

All liquids have a different boiling point. The temperature in a still is regulated so that the liquid that is boiled off is mainly alcohol. The escaping vapor is trapped and condensed—that is, turned back into liquid.

Whiskey and most other distilled beverages are made from grain, which is composed mainly of starch. This starch must be changed to sugar, and the sugar will then be fermented into alcohol. Tiny plants called yeasts go to work on the sugar, breaking it apart into alcohol and carbon dioxide.

To change the starch into sugar, so that the yeast plants can feed on it, malt is added to a cooked mash of grain mixed with water. The malt contains enzymes which convert the grain starch into sugar.

When the sugar has been fermented into alcohol, the alcohol is separated from the mash by distillation. We now have alcohol that has been obtained from the grain, and this might be called "raw whiskey."

Whiskey is stored in wooden barrels for aging. This eliminates any unwanted impurities and gives the whiskey a smooth, mellow taste. The wood for the barrels may first be charred, to give the whiskey a nutty flavor and help absorb impurities.

HOW IS WINE MADE?

Wine can be made from many fruits and plants that contain natural sugar. But most wine is made from grapes. The grape is nature's most suitable product for wine making. Grapes have enough natural sugar to ferment properly. And grapes carry the yeasts that begin the wine-making process when the juice is released.

As grapes ripen on the vines, they produce more sugar and less acid. The grapes are picked when they reach the exact stage of ripening necessary for the wine that is to be made. Mechanical grape crushers break the fruit and release the juice gently, so that the seeds are not

broken. Natural wine yeasts on the grape skins ferment the juice, changing the grape sugar into alcohol and carbon dioxide.

White wines are made by fermenting the juice of the grapes without the grape skins. Red wines are made by fermenting the juice with the grape skins. The color of wine comes from the skins of the grapes. When the wine is the right color, the skins are removed and the wine continues to ferment without the skins.

If a wine maker wants a sweet wine, he stops the fermenting process before the sugar is all turned into alcohol and carbon dioxide. If a dry wine is wanted, the wine is allowed to ferment until almost all the sugar is gone. At the end of the fermenting process the wine is put into a cask or tank to begin aging.

The aging is divided into two stages. In the first stage wooden casks or barrels are used. In the second stage, the wine is placed in bottles. The length of time it takes for a wine to age to perfection depends on the type. Aging makes a new, harsh-tasting wine into a smooth-tasting wine.

WHAT IS FERMENTATION?

Fermentation is a chemical change in which certain chemical compounds are broken down into simpler forms. The change is caused by substances called enzymes, which are produced by tiny living plants or animals. Yeasts, for example, are one-celled plants which produce enzymes.

There are three main kinds of fermentation: alcoholic, acetic, and putrefactive. Each is caused by the presence of bacteria—yeasts or molds—which produce the particular enzyme responsible for the chemical change. Fruit syrups become alcoholic when yeast, containing an enzyme called zymase, is added.

Wine or cider turns to vinegar when certain bacteria, called "mother of vinegar," are present. This is acetic fermentation. Meat and animal matter decay in putrefactive fermentation after certain molds have formed on them.

Fermentation helps in the digestion of food. An enzyme called ptyalin in saliva changes the starch of foods into soluble sugar—the first step in digestion. Enzymes are also present in the stomach, the intestines, the pancreas, and in various other organs.

Yeast is put into dough to make bread light by producing bubbles of carbon dioxide which form as the enzymes attack the starches and sugars present.

Sometimes fermentation is harmful. To keep foods from spoiling, they are kept in cool places or refrigerators where the low temperature checks the growth of bacteria, yeasts, and molds. Food can be preserved by killing the fermenting agents with heat and then sealing it. This is done in canning.

WHAT THINGS ARE MADE FROM OIL?

Petroleum, or crude oil, is one of the world's most important substances. Through a process called refining, petroleum can be changed into more than 2,000 useful products. Here we can give only a general idea of what some of these are.

The best-known petroleum products are the high-energy fuels—gasolines, kerosenes, and diesel and fuel oils. Bottled gas is derived from petroleum. Much of the food we eat and the clothes we wear depend on substances from oil. Vegetable oil is used to prevent bread from sticking when it is being mixed. Petroleum-derived plastic film wraps much of our food. Many of our garments are made with synthetic fibers derived from petroleum.

Over a thousand different kinds of oils and greases are made from petroleum. The lubricants are used for everything from watch and machine parts to locomotives and electric generators.

From oil comes asphalt for roads and rooftops. Wax obtained from oil is used in making candles, waxed paper, and cellophane. Other products that come from oil are used in making carbon paper, ink to print books and newspapers, and detergents.

On farms, synthetic ammonia, made from petroleum, is used as a fertilizer. Oil-based sprays kill insects and weeds. And petroleum is used to manufacture petrochemicals. These are raw materials from which other chemical products, such as plastics and synthetic fibers, are made.

From petrochemicals the products made include such things as synthetic foam rubber, plastic tile, plastic film, and detergents.

HOW IS SYNTHETIC RUBBER MADE?

Natural rubber is made from latex, a white fluid of the rubber tree. The latex is held in a network of tiny tubes under the bark of the tree. When the bark is cut, the white, milky juice oozes out. Tiny particles of rubber float in this liquid.

People have learned to manufacture latex by combining chemicals in certain ways. This rubber is called synthetic rubber. The kind of synthetic rubber produced in the largest amount is known as general-purpose rubber. Its two main ingredients are butadiene and styrene. Butadiene is a gas made from petroleum, and styrene is a liquid made from petroleum or coal.

The butadiene and styrene are pumped into a large tank containing a soapy mixture. The soapy solution makes it easier for the rubber particles to form. A catalyst (a substance that speeds up the reaction) is added. As the mixture in the tank is stirred, it gradually changes to a milky white liquid. This is synthetic latex.

Synthetic latex is very similar in appearance to the natural latex that comes from the rubber tree. When the synthetic latex has developed to the proper state, a chemical is added to stop the reaction.

The latex is then pumped into another tank with acids and brine (saltwater). The mixture is stirred to coagulate it. The coagulated piece of synthetic rubber looks like gray crumbs. After being washed to remove any extra chemicals, the synthetic rubber is dried and pressed into bales. Basic synthetic rubber can be varied by adding other ingredients or combining them in different ways.

HOW ARE SYNTHETIC FIBERS MADE?

Some fibers, such as cotton, wool, silk, linen, and hair, are natural. They are produced by plants and animals. Others, such as rayon, nylon, Dacron, Saran, are man-made. To understand how man-made, or synthetic, fibers are made, we have to know something about fibers.

Most fibers are made up of organic (carbon-containing) chemicals, such as are found in all living things. Some organic chemicals have a special quality. Their molecules (groups of atoms) attach themselves to one another somewhat like the links of a chain. This is called polymerization. Each fiber consists of millions of such molecular chains held together by natural forces called chemical bonds. Different fibers contain different numbers of each kind of atom in their molecules, and the atoms are arranged differently.

In making synthetic fibers, chemists take atoms of carbon, hydrogen, oxygen, and other elements, and combine them in such a way that new substances are created. The raw materials for synthetic fibers are coal, oil, air, and water.

Atoms from these raw materials are combined and arranged into long molecular chains called polymers. In other words, the polymerization is created by the chemists, instead of by nature.

These polymers are liquid when they are hot. They can be cast into solid plastics and films like Saran wrap, or they can be extruded through spinnerets (nozzles with tiny openings) to form filaments. From these filaments fabrics are made.

Of all the fibers produced every year, about one-fifth are synthetic fibers.

WHERE DO WE GET WAX?

Many fruits and vegetables and some plant leaves have a thin protective coating of wax. Waxes are also produced by animals and are found in minerals and petroleum. And there are synthetic, or man-made waxes. We obtain wax from many sources.

Carnauba wax is obtained from the leaves of the carnauba palm tree of Brazil. This wax is hard and gives an excellent luster when it is used in floor and furniture polishes. Candelilla wax comes from a plant of the same name that grows in Mexico and the southwestern United States. It is a brown wax used in phonograph records, floor dressings, and candles.

Bayberry wax, from the berries of the shrub, is used for making candles. Worker bees secrete wax that they use in making their honeycombs. This wax, beeswax, is used for making cosmetics, church candles, polishes, crayons, and artificial flowers.

Wool wax from wool-bearing animals is called lanolin when it is purified. It is used in some ointments, cosmetics, and soaps. More than 90 percent of all commercial wax used today is petroleum wax. Petroleum wax has a wide variety of uses, because it is odorless, tasteless, and chemically inactive. It does not react easily with most other substances.

A hard sort of petroleum wax is called paraffin. Paraffin's most important use is as a coating for paper products. Soft petroleum waxes, such as petroleum jelly, are used for medicinal purposes. Synthetic waxes are chemical combinations of hydrogen, carbon, oxygen, and sometimes chlorine. They are tailor-made to have definite properties.

HOW DOES HEAT INSULATION WORK?

Heat insulation slows down the flow of heat from one place to another. For example, heat insulation keeps a house comfortable in winter by keeping the heat in. It also keeps a house cool in summer by keeping the heat out.

It is also used on hot pipes and tanks to keep them from losing heat; in refrigerators and cold-storage rooms to keep heat out; and it is used in refrigerated freight cars and trucks.

One form of manufactured insulation—that is, not natural insulation, but insulation made by people—is called mass insulation. It works by preventing the movement of heat. This is done by using materials that conduct heat poorly. These materials are filled with tiny closed-in spaces of air or gas, which are also poor conductors.

Different materials conduct heat differently. Some materials allow heat to flow through them easily, while others prevent the movement of heat. For example, silver is a good conductor of heat. It conducts heat about 19,300 times better than air does.

One of the best and most commonly used insulating materials is rock wool. The fibers of this material are made by dropping a certain kind of molten rock onto a whirling wheel. The wheel tosses droplets of molten rock into a current of air, which cools them into thin fibers.

Rock wool prevents the movement of heat (that is, it insulates) about 44 times better than glass, seven times better than wood, and even four times better than asbestos.

INDEX

206